LOCAL GREENS

In the face of the federal government's failure to tackle climate change in the early decades of this century, large cities in the U.S. started to take action. Networks of city governments and philanthropists offered cities support, and cities invested their own resources in sustainability offices. However, cities made limited progress in reducing their greenhouse gas emissions in the first two decades of this century. This book provides a clear-eyed analysis of the potential for big city governments to address society's most pressing environmental problems, including limiting and adapting to climate change. It includes original case studies of New York's environmental policy efforts in the first two decades of this century, which ground its analysis of the promise and perils of turning to cities to address climate change and other environmental issues. Drawing on the book's analysis of cities' strengths and weaknesses, it outlines a high-level agenda for urban environmental policy for the near term. With President Trump's return to power in 2025, and his promises to undo many aspects of federal environmental law, it is more important than ever for environmental advocates and scholars to understand the potential and limits of local action to fill the gap.

Katrina M. Wyman teaches and researches environmental law at NYU School of Law, where she is the Wilf Family Professor of Property Law and Faculty Director of the Guarini Center on Environmental, Energy and Land Use Law. She has published extensively on local environmental law and policy.

Danielle Spiegel-Feld spent nearly a decade as Executive Director of the Guarini Center on Environmental, Energy and Land Use Law at NYU School of Law, where she often worked closely with New York City officials to advance local environmental policy, and was an adjunct professor of law. She is an editor of *Global Sustainable Cities* (2023).

Local Greens

CITIES AND TWENTY-FIRST CENTURY ENVIRONMENTAL PROBLEMS

KATRINA M. WYMAN
New York University School of Law

DANIELLE SPIEGEL-FELD
New York University School of Law

CAMBRIDGE
UNIVERSITY PRESS

CAMBRIDGE
UNIVERSITY PRESS

Shaftesbury Road, Cambridge CB2 8EA, United Kingdom

One Liberty Plaza, 20th Floor, New York, NY 10006, USA

477 Williamstown Road, Port Melbourne, VIC 3207, Australia

314–321, 3rd Floor, Plot 3, Splendor Forum, Jasola District Centre, New Delhi – 110025, India

103 Penang Road, #05–06/07, Visioncrest Commercial, Singapore 238467

Cambridge University Press is part of Cambridge University Press & Assessment, a department of the University of Cambridge.

We share the University's mission to contribute to society through the pursuit of education, learning and research at the highest international levels of excellence.

www.cambridge.org
Information on this title: www.cambridge.org/9781009011976

DOI: 10.1017/9781009025195

When citing this work, please include a reference to the DOI 10.1017/9781009025195

First published 2025

A catalogue record for this publication is available from the British Library

Library of Congress Cataloging-in-Publication Data
NAMES: Wyman, Katrina Miriam, author. | Spiegel-Feld, Danielle, author.
TITLE: Local greens : cities and twenty-first century environmental problems / Katrina M. Wyman, New York University; Danielle Spiegel-Feld, New York University.
DESCRIPTION: Cambridge, United Kingdom ; New York, NY : Cambridge University Press, 2025. | Includes bibliographical references and index.
IDENTIFIERS: LCCN 2025000974 | ISBN 9781316515419 (hardback) | ISBN 9781009025195 (ebook)
SUBJECTS: LCSH: Environmental law – New York (State) – New York. | Climatic changes – Law and legislation – New York (State) – New York. | Carbon dioxide mitigation – Law and legislation – New York (State) – New York. | Pollution – Law and legislation – New York (State) – New York. | Municipal corporations – New York (State) – New York.
CLASSIFICATION: LCC KFN5610 .W96 2025 | DDC 344.747/1046–dc23/eng/20250114
LC record available at https://lccn.loc.gov/2025000974

ISBN 978-1-316-51541-9 Hardback
ISBN 978-1-009-01197-6 Paperback

For Michael, Anna and John: Memories of you are a blessing. Inspired by Nana and Sarah, I walked around Manhattan by myself and with Rosa as I tried to absorb what happened to you. Through these walks, you taught me many lessons about the city and life.

For Jonathan, Jeremiah and Hannah: I love you so much. Thank you for your patience in letting me spend many hours on this book. May you lead long, happy and healthy lives and pursue your dreams and passions.

Katrina

For my children, Jonah and Reuben, in the hope they'll be able to live their lives in a world full of beauty and thriving nature. And for my husband, Jonathan, for never questioning the value of my work and always supporting me. You three mean the world to me.

Danielle

Contents

List of Figures — *page* ix
List of Tables — xi
List of Photographs — xiii
Acknowledgments — xv

Introduction — 1

1 **A Brief History of Cities in Environmental Policy** — 17

2 **An Analytical Framework** — 25

3 **Local Environmental Protection in NYC** — 36

4 **Decarbonization Efforts in NYC** — 55

5 **Adapting to Climate Change in NYC** — 72

6 **An Urban Climate Change Agenda for the Early Twenty-First Century** — 87

Coda — 105

Notes — 107
Index — 259

Figures

I.1 Map of Lower Manhattan *page* 2
4.1 Cumulative number of cities among the twenty most populous cities in the United States with GHG reduction targets, by year 56
4.2 Cumulative number of cities among the twenty most populous cities in the United States with published GHG inventories, by year 59
4.3 Cumulative number of benchmarking and auditing laws in the twenty most populous cities, by year first adopted 62
4.4 Cumulative number of the twenty most populous cities with membership in ICLEI and C40, by year first joined 64

Tables

3.1 Examples of parks over 5 acres opened in whole or part in New York City between 2002 and 2021, listed by borough *page* 41
3.2 Total acreage devoted to parks in the twenty most populous U.S. cities according to Trust for Public Land 42
5.1 Selected Army Corps projects to protect against climate change related coastal flooding 83

Photographs

P.1 *Plaque, Battery Playscape at the Battery, Lower Manhattan, March 2024* *page* 3

P.2 *Slides representing the "bluff" landscape, Battery Playscape at the Battery, Lower Manhattan, March 2024* 3

P.3 *Near South Street Seaport along the East River, Lower Manhattan, March 2024* 3

P.4 *Pier 26 in Hudson River Park, Lower Manhattan, March 2024* 4

P.5 *Little Island, along the Hudson River, Lower Manhattan, March 2024* 4

P.6 *Construction of the East River Coastal Resiliency Project, Lower Manhattan, May 2024* 4

P.7 *Notice of the closure of Wagner Park for the South Battery Park City Resiliency Project, on the west side of Lower Manhattan near the Museum of Jewish Heritage, March 2024* 5

P.8 *Construction of the South Battery Park City Resiliency Project, on the west side of Lower Manhattan near the Museum of Jewish Heritage, March 2024* 5

P.9 *Low-tech interim flood protection measure near the Brooklyn Bridge, on the east side of Lower Manhattan, March 2024* 5

Acknowledgments

This book emerged from our shared interest in taking seriously the role of cities in environmental protection. Danielle was the first of us to become interested in local environmental law and policy. While executive director of the Guarini Center on Environmental, Energy and Land Use Law at New York University School of Law (NYU Law), she made important contributions to environmental law in New York City, for example, by encouraging the city to pass a law requiring buildings to post letter grades signaling their energy efficiency. You can view these grades today when you walk into large buildings in the city. Her enthusiasm for urban environmental law drew in Katrina. In 2018, we started teaching a seminar on the subject, which prompted us to publish an article on twenty-first century urban environmental law and policy, *The Urban Environmental Renaissance*, 108 Cal. L. Rev. 305 (2020). The article appeared around the time when the COVID-19 pandemic brought life in large cities to a halt, making us wonder if we should have included a question mark in the title. Nonetheless, the article led Matt Gallaway from Cambridge University Press to suggest to us that we author a book on urban environmental issues, which we were eager to do.

Donald Trump was president for the first time when we started teaching about climate change and environmental law in urban areas, and blue cities and states seemed like the only governments who would address these issues. The Biden administration subsequently reasserted some federal leadership in climate and environmental law. However, even with the federal government taking some forward-looking action, it became clear that governments at all levels need to continue to push the envelope if American society is to meet the challenges of limiting and adapting to climate change and addressing long-standing environmental inequalities. As this book goes to print in 2025, with the second Trump administration already working diligently to unravel the Biden administration's environmental efforts, local and state actors that want to address climate and environmental challenges are left to their own devices once again.

This book has been many years in the making, and we are grateful to everyone who helped us along the way. Many people with expertise and experience in government and environmental advocacy gave their time to speak with us, including Costa Constantinides, Ben Furnas, Cas Holloway, Cullen Howe, Al Huang, Laurie Kerr, John Lee, John Mandyck, Thaddeus Pawlowski, Seth Pinsky, Samara Swantson, and Dan Zarrilli; the book refers to only some of the conversations from which we benefited to preserve people's anonymity. Over the years in which we taught together we also learned about the factors driving local environmental law from the many guest speakers we had in our classes, including Malcolm Araos, Kate Boicourt, Lia Cairone, Samantha Maldonado, Laura Popa, Cecil Scheib, Pete Sikora, Vernice Miller-Travis, and Russell Unger.

We would not have been able to complete this book without all the help that we received from research fellows and research assistants at NYU Law and financial support from the school. There are so many people who helped pull together material over the years, and we apologize to those who we fail to name here. At the top of the list of those who helped is Sara Savarani, who as a legal fellow at the Guarini Center gathered information on local environmental law and policy, initially for our 2020 article and then this book, and assisted in pulling together the book. Other people who provided assistance at various stages include Janet Bering, Joseph Brau, Lucy Carlson, Elena De Nictolis, Nardos Girma, Ethan Goldman, Glenn Korman, Nathan Lee, Nate Mattison, Kyle McKenney, Max Miller, Adalene Minelli, Quetin O'Berry, Josh Podolsky, Corban Ryan, Grace Soutter, Griffith Tai, and Alisa White. Dana Rubin in the NYU Law library found many items that we were not able to locate on our own.

We are grateful to the comments we received on draft chapters from Christine Billy, William Buzbee, Elena De Nictolis, Michael Gerrard, Eric Goldstein, Mark Izeman, Bethany Davis Noll, Michael Oppenheimer, Elizabeth Stein, Richard Stewart, Frank Upham, and others. The book also benefited from presentations at the NYU Law summer faculty workshop, the University of Toronto Faculty of Law, the Fordham Urban Law Journal symposium on Building a Greener Future Through Urban Sustainability, and the Cities seminar taught by Clay Gillette and Andrew Haughwout at NYU Law. A special thank you to the students in the Urban Environmental Law and Policy seminar in spring 2023 who read many of the draft chapters and whose comments and questions led us to clarify our thoughts. The insights and enthusiasm of the students in the various iterations of the seminar that we co-taught over the years repeatedly spurred us to deepen our thinking. At the outset of this project, three anonymous reviewers of the book proposal provided useful feedback on the proposal.

As we were working on this book, we published two articles that drew from material from it, especially Chapter 4: *Local Action, Global Problem: Why and How New York City Is Tackling Climate Change*, 50 FORDHAM URB. L. J. 1187 (2023); and *Building Efficiency*, 40 ENV'T F. 24 (Mar./Apr. 2023). Various chapters of this book also draw from our 2020 article *The Urban Environmental Renaissance*. The editors of these three articles provided suggestions that have influenced the book.

Conversations over many years with our colleagues at NYU Law, including Vicki Been, Clay Gillette, Rick Hills, Richard Revesz, and Richard Stewart, helped to shape this book in countless ways. Richard Stewart, who passed away in the fall of 2023, was a mentor to both of us and a professor to Danielle. He encouraged our work on cities from its early stages. In the summer of 2023, several months before he passed away, he read draft chapters and participated in the NYU Law summer faculty workshop on the chapters. We miss him dearly and think of the wise advice he provided over many years.

Not everyone will agree with everything in this book, but we hope that it adds to the conversation about cities and environmental protection. All errors and omissions are ours.

Introduction

In the late twentieth and early twenty-first centuries, New York City reinvented its formerly industrial waterfront. Manhattan's shoreline was once prized for the port and piers that in 1860 processed "52 percent of the nation's combined imports and exports."[1] In the 2020s, New Yorkers and tourists flock to the waterfront's interconnected series of verdant paths and parks. The Battery at Manhattan's southernmost tip now includes a children's playground that simulates different natural ecosystems and is built to accommodate flooding.[2] Five slides made from granite from the Adirondacks are intended to give children a feel for bluffs, according to an informative plaque that reassures the supervising adults that a visit to the playground is educational, not just a means of burning off youthful energy.[3] Along the East River, which runs north of the Battery, lies the South Street Seaport, which is full of touristy restaurants and shops. Running north of the Battery on the west side of Manhattan that borders the Hudson River, a series of parks flow into each other, including Hudson River Park. Pier 26, a part of the park that opened in 2020, recreates the native grasses, trees, and rocks that existed when Henry Hudson explored the area in 1609 when the Lenape people controlled it (Figure I.1).[4] Further north along the Hudson, Little Island rises from the river like a bundle of blooming concrete tulips; it is a human-made play space for adults with open-air performance spaces. Like the Battery Park playground, Little Island opened in 2021.[5]

The waters beyond the shoreline have been similarly transformed. In 2018, the city's Department of Environmental Protection proudly declared that no one alive had ever before seen New York Harbor "as clean and healthy."[6] In the summer, the water is sufficiently clean that people kayak, fish from piers, and occasionally even swim in the Hudson River, although most of the river is not swimmable and there are state advisories about eating the fish.[7] The website for Hudson River Park boasts that "[t]he Hudson River has been on a remarkable journey. Once very polluted, water quality has vastly improved – the result of 40 years of environmental regulations and advocacy."[8] Aquatic species not seen in the river for many years are returning.[9] In 2019, a local team of whale enthusiasts identified 134 whales off New York's shores, up from just four sightings in 2012.[10]

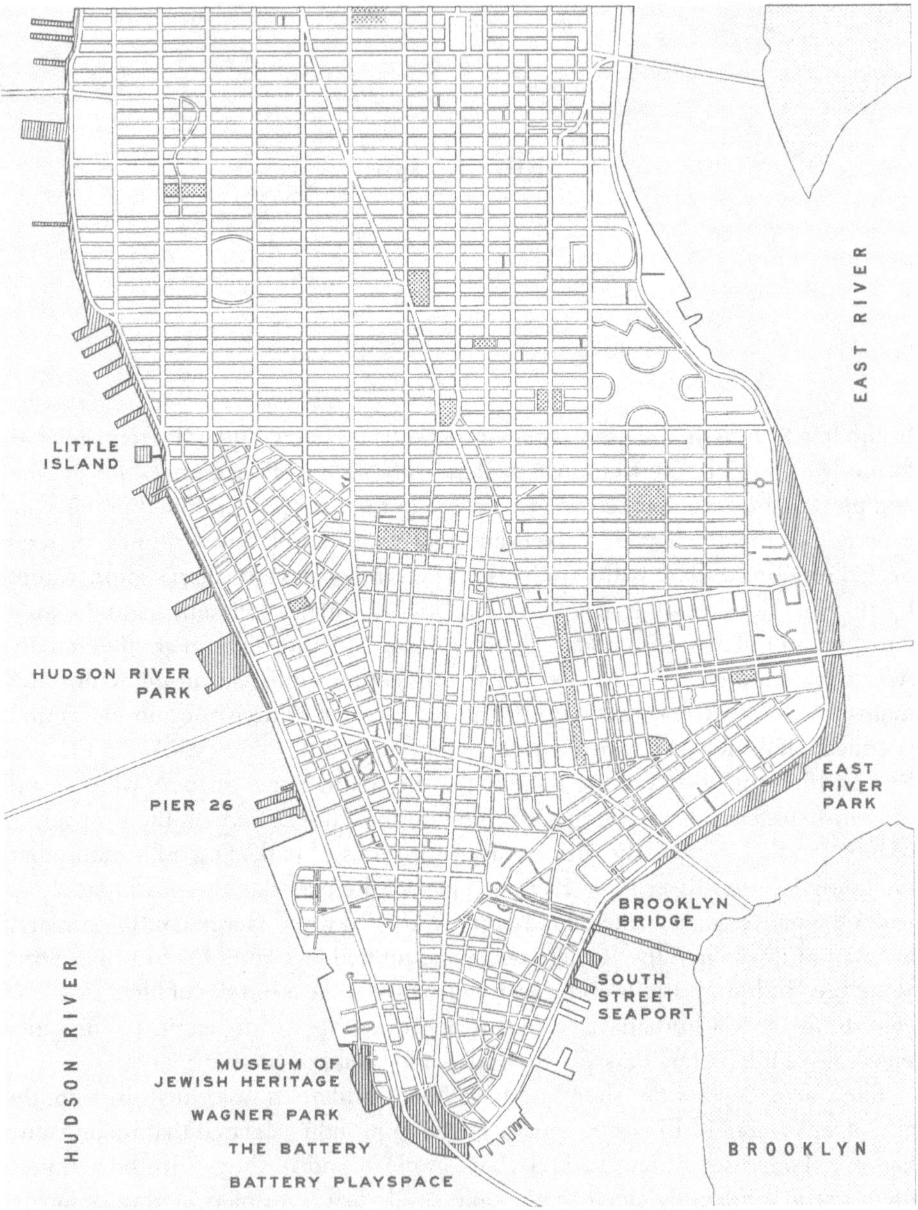

FIGURE I.1 Map of Lower Manhattan
Credit: Karen Messing

More ominously, the paths around Manhattan also offer clues about city leaders' anxieties about the environmental threats facing the city as the climate warms. As of 2024, there are four construction projects underway along the shores of lower Manhattan to increase resilience to flooding from sea level rise and the sort of storm surge that badly damaged large areas of the city during Superstorm Sandy in 2012,

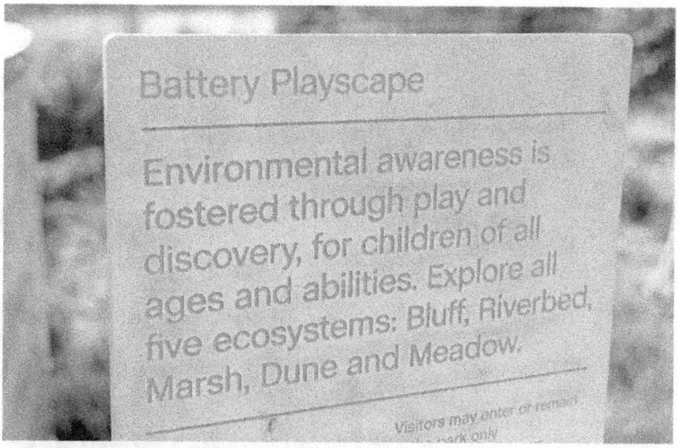

PHOTOGRAPH 1 *Plaque, Battery Playscape at the Battery, Lower Manhattan, March 2024.* Credit: Photography by Samuel Stuart Hollenshead

PHOTOGRAPH 2 *Slides representing the "bluff" landscape, Battery Playscape at the Battery, Lower Manhattan, March 2024.* Credit: Photography by Samuel Stuart Hollenshead

PHOTOGRAPH 3 *Near South Street Seaport along the East River, Lower Manhattan, March 2024.* Credit: Photography by Samuel Stuart Hollenshead

PHOTOGRAPH 4 *Pier 26 in Hudson River Park, Lower Manhattan, March 2024.* Credit: Photography by Samuel Stuart Hollenshead

PHOTOGRAPH 5 *Little Island, along the Hudson River, Lower Manhattan, March 2024.* Credit: Photography by Samuel Stuart Hollenshead

PHOTOGRAPH 6 *Construction of the East River Coastal Resiliency Project, Lower Manhattan, May 2024.* Credit: Seymore Fleck

PHOTOGRAPH 7 *Notice of the closure of Wagner Park for the South Battery Park City Resiliency Project, on the west side of Lower Manhattan near the Museum of Jewish Heritage, March 2024.* Credit: Photography by Samuel Stuart Hollenshead

PHOTOGRAPH 8 *Construction of the South Battery Park City Resiliency Project, on the west side of Lower Manhattan near the Museum of Jewish Heritage, March 2024.* Credit: Photography by Samuel Stuart Hollenshead

PHOTOGRAPH 9 *Low-tech interim flood protection measure (resembling sandbags) near the Brooklyn Bridge, on the east side of Lower Manhattan, March 2024.* Credit: Photography by Samuel Stuart Hollenshead

when 17 percent of the city's land mass flooded.[11] The most notable of these projects is the East Side Coastal Resiliency project, New York City's most ambitious climate flood protection initiative as of the early 2020s.[12] It involves rebuilding and elevating East River Park on landfill to protect the area against flooding expected from more frequent and ferocious storms due to climate change.[13] South of the park reconstruction, the city is installing floodwalls and "flip-up barriers."[14] At the bottom of Manhattan, the city is rebuilding part of the Battery to address flood risks, and New York State's Battery Park City Authority is building new flood protections on the west side.[15] Meanwhile, the city has installed barriers that look like large sandbags near the Brooklyn Bridge as a low-tech interim flood protection measure, pending the implementation of a better plan to protect the South Street Seaport and Financial District from the waters of the East River.[16] Manhattan's vulnerability to flooding from storms and sea level rise is hard to miss.

This book is concerned with the role of cities in safeguarding the environment in the early twenty-first century. Most American environmental law scholarship overlooks the role of cities in developing environmental law and policy.[17] Instead, scholars typically focus on federal environmental law. When they do look to lower levels of government, they often concentrate on the role of states, most notably California.[18] Legal scholars mainly seem to pay attention to the potential to advance an environmental agenda in states and localities when Republican dominance in Washington leaves the federal government inhospitable to environmental regulation.[19]

This book draws attention to the role of large cities in environmental protection historically and in the present. It examines the factors driving large American cities such as New York to address environmental problems in the early twenty-first century and those constraining cities' environmental policy choices. A clear-eyed view of cities' role in environmental law and policy and of the determinants of local environmental policy should help scholars, policymakers, and advocates identify the responsibilities to which local governments are best suited and design the structures needed to support them in these tasks. Integrating municipal governments in this manner has taken on newfound urgency in the twenty-first century as all levels of government need to address climate change, which is almost certainly the most complex environmental challenge that they have ever encountered. The return of Republican dominance in Washington in 2025, as this book went into press, makes it all the more pressing to understand the scope for local action.

EXISTING SCHOLARSHIP

With 80 percent of the U.S. – and over 50 percent of the world – population living in urban areas,[20] and cities accounting for over "70% of [U.S. and] global carbon dioxide emissions,"[21] twenty-first century charitable and nongovernmental organizations have shown considerable enthusiasm about the potential for cities to address climate change and other environmental issues. Major foundations, such as Bloomberg Philanthropies and the Kresge Foundation, fund efforts in cities to address climate change and improve sustainability in the U.S. and abroad.[22] Prominent global networks of city governments bring together local officials committed to limiting climate change. The C40 Cities Climate Leadership Group is likely the most notable; as of 2024, it included almost 100 cities accounting for approximately 20 percent of "the global economy," including fourteen U.S. cities, such as New York and Los Angeles.[23] City governments are themselves allocating resources to environmental policy. According to a 2015–2016 survey of 504 U.S. cities with populations over 20,000, "46 percent … have staff whose jobs are dedicated to sustainability."[24]

Scholars have also written several books for popular audiences arguing that cities are well placed to combat climate change and promote sustainability. Perhaps the most well-known is *Cool Cities*, by the late political theorist Benjamin Barber.[25] Published in 2017, in the first year of the first Trump administration, *Cool Cities* argued that cities around the world have a right to spearhead efforts to reduce greenhouse gas (GHG) emissions, given the failure of nation-states to aggressively pursue decarbonization. Barber also saw cities as having the opportunity to make a major dent in GHG emissions, especially if they work together through forums such as the Global Parliament of Mayors that he helped to found.[26] Barber emphasized that the large share of GHG emissions attributable to cities means that they have the ability to be part of the solution to limiting climate change. He thought that the politics of addressing climate change would be easier at the local than the national level because city governments are closer to people, and therefore more likely to respond to popular concerns about climate change.[27]

The optimism that C40, Barber, and others evince about the potential for local governments to address climate change stands in sharp contrast to a long-standing view in American legal scholarship that cities and states – apart from California – are incapable of dealing with pressing environmental problems. A well-known 1977 *Yale Law Journal* article by our late colleague Richard Stewart, the leading environmental law professor of his generation, articulates several rationales for federalizing environmental law in the face of the failure of local and state governments to limit air and water pollution.[28] Writing just a few years after Congress passed the Clean Air and Water Acts in the early 1970s, Stewart refers to a lack of capacity at the local and state levels to deal with pollution problems, the vulnerability of these lower levels of government to influence from polluting industries, and the inability of subnational governments to limit pollution harming their residents that originates elsewhere, among other reasons.[29]

Early twenty-first century legal scholarship continues to be skeptical of the ability of local governments to successfully address society's most important contemporary environmental problems, such as climate change. Some legal scholarship emphasizes that limiting GHG emissions is an interjurisdictional pollution problem and that local efforts to reduce these emissions will merely displace them to nonregulating jurisdictions.[30] Other scholarship goes further and suggests that local governments are likely not only to be ineffective in limiting climate change but also to delay or thwart societal decarbonization. There are concerns that local governments, responding to the opposition of local residents to disrupting their local environment, will block building renewable generation and transmission infrastructure necessary to decarbonize electricity supplies, and new, denser residential housing that would lower GHG emissions by reducing car travel and the energy needed to cool and heat homes.[31] While the precise concerns about local governments may have changed since the 1970s, the skepticism about their potential to contribute to addressing environmental issues endures.

THIS BOOK'S CONTRIBUTIONS

This book charts a middle path between enthusiastic optimism and the skepticism about the potential for cities to address climate change and other environmental issues. Centering urban politics, we argue that large cities have strong incentives to tackle environmental problems that local residents mainly benefit from solving. In addition, community-based advocates can prompt cities to attend to global environmental problems, such as the need to limit planetary warming. However, there are more challenges to cities acting aggressively on their own to tackle global problems than the optimists about cities tackling climate change tend to acknowledge. In light of their status as constrained entities nested within states and a large federation, cities will struggle to effectively contribute to addressing society's most pressing environmental problems without support from higher levels of government. Breaking down our arguments, this book makes four contributions.

First, we emphasize the potential for leading cities to play a meaningful role in protecting the environment and argue that it is time to stop reflexively equating environmental law with federal law. Environmental protection is not, and has never been, an exclusively federal or state enterprise. Early twenty-first century literature arguing that cities should take on decarbonization and sustainability tends to imply that it is proposing a novel role for cities, thus overlooking the historical role of U.S. city governments in environmental protection going back to the nineteenth century, a role which was revived with new vigor in the first decades of the twenty-first century. Recognizing the history of local environmental protection efforts helps to establish the viability of a local role in addressing contemporary challenges – while also offering cautionary lessons about the extent to which local governments are well positioned to protect the environment.

Second, we offer a framework for understanding the factors that give rise to, and constrain, local environmental law and policy in the early twenty-first century and the categories of environmental problems that cities are likely to address.[32] We agree with the many scholars of urban politics who argue "that the central issue of local governance is economic development."[33] Created and constrained by state law and at the mercy of federal choices about interest rates, tax levels, and immigration policy, local governments have agency, but it is fragile.[34] They must tend to their economic base to be able to fund the services, such as policing and fire, which are their core responsibilities. Within the confines of the bounded agency that cities enjoy, there are two main reasons that local governments act on their own to safeguard the environment – without compulsion or subsidies from the federal or state governments: to make the city more attractive to the economic elites that shore up the city's tax base and to respond to political pressure from organized grassroots groups. The first is a top-down explanation, while the second is a bottom-up explanation.

Local environmental protection efforts sometimes emerge in a top-down fashion because local elites perceive such efforts as consistent with the overarching priority of promoting local economic prosperity. City policymakers may advance environmental protection measures based on their own assessment that the measures will promote the city's economic interests. Policymakers also might be influenced by advocacy from large businesses, major landowners and developers, and other powerful local interests that stand to obtain private economic benefits from the measures, such as higher property values or more business revenue. In the early twenty-first century, New York and other postindustrial cities built new parks to attract knowledge workers and tourists and began planning and, in some cases, investing in adapting their physical environments to protect their economic prosperity as the climate warms.

In contradistinction to the first explanation, local environmental protection efforts sometimes emerge from the bottom up in response to advocacy from local grassroots community groups who find allies within city government. Not all local environmental protection efforts are in the service of economic development; indeed, local efforts sometimes impose costs on local actors who argue that the efforts will jeopardize the city's economic prosperity. Grassroots advocacy is motivated by a variety of concerns. With the development of organized groups representing historically marginalized communities of people of color and low-income residents, city governments have faced calls in recent decades to address unfairness in the distribution of environmental burdens, such as garbage processing facilities, and benefits, such as green space.[35] In addition, as global warming has accelerated, some environmental activists frustrated by politics in Washington, D.C., have turned to city governments to make progress in reducing GHG emissions out of a belief that limiting climate change is a moral necessity. Sometimes, although perhaps not often, the politics align at the local level for grassroots groups to prevail, even though local business elites express concerns that policies that the advocates are proffering will impose local economic costs. A case in point: Prodded by local climate activists, in 2019, New York City officials who were committed to standing up to President Donald Trump enacted a law capping GHG emissions from large buildings starting in 2024 that could impose significant compliance costs on building owners.[36]

In short, we maintain that cities have heterogeneous motivations for protecting the environment. Sometimes they act based on a perception from elites inside and outside of government that environmental protection will benefit the local economy, even if it will be costly upfront. Less often perhaps, cities act in response to bottom-up advocacy from grassroots groups that find allies within city government for policies aimed at saving the planet or promoting a more equitable distribution of environmental benefits and burdens. Such policies are not obviously linked with promoting economic prosperity and indeed may impose economic costs on powerful local actors. Politics at the local level are not simple, and not all meaningful local government activity is focused on promoting economic development.[37]

However, the opportunities to achieve environmental progress at the local level through multiple paths – from the "top" and the "bottom" – should not be taken to imply that cities can address today's most salient environmental issues on their own. It is useful to distinguish two ideal types of environmental problems: local and global problems.

Both city policymakers and grassroots advocates are likely to focus on protecting local environmental quality, for example, by protecting green spaces and removing solid waste. They may disagree about how to order their priorities; policymakers concerned about economic development might most want to enhance the physical beauty of the city in wealthy or heavily touristed areas, while grassroots advocates might be most concerned about pollution in low-income neighborhoods. Nonetheless, addressing the local environment should be attractive to both policymakers and community advocates because people within the city – and the local economy – stand to benefit from local public goods such as parks, the remediation of contaminated lands, and waste removal. By extension, local governments should be motivated to tackle the early twenty-first century challenge of increasing the resilience of their populations and landscapes to the effects of climate change, such as hotter temperatures, flooding, drought, and wildfires. Increasing local resilience, for example, by reconstructing parks such as the East River Park, stands to create new amenities from which local residents can benefit in the short term, while also avoiding loss of life and property damage from future flooding. Yet, adapting urbanites and their environments to climate change is costly; the budget for the East Side Coastal Resiliency project alone is $1.45 billion.[38] Accordingly, cities will require financial and other assistance from higher levels of government to adapt to climate change, even though cities have humanitarian and economic motivations for increasing local resilience to climate impacts.

Cities have weaker incentives to take serious steps to address global environmental problems compared with local ones. Reducing GHG emissions to limit climate change is a paradigmatic example of such a global problem.[39] No single jurisdiction's actions will be sufficient on their own to stabilize the planet's temperatures and minimize planetary warming. Even the United States cannot unilaterally limit global warming by reducing its emissions; historically the world's largest GHG emitter each year, it is now the second largest source of GHG emissions annually after China, which emitted 27 percent of the world's GHGs in 2019 compared to the United States' 11 percent.[40] America's most populous city has even less of a chance of stabilizing planetary temperatures on its own; New York City accounted for just under one percent of U.S. GHG emissions in 2022.[41] Moreover, serious local government efforts to reduce GHG emissions in large American cities will likely impose upfront costs on local actors, such as the owners of buildings, which are the largest source of emissions in New York City.[42] Compounding matters, the principal beneficiaries of these GHG reductions will likely be people outside the city's borders. Given the structure of the benefits and costs of reducing GHG emissions from the local perspective, it is not clear that cities, left to their own devices, will do much to mandate their residents lower their emissions. Grassroots advocacy can extend the boundaries of what is possible at the local level to encompass policies that local elites think will be economically costly, such as New York City's 2019 law capping GHG emissions from large buildings. However, such advocacy requires sustained community mobilization to overcome the ever-present tendency in city governments to favor policies perceived as enhancing local economic development. Pondering the motivations of cities to engage in environmental protection leads us to be only cautiously optimistic about the potential for large cities to meet the challenge of climate change and to underscore the need for higher levels of government, especially the federal government, to help the nation's vast urban populations address climate change.

In addition to setting out a framework for analyzing the motivations of cities to protect the environment, the book's third contribution is a series of case studies of New York City's efforts in the first two decades of the twenty-first century to address three environmental problems: the local problem of improving the quality of the city's physical environment, the global problem of reducing GHG emissions to limit planetary warming, and the local problem of adapting the city's environment to increase its resilience to climate change. Drawing on original research, Chapters 3 through 5 cumulatively offer a partial history of local environmental policy in New York City in the first two decades of this century that we hope is of interest for its own sake, independent of the way in which the chapters illustrate the book's argument about the disparate interest group dynamics from which local environmental policies emerge. New York City's limited ability to make progress in reducing GHG emissions and adapting to climate change in the first two decades of this century reinforces our view that caution is warranted about its capacity – and, more importantly, that of the many other smaller cities without New York's resources – to address the most pressing environmental problems of our time unassisted by higher levels of government.

With a clear-eyed view of cities' motivations to protect the environment and the constraints that they face in doing so, this book's fourth contribution is to define at a high level an environmental agenda for large cities for the warming world of the early twenty-first century. Setting to the side the problems of providing local public goods, such as green space, that cities have been addressing for centuries, we focus on what cities should be doing to increase local resilience to warming that is already occurring, and to assist in the global project of decarbonizing to limit climate change. We also discuss the ways in which higher levels of government, in particular the federal government, should facilitate local efforts. As mentioned earlier, localities that adapt to climate change will likely reap economic – and human – benefits of environmental safety from floods, drought, heat, and fire. Cities should be regularly updating their understandings of the risks that they face from climate change, and the differential vulnerabilities of populations and geographies within their borders. To reduce these vulnerabilities, they need to invest in bolstering the social infrastructure that their populations enjoy, as well as local physical infrastructure, such as for drinking water and stormwater. Regulation of land use and buildings could also be an important tool for reducing vulnerability to hazards such as flooding, wildfires, and extreme heat. Given the upfront costs of adapting to climate change and the expertise required, local governments, even of very large cities, will require ongoing assistance from the federal government, including in the form of predictable, annual federal funding for local climate resilience.

Since reducing GHG emissions will impose upfront costs on local actors largely for the benefit of people beyond local borders, cities lack clear incentives to require local actors to reduce these emissions. In 2022, Congress passed the Inflation Reduction Act (IRA),[43] which, if it lives up to its proponents' aspirations, may alter the economic calculus at the local level and induce local governments to undertake some actions, such as electrifying municipal vehicle fleets and installing solar panels on city government-owned buildings, that localities may not otherwise have pursued. Assuming the core elements of the IRA survive during the second Trump administration, accessing the subsidies that the IRA provides for decarbonization should be a central priority of city governments if for no other reason than any funding that cities leave on the table presumably will be taken up by other cities with which they compete for residents and industry. However, it would also be desirable for large cities to do more than access IRA funding. They should pursue a regulatory agenda to decarbonize privately owned sources of GHG emissions in their communities often under local authority, such as buildings. Large cities should also use their authority over land use regulation to promote societal decarbonization by increasing allowable residential density and facilitating the development of renewable energy infrastructure. Until Congress can legislate mandating economy-wide decarbonization, federal regulatory efforts are legally and politically precarious and cities, along with progressive states, may be able to fill some of the voids left by inadequate federal policy. Activists in cities likely will need to mobilize to promote this local decarbonization regulatory agenda. Given that decarbonization is often perceived as imposing costs on local actors for the sake of the world, local policymakers are unlikely to mandate decarbonization without pressure from activists.

Other commentators have noted that effectively addressing the climate crisis requires a "whole-of-government approach."[44] Yet, the "whole government" of which they speak is often the federal government alone,[45] and the federal government cannot be consistently relied upon to assist in the fight against climate change. Going forward, policymakers, environmental advocates, and scholars must look beyond the federal – and to a lesser extent, state – governments that have been the main focus of environmental law since the 1970s and recognize the importance of supporting urban municipalities in addressing contemporary environmental challenges, especially in adapting to climate change.[46]

PLAN FOR THE BOOK

This book proceeds as follows.

Chapter 1 sets the stage for considering the role of large U.S. cities in environmental protection in the early twenty-first century. It highlights the historical role of cities in providing environmental protection in the nineteenth and early twentieth centuries, and the gradual emergence of state and then federal environmental law in the latter third of the twentieth century as subnational governments proved inadequate at addressing the nation's environmental problems. This chapter concludes by emphasizing the potential, depending on state law, for cities to address environmental policies notwithstanding the significant federalization of environmental law, in part because federal environmental law typically imposes minimum standards that cities and states can exceed.

Chapter 2 elaborates our analytical framework for understanding why cities adopt environmental policies in the early twenty-first century, and the implications we draw from this framework about the constrained ability of cities to address pressing environmental problems such as climate change.

Chapters 3 through 5 turn from abstraction to real-world local environmental policy. These chapters analyze environmental policy in New York City in three issue areas in the first two decades of the twenty-first century. Readers interested in local environmental history could dispense with Chapter 2 and proceed directly to Chapters 3, 4, and 5.

Chapter 3 focuses on New York City's efforts to reconfigure the local environment to promote economic development as the city emerged from deindustrialization by creating new parks, redeveloping waterfront areas, cleaning up polluted sites, and improving air quality. This chapter also underscores the nascent incorporation of equity into environmental policy in the city in the first decades of the twenty-first century in response to community-based advocacy. It highlights the city government's efforts to center equity in the siting of facilities for processing the city's garbage.[47]

Chapter 4 analyzes the steps that New York City took starting in 2007 to reduce GHG emissions from buildings. Until the late 2010s, city policymakers did not impose any significantly costly regulatory requirements on local actors to decarbonize, and relied instead on information tools that did not threaten local economic interests. As mentioned earlier, in 2019, partly in response to grassroots community advocacy, New York City legislated declining caps on GHG emissions from the city's large buildings, which, if the caps are enforced, will be expensive for many owners to achieve.

Chapter 5 addresses early efforts on the part of New York City policymakers to adapt the city to climate impacts, focusing in particular on efforts to protect the city against coastal flooding. Until 2012, when Hurricane Sandy caused massive flooding in the city, city policymakers mostly focused on gathering information about the climate risks facing the city, but took few tangible actions to address these risks, apparently perceiving them as distant, uncertain, and not yet worth the costs of addressing. The lived experience of Sandy, and a massive injection of federal funding into the city after the storm, changed the calculus for policymakers, who developed the city's first plan for protecting its coastline. However, after Sandy, policymakers were slow to build coastal protection infrastructure. In the first two decades of this century, adaptation efforts, at least concerning coastal protection, appear to have been largely driven from the top, and community-based advocates have not to date exerted influence over adaption equivalent to their impact on local decarbonization efforts.

Chapter 6 outlines a high-level agenda of actions that local governments in large cities should undertake to adapt to climate change and contribute to decarbonization, taking into account the opportunities and constraints at the local level. The chapter also highlights the assistance that even large cities require from the higher levels of government, especially the federal government, the best resourced level of government, to address the challenges of a warming world. We then offer a brief coda that recapitulates the book's main themes.

New York City as a Reference Point

New York City is a central reference point in this book, although we also discuss environmental law and policy in other cities as well. As residents of New York – one of us is a native New Yorker and the other has lived in the city for over two decades – we are sensitive to the city's famous parochialism that *The New Yorker* magazine captured in a 1976 cover of a map of the United States that showed essentially nothing of interest between the Hudson River and the Pacific Ocean.[48] There also are reasons to doubt the generalizability of findings from studying local environmental policy in New York to other cities. New York City is the country's most populous city, and it has outsized wealth and resources, and extreme poverty and economic and racial inequality. Moreover, cities differ widely in the environmental challenges that they face; their political structures; their latitude to address environmental challenges based on their topographies, climates, and economies; and the politics of the states that empower them.[49]

Nonetheless, there are strong reasons for using New York as a reference point for thinking about the role of cities in environmental policy. As a large, diverse city, New York City faces many environmental challenges that other cities face on a smaller scale, such as adapting to rising temperatures, increased risks of flooding and poor air quality due to wildfires outside local borders, decarbonizing the local building stock and a history of people of color and low-income communities being disproportionately burdened by pollution. As the leading American city, its approach to environmental issues is often emulated by other cities, a phenomenon that Chapter 4 documents. Since New York's approach is a reference point for other cities, it makes sense that the city could be a reference point for scholarship too.[50] Moreover, our vantage point as New Yorkers enables us to understand local environmental policy in the city in a way that we would be hard pressed to do for other cities. Indeed, one of us (Spiegel-Feld) has contributed to the development of local New York environmental law. Drawing on our knowledge of New York, we identify patterns and frameworks whose relevance can be considered for other cities in future work.

A Note on Terminology

The book takes a broad view of what falls within the rubric of environmental law and policy. We include within *environmental* law and policy measures affecting air, water, land, the atmosphere and other resources that will protect and improve human health and biodiversity. Historically, some of the measures that we label as environmental policy measures – such as the construction of water supply systems, improving air quality, or the development of systematic garbage collection – were probably not viewed by many people as environmental measures. Supplying cities with clean water and sewers or reducing air pollution were regarded as public health measures;[51] systematizing garbage collection might have been seen as a "housekeeping" function.[52] Without denying that the policy measures that we bring under the environmental rubric might also be characterized in other ways, we think of them as environmental policy because we take a capacious view of the scope of the environment and what affects it.[53]

We are also mindful that the word "city" has several meanings.[54] As used in this book, the word "city" refers to a local authority – that is, a nonstate and nonfederal authority – that has general jurisdiction to govern a given geographic area, irrespective as to whether it is formally organized as a city, county, parish, or other.[55] As mentioned earlier, the book is primarily concerned with large cities, by which we generally have in mind cities with populations of at least 500,000. For example, in several places in the book, we provide data about patterns in environmental policy in the twenty most populous cities in the United States, which as of 2022, ranged from

New York City, with a population of over eight million, to Oklahoma City, which had a population of just over 694,000.[56] The book focuses on large cities because it is often these cities that people seem to have in mind when they emphasize the economic importance of cities and their potential to address climate change and other environmental issues. While there are differences in the resources available among the top twenty cities, the differences between the resources of these cities and the many smaller cities are likely even more vast.[57]

1

A Brief History of Cities in Environmental Policy

Contemporary discussions about the potential for cities to address climate change are often ahistorical. Both the proponents of local climate action and those who are skeptical that local governments are up to the task tend to speak as if the idea of cities tackling environmental problems is novel.[1] A look at American history underscores that this is far from the case. Indeed, in the nineteenth and early twentieth centuries, cities were often the first level of government to seek to provide many Americans with environmental protection.

Drawing on existing scholarship, this chapter sets the stage for the book's analysis of the potential for cities to address the environmental challenges of the early twenty-first century by resurrecting the contributions cities historically made to environmental protection. The historical role of cities provides support for an optimistic narrative that city governments can positively contribute to environmental protection. However, the shortcomings of the nineteenth- and early twentieth-century local efforts that led to higher-level interventions also suggest that enthusiasm for achieving environmental goals at the local level should be tempered.

In the nineteenth and early twentieth centuries, cities made some important strides to improve the local environment within their borders by developing systems to supply drinking water and collect wastewater, stormwater and solid waste, building green spaces, and attempting to address air pollution. However, cities – and states – struggled to address air and water pollution problems that crossed jurisdictional borders. In some cases, cities even exacerbated transboundary pollution problems, for example, by dumping sewage into waters on which other jurisdictions depended for drinking water. As Chapters 2 and 3 emphasize, there is a similar tendency in the early twenty-first century for cities to focus on supplying local public goods that benefit their communities, such as green spaces and local air quality.[2] As in the past, cities today have fewer incentives and tools for addressing large-scale problems, such as greenhouse gas emissions contributing to climate change, that extend beyond their borders.

CITIES AS ENVIRONMENTAL FIRST RESPONDERS

Before the emergence of administrative states at the state and federal levels, local governments, under authority states granted to them, took the lead in addressing environmental problems.[3] Supplying safe drinking water was an early priority for expanding cities. As urban populations grew during the late eighteenth and early nineteenth centuries, local waters became highly polluted and proved inadequate to meet local requirements.[4] In the older cities in the Northeast, such as New York and Philadelphia, and the newly emerging cities of the Midwest, such as Chicago, local governments and agencies built water supply systems to provide city residents with clean drinking water to improve public health and fight fires.[5]

Philadelphia was the first city in the United States to establish a public water supply system in 1801, after a devastating yellow fever epidemic in 1793 "shut down" the city, then "the country's capital and busiest shipping port."[6] It took New York City longer to establish its own water supply system to import water into the city.[7] A New York State-appointed Board of Water Commissioners built the Croton Aqueduct, which opened to much fanfare in 1842.[8] The impetus for constructing the city-owned water supply system came from the city and city-issued bonds paid the entire cost of building the system, which exceeded $10 million.[9] "By 1860, the nation's sixteen largest cities, as well as many smaller ones" had water supply systems.[10] The introduction of these systems, combined with growing urban populations, led to increased demand for water.[11]

With water more readily available, people started introducing indoor water closets. To remove wastewater, American cities then built sewage systems, which often dumped untreated sewage into nearby waterbodies.[12] Cities were also the first level of government to seek to address air pollution starting in the late nineteenth and early twentieth centuries.[13] With coal as the dominant source of energy, cities were covered in smoke, especially Pittsburgh and other places in the Midwest where bituminous coal was burned.[14] In response, local community groups, including initially many formed by "middle-class women," organized to pressure local governments to enact anti-smoke ordinances to clean the air.[15]

A key way in which America's nineteenth- and early twentieth-century cities addressed environmental problems was through governmental choices about local land uses. Local governments have long played a role in determining how land is used within their borders, and their ability to control land use remains one of the most important levers that they use to pursue economic development and other objectives. In the nineteenth and twentieth centuries, cities employed this land use authority to build pioneering parks, and clean air was one of the reasons cited for building them.[16] Central Park, which opened gradually starting in 1858, was the "first landscaped public park in the United States" and led to the creation of other urban parks.[17] The establishment of urban parks also influenced the development of national parks.[18] In addition to introducing green spaces, nineteenth- and early twentieth-century local governments prohibited activities, such as brickyards and livery stables, from city neighborhoods to reduce smells, air pollution, and other environmental harms.[19]

Originally devised in Germany, the technique of zoning land for residential, industrial, commercial, and other purposes spread rapidly in the United States in the early twentieth century after New York City adopted its first zoning resolution in 1916.[20] By restricting industry and commercial establishments to particular areas of the city, and protecting residential areas from industrial and commercial development, zoning offered the potential to avoid environmental harms in residential areas that might have given rise to what the courts would have considered nuisances in the nineteenth century, such as air pollution in residential areas from factories.[21] Of course, there was a less favorable side of zoning as well, which observers recognized early on: it can be used to segregate people based on race and income.[22]

Around the same time in which America's urban elite endeavored to build new parks, and separate incompatible land uses, the nation's cities started to swell with refuse[23] and the "garbage nuisance came to be seen as a serious environmental problem."[24] The prevailing system of the early nineteenth century, whereby individuals were left to dispose of their garbage on their own or use private contractors,[25] proved unworkable as urban areas became more densely populated and cities' increasingly unsanitary conditions were blamed for a number of public health problems.[26] Urban inhabitants looked to local governments for relief.[27] In cities such as New York and Chicago, women's organizations were formed in the late nineteenth century to persuade local governments to improve sanitary conditions, including improving street cleaning.[28] In response, many local authorities developed municipal garbage collection and street cleaning services. For most of the nineteenth century, the resulting services were far from exemplary.[29] But around the turn of the twentieth century, George Waring, a sanitary engineer who was New York City's street-cleaning commissioner, developed the city's first comprehensive waste management strategy and started to bring the city's garbage problem in check.[30] Waring's reforms inspired other cities to improve their own waste management plans too.[31] It took more than half a century following Waring's death for the federal government to make its first serious attempt to regulate solid waste.[32]

STATE INTERVENTIONS AND THEN FEDERALIZATION

While local governments were often the first level of government to undertake measures to protect the environment, there were clear limitations to these local efforts. Local governments exported pollution problems to other places, for example, by dumping untreated sewage into water bodies that other jurisdictions relied upon for drinking water.[33] In 1889, the state of Illinois established a regional sanitary district to deal with the problem of Chicago's sewage polluting Lake Michigan, from which the city drew water supplies.[34] The regional authority built a canal that reversed the flow of the Chicago River to avoid the city's sewage being dumped into the Lake. However, the effect of the project was to send Chicago's sewage into rivers from which other Illinois communities and St. Louis, Missouri drew their water.[35]

As twenty-first-century histories emphasize, people in poor neighborhoods did not initially benefit from local environmental protection measures such as drinking water supply and sewage systems to the same degree as people in wealthier enclaves.[36] In the south, some "black communities were provided with these services only to prevent diseases from spilling over into white neighborhoods."[37] In other cases, people in marginalized communities bore the costs of environmental improvements that mainly benefited others. When Central Park was built in the nineteenth century, Black landowners and "poor whites" were displaced from land incorporated into the park.[38]

In the late nineteenth and early twentieth centuries, state governments intervened in an attempt to overcome local governments' incentives to address local environmental problems in ways that harmed other localities in the state. The spread of typhoid prompted states to establish state boards of health starting in the late nineteenth century to regulate sewage disposal and to prohibit new sewer systems from dumping sewage into water bodies.[39] "By 1927, all but four states had boards of health with divisions of sanitary engineering" to regulate water pollution, but enforcement "was lax" and "state boards preferred" cooperating with industry.[40] The development of state capacity in the late nineteenth and early twentieth centuries in the environmental area was consistent with a general trend at the state level to assert greater control over functions that the states had previously delegated to local governments as the bounds of economic activity expanded, and greater expertise and funding were needed to address contemporary challenges than many local governments could supply.[41]

As the twentieth century unfolded, the scale of environmental problems extended beyond the capacity of even state governments to address and the federal government eventually assumed a dominant role in environmental protection in the 1960s and 1970s. The federalization of environmental law loosely tracked the more general rise of the federal government as a domestic policymaker in the twentieth century.[42] The Depression had demonstrated the limits of state and local governments, and the federal government had intervened to help the nation recover from the economic crisis.[43] After taking on foreign powers in World War II and the Cold War, the federal government assumed a leading role in dismantling racial segregation at home.[44] States seemed like backwaters, with southern state leaders defending racial segregation during the Civil Rights Movement, while the federal government appeared to be the champion of "social progress."[45] The rights-based discourse of the era influenced the federalization of environmental law.[46] As an illustration, in 1970, the year that popular concern with the environment culminated in massive Earth Day rallies across the country, President Nixon stated in "his … State of the Union address, … 'Clean air, clean water, open spaces – these would once again be the birthright of every American.'"[47]

The scale of the nation's environmental problems was another reason for the federalization of environmental law in the latter part of the twentieth century.[48] As the country's economy became more nationally and internationally integrated, pollution problems crossed not only local but also state borders.[49] The motor vehicles that contributed to air pollution traveled between municipalities and states; it would therefore do little good for a state – let alone a city – to impose emission standards on cars and trucks if owners could avoid these standards by buying cars in other places that did not regulate vehicular emissions and driving the cars into regulating jurisdictions. National standards for new cars would also be more palatable to the auto manufacturers who wanted to avoid a patchwork of state standards if governments were to regulate auto emissions. Congress legislated in 1965 that the federal Department of Health, Education, and Welfare establish emission standards for new cars.[50]

Similarly, air pollution from large stationary sources, such as power plants and steel mills, crossed state borders, as did water pollution, fueling conflicts that the states themselves struggled to resolve. For example, in the New York City metropolitan area, pollution from New Jersey's heavy industries was a major source of air pollution and associated health problems in Manhattan and Staten Island.[51] In the decades leading up to the Clean Air Act of 1970, New York and New Jersey were never able to agree on a mechanism to address the regional air pollution problem, in large measure, it seems, because New Jersey was reluctant to regulate its industries.[52] New York City and state officials appealed for federal assistance in addressing interstate air pollution in the region in the 1960s.[53] In 1964, for example, New York City's Mayor Wagner bluntly described the pernicious status quo in testimony to the United States Senate. "A great deal of the smoke and dirty air in New York City comes each morning from the large industrial areas of Jersey,"[54] Wagner explained. 'We return the compliment each afternoon, depending on the prevailing winds, or we pass some of our smoke and gases on to our Long Island or Connecticut neighbors.'"[55] The inability of cities and states to resolve air pollution problems in major interstate metropolitan regions "became a prime justification for increased federal intervention in interstate air pollution control."[56] Federal legislation also held out the hope of a more comprehensive resolution to interstate water pollution problems that localities and states were unable to resolve on their own.[57]

Part of the reason that states and local governments failed to curtail air and water pollution is that they had strong incentives not to hinder industrial development in their jurisdictions.[58] From the end of World War II until 1978, manufacturing was the "engine" of the U.S. economy.[59] Cities and states competed to attract manufacturing and other industry, and environmental standards were one axis on which they competed.[60] If one jurisdiction required its industrial sources to reduce their pollution, it risked losing industry to others.[61] And if the pollution crossed jurisdictional boundaries, any gains in environmental quality might be canceled out by another jurisdiction adopting lower environmental standards.[62] Illustrating how New Jersey used low environmental standards to attract industry, environmental historian Scott Dewey recounted that in 1967, New York Senator Robert F. Kennedy took a helicopter tour of the New York metropolitan area "to review the interstate air pollution situation. [H]e and his companions passed over a smoke-belching factory in New Jersey with a large sign offering an unsubtle reminder of the lax state of industrial regulation in the Garden State for New York industrialists considering relocation: 'Hoboken Welcomes Industry, Come on Over.'"[63]

Further stacking the odds against robust regulations, in the 1970s, many major U.S. cities had limited room to take steps that might alienate industry and residents. They were losing people to the suburbs; between 1950 and 1980, "[e]ighteen of the nation's twenty-five largest cities in 1950 suffered a net *loss* of population."[64] Employers also were decamping from cities, following people to the suburbs.[65] In an article published in 1980, Professor Gerald Frug wrote, "[t]he problem of the increasing exodus of wealthier taxpayers, including businesses, from the nation's major cities is notorious."[66]

Perhaps owing to their incentives to appease industry, few state or local governments invested substantially in developing the institutions that would be necessary to regulate pollution. According to Professor William Andreen, "[i]n 1961, only 43 percent of the communities with major or moderate air pollution problems had control programs whose budget exceeded $5,000 per year."[67] Even New York City, the nation's most populous city, "was never able" to set up an effective air pollution control agency after many years of trying, and the air quality in the city was dismal in the late 1960s.[68] Indeed, by the mid 1960s, New York reputedly had the worst urban air quality in the country.[69]

For all of these reasons, environmentalists in the 1960s and 1970s favored federalization.[70] They thought that the federal government would be more responsive to environmental concerns and less likely to be captured by industry in setting standards than local and state governments had been to date.[71] Also, uniform national pollution standards would limit the ability of industry to lower standards by playing one community "against another."[72] Industries sought to avoid federalization precisely because they thought that they had more influence at the local and state levels than they would have federally.[73] In a striking contrast to the political polarization today between Democrats and Republicans on environmental issues, there was bipartisan support for federalization. Both political parties supported more aggressive federal measures to protect the environment in the 1970s.[74] From this confluence of interests, the landmark federal environmental statutes of the 1970s were born.

CITIES' ROLE IN A FEDERALIZED FIELD

Federalization of environmental law meant that the federal government would henceforth establish standards that states and cities and industry would have to meet.[75] However, cities and states were differentially affected by the federal government's new role as a standard-setter. Federal law often includes provisions delegating authority to the states – but not to local governments – to implement federal standards within their borders by regulating industry.[76] Moreover, the federal delegation of authority to states sometimes newly empowered states to co-opt city governments to advance state objectives. Cities are subject to the federal standards that states administer because cities operate infrastructure, such as drinking water supply systems and wastewater treatment facilities, that federal standards regulate, similar to other industrial pollution sources. Thus, federal environmental law has required cities to spend funds on environmental protection that they otherwise might have allocated to other local priorities.[77] For instance, in order to meet the dictates of the federal Safe Drinking Water Act of 1974, New York City had to build a $3.2 billion water filtration plant to filter water from the old Croton system,[78] to more strictly regulate land use near its reservoirs, to upgrade sewage treatment plants, and more.[79] Cities also have had to make similar infrastructure investments to meet federal water quality objectives embedded in the Clean Water Act and applied to cities by states under delegated federal authority.[80]

Even so, federalization has preserved space for cities and states to innovate in some very important areas. First, the application of federal standards to locally provided services, such as water supply and sewage treatment, has motivated localities to develop novel, and lower-cost, means of achieving these standards.[81] While the Clean Water Act initially led local governments to build sewage treatment plants, in the 2000s, cities began embedding green infrastructure, such as green roofs and bioswales, as a way of meeting Clean Water Act standards without having to expand the sewer system by building new pipes, reservoirs, and other forms of "gray infrastructure."[82]

More significantly, cities retain the ability to address issues that are not the subject of federal regulation, such as greenhouse gas emissions from buildings. In addition, where the federal government has regulated an issue, cities often can develop standards that exceed federal standards. Federal standards typically set a regulatory floor, not ceiling, in the common parlance of the literature.[83] Exceptions to this rule, such as energy efficiency standards for appliances and emission standards for new motor vehicles, involve clear economies of scale to create uniform national product standards; in such cases, local and state governments generally cannot exceed (or undercut) the federal standards.[84] Outside of these contexts where federal regulations impose uniform product standards, cities and states have the authority under federal law to adopt standards that surpass federal minimums.[85]

Cities also maintain primary responsibility for regulating land use within their jurisdictions, which can materially influence the amount of pollution that urbanites produce. As an example, cities typically establish zoning, which enables them to influence density and travel distances, and hence demand for energy. Cities also can choose how to allocate space on their streets, which influences residents' transportation choices. If all the streets are reserved for motor vehicles, residents will naturally rely more on private cars for transportation than if large portions of the roads are reserved for bicyclists, buses, and pedestrians.

CONCLUSION

The rest of this book is about how cities are using – and might use – the authority that they enjoy in the early twenty-first century to address contemporary environmental problems. With the development of state and federal environmental regulation, there are more potential sources of environmental protection for urban residents than there were in the nineteenth century, though these other levels of government may not necessarily provide the protections urbanites desire.

Chapter 2 outlines a framework for examining the kinds of environmental problems that large cities are most incentivized to tackle. There are important continuities with the nineteenth- and early twentieth-century histories of local efforts. As in the past, large cities seem more motivated to act to invest in their local environment, than to tackle environmental problems that extend beyond their boundaries. This is especially the case where investments in the local environment will yield quick, visible payoffs. However, the permeability of local governments to interest groups, including environmental groups, means that sometimes these governments will take steps to address large-scale problems – such as limiting global climate change – even where the benefits to local actors are attenuated.

2

An Analytical Framework

In 2018, the city council in Washington, D.C., passed the first local law in the nation mandating that large existing buildings reduce their energy use to help limit climate change.[1] As of 2023, at least eight other cities – and four states – had legislated requirements that existing buildings reduce their greenhouse gas (GHG) emissions or improve their energy efficiency.[2] To comply with these requirements, building owners may need to make costly changes to reduce energy consumption; the GHG standards also may necessitate expensive investments in electrifying heating and cooling systems and removing natural gas and oil boilers.[3] For example, the president of a residential cooperative suing New York City over its GHG-based building performance standard argues that it will cost $35 million to electrify the heating systems serving the cooperative's 10,000 "middle-and-working class" residents.[4] The residents may have to pay higher maintenance fees or special assessments to help finance the transition.[5]

What leads a city government to pass a law that may require local building owners to spend significant sums of their own funds to reduce energy use or GHG emissions to limit planetary climate change?[6] This chapter provides a framework for understanding what drives city governments in the early twenty-first century to engage in environmental protection efforts in the absence of mandates or generous subsidies from higher levels of government. We start with the reality, widely acknowledged in scholarship about local governments, that promoting local economic growth is a "central preoccupation" of these governments.[7] The importance that city policymakers attach to local economic development reflects the precarious position of U.S. local governments. Even populous cities, such as New York and Los Angeles, are relatively small jurisdictions nested within larger states and a federation, competing with other localities for residents and businesses to maintain a tax base to fund an array of services, such as police and fire.[8]

Within the confines within which cities exist, two interest group dynamics can give rise to local environmental protection efforts. First, such efforts can emerge from the top down in reflection of the preferences of local elites. Sometimes city policymakers, such as mayors or top civil servants, perceive that environmental policies will promote local economic prosperity. They might come to this view on their own, or as a result of arguments advanced by powerful local interests with whom they are in contact, such as leading business people or real estate owners, that perceive some environmental protection to be in their private economic interests. For example, property developers might support revamping industrial waterfronts into parks to increase the value of neighboring land; the developers might argue to city policymakers that the parks also stand to benefit the wider neighborhood and the city as a whole.

Second, in contradistinction to the first explanation, local environmental protection efforts might emerge "from the bottom up," in response to grassroots advocacy. Such groups may be motivated to participate in the political process for many reasons, including a moral commitment to saving the earth, a belief that undesirable land uses, such as garbage collection facilities or bus depots, should be more equitably distributed in the city, or a desire to improve public health. Notably, the grassroots advocates might propose policies that elites fear will harm the local economy or at least the interests of economic elites. Nonetheless, the grassroots advocates might be able to prevail under certain circumstances, such as where they are well organized and can credibly influence local elections.[9]

That there are multiple paths that can lead to the development of local environmental protection policies highlights the scope for such initiatives to emerge. Yet there are also limits on the environmental policies that local governments can adopt. The position of local governments as small actors requiring a tax base, nested within larger political units that define the bounds of local authority, severely constrains cities' ability to solve many of the most pressing contemporary environmental problems, such as climate change, on their own.

This chapter begins by emphasizing the precarious position of cities in the U.S. context; this precarity provides the starting point for understanding the determinants of local environmental protection efforts. The chapter then elaborates the top-down and bottom-up hypotheses for why cities have developed a substantial amount of environmental policy notwithstanding the many constraints they face. Finally, the chapter analyzes the implications of these hypotheses for the potential to rely on local governments to address environmental problems.

THE PRECARIOUS POSITION OF CITIES

In a seminal book published in 1981, political scientist Paul Peterson argued that local governments are buffeted by forces beyond their control.[10] *City Limits* came out just a few years after New York City almost went bankrupt in the mid-1970s, and the shadow of that fiscal crisis likely influenced Peterson's perception of cities as economically vulnerable actors that had to focus on maintaining their tax base.[11] However, as Peterson and others argue, there are structural reasons for regarding cities as precarious political entities, even setting aside New York's famous fiscal crisis.

The boundaries of local governments' authority are typically defined by state law. While state law usually authorizes local governments to deliver a range of services, it also often limits the tools that localities can use to provide and fund these services, and circumscribes localities' ability to run annual deficits.[12] Complicating matters, the state law establishing the bounds of local action is not necessarily stable; cities are vulnerable to the whims of state lawmakers, who may curtail local power.[13] Indeed, local government scholars have suggested that state preemption of local governments has recently increased due in part to the contemporary partisan divide between Democratic cities and Republican rural areas.[14] Federal law and policy can further constrain local governments' ability to deliver the services for which they are responsible. Federal monetary, fiscal, and immigration policies influence the economic and social environments in which cities exist, affecting the stability of their revenues, the interest rates that they pay on debt, and the size of local populations.[15] Federal law also may preempt local and state laws, or, like state law, be interpreted by the courts as preemptive.[16]

Given the narrow space in which they operate, local governments tend to focus on promoting economic prosperity in order to maintain, and expand, the local tax base that largely funds municipal services.[17] In so doing, they compete with other local governments for the businesses and individuals that make up their tax base.[18] For decades, academics have theorized about, and provided empirical evidence of, the "central preoccupations" of local governments with economic growth and development, and the competition among localities for businesses and individuals that will contribute to achieving these goals.[19]

In a book about his time as Deputy Mayor of New York City for Economic Development and Rebuilding from 2002 to 2007 under Mayor Michael Bloomberg, Daniel Doctoroff explicitly describes his focus on competing to attract residents and businesses to enhance the city's fiscal position. In one passage, Doctoroff reflects on how he saw his job as selling the city to grow its population.[20] "In my mind," Doctoroff writes, "a city was like any other product. It had customers. It had competitors. It had to be marketed. How would you know if you were doing your job successfully? The answer: more people would choose New York over other places to live, and the population would grow."[21] A bit later, Doctoroff explains why growth is desirable from a budgetary perspective for the city:

> For a city, each new resident is attractive as long as the marginal tax revenues from that one additional person are greater than the marginal costs of supporting him or her. Because cities have already invested so much money in infrastructure (at least those in the developed world), adding the average new person will typically allow a city to make a "net profit" on him or her.[22]

Doctoroff's description of the city government as selling a product to expand its budget might strike some readers as cold and calculating. The ease with which Doctoroff assimilates the city government to a market actor likely owes something to his private sector career, including in private equity, before becoming deputy mayor.[23] Indeed, the Bloomberg administration has been characterized by observers, such as anthropologist Julian Brash, as highly focused on marketing New York City as a "luxury product" to global businesspeople and professionals with backgrounds similar to key figures in the administration.[24] But in a few words, Doctoroff bluntly provides evidence for the long-standing academic hypothesis that local governments compete for residents by offering different packages of goods and services.[25]

TWO HYPOTHESES FOR LOCAL ENVIRONMENTAL ACTION

As indicated earlier, within the narrow bounds within which local governments operate, there are two disparate interest group dynamics that give rise to local environmental protection efforts in the early twenty-first century: They may emerge from the top down, at the urging of local elites, who view environmental protection as consistent with cities' economic interests, or they may emerge from the bottom up, following organized pressure from grassroots advocates for whom such protection is part of a broader social justice or environmental agenda.

Elite Perceptions that Environmental Protections Promote Economic Prosperity

City policymakers focused on promoting local economic growth sometimes pursue environmental measures, such as building parks or cleaning up contaminated land, because the policymakers perceive these measures as benefitting the city's economy, notwithstanding their upfront costs. In promoting such measures, city policymakers may be following their own assessment that the measures will grow the city's economy, or they might be influenced by advocacy from large businesses or real estate interests that stand to obtain private economic benefits from the measures, such as higher property values or more business revenue.[26]

Scholarship on urban politics has long emphasized the power of local elites to dictate city policy in various areas, such as land use, and it is logical that such elites would influence the related field of local environmental policy as well.[27] The composition of local elites varies across time and place, and members of elites disagree with each other.[28] In *The Permanent Government*, published in the early 1980s, writers and social activists Jack Newfield and Paul Du Brul argued that "about 1500 or 2000 people" governed New York City, but that power was more decentralized than in other places because "[t]here [was] … no one political boss like the late Richard Daley of Chicago … [or] controlling financial family[.]"[29] According to Newfield and Du Brul, many of the city's power brokers were from "the banks and financial institutions" and the real estate industry.[30] The city's elite also included top elected and appointed city and state officials, such as Robert Moses in his prime.[31]

In the early twenty-first century, city elites, such as Bloomberg era power broker Doctoroff, often seem to subscribe to the "Creative Class" theory of economic development. This theory posits that making postindustrial cities attractive to today's high-income earners is key to expanding a city's economy and tax base.[32] City officials and others commonly think of new parks, bicycle paths, and clean air and water as amenities that appeal to the Creative Class of high-income professionals in technology, finance, and professional services, as well as tourists. As discussed in Chapter 3, in the first two decades of this century, New York and many other cities pursued a green economic development strategy that involved reconfiguring their physical environments to adapt to the deindustrialization of their economies and the departure of manufacturing jobs in the twentieth century.

The idea that protecting the environment might promote economic growth is not novel.[33] In the nineteenth and early twentieth centuries, cities in the Northeast, the Midwest and the West would not have grown if they had not invested in securing drinking water for their residents. Building drinking water supply systems to bring safe water for residents to drink and to fight fires was an economic development project. New York apparently sought to build a water supply system in part because it saw that Philadelphia had suffered fewer deaths from an epidemic after the city built such a system, and the construction of the water supply system likely helped New York become the economic metropolis that it remains today.[34] Building sewer systems and organizing garbage collection were also necessary to remove wastes from cities to make them livable.[35] Establishing landmark public parks, such as Central Park, increased neighboring land values, and real estate interests supported the creation of new parks.[36]

As discussed in Chapter 1, in the mid-to-late twentieth century, when industries were leaving cities, few observers thought that city governments had an economic interest in protecting the environment. Although Peterson recognized the provision of sewers (an environmental amenity in our terms) as consistent with the local goal of attracting businesses, he argued that cities had an incentive to lure businesses with lax regulation of air and water pollution.[37] Many other observers concluded that cities and states would not impose strict pollution standards on industries for fear that they would relocate to other areas; the perception that subnational governments were unable to regulate pollution due to the competition in which they were engaged for business was an important argument for federalizing environmental law in the 1970s.[38] However, the experience of the mid-twentieth century should not obscure the potential that early twenty-first century local governments might perceive environmental policy as developmental policy, at least when the city's economy depends on service rather than extractive industries.

Grassroots Advocacy

The second pathway through which local environmental protection efforts can emerge is from the bottom up in response to grassroots community advocacy. Coincident with the revival of major cities in the late twentieth and early twenty-first centuries, Professors Clay Gillette, Richard Schragger, and others argued that cities have the ability to do more than promote economic development by competing for mobile businesses and residents, and can indeed engage in redistribution from rich to poor, contrary to Peterson's argument in *City Limits*.[39] Interest groups, including environmental groups, can form within cities and influence local government policy, sometimes even if the groups' policy preferences will impose costs on powerful local actors, such as large property or business owners, and potentially run counter to the city's overall economic interests.[40] To be sure, grassroots advocates need allies within local governments, such as city council members or influential civil servants, to implement the groups' policy preferences. But grassroots advocates can catalyze interest in such policies and help bring them to fruition.

Grassroots advocates have organized at the local level in recent decades to achieve a variety of environmental goals. In an era of pronounced global warming, some climate activists are pushing local governments to decarbonize local sources of GHG emissions, such as transportation and buildings, even though doing so is costly for local actors. As will be discussed in Chapter 4, local climate activists played an important role in persuading New York City to adopt legislation in 2019 capping GHG emissions from large buildings in the face of federal inaction during the first Trump administration.

Other grassroots groups advocate local environmental protection efforts to overcome disparities in pollution burdens and access to environmental amenities, such as parks, that have harmed low-income people and people of color. Chapter 3 recounts the decades-long efforts of community-based advocates in New York City to redistribute the waste transfer stations that process large amounts of the city's solid waste from a small number of communities populated by many low-income people and people of color and the willingness of the Bloomberg and de Blasio mayoral administrations to adopt the policy goals of these advocates. Invoking the idea of "equity" in allocating responsibility for waste, these advocates seem motivated by concerns about racial and economic justice, not principally local economic development.

Still other individuals advocate environmental protection at the local level to protect nonhuman animals and species. In 2019, advocates for birds in New York City, including the NYC Audubon Society, persuaded the city council to pass a law requiring the use of "bird-friendly materials" on the exteriors of new buildings and substantially altered buildings in the city to reduce bird deaths from collisions with buildings.[41] The legislation was the culmination of years of work, including community monitoring of bird collisions with buildings, which was started by NYC Audubon in 1997.[42]

There are several reasons why cities are permeable to the advocacy of climate, environmental justice, animal, and other environmental activists in addition to the business interests that have long dominated local politics.[43] Lacking the "time and resources" to sift through technical documents to devise novel policies, members of local legislatures and policy staff in local governments may welcome ideas from outside interest groups, including environmental and social justice groups.[44] Compared with the federal and state governments, local governments are easier to access.[45] City council members and civil servants in executive agencies often work and live in the same communities as residents, meaning that local advocates do not have to travel far to meet in person. Formally, the process for passing local laws is often relatively straightforward, with many fewer hurdles for interest groups to overcome than exist at the federal and state levels. Local legislatures usually have a single body, not two as at the federal and state levels.[46] Voter turnout in local elections is often low, which means that interest groups that can turn out members to vote – or credibly threaten to do so – may have substantial sway with local elected officials.[47] Because local politicians represent small geographic areas, big media buys are not as relevant in these campaigns, which means that the most well-heeled interest groups are not necessarily the most powerful.

As Chapter 4 indicates, local governments were particularly attractive targets of opportunity for climate activists during Republican presidential administrations in the first two decades of this century, when the gap between what was achievable locally and federally to address climate change was great.[48] Two defining features of politics in the early twenty-first century are that Democrats are much more concerned about climate change than Republicans,[49] and Democrats tend to cluster in cities, while Republicans dominate in rural areas.[50] That people who are more likely to be concerned with climate change tend to concentrate in cities suggests that local officials may have greater political scope to address the issue than state or federal institutions. These higher levels of government also must be responsive to rural residents, more of whom seem to oppose climate action.

In addition to the political latitude that big city governments may have to pursue global public goods such as limiting climate change, large cities, especially marquee cities, have some latitude to adopt environmental measures that impose costs on local actors without causing a contraction of their tax base. As the revival of large U.S. cities in the late twentieth and early twenty-first centuries showed, many people and businesses are eager to locate in highly populated areas in the postindustrial era notwithstanding the higher cost of living and the hassles associated with these areas, such as traffic congestion. They derive compensating benefits from the agglomerations of people and firms in cities. Individuals enjoy more opportunities to engage and learn from other people and employment opportunities than they would in small communities. Firms have access to more workers, customers, and other firms in similar businesses, all of which seem to be especially beneficial in knowledge industries.[51] The downsides of living in large densely populated cities became more visible during the COVID pandemic and remote work expanded, prompting people to leave these cities and leading to concerns that these cities will soon face economic crises comparable to those of the 1970s.[52] But there likely are still enduring agglomeration benefits to being in large cities,[53] and these benefits probably offer large cities some latitude to adopt environmental protection requirements that impose costs on private firms within their borders that might not usually be seen as within localities' economic interests.[54] Still, there is presumably a tipping point – hard to specify in the abstract – beyond which local governments cannot impose further costs without leading some individuals and firms to relocate. The individuals and firms likely to bear the costs of local government actions will be incentivized to bring these costs to the attention of local governments, and they will be able to avail themselves of the same highly permeable channels of influence as the advocates of environmental protection.

IMPLICATIONS FOR LOCAL ENVIRONMENTAL POLICY

Since local environmental policy can emerge from the bottom up, as well as the top down, there is more scope for cities to engage in environmental protection than is suggested by the common image of city governments as beholden to policymakers and business interests focused on promoting economic development. However, the scope for local environmental protection efforts is not limitless in the early twenty-first century, especially, as mentioned earlier, when the constraints imposed by state and federal laws and market forces are taken into account. What are the implications of the internal top-down and bottom-up political dynamics and external constraints described earlier on city governments for the types of environmental issues that local governments might address?

Local Public Goods

One implication is that cities are most likely to focus on improving their local physical environment, or to use different terms, providing local public goods such as green spaces, garbage collection, and sewer systems.[55] City policymakers focused on increasing local prosperity so as to maintain and grow their tax base seem likely to have a particular incentive to improve the quality of the local environment by building new parks, improving local air quality by reducing in-city pollution, protecting the city against flooding, and reducing waste; this incentive is especially strong where city economies depend on services rather than natural resource extraction. Some of the business interests that so much scholarship indicates have the ear of city policymakers also are likely to favor improvements to the local physical environment. Such improvements stand to benefit the value of corporate assets in the city (such as landholdings) or increase the attractiveness of cities to employees in the knowledge economy and tourists. Grassroots advocates also are likely to support improving the local environment since they stand to benefit, though they may disagree about what counts as an improvement and where in the city improvements should occur.[56] For example, community advocates may favor investments in neighborhood parks over destination waterfront green spaces or sites for new commercial or residential development, or prioritize reducing sources of air pollution in low-income neighborhoods, such as solid waste facilities.[57]

Yet, while cities are incentivized to focus on providing local public goods to improve their economic prosperity, they are limited in their ability to do so by the legal and market constraints mentioned earlier. They cannot devote unlimited resources to improving and maintaining their local physical environments. Doing so would require huge increases in taxes, which at a certain point would lead businesses and individuals to exit for lower cost jurisdictions.

Furthermore, the distribution of political power within a city when an environmental measure is adopted will influence who benefits and who pays for the enhanced environmental protection, and how quickly different groups will receive benefits. There are well-known instances of cities improving their local environment for some people at the expense of historically marginalized communities. When sewers were built in New York City in the nineteenth century, "[i]t was common for sewer outfalls to terminate in poor or minority neighborhoods."[58] When New York City built a sewage treatment plant along the Hudson River to comply with the federal Clean Water Act in the late twentieth century, the city built it near a predominantly Black and Latino neighborhood.[59] When cities have invested in environmental protection, low-income people and people of color also have historically been slower to benefit from these investments, and not received a proportionate share of the benefits. Professor Dorceta Taylor explains that in the nineteenth century,

> [g]rave inequities existed in the delivery of urban services in New Orleans and other parts of the South. Black neighborhoods were not provided with sewage systems, clean water, paved streets, or garbage removal as early or as frequently as white neighborhoods. In some cases black communities were provided with these services only to prevent diseases from spilling over into white neighborhoods.[60]

There remain vast disparities based on race in access to high-quality green space in urban areas.[61]

Global Public Goods

If the internal political dynamics within cities incentivize city governments to improve the local physical environment, albeit sometimes in inequitable ways, these same dynamics raise questions about the likelihood that city governments are motivated to aid in improving the global environment, for example by aggressively decarbonizing to limit climate change.[62]

Start with the top-down dynamic that postulates that local environmental policy sometimes emerges from a perception among city elites that improving the local environment in a particular way will be economically beneficial for the city. Reducing GHG emissions within the city benefits the whole world; while city residents enjoy some benefits from the lowered GHG emissions (and reductions in co-pollutants, such as particulate matter), the GHG reductions mainly benefit people outside the city. Moreover, decarbonizing the main sources of GHG emissions in cities, transportation and buildings, will impose high upfront costs on local actors.[63] The paucity of city policies to aggressively decarbonize local communities in the first two decades of this century suggests that city policymakers focused on local economic prosperity are unlikely to implement on their own climate policies with such a lopsided local cost-benefit structure.[64]

The bottom-up explanation for local environmental policy suggests that there is more scope at the local level for acting to confer global public goods, such as reductions in GHG emissions, than the top-down explanation. However, grassroots advocates have to mobilize effectively to persuade city governments to act to confer benefits on the world at the expense of local actors. The need for effective mobilization at the local level counsels caution about the prospect that cities will lead in limiting climate change. The scale of the necessary mobilization would be vast; environmentalists and others will need to engage in sustained advocacy and mobilization in cities across the country to persuade them to adopt and implement local decarbonization policies that would impose upfront costs on local actors.[65] This scale of mobilization would require significant philanthropic investments in grassroots advocacy, with no guarantee of the nation-wide results necessary to set the country on the path to decarbonization. For even city policymakers sympathetic to the need to decarbonize must consider the impact on their local economies of mandating aggressive decarbonization given the importance for local governments to maintain their tax base to fund service provision.

In sum, the two interest group explanations for the emergence of local environmental policy suggest caution is in order about the likelihood that city governments will of their own volition seek to aggressively decarbonize their communities. Through the Inflation Reduction Act of 2022, and components of the Bipartisan Infrastructure Law from 2021, the Biden administration sought to alter the cost-benefit calculus of cities (and many other public and private actors) to further decarbonization. As this book goes to press in 2025, it is unclear whether the financial incentives that these statutes provided to decarbonize will survive the second Trump administration, and if they do, whether they will spur considerable decarbonization at the local level.

While we are less optimistic about the potential for cities to play a meaningful role in decarbonization than some of those who have invested time and resources in building up municipal capacity on climate change,[66] we are more optimistic than some of the legal scholarship spanning decades doubting that subnational governments can develop robust environmental law.[67] The urban enthusiasts tend to underestimate the legal and market constraints on local governments, even large ones such as New York City, which must compete for residents and industry to maintain a tax base to fund an array of services subject to state, and to some extent, federal, law constraints. In emphasizing the constrained nature of cities, we offer a corrective to the enthusiasm for local climate policy that appeared in the late 2010s amid the first Trump administration's hostility to climate policy.[68] Conversely, the latter legal scholarship sometimes seems to assume that the actions of local governments are based solely on economic self-interest, to define that self-interest narrowly, and to underestimate the potential – illuminated in early twenty-first century scholarship on urban politics – for grassroots political advocacy to lead cities to adopt policies that might appear to be inconsistent with local economic self-interest. Our measured optimism suggests that large cities can play a role in decarbonization, even though it conveys a global public good. But for them to be effective, climate activists will need to mobilize over a sustained period at the local level to maintain the pressure on local officials who are highly sensitive to cities' needs to cultivate local economic prosperity to sustain the tax base.[69]

CONCLUSION

Recognizing that large cities have some incentives to address environmental issues on their own initiative in the early twenty-first century underscores the importance of defining how these cities might contribute to tackling contemporary environmental challenges, such as climate change. Leading environmental federalism scholarship tends to focus on what responsibilities each of the federal and state governments should assume in protecting the environment given the diversity of problems and preferences across the country.[70] Yet, after decades, there is no resolution to the debate about the comparative benefits of federalization versus decentralization.[71] Moreover, it is valuable to consider the potential for cities in particular, not merely as adjuncts to states, to help meet the environmental challenges of the early twenty-first century given current local incentives. Taking into account our analysis of cities' incentives to confront local and global environmental problems, Chapter 6 considers what city governments should do to adapt to and limit climate change. It also explores what higher levels of government might do to assist cities in light of the constraints that they face if the higher levels of government are interested in advancing environmental protection. However, before sketching an urban environmental agenda for the early twenty-first century, the next three chapters recount the recent history of environmental policy in New York City to illustrate cities' multifaceted motivations for pursuing environmental protections. This history also eludicates cities' relatively greater competence to address geographically constrained environmental problems such as waste management or lack of green space as opposed to the global problem of limiting climate change.

3

Local Environmental Protection in NYC

When Michael Bloomberg became mayor of New York City in 2002, the city was reeling.[1] The attacks of September 11, 2001 on the World Trade Center had traumatized the public and left many wondering whether there would be a mass exodus from the city.[2] The economy was in recession, and the city government projected deficits for the next three years.[3] For many New Yorkers, the Bloomberg administration had one main job: stabilize the local economy and bring back growth. Improving the quality of the local environment was part of the administration's strategy to achieve those aims.

The Bloomberg administration's approach to reviving and then growing the city's economy over its twelve years in office reflected the private sector backgrounds of the mayor and Daniel Doctoroff, whom Bloomberg handpicked to be his first Deputy Mayor for Economic Development and Rebuilding. Bloomberg had made a fortune building a financial information empire and Doctoroff had been a successful investment banker and private equity fund manager.[4]

Bloomberg and his team thought of the city as a product that was competing with other metropoles for leading postindustrial businesses and highly trained professionals.[5] The businesses and individuals they wanted to retain and attract to New York would pay the higher costs of operating in the city in exchange for a high "value" proposition.[6] Like other city governments in the early twenty-first century, the Bloomberg administration recognized that its local economy had deindustrialized with the decline of manufacturing, and that to grow the city needed to compete for the Creative Class and their employers in finance, information, technology, and other service industries.[7] New York City could not do so by offering low living and operating costs; instead, the city would have to show that it was worth the higher prices that they would pay to inhabit it.[8] New housing, modern office districts, and amenities – including environmental ones such as parks – would help to establish the value proposition.[9] While a lax approach to the environment may have helped cities attract heavy industry in the "smokestack chasing" era of the early twentieth century, it would not lure entrepreneurs, technology workers, financial service professionals, and architects.[10] Under Bloomberg, the city government set to work "physically remaking" New York City to help make it into a "luxury product."[11] In Doctoroff's words, "[a] healthier, more convenient, more environmentally forward city would attract more people, who would pay more taxes, which we would invest back into the city."[12] This was a paradigmatic example of a city government promoting local environmental improvements from the top to advance its agenda for local economic prosperity.

The administration's focus on increasing the city's attractiveness to the Creative Class provoked strong reactions from the progressive left. Its land use and housing policies were criticized as increasing inequality, displacing low-income people and people of color, and gentrifying affordable areas of the city; the "stop-and-frisk" policing that it pursued in the name of public safety was held by a federal district court judge to be unconstitutional for targeting Black and Latino men.[13] The critiques of Bloomberg spilled over into some of his environmental policies; critics argued that the administration's investments in public parks benefited elites and neglected the needs of low-income people for public spaces.[14]

In 2014, Bill de Blasio succeeded Bloomberg as mayor after he was term-limited.[15] A longtime left-leaning progressive Democrat, de Blasio had been a city council member from Brooklyn and public advocate, and regional director for the Department of Housing and Urban Development under President Bill Clinton.[16] De Blasio's campaign was a rebuke of the Bloomberg era; he proclaimed that New York had become a "'Tale of Two Cities,' one where 'city hall too often has catered to the interests of the elite rather than the needs of everyday New Yorkers.'"[17] He promised to establish programs that would help low- and moderate-income New Yorkers, such as free, universal prekindergarten and improved sick leave policies "for low-wage workers."[18]

Governing mostly during a period of economic bounty, Mayor de Blasio could afford to focus on addressing inequalities. However, even his administration pursued economic growth, and recognized the importance of the city's local environment, such as its green spaces, for the local economy.[19] In line with its focus on reducing inequalities, though, the de Blasio administration invested in local environmental goods, such as community-based parks, to promote greater access to these goods in disadvantaged areas.[20]

Notably, in both the Bloomberg and de Blasio eras, policies to improve the local environment emerged not only from city hall but also from community-based activism. Consistent with Bloomberg's concern with public health,[21] his administration embraced some of the ideas that community advocates advanced for reducing the burden of the city's solid waste in a small number of low-income communities of color.[22] Eddie Bautista, a long-standing environmental justice advocate in the city, joined the Bloomberg administration as a senior official, and the concept that Bautista and others promoted of allocating responsibility for processing the city's garbage more equitably was incorporated into the city's solid waste management plan.[23] The de Blasio administration took further steps to reduce the disproportionate burden of garbage collection on low-income communities and communities of color in response to pressure from environmental justice groups, for example, by developing a franchising system for commercial waste collection. The ability of community advocates to advance "waste equity" and commercial waste zones illustrates the permeability of New York City government in the early twenty-first century to influences from outside the economic elite, even during the Bloomberg era when the mayor was regarded by many as a representative of that elite.[24]

Taken as a whole, New York City's experience in the first decades of the twenty-first century underscores the potential for local governments to materially improve local environmental quality. At the same time, the history highlights the constraints cities face in addressing environmental problems within their borders, including the unequal distribution of environmental amenities and burdens. Using the Bloomberg and de Blasio administrations as case studies, this chapter examines how the pull and push to improve the local environment from the "top" and through community advocacy played out in America's largest city in the first two decades of this century.

BLOOMBERG'S GREEN GROWTH STRATEGY

Michael Bloomberg was not known as an environmentalist when he first took office in 2002. In fact, in his first year as mayor, struggling to deal with a budget deficit, he proposed a moratorium on the city's recycling program.[25] Yet, by the end of 2007, the Bloomberg administration had created a pioneering Office of Long-Term Planning and Sustainability, and published a groundbreaking sustainability plan called PlaNYC with 127 action items, including a commitment to reducing the city's GHG emissions by 30 percent below 2005 levels by 2030 discussed in Chapter 4.[26] It was a 180-degree turn. Writing in 2009, a journalist for *The New Yorker* magazine mused, "Who would have guessed, back in 2002, when the businessman Mayor seemed to regard recycling as a discretionary luxury, that his physical legacy might come to be defined as much by the planting of a million trees and by lawn chairs in the middle of Times Square as by gleaming (and empty) new office towers."[27]

What sparked the change of heart? Key voices in the administration came to believe that improving the city's "physical environment" is important to promoting and managing local prosperity.[28] Doctoroff was an especially important voice in this respect. Odd as it may seem, the Bloomberg administration's interest in sustainability emerged in part from Doctoroff's failed efforts to bring the 2012 Olympic Games to New York City.[29]

Back in the 1990s, when Doctoroff still worked in the private sector, he became "obsessed" with the idea that New York City should host the Olympics.[30] As Doctoroff recounts in his memoir, *Greater than Ever*, he came to believe that hosting the Olympics would enable New York to make the infrastructural upgrades that it needed to unbury itself from three decades of economic hardship and decay. The Olympics would create the occasion – and the urgency – for the city to proceed with public works projects and developments that were necessary to revitalize the city and bring it into the twenty-first century.[31] Once Doctoroff joined the

Bloomberg administration, he had the support of City Hall behind the bid for the Olympics.[32] Eventually, New York City won the support of the United States Olympic Committee as well, and the city represented the United States in its bid to the International Olympic Committee.[33] But in 2005, London, the world's other financial capital, ultimately won the Games.[34]

Studies that the city conducted during the preparation of the Olympics bid indicated that the city's population would grow by a million more before 2030, bringing the total number of inhabitants to over nine million.[35] That meant one million more people traveling through the city's streets, competing for scarce green space, drawing water from the city's reservoirs, and taking electricity from the city's grid. Throughout Bloomberg's first term in office, the city's economy rebounded from the September 11th attacks. Looking at the forecasts, Doctoroff came to believe that "it was logical to think that if we didn't manage the growth, we might even choke off the virtuous cycle [of growth] that we had set in motion."[36]

The fact that London had a sustainability plan and congestion pricing in place by 2004 also influenced Doctoroff.[37] When a staffer at the NYC Economic Development Corporation brought up London's advances in this field, it set off Doctoroff's competitive instincts. "I was acutely sensitive to anything London did that would make us less competitive because it had just beaten us out for the Olympics," he later explained.[38] In the words of Laurie Kerr, who as a senior policy advisor in the Office of Long-Term Planning and Sustainability was involved in preparing PlaNYC, between concerns about the impact of population growth on the city's infrastructure, competition with London, and concerns about a looming energy crisis,[39] the idea that New York City would develop a sustainability plan was "almost overdetermined."[40]

The plan that was released in 2007 reflects the multifaceted pressures to improve the local environment in New York City.[41] Three of PlaNYC's environmental initiatives – the initiatives for creating new green spaces, remediating contaminated lands (brownfields) to create additional land for development, and reducing air pollution – highlight the tight connection between the Bloomberg administration's interest in environmental protection and promoting economic development.

Creating New Green Spaces

Early on, Bloomberg recognized that improving the city's parks could help achieve his central objective of improving the city's economy. In his first State of the City speech in 2002, just five months after September 11th, when there were widespread fears that the city was in economic decline, Bloomberg identified parks and waterfront revival as a priority,[42] and called for creating a recreational path around the entire island of Manhattan and building new parks on Manhattan's far west side.[43] Parks are an amenity that can help attract new businesses and residents.[44] They increase the value of neighboring land, which increases the city's property tax revenues.[45] Parks are also a destination for tourists, and tourism is a major source of employment for low-skilled workers who no longer have access to many manufacturing jobs in New York City.[46] Bloomberg made this point explicit in his 2003 State of the City speech, declaring that "[tourism] provide[s] hard-working New Yorkers, from all five boroughs, with the kind of opportunity to climb the ladder into the middle class that manufacturing jobs once did."[47]

PlaNYC proclaimed the late twentieth and early twenty-first centuries the third "great age[] of parks development" in New York City, building upon the creation of Central Park and other parks in the late nineteenth century and the increases in park acreage between 1930 and 1960 with help from federal funding.[48] The plan boasted that over "300 acres of new parkland" had been "added" in the city in the previous five years (coincidentally the time that Bloomberg had been mayor).[49] It also set out plans for further increasing parkland in the city to maintain and improve quality of life as well as improving public health and addressing inequitable access to parkland across the city's neighborhoods.[50] A key goal was ensuring that "nearly every New Yorker lives within a 10-minute walk of a park by 2030."[51] Over the course of the Bloomberg administration, approximately 427 acres of land came under the jurisdiction of the city's parks department.[52] In 2014, a former official in the Bloomberg administration noted that as of 2013, Bloomberg's last year as mayor, "76% of New Yorkers lived within a 10-minute walk of a park or playground."[53]

Table 3.1 identifies examples of new parks of five or more acres opened in whole or in part between 2002 and 2021. Some of the early twenty-first century parks were established with the help of the state and federal governments, and private entities, as the city leveraged its zoning authority to increase public access to areas such as the waterfront.[54] Notably, of the almost 683 acres of land that came under the jurisdiction of the City Parks department between 2002 and 2021, approximately 73 percent of the acreage was on the waterfront.[55]

Indeed, the waterfront has been a particularly popular site of park and path building in the early twenty-first century in New York and other cities with vacant land near waterbodies in the wake of urban deindustrialization.[56] Proposals to build new parks and public spaces along New York's waterfront dated back to at least the late twentieth century.[57] There were many "underutilized" waterfront areas[58] after changes in the shipping industry in the mid-twentieth century rerouted traffic away from New York City harbor, contributing to the economic decline of the "working waterfront."[59] By the early twenty-first century, the waterfront was also a much more desirable place to spend time and live than decades earlier; water quality had improved with the decline of heavy waterfront industries and the cleaning up of polluted waters set in motion by the enforcement of the federal Clean Water Act of 1972.[60] "[U]nderutilized" waterfront areas were the sites of some of Mayor Bloomberg's most ambitious redevelopment efforts in the city.[61] By 2004, just two years after Bloomberg took office, a local NGO "identified sixty-one waterfront redevelopment projects underway, mostly emphasizing commercial, residential, and recreational uses, with several more in the pipeline."[62]

TABLE 3.1 *Examples of parks over 5 acres opened in whole or part in New York City between 2002 and 2021, listed by borough*[63]

NAME OF PARK	TOTAL ACREAGE	YEAR OPENED
	BRONX	
Barretto Point Park	12.22 acres[64]	2006[65]
Bridge Park	7.16 acres[66]	2015[67]
Concrete Plant Park	6.28 acres[68]	2009[69]
Locust Point Marina	22.07 acres[70]	2003[71]
Mill Pond Park	11.57 acres[72]	2009[73]
	BROOKLYN	
Brooklyn Bridge Park	21.38 acres[74]	2010[75]
Bush Terminal Park	22.12 acres[76]	2014[77]
Bushwick Inlet Park	35.53 acres[78]	2010[79]
Domino Park	5.0 acres[80]	2018[81]
Marsha P. Johnson State Park (East River State Park)	7.0 acres[82]	2007[83]
WNYC Transmitter Park	6.61 acres[84]	2012[85]
	MANHATTAN	
Governors Island[86]	172 acres[87]	2006[88]
Hudson River Park	550 acres[89]	2003[90]
Southpoint Park, Roosevelt Island	~7.0 acres[91]	2011[92]
The High Line	6.73 acres[93]	2009[94]
	QUEENS	
Elmhurst Park	6.22 acres[95]	2011[96]
Hunter's Point South Park	22.81 acres[97]	2013[98]
Park at Beach 108 Street	13.83 acres[99]	2007[100]
Sunset Cove Park	9.38 acres[101]	2019[102]
	STATEN ISLAND	
Brookfield Park	258.72 acres[103]	2017[104]
Fairview Park	42.60 acres[105]	2021[106]
Freshkills Park	2,200 acres[107]	2012[108]
Goodhue Park	26.53 acres[109]	2013[110]
Heritage Park	9.93 acres[111]	2014[112]
Old Place Creek Park	44.73 acres[113]	2016[114]
Richmond Terrace Park	11.19 acres[115]	2019[116]

Along the west side of Manhattan, miles of "dilapidated piers and parking lots" were converted into a sprawling "Hudson River Park" replete with lush lawns and manicured boardwalks that started opening to the public in 2003.[117] Just east of the Hudson River Park, a decaying elevated freight railway that had not been used in decades was converted into a greenway with over 500 species of plants and trees that began opening to the public in 2009.[118] The metamorphosis of this relic from the city's industrial past into an urban oasis has made the High Line a tourist sensation, spurred the creation of similar linear parks in other cities, and even inspired a best-selling children's book called *The Curious Garden* by Peter Brown.[119] In Brooklyn, new waterfront parks, such as Brooklyn Bridge Park, which opened in 2010, draw visitors from throughout the five boroughs and beyond.[120] On Staten Island, the city began working on the multidecade-long project to convert the closed Fresh Kills landfill into a park.[121] Occupying an area that is almost three times the size of Central Park, Freshkills Park will be the biggest park created in New York City in over a century once it is completed.[122]

New York City was far from alone among U.S. cities in its quest to increase parklands in the early twenty-first century. According to data compiled by the Trust for Public Land, which is reproduced in Table 3.2, thirteen of the nineteen most populous American cities for which there are data increased the total amount of land that they devote to parks between 2013 and 2021.[123] What's more, all but one of the six cities that the Trust for Public Land codes as having a "high" population density increased park acreage. Thus, even in cities where land is most scarce, local officials prioritized the creation of new parks over competing land uses. This speaks volumes about the value that local leaders in these cities assigned to new green space.[124]

TABLE 3.2 *Total acreage devoted to parks in the twenty most populous U.S. cities according to Trust for Public Land*[125]

	Density level	2013 Total Park Acreage	2021 Total Park Acreage
Austin	Medium-low	27,398	18,974
Charlotte	Low	20,472	22,208
Chicago	High	12,485	13,865
Columbus	Medium-low	10,861	13,895
Dallas	Medium-low	23,331	20,632
Denver	Medium-high	5,900	6,456
Fort Worth	Medium-low	11,667	12,913
Houston	Medium-low	49,487	44,480
Indianapolis	Low	11,203	No Data
Jacksonville	Low	65,107	84,333
Los Angeles	High	36,113	38,283
New York	High	38,606	39,766
Oklahoma City	Low	26,154	18,588
Philadelphia	High	10,929	10,794
Phoenix	Medium-low	49,254	50,897
San Antonio	Medium-low	24,662	33,911
San Diego	Medium-low	48,468	39,987
San Francisco	High	5,685	6,165
San Jose	Medium-high	16,463	17,376
Seattle	High	5,546	6,618

Brownfields

PlaNYC included other initiatives for greening New York in addition to establishing new parks and renovating existing parks and playgrounds. The city committed to planting over one million new trees by 2017, a goal that it achieved two years ahead of schedule in 2015.[126] The plan also promised a program to remediate contaminated land to increase the amount of land available to build new residential housing to accommodate population growth. Since the supply of land is "fixed," the plan explained, the city had to use land "more efficiently" to meet the needs of its growing population.[127] Greening would facilitate growth.

New York City has had a shortage of affordable housing for decades; in a city where most people rent, since the 1970s, over 40 percent of households in the city have been "rent burdened," meaning they pay over 30 percent of their income in rent.[128] The long-standing shortage of affordable housing, combined with the expectation that the city's population would increase, meant there was a need for new housing construction. Moreover, there was land that could be repurposed for housing. At the beginning of the twenty-first century, "many areas of New York were still zoned exclusively for manufacturing and industry"[129] even though manufacturing did not account for a large share of jobs in the city. The Bloomberg administration (and the de Blasio administration that succeeded it) pursued aggressive policies of rezoning neighborhoods to boost the supply of land available to build housing.[130] Bloomberg-era city officials boast that his administration rezoned 40 percent of the city's land mass, although it bears emphasizing that many of these rezonings did not increase the supply of land available for new housing.[131]

Zoning alone will not make land useable for housing if the land is contaminated, and in PlaNYC 2007, the city estimated that contaminated land, which is often in low-income areas, amounted to "eight times the size of Central Park."[132] In 2009, fulfilling a commitment in PlaNYC to help create new sites for residential development, the Bloomberg administration established the first municipal brownfield remediation program in the United States for sites not in New York State's Brownfield Cleanup Program.[133] The city program is open to those who want to participate and has several elements, including a certification for properties that have achieved cleanup standards, some limited protection against liability, and grants for eligible cleanups which can be substantial for land for "affordable or supportive housing."[134] A 2018 policy brief from NYU's Furman Center found that the sites enrolled in the program were heavily concentrated in a small number of areas in the city, many of which were "gentrifying neighborhoods."[135] Indeed, 24.56 percent of the sites enrolled for cleanup in the program at the time of the Furman Center analysis were in Brooklyn's Williamsburg-Greenpoint, the area of the city that gentrified the most between 1990 and 2010–2014 based on the magnitude of rent increases.[136] Extrapolating from the Furman Center's findings, it seems that the cleanup of brownfields in New York City has been tightly connected with development, with property owners seeking to remediate brownfields in rapidly changing areas of the city, presumably to build on the land.[137] In other words, cleaning up land appears to have quite literally been a foundation for development.

Reducing Air Pollution

After the federal government began regulating air pollution under the 1970 Clean Air Act, air quality improved in New York City.[138] The decline of heavy industry in the city as its economy shifted more toward service and creative sectors likely also helped to reduce urban air pollution.[139] Nonetheless, when PlaNYC was released in 2007, and even as of 2024, air quality still did not fully satisfy the federal ambient air quality standards that the Environmental Protection Agency establishes under the Clean Air Act.[140]

PlaNYC proposed to increase air quality citywide through a variety of initiatives. Recognizing that transportation is the source of over 50 percent of the city's "criteria pollutant emissions," the plan included a proposal to pilot congestion pricing for driving into, and out of, Manhattan's Central Business District.[141] Perhaps the most politically controversial recommendation in PlaNYC, the congestion pricing pilot, which was inspired by London's congestion charge, never came to fruition during Bloomberg's tenure because New York State legislators blocked it.[142] The PlaNYC proposal would have reduced traffic congestion, which has economic as well as environmental costs, improved air quality, and generated funds for mass transit.[143] It took until January 2025, and a series of twists and turns, for congestion pricing to come into effect as a result of a New York State initiative to raise funds for mass transit, lower traffic congestion, and improve air quality in Manhattan.[144]

PlaNYC was more successful in reducing pollution from the use of dirty heating oils in buildings. It tasked the city's Health Department with developing a New York City Community Air Survey (NYCCAS), which was to be "one of the largest urban air pollution studies conducted"[145] up to that date. A key goal was to understand local sources of pollution at a more granular, neighborhood level than was feasible using the twenty-four monitors that then existed across the city to monitor compliance with federal air quality standards so as to promote "public health and environmental justice."[146]

The first iteration of the NYCCAS report showed that "the strongest predictor" of wintertime concentrations of fine particulate matter and sulfur dioxide in an area "was the density of nearby buildings and specifically the density of buildings burning fuel oil."[147] A second iteration of the study found that fuel oils #4 and #6 – two types of residual oils, which are heavy types of oil that remain after the lighter oils are removed in the refining process – were especially potent contributors to air pollution in the vicinity in which they burned.[148] Fortunately, less than 10,000 out of an approximate 1,000,000 buildings in New York City used either heating oil #4 or

#6 at that time – just 1 percent.[149] As such, the city believed that it could make a substantial improvement in local air quality for a relatively low cost by targeting just the tiny fraction of buildings that used the dirtiest types of fuels.

Experience has borne out these predictions: New York City's program to phase out residual fuels has been extensively studied and has been credited with reducing particulate, sulfur dioxide and nitrogen dioxide pollution within the first four years of the program's operation.[150] Implementation of the Clean Heat Program reduced air pollution on an average citywide basis *and* reduced disparities in air pollution concentrations in different neighborhoods. Looking at sulfur dioxide levels, for example, the "difference between the most and least polluted neighborhoods dropped from over 10 parts per billion (ppb) in the winter of 2008–2009 [before the Clean Heat Program was implemented] to about 1 ppb in 2014–2015."[151] There is also reason to believe that low-income communities have reaped more substantial health benefits from the Clean Heat program than high-income communities.[152] Between 2010 and 2019, not just New York but also Boston and Philadelphia passed laws[153] phasing out the use of the dirtiest types of heating oils. The residual heating oil bans embody a form of downstream regulation of fuel consumption (by building owners and residents) by local governments.[154]

DE BLASIO'S EQUITABLE GREEN GROWTH

In 2014, longtime progressive Democrat Bill de Blasio became mayor on a platform of addressing growing inequality in the city. "In so many ways, New York has become a Tale of Two Cities," the opening pages of de Blasio's campaign platform intoned.[155] "Nearly 400,000 millionaires call New York home, while nearly half of our neighbors live at or near the poverty line. Our middle class isn't just shrinking; it's in danger of vanishing altogether."[156] De Blasio's campaign tapped into a lived reality for many New Yorkers at the end of the Bloomberg era. As journalist Juan González explained in his book about de Blasio's election, "While in 2002 the top 1 percent of New York City residents had taken in 27 percent of all income, by 2012 that share had nearly doubled to 45 percent – a spiraling divide far greater than in the rest of the nation, where the 1 percent's share of income rose from 17 to 23 percent over the same period."[157] Stagnating incomes, combined with population growth, had translated into an affordable housing crisis that touched the middle class.[158] Responding to the economic insecurity underpinning these statistics, de Blasio's platform included promises to protect and increase affordable housing, improve the school system, and protect low-wage workers. It was surprisingly thin on environmental issues and, notwithstanding de Blasio's focus on inequality, did not once use the term "environmental justice."[159]

What did de Blasio's election mean for the city's local environment?[160] The de Blasio administration was much less focused on promoting economic growth by physically reshaping the city to appeal to the Creative Class than its predecessor.

Yet, reflecting local economic imperatives, the administration still sought to promote growth, and it still conceived of improving the city's physical environment through parks and cleaning up brownfields as helping to achieve that growth.[161] But the de Blasio administration elevated equity as an objective on par with promoting economic growth, and, responding to critiques of the Bloomberg era, it sought to promote environmental equity, for example, by investing more in community parks.

Adding Equity to Growth

The de Blasio administration departed from the Bloomberg administration's strategy of initiating changes to the city's physical environment to appeal to postindustrial elites. Not only was de Blasio elected on a platform of addressing inequality, but as mayor he had less need to focus on economic development than his predecessor. Bloomberg had to deal with two major economic crises – the 2001 recession, exacerbated by the economic fallout from the terrorist attack on September 11, 2001, and the 2008 recession.[162] De Blasio enjoyed a growing economy for seven straight years from when he became mayor in 2014 until March 2020, his second-to-last year in office, when the COVID pandemic severely disrupted the city's economy.[163] Governing mostly during a period of economic bounty, de Blasio could afford to focus more on addressing inequalities in the city than Paul Peterson, writing against the backdrop of the city's near-bankruptcy in the 1970s, might have expected of a local government; city government spending and employment increased substantially under de Blasio.[164]

Reflecting the imperative to foster local prosperity to sustain the city's budget, the de Blasio administration still sought to spur economic growth and saw environmental policy as a tool that could be used toward that end. The difference was "[t]he explicit addition of equity" as a goal[165] which, at least rhetorically, was set on equal footing with growth.[166] The coupling of efforts to promote economic growth and equity was reflected in a range of policy areas. Similar to its predecessor, the de Blasio administration rezoned neighborhoods in the city to enable the construction of new housing to accommodate population growth and bring down housing prices.[167] Many of the neighborhoods that the city initially rezoned have large populations of low-income people of color, which fueled criticisms, including that the rezonings would increase displacement and gentrification.[168] But the city tried to ensure that at least some of the new housing that would be built in rezoned areas would be affordable to middle- and low-income people by instituting a mandatory inclusionary housing policy that requires developers to set aside a certain portion of new development as affordable.[169] The city continued the Bloomberg effort to "reclaim" contaminated land for new development by encouraging the cleanup of contaminated sites.[170] But through cleaning up brownfields, the de Blasio administration also explicitly aimed to improve environmental conditions in environmental justice communities and enable communities to realize their visions for their surroundings.[171]

Parks

The de Blasio administration's approach to parks exemplifies its efforts to marry economic growth and reducing inequality through investments in the city's physical environment, as well as some of the limits of the administration's efforts to tackle inequality. In a line that could have come straight from a Bloomberg-era PlaNYC, de Blasio's OneNYC plan released in 2015 declared that "Parks and public space are essential to economic development[.]"[172] The city parks department also continued to acquire more land in the de Blasio era, an overwhelming share of which was on the waterfront.[173] Yet, in 2014, his first year as mayor, de Blasio also launched the Community Parks Initiative to improve "local parks in dense and growing neighborhoods that have not seen significant capital investment in a generation."[174] OneNYC emphasized the administration's commitment to investing in parks in "underresourced and growing neighborhoods."[175]

The Initiative responded to a critique that the Bloomberg administration's approach to parks neglected low-income people and people of color.[176] The sociologist Kevin Loughran articulates the critique in a book published in 2022, explaining that cities' use of urban parks to boost property values, new development, and tourism encourages lopsided investment in marquee parks in areas that house the wealthy or hold tourist appeal.[177] The Community Parks Initiative sought to invest in the very parks that Loughran and others argue are likely to be neglected when parks are primarily conceived of as tools for promoting economic growth. Notably, however, Bloomberg also made investments in parks in low- and moderate-income neighborhoods throughout the city, for example, by creating Barretto Point Park in the South Bronx, and his administration set aside funding that helped to lay a basis for the Community Parks Initiative.[178] Thus, there may be less difference between the two administrations' approach than some of Bloomberg's critics appreciate.

Moreover, even with the Community Parks Initiative, the city was far from equitably investing in parks in low- and high-income neighborhoods or overcoming the long-standing underinvestment in green space in communities of color and low-income neighborhoods.[179] The Community Parks Initiative also failed to address another critique of city investments in parks, namely that they may displace low-income people and lead to neighborhood gentrification as the green infrastructure increases property values and rents.[180] Adding parks and cleaning up brownfields in degraded waterfront areas certainly make the area more pleasant, but what if they simultaneously make the area more attractive to a new group of wealthier, whiter households? Melissa Checker succinctly captures the anxiety about "green gentrification" in describing the greening of two waterfront communities in Brooklyn:

> In Williamsburg and Sunset Park, for instance, activists finally won hard-fought battles for green space and other environmental improvements, only to find that those initiatives led to new development that threatened to price them out of their own

> neighborhoods. Without diminishing the hard work and commitment of grassroots environmental justice activists, I wondered whether their successes were being co-opted. Had their activism unintentionally caused environmental gentrification?[181]

The critiques of new parks as pricing low-income people out of neighborhoods are part of broader concerns about neighborhood change, and as mentioned already, similar criticisms are directed at large-scale neighborhood rezonings in early twenty-first century New York City to promote more residential development.[182] Whether new residential housing displaces low-income people and leads to gentrification of neighborhoods are complex empirical questions.[183] Similarly, the relationships between new green infrastructure, such as parks, and displacement and gentrification are also difficult to disentangle empirically. Research by sociologists such as Kenneth Gould, Tammy Lewis, and others supports the idea that urban greening is a cause of gentrification.[184] However, there are also suggestions in existing literature that the relationship between greening and gentrification runs the opposite way; gentrification may contribute to greening insofar as new higher-income residents demand more amenities or add to calls of long-term residents for such amenities.[185]

Assuming that new green infrastructure such as parks contributes to more higher-income people moving into a neighborhood and low-income people relocating because rents rise, it is not clear how policymakers should respond. Indeed, the difficulty of formulating a response may explain in part the limited response of the de Blasio administration to the concerns about green gentrification. The idea that governments should not invest in improving the environment in historically marginalized communities to prevent gentrification is problematic. How can inequalities be overturned without changing the status quo? At the same time, especially in cities such as New York where the affordable housing crisis looms large, it would be irresponsible not to take measures to ensure that urban greening does not make housing even more unaffordable for those in need. Ultimately, solutions to concerns about green gentrification may have to come from policies in a range of areas, including housing law.[186]

"WASTE EQUITY"

Long before the Bloomberg and de Blasio administrations sought to put their stamp on the city's environment, community-based advocates had developed ideas for improving environmental conditions in predominantly Black, Latino, and low-income communities in the city. In New York City, as in other parts of the country, communities of color and low-income neighborhoods have borne a disproportionate share of the burden of collecting and processing garbage, and other polluting infrastructure such as bus and truck depots that is vital for urban life.[187] Reflecting this reality, some of the earliest campaigns mounted by environmental justice groups formed in the city in the latter twentieth century focused on the inequitable allocation of responsibility for waste management in the city.[188] Although the Bloomberg administration often seemed to focus on remaking the city to appeal to elites, it adopted environmental justice advocates' goal of achieving "waste equity," and brought into the administration a longtime environmental justice advocate to help advance this objective. The de Blasio administration also responded to environmental justice advocates' concerns about waste. In the de Blasio era, the city council legislated a version of the franchising system for collecting commercial solid waste that advocates advanced to reduce truck traffic in the communities where waste facilities cluster. The ability of environmental justice advocates to fundamentally shape the Bloomberg administration's 2006 solid waste management plan and persuade the city to adopt the franchising system illustrates the openness of the city's politics in the early twenty-first century to community-based proposals to increase environmental protection to improve public health and increase fairness, not merely as an adjunct to economic growth.[189]

For a significant part of the twentieth century, New York City mostly dealt with its garbage within its borders, relying on a mix of incinerating its trash and sending it to landfills, the largest of which was the Fresh Kills landfill on Staten Island.[190] Allegedly the largest landfill in the world while it operated from 1948 to 2001,[191] Fresh Kills was a dumping ground for the residential waste that the city government collected and the commercial trash collected by private carters.[192] The trash arrived at Fresh Kills by barge from marine transfer stations located throughout the city, which reduced the use of trucks to transport garbage.[193]

In a sense, sending trash to Staten Island represented an attempt by the city to externalize the cost of its trash. Staten Island is the least populous of the city's five boroughs and is also the least geographically connected part of the five boroughs. There was not even a bridge connecting Staten Island to the rest of New York City until 1964.[194] The borough is also a political anomaly: in a majority-minority City that overwhelmingly votes Democratic, Staten Island, where the population is predominantly white people, has long been a Republican stronghold.[195] So while Staten Islanders complained bitterly about their role as the trash can of New York over the decades, in a city that is consistently run by Democratic officials for whom Staten Islanders didn't vote, it was relatively easy for elected officials to turn a deaf ear.[196]

Responsibility for the city's garbage began to shift to low-income communities of color in the city in the late 1980s, when New York City increased the tipping fees charged to private carters for depositing commercial trash at Fresh Kills "in an effort to preserve landfill space."[197] The fee increase led the carters to take more commercial waste to transfer facilities where it could be trucked out of the city.[198] The number of these facilities grew in a small number of predominantly low-income communities of color in the city.[199] Community advocates mobilized, and in 1991, groups concerned about the clustering of waste transfer facilities in a small number of predominantly low-income communities of color formed the New York City Environmental Justice Alliance.[200]

Fatefully for these communities, in the mid-1990s, Staten Island's political star rose, after it was pivotal to the razor-thin electoral victory of Republican Rudolph Giuliani as mayor over incumbent Democrat David Dinkins in 1993. The get-out-the-vote efforts of Staten Island Republican borough president Guy Molinari were credited with helping to bring so many Staten Islanders to the polls.[201] In late May of 1996, Giuliani, Molinari, and New York State Republican Governor George Pataki held a press conference to announce that Fresh Kills would receive its last shipment of waste on December 31, 2001.[202] Conveniently for Giuliani, that also would turn out to be his last day as mayor.[203]

Without Fresh Kills, New York City began exporting much more waste out of the city by truck than it had in the past, and marine transfer stations fell into desuetude.[204] Waste that would have been transported across New York Harbor via barge to Fresh Kills was now trucked to land-based waste transfer facilities in the city to be driven out of it in larger trucks.[205] The number of waste transfer facilities and diesel-powered truck traffic increased, especially in local communities surrounding major truck routes, as the facilities became the transit point for the city's residential as well as its commercial waste on its way out of the city in long-haul trucks.[206] In a classic instance of environmental injustice, a small number of low-income communities of color with high rates of asthma – "Williamsburg/Greenpoint and Sunset Park/Red Hook in Brooklyn, and the South Bronx"[207] – bore the brunt of the truck traffic and the waste transfer facilities, and the environmental and health harms to which they contributed.[208] The system was economically problematic as well for the city because transport costs were increasing as nearby landfills filled up and the city had to rely on long-haul trucking to more distant landfills.[209]

In 1997, anticipating the consequences of the closure of Fresh Kills, the New York City Environmental Justice Alliance, New York Lawyers for the Public Interest, and others had established the Organization of Waterfront Neighborhoods (OWN), a coalition of community groups from the waterfront areas where waste transfer stations were already concentrated.[210] OWN advocated for "borough equity," the principle that each of New York City's five boroughs should manage its own trash, and also called for reviving the marine transfer stations to take trash out of the city by barge or rail, rather than trucks.[211] According to Professor Julie Sze, Manhattan was the largest hurdle to requiring each borough to manage its garbage.[212] "[T]he richest borough[,]" Manhattan produced "40 percent of the city's commercial waste," and directed all of this waste to "Brooklyn, Bronx, and Queens"[213] because it did not have any waste transfer stations of its own.[214]

In 2006, Eddie Bautista, who had helped found OWN, transitioned to insider when the Bloomberg administration hired him to get the city council to pass its solid waste management plan.[215] Years later, Bautista recalled that as far back as 2001, Bloomberg had framed his plan as a means of achieving "equity, environmental justice, and public health."[216] The Bloomberg plan, which the city council adopted in 2006, embraced borough equity and advocated reviving the marine waste transfer stations.[217] In furtherance of these goals, and over intense community opposition, Mayor Bloomberg forced Manhattan's predominantly white, upscale Upper East Side to accept the construction of a new marine transfer station.[218] The plan also committed the city to diverting more waste from landfills by increasing recycling.[219]

The incorporation of equity into the city's 2006 solid waste plan was a historic accomplishment for community groups.[220] Yet, the achievement did not fundamentally change "the racial geography of New York City garbage," to borrow a term from Professor Sze.[221] Bloomberg's solid waste plan did not mandate reductions in the waste or trucks passing through the small number of low-income communities of color where waste transfer facilities cluster.[222]

In the fall of 2013, as Bill de Blasio was about to win his first term as mayor, environmental justice advocates joined with advocates from labor and other groups to establish the "Transform Don't Trash NYC" coalition to address the continuing inequities in waste management after the solid waste management plan.[223] The coalition aimed to persuade the next administration to adopt a "franchising system" for the private collection of commercial waste to reduce the number of trucks passing through the communities where waste transfer stations cluster and to improve the safety, environmental record, and working conditions in the commercial waste sector, in which the workers are predominantly poorly paid people of color.[224] The press release announcing the coalition acknowledged that the Bloomberg administration had adopted "a plan to more fairly distribute waste facilities throughout [the city's] five boroughs," but it emphasized that the burden of dealing with the waste from the city's commercial businesses, such as restaurants, hotels, and office buildings, was still borne disproportionately by a small number of low-income communities of color.[225]

In 2019, the city council passed the Commercial Waste Zones Law.[226] It was another victory for environmental justice advocates, who found allies in the Department of Sanitation and Antonio Reynoso, chair of the city council's Sanitation committee.[227] The law requires the city's Department of Sanitation to divide the city into zones and select up to three private carters for each zone.[228] The nonexclusive franchise system means that commercial customers will have some choice, but the number of trucks driving around the city to pick up commercial trash should fall significantly compared to the prior system in which an unlimited number of private carters pick up trash.[229] Lowering the number of trucks collecting commercial waste should reduce air pollution and greenhouse gas emissions, including in the low-income communities of color with waste transfer facilities where the trucks converge.[230] Since the city could better enforce labor standards against a smaller number of carters, pay and working conditions also might improve for the workers in the private carting industry.[231] In addition, with fewer companies competing for business and tighter regulation of the carters, the carting industry's poor safety record might improve.[232]

With the passage of the Commercial Waste Zones Law and other laws legislated by the city council in the 2010s, legal tools are in place to lessen the burdens of the city's waste on the small number of low-income communities of color where they are concentrated.[233] The city has been delayed in implementing the commercial waste zones law, but is moving forward and the first zone became "fully operational" in January 2025.[234] However, until the city generates less waste, collection and disposal are bound to be sources of conflict, pitting different neighborhoods of the city against each other and burdening less politically powerful communities outside the city as well as within it with New York's garbage.[235]

In addition to the Commercial Waste Zones law, the city council passed other laws during the de Blasio era to address environmental inequalities. In 2017, the council legislated two local laws that recognize the systemic character of environmental injustice.[236] The laws require that the city identify and map environmental justice areas in its borders.[237] They also require that the city prepare a study identifying "environmental justice concerns" in these areas, among other topics, and develop a plan "that provides guidance for incorporating environmental justice concerns into city decision-making, identifies possible citywide initiatives for promoting environmental justice and provides specific recommendations for city agencies[.]"[238] The laws created an Environmental Justice Advisory Board, currently chaired by Peggy Shepard, head of WE ACT, one of the premier environmental justice groups in the city.[239]

The two environmental justice laws are legally toothless in the sense that they do not create any binding legal obligations on the city government to remedy any environmental injustice. Nor do they create any private right of action that would allow individuals or environmental justice groups to sue the city for failing to remedy environmental injustices.[240] The city has also been slow to comply with the 2017 laws. In April 2024 it finally released the mandated study documenting the many environmental inequities in the city, over five years after the study was due under local law; as of early 2025, the city has yet to finalize a plan for addressing these inequities, which local law required be finalized by 2021.[241] But the existence of the laws is an indication of the attention that city policymakers increasingly paid to environmental injustices in the de Blasio era, consistent with the growing attention to such injustices in New York State in the late 2010s, and at the federal level in the Biden administration in the early 2020s.[242]

CONCLUSION

New York City's experiences during the twenty-first century demonstrate the potential for local governments to effectively address quintessentially local environmental problems where leaders perceive that there will be local economic benefits from environmental protection. The Bloomberg administration's interest in New York City's environment provides strong evidence for this proposition. Perhaps because Bloomberg and his key lieutenant Doctoroff came from the private sector, they seem to have come to environmental protection based on a cost-benefit analysis that adjudged safeguarding the environment to be helpful in growing the city's economy and managing the effects of that growth. Indeed, as PlaNYC was prepared, city agencies were apparently encouraged by the Mayor and Deputy Mayor "to think creatively and to analyze the costs and benefits of a variety of solutions before recommending a preferred path forward."[243]

Yet, the history of local environmental protection efforts in New York City in the early twenty-first century suggests that the perceptions of top city policymakers and elites that environmental protection will enhance local economic prosperity are by no means the sole reason that city governments seek to improve the physical environment under their jurisdiction. Community-based advocacy proved highly influential in the incorporation into the 2006 solid waste plan of the idea that each borough should bear some responsibility for managing its trash, and the adoption of the 2019 law to establish zones to reduce the truck traffic associated with the collection of the city's commercial trash. As Eddie Bautista stated in the fall of 2019, "This commercial waste reform agreement was a generation in the making … Environmental justice communities – neighborhoods like North Brooklyn, South Bronx, Southeast Queens, and Sunset Park long condemned to handle over 75% of NYC's waste – have sought relief from a chaotic and unjust commercial waste system for 30 years."[244] Moreover, even top city policymakers are not solely motivated by economic concerns. The Bloomberg administration's interest in improving local air quality seems to have been motivated in significant measure to a desire to improve public health, and linked only loosely to promoting economic growth.[245] The de Blasio administration's Community Parks Initiative was intended to reduce long-standing inequalities in high-quality public spaces.

Overall, the history of New York City's efforts to address problems such as lack of green space, contaminated lands, and solid waste management in the early twenty-first century underscores that city governments have significant agency to improve local environmental quality. The history further highlights that pressures from city policymakers and elites *as well as* community advocates can lead to meaningful local environmental law and policy development. Neither the top-down nor the bottom-up pathway is strictly dominant.

However, the history also emphasizes the constraints that hinder cities from addressing what are often thought of as paradigmatically local environmental problems. Some of these are legal constraints, such as the need for state legislative approval that stymied the Bloomberg administration's efforts to implement a city pilot of congestion pricing to reduce traffic entering the Central Business District, or the preemptive effect of federal environmental law that thwarted the Bloomberg effort to reduce air pollution from the city's taxi fleet.[246] Others are fiscal. A number of the parks built in the early twenty-first century, such as Hudson River Park and Brooklyn Bridge Park, were built with funding from higher levels of government as well as the city.[247]

An important question is why there remain significant environmental inequalities in New York City, for example, in access to green space and the allocation of responsibility for managing the city's solid waste, notwithstanding decades of community-based advocacy to center environmental justice and some of the legal and policy responses from city policymakers described earlier.[248] Some of these inequalities are no doubt due to limited political power on the part of low-income communities and communities of color and the effects of long-standing racism.[249] However, it also seems plausible that the city's position as a jurisdiction nested within larger polities that must compete within other cities for residents and businesses constrains the city's ability to fundamentally address the inequalities in the allocation of environmental benefits and burdens within its borders. As scholars have argued for decades, maximizing the local tax base to fund municipal services is a central concern of local policymakers.[250] Unless state law is changed to enhance the fiscal flexibility of local governments, or the federal government significantly increases funding for local governments, local governments such as New York may need to continue to focus on allowing new development to enhance their property tax base and attracting high-income earners to boost other tax revenues.[251] In this regard, it is worth recalling that amid the de Blasio administration's focus on reducing environmental inequalities, the OneNYC plan still mentioned that "a great open space can attract residents and businesses."[252] Even the de Blasio administration sought economic development and treated public spaces partly as tools for promoting that development.

4

Decarbonization Efforts in NYC

INTRODUCTION

As New York and other cities started to improve the quality of their local environments in the early twenty-first century, some local governments also started to take action to try to limit the global problem of climate change. Limiting greenhouse gas (GHG) emissions is not an obvious task for local governments because reducing GHG emissions benefits everyone in the world. No single city emits enough GHGs that its actions alone can materially affect global temperatures. Since GHGs produced in any particular location mix globally and create global impacts, cities that take action to reduce GHG emissions will bear the full cost of whatever investments they make toward reducing GHGs but will only receive a small fraction of the benefit.[1]

Local actions to address climate change are also perplexing because higher levels of government significantly constrain the tools that cities can use to regulate GHG emissions.[2] American cities generally cannot directly regulate emissions from the production of electricity or the use of motor vehicles, which are under federal or state control.[3] Yet, together, electricity generation and transportation account for more than half of U.S. GHG emissions.[4] Cities can affect the demand for fossil fuels through measures including land use planning, local procurement, educational campaigns, and subsidies for low-carbon alternatives. However, due to state law limits on local taxation authority, the tools that localities can use to reduce demand are circumscribed and many cities cannot unilaterally impose taxes on carbon-intensive products, which many economists believe would be the most efficient means of spurring decarbonization.[5] In short, cities that want to engage in regulating GHG emissions must operate within a sea of second bests.

Given the structure of the climate change problem, and the limitations on local authority to address it, it is not surprising that few U.S. cities have implemented measures to materially reduce GHG emissions. In a 2020 study, the Brookings Institution found that of the 100 most populous cities in the U.S., "[s]lightly less than half … have established GHG reduction targets."[6] Research for this book found that seventeen of the twenty most populous cities in the U.S. – 85 percent – had established GHG reduction targets as of 2020, which is consistent with the suggestion in existing scholarship that larger city size correlates with actions to reduce GHG emissions (Figure 4.1).[7] However, adopting a GHG reduction target does not mean that cities are acting to achieve the target, let alone imposing costly requirements on local actors to reduce their emissions. Indeed, the Brookings Institution study provided suggestive evidence that few of the cities that have adopted targets have implemented policies with the ambition necessary to meet the cities' GHG reduction commitments. It found that "[d]espite genuine achievements in many cities, roughly two-thirds of cities are currently lagging their targeted emission levels."[8] A similar share of our list of the top twenty cities by population also seems to be lagging in achieving their targets according to the data in the Brookings report.[9]

This chapter analyzes the gradual emergence of local decarbonization policies in New York City. New York is one of the small number of U.S. cities that have taken meaningful actions to reduce GHG emissions in the early twenty-first century (though, as we will describe, the city is lagging in achieving its climate goals,[10] and there are questions about whether progress will slow further in the post-COVID reality). The chapter examines the motivations in NYC for local efforts to reduce GHG emissions and traces the trajectory of New York City policies to limit GHG emissions. It concentrates on policy efforts to reduce emissions from buildings, which are by far the largest source of NYC's GHG emissions under the standard geographic approach for measuring emissions in cities, and a sector over which the city government has significant regulatory control.[11]

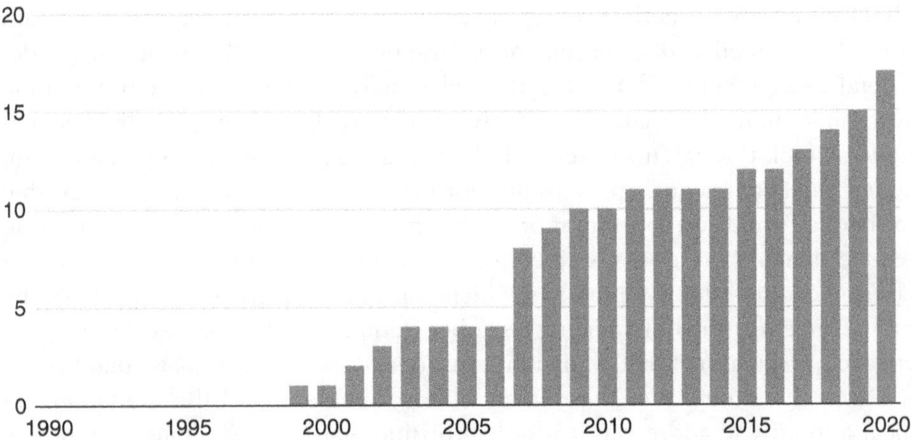

FIGURE 4.1 Cumulative number of cities among the twenty most populous cities in the United States with GHG reduction targets, by year[12]

The city government set its first target to reduce its emissions in 2007.[13] Top officials in the administration of then-Mayor Michael Bloomberg seemed to believe that reducing the city's emissions would help with local economic development, because energy conservation would reduce the need to build new energy infrastructure to accommodate economic growth, and would also generate employment.[14] To advance energy conservation, the administration, working with the city council, adopted a number of policies geared toward encouraging more energy-efficient buildings. However, until 2019, when the city council passed a law mandating emission reductions from large buildings, the city's efforts to reduce its emissions imposed few costs on private actors. Thus, the first twelve years of city efforts to reduce emissions are consistent with the traditional local focus on promoting economic development in the sense that they emerged from a plan for the city's growth and they did little to threaten such development.

Local Law 97, the innovative law that the city passed in 2019 to cap and reduce GHG emissions from large buildings, marks a break with the city's prior efforts. It portends real costs on private actors in the city – in particular building owners, including the owners of residential real estate – if the city implements and enforces the law.[15] The law is thus difficult to reconcile with the traditional local focus on economic development. We argue that this law emerged from the efforts of insiders in city government and local progressive interest groups focused on a mixture of environmental, social justice, and labor concerns. During President Trump's first term in office, when progressive politicians were ascendant in deep-blue enclaves such as New York City, local environmental and social justice activists had allies in city government, and the political power of large property owners waned with an unpopular real estate developer in the White House. This particular allocation of political power made way for progressive local climate action that might not otherwise have been possible. The passage of Local Law 97 in 2019 amid a progressive wave in New York City shows that the porousness of local political institutions can generate climate action that imposes costs on powerful local actors such as the real estate industry, at least on paper.

However, passing a law is one thing; implementing it is another. A key test of the city's commitment to locally costly climate regulations will be whether the city fully implements Local Law 97, especially after 2030 when the caps become more stringent, more buildings have to reduce their emissions, and the city may have to fine more building owners for noncompliance.[16] Already, there are growing concerns about the costs of the building retrofits that Local Law 97 may require of some buildings, especially from the owners of residential properties. The city may yet weaken the law through either legislative changes or deficient implementation. Only time will tell whether the trajectory of local decarbonization efforts in New York City provides support for the distrust that many scholars have about the potential for local governments to lead decarbonization efforts. If a large and resourced liberal city such as New York, with a vibrant community of climate activists, cannot enforce costly mandates on local actors to decarbonize, then it seems likely that many other cities will also struggle to take the lead in decarbonizing. On the other hand, if the city is able to implement Local Law 97, that will suggest that there may be a regulatory role for cities in the societal project of decarbonization, perhaps especially large ones.

This chapter begins by analyzing the original linkage between local climate policy and economic development in New York City. Then the chapter shifts to discussing how a group of policy insiders and outside activists were able to legislate mandates on large buildings to reduce their GHG emissions during the first Trump presidency. It concludes by considering the implications of the arc of New York City's decarbonization efforts to date for the role of cities in addressing the central challenge of reducing GHG emissions to limit climate change.

GREEN GROWTH REDUX

As discussed in Chapter 3, on Earth Day in 2007, Mayor Michael Bloomberg released New York City's first sustainability plan, PlaNYC. Intended to be a comprehensive plan to prepare the city's physical environment for an expected increase in the city's population to over nine million by 2030, the plan included the city's first target to reduce GHG emissions.[17] The city's climate initiatives were a central component of PlaNYC's broader strategy for preparing the city for population and economic growth.[18]

Local officials were quite concerned about future energy constraints in the 2000s. In 2004, the New York City Energy Policy Task Force concluded that "New York City has adequate electricity resources today, but only by a slim margin."[19] The report went on to explain that "[a] projected increase of approximately 1.5% annually in electricity demand in the next five years will necessitate new generation and transmission facilities and expanded distribution resource measures."[20] The following year, oil prices reached record highs and concern about the U.S. dependence on foreign energy sources pervaded the halls of Congress.[21] Bloomberg administration officials made no secret of the fact that their plans to reduce energy use were motivated in large part by a desire to safeguard the city's energy supply. Testifying at a city council hearing on a proposed bill to increase building energy efficiency that would arguably become the Bloomberg administration's signature climate law, Rohit Aggarwala, who headed the Mayor's Office of Long-Term Planning and Sustainability that developed PlaNYC, explained the rationale behind the proposal as follows:

> one of our key findings from PlaNYC [is] that we cannot think about energy infrastructure without treating our buildings as part of that infrastructure, because

> you can't just think about the power plants and the transmission lines, you also have to think about demand, whenever you think about energy challenges .... Economically, there is no better time than today to make emissions reduction[s] and energy efficiency within our buildings a priority. New Yorkers currently spend well over $13 billion each year on energy, and during the past decade, demand for energy has increased by 23 percent.[22]

PlaNYC itself proffered a similar economic rationale for its climate actions. "These efforts will require substantial investments – but each will provide an even greater return,"[23] the plan noted.

None of this is to suggest that New York City officials were not genuinely motivated to reduce climate change. They were. As a coastal city, NYC officials were deeply concerned about the risk of flooding that climate change would bring.[24] However, the actions that the city proposed to tackle climate change also directly aligned with its economic priorities.

PlaNYC's target to reduce New York City's GHG emissions by 30 percent below 2005 levels by 2030 was ambitious for the era in which it was adopted.[25] But what distinguished PlaNYC from other municipal climate plans that came before was its data-driven approach to tracking progress toward the stated goal and educating the private sector about their contributions to emissions.[26] As an initial step, in 2007, the city published the first of its annual GHG inventories, which report emissions released from activities in the city and the generation of electricity supplied to the city.[27] As Figure 4.2 shows, New York City acted before many other U.S. cities to publish an inventory of GHG emissions.

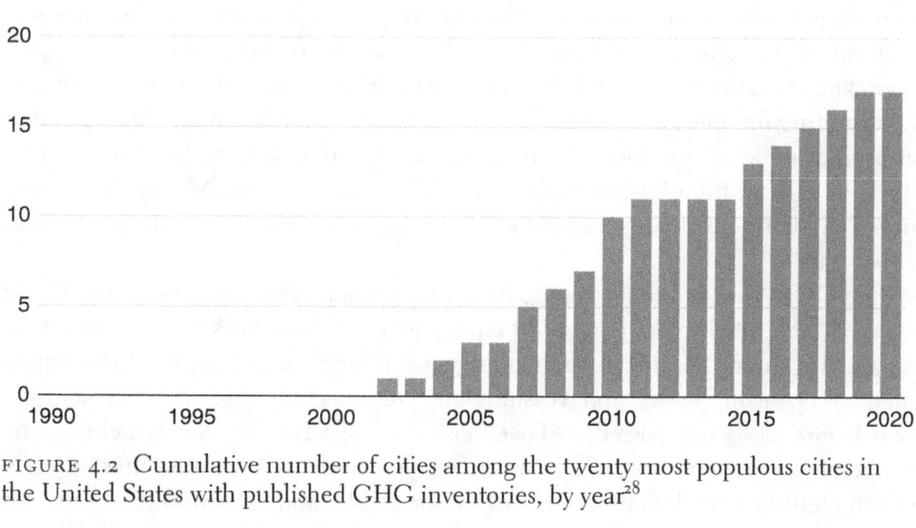

FIGURE 4.2 Cumulative number of cities among the twenty most populous cities in the United States with published GHG inventories, by year[28]

In 2009, at the urging of a Bloomberg administration seeking to implement PlaNYC, the city council passed the *Greener, Greater Buildings Plan* (GGBP)[29] to enlist the real estate industry in achieving the city's climate goals.[30] New York focused its efforts on real estate, as opposed to other sources of emissions such as transportation, because energy use in buildings accounts for the lion's share of local GHG emissions in New York and other densely populated urban areas under the standard geographic approach to measuring city emissions.[31] Some cities also have more authority to regulate emissions from buildings than transportation, which makes buildings a more natural regulatory target.[32] Indeed, around the same time that the city passed the GGBP, the Bloomberg administration tried to adopt rules to regulate emissions from taxis and introduce congestion pricing to drive into the central business district, but these efforts were thwarted by the federal courts[33] and state legislators,[34] respectively.

The GGBP included four distinct components. Local Law 84 (LL84) requires buildings to annually report to the city how much energy and water they consumed; the buildings then receive a "benchmarking" score that indicates how their consumption compares to similar properties. Local Law 85 requires buildings to meet the requirements of the most current energy code when they conduct major renovations. Local Law 87 requires buildings to conduct periodic energy audits that identify opportunities for cost-effective retrofits and retro-commissioning of Heating, Ventilation and Air Conditioning (HVAC) equipment.[35] Local Law 88 requires nonresidential buildings to make certain lighting upgrades and separately charge large tenants for their electricity consumption (i.e., "submeter") instead of charging them a fixed percentage of the building's total electricity bill (which had previously been common practice[36]).

The legislative package also established two programs to assist building owners in making energy upgrades: a jobs training program to bolster the local workforce with the required technical expertise, and an energy efficiency-financing corporation known as the New York City Energy Efficiency Corporation to provide low-cost funding for energy upgrades.[37] New York City officials touted climate action as promoting local employment. In 2009, for example, Aggarwala predicted that the four bills in the *Greener, Greater Buildings* package that Mayor Bloomberg urged the council to adopt would create "19,000 construction related jobs over … 12 years."[38]

The GGBP was groundbreaking. At the time it was passed, the buildings that it covered accounted for 45 percent of energy usage in New York City.[39] Local Law 84 was also among the first benchmarking laws in the U.S. and the first to be implemented[40] (Austin, Texas, and Washington, DC enacted benchmarking laws the year before LL84 was passed).[41] Together with Local Law 87, this benchmarking law created a vast repository of data on energy use and retrofit opportunities throughout the building stock that could educate the public and inform future emissions mandates. That the Bloomberg administration would emphasize the collection of energy and emissions data was perhaps natural given that the mayor built his fortune collecting data about financial markets for Wall Street.[42]

But the GGBP was also modest. Apart from the requirements to tune up HVAC equipment and make lighting upgrades in nonresidential buildings, none of the regulations obligated building owners to reduce energy consumption. Nor did the regulations create a direct financial incentive for owners to reduce their energy consumption. Instead, the laws' principal aim was to overcome information deficits among building owners regarding how inefficient their properties may be in order to incentivize voluntary, cost-effective improvements.[43] As a testament to just how nonconfrontational the GGBP regulations were, at a city council hearing about the benchmarking bill, a representative of an industry-connected nonprofit organization, stated that there was a "strong drive" for benchmarking in the industry.[44] "[B]uildings are already going this way,"[45] he explained.

It was far from accidental that the GGBP adopted such a nonconfrontational approach. Mayor Bloomberg would have preferred to impose legally binding obligations on building owners to implement measures to improve their energy efficiency, but he backed down in the face of opposition from real estate owners and an economic recession.[46] Instead of taking on the industry, the city "join[ed] forces with the real estate industry" in its quest to make their buildings greener.[47]

Although the cooperative approach was a second best adopted in the face of the real estate industry's political clout, there was an economic rationale for thinking it might yield some improvements in energy efficiency. Contrary to other polluting industries, such as energy producers, real estate does not inherently benefit from intensive energy consumption and could actually benefit from lower energy costs from reducing its energy use. In any event, the mayor who had made a fortune in supplying data to the finance industry would be responsible for the collection of a large amount of data about building energy usage in New York City that would enable his successor to design mandates to require buildings to reduce their GHG emissions.

The GGBP had a catalytic effect, perhaps in part because Bloomberg Philanthropies helped to fund work to export ideas about improving building energy efficiency that the Bloomberg administration had developed in New York City.[48] As Figure 4.3 indicates, twelve of the twenty most populous cities, including New York City, adopted some sort of benchmarking law between 2009, when the GGBP was passed, and 2022. Seven of these cities also adopted some sort of energy audit law in the years that followed as well or included an audit requirement as a component of their benchmarking law.[49]

Important as these developments were, by the mid-2010s, it was evident to people following climate policy in New York City that the GGBP's light-touch approach was not going to get the city all the way to where it wanted to go. Building emissions fell 19 percent below 2005 levels between 2005 and 2013, but much of the decrease was attributed to reductions in the carbon intensity of electricity brought about by

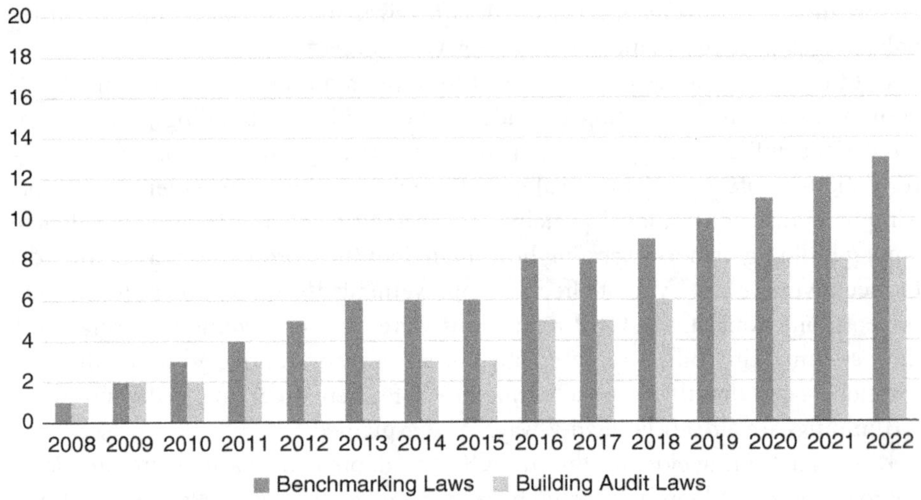

FIGURE 4.3 Cumulative number of benchmarking and auditing laws in the twenty most populous cities, by year first adopted[50]

greater use of natural gas to generate electric power due to the fracking revolution and declines in the price of natural gas, rather than actions that building owners had taken.[51] Benchmarking itself was associated with more modest impacts; a 2016 city-funded study of properties that regularly submitted benchmarking data between 2010 and 2015 found that such properties reduced their energy use by 10 percent during that time period.[52] Another study that examined the effects of benchmarking laws in Austin, New York, San Francisco, and Seattle found that, on average, the benchmarking laws led to a 3 percent decline in utility expenditures.[53] As for the energy audits that LL87 mandated, the only study to have systematically assessed their impact found the audits to have modestly reduced energy use by between 2.5 and 4.9 percent, depending on the type of building.[54]

Late in the Bloomberg administration, officials started to contemplate more ambitious GHG reduction targets, as climate scientists underscored a need for deeper reductions and Hurricane Sandy decimated large parts of the city in 2012.[55] In fact, on December 31, 2013 – the very last day in which Bloomberg was in office – the Mayor's Office of Long-Term Planning and Sustainability published a report suggesting a goal of reducing the city's emissions by 80 percent below 2005 emissions by 2050 (80 × 50), and laid out steps the city could take to reduce its emissions by this much.[56] To achieve the 80 × 50 goal, the city would have to adopt stricter, more politically complicated regulations than it had to date. Reviving a strategy that was laid to waste in the GGBP negotiations, the report mentioned mandatory building performance targets as an option for helping to achieve an 80 percent reduction in citywide GHG emissions by 2050.[57] President Trump's election in 2016 provided the political context that enabled local leaders in New York and several other cities to pledge stronger action. With an avowed climate skeptic in the White House, protest politics were a powerful force in local climate policy.[58]

PROTEST POLITICS

On June 1, 2017, news broke that President Trump had formally decided to withdraw the United States from the Paris Agreement on climate change.[59] The news angered climate activists who had hoped that people in Trump's inner circle might prevail upon him to uphold the agreement.[60] The day before, anticipating that Trump would withdraw the country from the agreement, New York City's Mayor Bill de Blasio had warned that "[t]his is a dagger aimed straight at the heart of New York City."[61] De Blasio explained that federal withdrawal would amplify the need for local actions:

> [W]e in New York City are going to have to take matters into our own hands. And by the way, that's what cities all over the country and all over the world are going to do. That's what states and provinces are doing. It shouldn't be this way, but it's what is necessary. We have to take matters into our own hands when it comes to climate change.
>
> We plan, later this week, to sign an executive order maintaining New York City's commitment to the Paris Agreement. We will partner with cities big and small around the country to support them in doing the same. It's obvious that when our federal government fails us, local governments have to step up.[62]

History was repeating itself. Shortly after taking office in 2001, President George W. Bush had declared that the United States would not implement the Kyoto Protocol negotiated under the Clinton administration that required developed countries to reduce their GHG emissions.[63] Many cities responded to the presidential decision to abandon the Protocol by pledging to reduce their emissions in line with the Protocol. For example, eighteen of the twenty most populous cities signed the Mayors Climate Protection Agreement, under which cities pledged to aim to achieve or exceed the GHG reduction targets that would have applied to the United States if it had implemented the Kyoto Protocol.[64] U.S. cities, including NYC, also joined the International Council for Local Environmental Initiatives (ICLEI) network,[65] and the C40 Group for Climate Leadership, which began with an initial meeting in 2005 held at the initiative of Ken Livingstone, the Mayor of London, England, at the time (Figure 4.4).[66]

After President Trump announced that he planned to withdraw the U.S. from the Paris Agreement, New York, Chicago, Dallas, and hundreds of other cities, including seventeen of the twenty most populous cities, pledged to reduce their own emissions to align with the Paris targets.[67] Once again, cities were promising to take up climate change in protest against federal backsliding.[68] The support from city governments for international climate commitments was consistent with the partisan divide between Democrats and Republicans over climate change that emerged in the 1990s, and the concentration of Democrats in cities.[69]

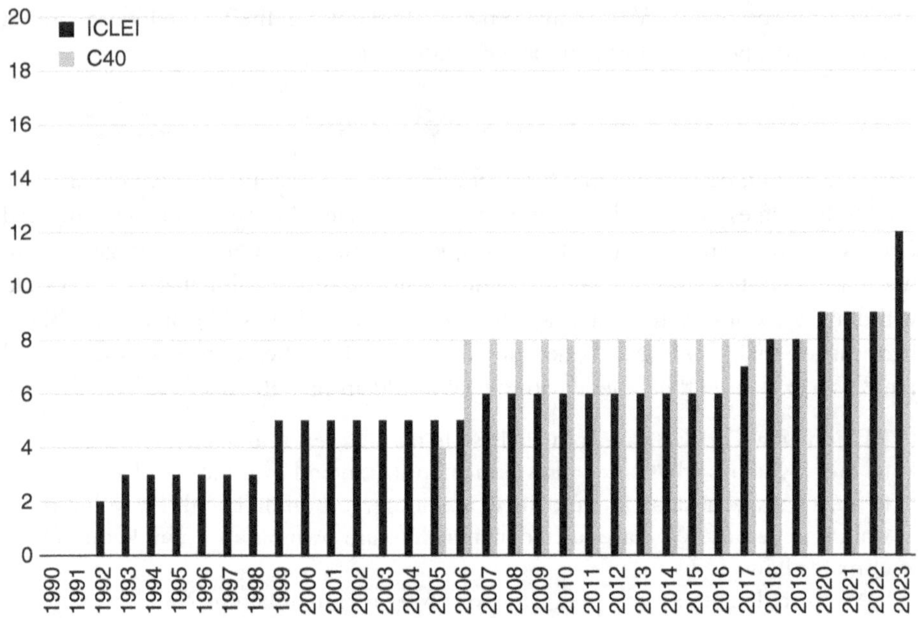

FIGURE 4.4 Cumulative number of the twenty most populous cities with membership in ICLEI and C40, by year first joined[70]

But there were also some important differences between 2017 and 2001. With the climate crisis intensifying – 2017 was the hottest summer New York City had ever recorded to that date[71] – the memory of 2012's Hurricane Sandy still plainly in view, and a deeply unpopular president who for many personified the excesses of the real estate industry, the stars were finally aligned for New York City to impose stricter climate regulations to curtail building emissions.

In September 2017, two months before he was handily reelected to a second term, Mayor Bill de Blasio sketched the centerpiece of a more aggressive climate strategy: New York City would set a cap on the amount of fossil fuels that large buildings could use each year and fine buildings that exceeded their caps.[72] The caps would apply to buildings with more than 25,000 square feet, thus capturing tens of thousands of buildings.[73] The mayor offered few details about the plan in making the announcement. However, he made clear that the fines could be substantial, up to millions of dollars per year. "We gave people a very fair amount of time for the private sector to come forward and really agree to voluntary goals that will be sufficient,"[74] de Blasio said. "It [is] time to move to mandates."[75] Nineteen months later, the city council passed Local Law 97 of 2019 (LL97), which wrote the envisioned mandate into law. The bill passed by a vote of 45–2, with the only two no's coming from the Republican-trending borough of Staten Island.[76]

As indicated earlier, the idea of mandating that buildings meet certain performance standards was far from new;[77] Bloomberg officials wanted to require certain efficiency improvements as part of the GGBP and revived the idea in their waning days in office.[78] The de Blasio administration drew heavily upon its predecessor's work on climate change. As a case in point, the de Blasio administration's very first sustainability plan, *One City: Built to Last*, formally adopted the goal of reducing citywide GHG emissions by 80 percent by 2050, which Bloomberg officials had floated earlier, and signaled that building mandates might be necessary to achieve the goal.[79] The continuity in climate policy was likely facilitated by a continuity in officials between the two administrations. Inside the mayoral offices working on climate change, Dan Zarrilli and John Lee were both key figures in the Bloomberg administration and stayed on well into the de Blasio era.[80] Costa Constantinides, the chair of the city council's environmental protection committee starting in 2015, spearheaded the drafting of Local Law 97. He had worked as a staffer for the chair of the committee he was now heading in 2009, when the Bloomberg era building laws were adopted and mandates were considered but dropped.[81]

So why were city policymakers and legislators more successful in pushing through mandates in 2019 than their predecessors in the Bloomberg era? Part of the answer is that community-based interest groups in New York City were more active and more powerful this time around than they had been in the past.[82]

Several political developments, both inside and outside of New York City, laid the groundwork for these community groups' ascendance and for performance mandates to finally pass in 2019. After the People's Climate March brought more than 300,000 climate activists into the New York City streets in September 2014,[83] pressure from grassroots interest groups in the city for GHG mandates began to coalesce.[84] In 2015, the Alliance for a Greater New York (ALIGN), an alliance of labor and community groups, formed the Climate Works for All coalition and issued a report calling for mandatory "energy use performance targets" for buildings.[85] The Alliance saw mandatory targets for buildings as a way of addressing climate change *and* an economic policy that would benefit low-income New Yorkers and people of color.[86] Retrofitting buildings would increase demand for labor and more efficient buildings would reduce utility costs for their inhabitants. It was the perfect alignment of the climate and economic interests of the Alliance's members.[87]

Trump's election in late 2016 and his withdrawal from the Paris Agreement greased the wheels further.[88] After Trump announced that the U.S. would withdraw from the Paris Agreement, progressive council member Jumaane Williams proclaimed that mandatory energy efficiency standards for buildings were "one of the immediate ways New York City can really lead" on reducing GHG emissions "and truly resist."[89] Activists at ALIGN used the Trump family's real estate holdings in New York City as a reason to mandate building energy improvements, warning that "[w]ithout requiring significant energy use reductions at Trump Tower, Trump International Hotel, Kushner's 666 Fifth Avenue office tower, and others, the city will not be able to meet its ambitious 80 × 50 goal."[90] Pete Sikora, a veteran grassroots climate change organizer for New York Communities for Change (NYCC), was even blunter in his assessment: "Trump being in the White House helped us because it removed the idea that the Feds would come in and save us,"[91] according to Sikora. "Trump also got people really revved up," he added.

By mid-2017, political momentum was moving quickly in the direction of mandates. However, there were still disagreements between various interest groups over the details. ALIGN, for its part, praised de Blasio's coming out for building performance mandates but wanted to make sure that any such mandate would count emissions from electricity used in buildings, not just fossil fuels burned on-site.[92] They also insisted that tenants in rent-regulated buildings not face any rent increases as a result of the mandates; such rent hikes could harm low-income tenants.[93] In August 2018, the Urban Green Council, a nonprofit with connections to sustainability minded real estate owners, produced a "consensus-based" report from a process involving building owners and climate activists that recommended that large buildings collectively be required to improve their energy efficiency by 20 percent by 2030, with additional improvements to follow.[94]

Climate activists in New York City linked their goal with the broader wave of popular progressive politics, emphasizing the connection between building mandates and standing up to Trump. As 2018 wore on, progressive Democrats scored eye-popping victories in Democratic Party politics in the New York area. In June 2018, insurgent progressive Alexandria Ocasio-Cortez unexpectedly defeated a long-time Democratic incumbent in the party primary for a safe Democratic federal House seat covering the Bronx and Queens; addressing climate change was one of her priorities.[95] In November 2018, the Democrats took control of the New York State senate for "the first time in a decade" after campaigning against Trump.[96] Testifying at a December 2018 City Council Environmental Protection Committee hearing on the proposed buildings legislation, grassroots organizer Pete Sikora from NYCC said that "[w]ith Trump in office, this legislation rises to the challenge of the climate crisis where the federal government is destroying the progress the world needs at the exact moment when there's no time left."[97] "The world will be watching this bill," he continued. "It will be a model for bold action worldwide … It truly is a green new deal for New York City."[98]

The Climate Works for All coalition embodied the type of multiracial model of climate activism that Sikora argues is important for spurring the adoption of climate policy in New York City. In a 2022 piece recounting the history of a successful grassroots effort to ban natural gas combustion in new buildings, Sikora suggests that "[i]n a politically 'blue' place" such as New York City, where a majority of residents are members of racial and ethnic minorities, "a multiracial coalition" comprised of people of color and "predominantly white progressive climate activists" that targets key decision-makers can persuade the city government to adopt climate policy even if the coalition has a relatively small number of active members at any given time.[99] A key reason is that local Democratic politicians in New York pay attention to groups that can credibly claim to influence the outcomes in the low-turnout Democratic primaries that largely determine who wins political office in the city.[100] Under this theory of social change, local climate laws emerge from local interest groups wielding – or threatening to wield – influence in Democratic primaries, not the Democratic leanings of the majority of the city's voters, most of whom rarely vote in Democratic primaries or local general elections.[101] The Climate Works for All coalition included not only ALIGN and NYCC, but also District Council 37, the largest public sector union in the city, WE ACT for Environmental Justice and the New York City Environmental Justice Alliance, among others.[102] The coalition's ability to credibly assert that representatives of low-income communities, people of color, *and* a prominent local union supported the bill likely signaled to some council members that it was safe to support it.

Mainstream environmental advocacy groups such as the Natural Resources Defense Council (NRDC) and the League of Conservation Voters were not part of the Climate Works for All coalition.[103] While supportive of the bill's goals, some of these more well-established groups had different visions for what the mandates should look like. They also seemed to espouse a different theory of change from Sikora and his allies, continuing to believe that collaboration with industry players was key. As a case in point, at a 2018 hearing of the City Council Committee on Environmental Protection on a draft of the legislation to establish the mandates, NRDC testified jointly with the Real Estate Board of New York (REBNY), the main group representing building owners targeted by the proposed law, and the Service Employees International Union Local 32BJ, which represents building employees, such as doorpersons, who often work for REBNY members.[104] NRDC's testimony with REBNY may have reflected a pragmatic desire to craft a policy that industry could effectively implement, while also advancing the goal that NRDC shared of equitably decarbonizing buildings.[105] During the Bloomberg era, collaborating with industry might have seemed like a strategy for success.

REBNY may also have made it relatively palatable for NRDC to collaborate with them this time because they did not outright oppose the bill or try to strike down the bill in its entirety (at least not publicly).[106] Instead, they took aim at specific aspects of the draft bill. REBNY was particularly against the idea of exempting all rent-regulated buildings from the performance mandates,[107] which was a key demand of members of the Climate Works for All coalition, who wanted to protect low-income tenants from rent hikes.[108] Real estate officials opposed exemptions for rent-regulated housing because they believed that if "too many types of buildings were given exemptions … [it would place] an undue burden for reducing the city's greenhouse gas output on the remaining buildings."[109] NRDC and 32BJ joined REBNY in opposing the exemption for rent-regulated housing.[110] The final bill that was passed in 2019 exempted all buildings with one or more rent-regulated units from having to meet the emissions caps.[111] In a provision supported by ALIGN, NYCC and NRDC, among others, the law requires these buildings to implement low-cost measures to increase energy efficiency that would not meaningfully increase rents.[112] Real estate's power was clearly on the wane in 2019.[113] With progressive activists electrified and Trump symbolizing for many the excesses of the New York City real estate industry, the time was ripe to mandate performance standards aligned with the preferences of the left flank of the local environmental movement.[114]

Consistent with the priorities of the Climate Works for All coalition, LL97 explicitly incorporates environmental justice concerns. As mentioned earlier, to protect low-income tenants from rent increases, the law exempts properties with rent-regulated apartments from the emissions caps, while requiring that the owners of buildings with such apartments implement low-cost energy efficiency measures, which could benefit tenants.[115] LL97 requires the creation of an advisory board to assist in implementing the law and requires that environmental justice organizations be represented on that board (in addition to advocates from traditional environmental groups); strikingly, the law calls for two environmental justice representatives as contrasted with "one building owner or manager" to participate in the advisory board.[116] This is a marked change in tenor from the Bloomberg era. Whereas the Bloomberg administration went through pains to collaborate with real estate, the de Blasio administration and the city council that was in office during the first Trump presidency seemed concerned with other stakeholders.[117]

Mechanically, LL97 embodies a traditional approach to environmental regulation. It imposes regulatory requirements on individual buildings without incorporating economic ideas popularized at the federal and state levels since the 1990s that allow pollution sources to trade responsibility for achieving pollution reductions among themselves to lower the overall cost of achieving the environmental objective.[118] The law works as follows: buildings are grouped into different categories based on their type of use (multifamily residential, museums, financial offices, etc.). Each building type is permitted to emit up to a specified amount of carbon dioxide equivalent (CO_2e) per square foot. For example, laboratories are allowed to emit more than hotels per square foot.[119] A building's limit (or cap) is determined by multiplying the building's square footage and the allowable amount of CO_2e for its type of use. Building owners that exceed their emissions caps are liable to pay up to $268 per ton of excess emissions, an amount intended to incentivize building upgrades.[120] To calculate a building's annual emissions, owners must multiply the total amount of energy consumed by the carbon intensity coefficient that the city assigns for the relevant type of energy (electricity procured from the grid, natural gas, fuel oil, etc.).[121] The first compliance period runs from 2024 to 2029, and the caps get progressively stricter until 2050.[122] The law also contains some flexibility mechanisms to lessen the burden on owners. For example, if an owner exceeds the permissible amount of GHG emissions per square foot, he can purchase renewable energy credits to offset the emissions attributed to his energy use.[123] Environmentalists have sought to constrain the use of the renewable energy credits, concerned that the use of these credits could reduce the incentive for building owners to invest in building retrofits.[124]

BEYOND LOCAL LAW 97

As was the case with the GGBP of the Bloomberg era, Local Law 97 may lead to legislation to decarbonize buildings in other cities and states. In fact, at least eight other cities have passed legislation that sets some sort of mandatory energy or emissions limits for buildings, including Washington, D.C., which legislated its building performance standard before New York City passed its law.[125] In an example of how local climate initiatives can spur action at higher levels of government, one of the key officials in the de Blasio administration who worked on Local Law 97, Mark Chambers, became Senior Director for Building Emissions and Community Resilience in the Biden administration's Council on Environmental Quality.[126] In this role, Chambers helped to form the National Building Performance Standards Coalition to spur the adoption of similar laws in cities and states throughout the country.[127] In December 2022, the Biden administration also adopted "the first-ever" performance standards for federal buildings to increase energy efficiency and electrification of these buildings.[128]

There are some important differences between the forms that existing building performance laws have taken. Arguably the most important distinction is that some of the laws require that buildings reduce the amount of energy they use, while others, such as Local Law 97, limit the amount of GHG emissions they can release.[129] This distinction is critical because the laws that limit GHG emissions do not necessarily encourage energy efficiency.[130] This is a major drawback given that building out the electricity grid more than is necessary imposes significant economic and environmental costs,[131] even if all the electricity in the grid comes from renewable sources.

However, there are also some important commonalities between many of the mandates. The same forces that have brought greater attention to the need to incorporate equity considerations into climate change policy in New York City have influenced local leaders in other major American cities.[132] For instance, both Boston and Washington, D.C. elevated community groups in the process of developing their building performance standards and the resulting laws prioritize investment in environmental justice communities. The Boston mandate, for example, calls for fines and compliance payments that are collected under the program to be invested in environmental justice projects.[133] And the particular projects that receive the investment will be recommended by a Review Board, whose members come mostly from community groups.[134]

Coincident with the spread of local and state laws to require existing and new buildings to decarbonize or improve their energy efficiency is the emergence of local laws prohibiting newly constructed buildings from including connections to natural gas infrastructure or combusting natural gas onsite.[135] The intent behind such "natural gas bans" is to avoid perpetuating demand for natural gas in newly built buildings that can often be electrified more cheaply than existing buildings.[136] The first ban on natural gas in new buildings was passed by the Berkeley City Council in 2019, and a number of other local governments, including New York City, quickly followed suit.[137] Using similar tactics as it had employed to secure passage of LL97, NYCC played a key role in the ten-month campaign that led to the passage of the ban at the end of 2021, this time in coalition with New York Public Interest Research Group and WE ACT for Environmental Justice.[138] The gas industry and some others oppose local laws to ban natural gas in new construction and the opponents are using various tactics to resist such laws.[139] In response to advocacy from the gas industry, "[a]t least 20 mostly red states" have preempted local government bans on natural gas.[140] In litigation brought by the California Restaurant Association, a panel of the Ninth Circuit Court of Appeals held in 2023 that Berkeley's ban is preempted by the federal Energy Policy and Conservation Act (EPCA), leading Berkeley to withdraw the law.[141] In May 2023, in an example of environmental advocates scaling up to the state level a policy for which they have successfully mobilized locally, NYCC, Food & Water Watch, WE ACT for Environmental Justice, and others persuaded New York State to follow New York City and adopt a state ban on natural gas connections in new buildings.[142] However, underscoring the vulnerability of subnational policies, opponents are challenging both the New York City and New York State bans as preempted by EPCA, relying on the Ninth Circuit precedent.[143]

CONCLUSION

Both PlaNYC and Local Law 97 emerged during times of economic bounty. Bloomberg even referred to the city's good fortune in his speech in 2007 announcing the launch of PlaNYC: "Our economy is humming, our fiscal house is in order and our near-term horizon looks bright," the mayor said. "If we don't act now, when?"[144] As for Local Law 97, the city council passed the law toward the end of a period of more than ten straight years of economic growth.[145]

Within a year of the Local Law 97's passage in 2019, the COVID-19 crisis threw the local economy into a tailspin, hundreds of thousands of people left the city, unemployment rates soared, and property values plummeted.[146] As of 2024, New York City had more than recovered all of the jobs lost in the pandemic, but the city's population was still lower than before COVID, almost 23 percent of Manhattan's office space was vacant, housing was increasingly unaffordable, and over 80,000 people were sleeping in city shelters every day.[147]

With such strong economic headwinds facing the city, one cannot help but wonder whether the city will implement its climate commitments, especially

LL97. Property owners are exerting considerable pressure to weaken the law.[148] Amid the housing affordability crisis, residential property owners are concerned that they will not be able to finance retrofits to their buildings to comply with the law and will face large fines.[149] While the NYC Department of Buildings is developing rules and hiring staff to implement LL97,[150] it is also creating by rule provisions that could delay the law's effectiveness in reducing GHG emissions. In late 2023, the city government promulgated rules allowing the owners of buildings failing to comply with their emissions caps as of 2024 to avoid paying fines for two years if they prepare a decarbonization plan.[151] As of 2024, twenty-five members of the city council, "one short of the majority," also supported a bill to reduce the emissions caps and penalties for residential condominium and cooperative buildings, and in effect reduce the onus on them to decarbonize.[152] The moves from the administration and the council give rise to the concern that the law could die a death by 1,000 cuts. On the other hand, as this book goes to press, the return of Donald Trump as president creates the potential that the protest politics that fueled the passage of LL97 might reemerge over time and support LL97 implementation.

In the end, whether LL97 will be faithfully implemented in New York City, and how widely it will be replicated, may depend on policymakers finding a way to redistribute some of the costs of decarbonizing buildings away from building owners. LL97 unapologetically allocated most of the cost of compliance to building owners. Amidst the bullish local climate politics of the first Trump presidency, this cost allocation made good political sense. In the present era, it is less clear that this is the case. Moving forward, the more that the transition costs of laws such as LL97 can be socialized, the more politically viable cities' decarbonization laws may be.

If New York City is able to implement LL97, the experience would suggest that a city can adopt and implement a law to reduce GHG emissions that imposes costs on local private actors, at least if there are people inside government *and* effective advocacy groups outside of it committed to the law. A reduction in building emissions attributable to the law would suggest that cities can indeed impose costly measures on local actors to address climate change, notwithstanding the apparent incentives of cities to ignore climate change because they have little sway over trends in world temperatures. Successful implementation also might vindicate the confidence of New York City policymakers dating back to the Bloomberg era that New York City's actions can make a difference. In 2022, fifteen years after the release of PlaNYC in 2007, Cas Holloway, who led the New York City Department of Environmental Protection under Bloomberg, explained that "New York City has always seen itself as a model for the urban world." "We always thought that ambitiously, hoping to inspire others."[153] But the precarity of Local Law 97 in 2024 emphasizes that the politics of limiting GHG emissions are no simple matter at the local level, even in a deeply Democratic city such as New York.

5

Adapting to Climate Change in NYC

INTRODUCTION

Cities need to adapt to global climate change to protect local residents against extreme heat, flooding, drought, fires, and other risks that are already manifest in urban areas.[1] Cities are also well positioned to promote adaptation to climate change given the extensive local control over land use. They can limit new development in areas at risk of flooding, fires, and other harms, and channel that development to safer neighborhoods.[2] They also can build more green spaces and plant more trees on city-owned land to reduce urban temperatures and risks to people from heat, which kills more people in the United States "than … all other natural disasters combined."[3] Indeed, large city governments may be better placed than the more distant federal and state governments to address at a granular level the variegated vulnerability to the effects of warming temperatures within their borders.[4]

Cities also stand to receive the majority of benefits from their investments in adaptation, unlike with their investments in decarbonization, which benefit the world as a whole.[5] Adaptation is a local public good, akin to urban parks and other locally beneficial changes to the local environment, such as clean air and cleaning up contaminated lands discussed in Chapter 3. Indeed, the same change to the local environment, such as improving a public park, can enhance climate resilience and provide individual wellness and aesthetic benefits. New York City's East Side Coastal Resiliency project illustrates the dual functionality: it involves rebuilding and elevating a stretch of parkland along the East River to protect it and the surrounding neighborhood, which includes 28,000 residents of public housing, from flooding as the climate warms.[6]

Given the benefits to cities of adapting to climate change and the tools available to them to do so, it is not surprising that cities began gathering information in the early twenty-first century about local climate impacts and started to develop relevant plans. Political science professor Sara Hughes concluded in an article published in 2015 that "most of the adaptation planning that is happening in the U.S. is taking place in cities and at the local level,"[7] and research published subsequent to

Hughes' article suggests that cities have continued to take the lead.[8] Suggestive of the local interest in climate impacts, research for this book found that as of 2020, ten of the twenty most populous cities in the U.S. had developed and published projections for the impacts of climate change in their areas.[9]

However, despite all the apparent motivations that cities have to adapt, and the efforts they have put into information gathering and planning, most cities actually had done relatively little adaptation as of the early 2020s. Hughes highlighted the lack of adaptation actions (as opposed to adaptation *plans*) in her 2015 article. Hughes found that while "most of the adaptation planning that is happening in the U.S. is taking place in cities and at the local level" the "concrete adaptation actions taking place in cities are quite limited."[10] Thus, notwithstanding the different economic structure of adaptation as compared with decarbonization from a local perspective, the picture for adaptation is similar to that for decarbonization as of the early 2020s: more talk than activity.

New York City is somewhat of an outlier among U.S. cities in the extent to which it has moved beyond planning to actually implement measures.[11] Yet, even New York's adaptation actions have been slow and halting, and thus far inadequate given the scale of the climate risks that the city faces over the twenty-first century from coastal and rainwater flooding and rising temperatures. If even New York City cannot adapt on its own, it is hard to imagine that other smaller, less resourced cities will fare much better without assistance from higher levels of government.

This chapter analyzes the trajectory of New York City's nascent efforts to adapt to climate change in the first two decades of the twenty-first century to shed light on why cities are falling short in implementing adaptation plans.[12] It focuses on the city government's efforts to protect against coastal flooding because this is a major risk facing New York City and was the primary focus of local adaptation efforts in the decade or so after Hurricane Sandy led to massive storm surge flooding in the city in 2012. However, in recent years, the city has also taken some steps to reduce vulnerability to heat and flooding from rainfall, both of which are important concerns for communities of color and low-income populations in the city, among others.[13]

Drawing on the framework set out in Chapter 2 for understanding local environmental action, the impetus for planning and implementing coastal protection adaptation measures has largely come from the "top." Specifically, they have been pushed by city policymakers concerned about the impacts of global warming for the city's residents and economic base.[14] While there has been community-based advocacy for coastal protection since approximately 2010, city policymakers largely defined the city government adaptation agenda, at least until the late 2010s and early 2020s.[15] The history of city policymakers driving adaptation planning and implementation in New York City is consistent with Hughes' findings that urban adaptation planning is typically initiated by city officials (as opposed to community members), and that these officials frequently characterize it "as a necessary strategy for protecting the city's assets and reducing the city's vulnerability to hazards and disasters."[16]

From 2000 until 2012, when Hurricane Sandy struck the city, New York policymakers did not perceive climate change as sufficiently threatening to the city's economic prosperity or residents to warrant significant investments of local government resources. During this time period, city policymakers focused on gathering information about the risks that climate change presents for the city, but they undertook few tangible actions to protect the city from the risks of storm surge flooding – or rainfall flooding or higher temperatures. While the information that policymakers collected revealed major climate risks to the city, uncertainty about the magnitude and timing of the risks, the long time horizon over which they seemed likely to emerge, and a lack of local, federal, and state funding for proactive adaptation likely contributed to the paucity of local action.[17]

Sandy increased policymakers' perception of the urgency of acting to adapt, and injected $15 billion of federal funding into the city that enabled it to invest in adaptation.[18] Yet, between 2012 and the early 2020s, the city had great difficulty implementing adaptation actions; by 2022, ten years after Sandy, the city had still not spent the full $15 billion that the federal government appropriated for it after Sandy, and the city had to secure a Congressional extension to avoid losing some of the federal appropriations.[19] On the tenth anniversary of Sandy, a journalist for *The New York Times* surveying the city's steps to adapt concluded that the city was "only just beginning to act."[20] Internal obstacles seem to have hamstrung New York City's efforts, including a lack of expertise at the local level in building novel coastal protection infrastructure, and the extensive public consultation and analytic requirements that have applied since the 1970s in New York and other places in the United States to the construction of infrastructure.[21]

Moreover, as New York City policymakers began grappling after Sandy with protecting the city's coastline, they, like their counterparts in cities and states along the eastern seaboard, seem to have realized that protecting local people and the economies will be too costly for local actors alone. New York City, like governments in Boston, Charleston, Miami, and other places, is currently working to externalize onto federal taxpayers some of the substantial costs of protecting their coastal areas against flooding as the climate warms, by developing coastal protection projects with the U.S. Army Corps of Engineers (USACE) that the Corps would build.[22] It is the Corps' efforts to design coastal protection infrastructure for the New York-New Jersey region that seems to have galvanized what to our knowledge is the first robust, citywide community advocacy concerning adaptation in the early twenty-first century. In late 2023, the local advocates scored a victory when they persuaded New York State to request that the Corps broaden its study and revisit its tentatively selected plan.[23] But as of early 2025, it is unclear whether the community advocacy will spur the federal – or the state and local – governments to better protect New York City against the severe flood risks that it faces from climate change, similar to the way that community advocacy has previously led the city to supply local public goods and even the global public good of decarbonization.[24]

This chapter begins by analyzing the efforts of New York City policymakers between 2000 and 2012 to gather information about the risks that climate change presents for the city. Then it discusses the adaptation strategy that the Bloomberg administration developed after Sandy, the challenges that the city faced in implementing aspects of this strategy, and the efforts to persuade the federal government, through the Army Corps of Engineers, to assume substantial responsibility for protecting the city's coastline. The chapter concludes by highlighting the implications of the difficulties that New York City has had adapting to climate change for the role of cities in adaptation, and the assistance that cities need from higher levels of government, most notably the federal government.

2000–2012: INFORMATION GATHERING

From 2000 to 2012, New York City's efforts to adapt to climate change were largely limited to gathering information about the risks facing the city. In 2001, Columbia University's Earth Institute published the first scientific assessment of the potential impacts of climate change in New York City.[25] For several years after the release of this federally commissioned study, the city's Department of Environmental Protection (DEP) seems to have taken the lead within the city government in assessing the impacts of climate change for the city.[26] DEP funded researchers at local universities to model the local impacts of climate change and study the possibility of building storm surge barriers to protect New York City, and it established a "Climate Change Task Force to oversee the Department's" analysis of climate risks and preparation for them.[27] DEP had an incentive to understand the implications of climate change for the New York region because it manages the city's water supply, wastewater and stormwater drainage systems, and spends a considerable amount on long-lived infrastructure for these systems.[28] The Department needed to incorporate the future impacts of global warming in its "planning and investments"[29] to ensure that its infrastructure and systems would continue to meet local needs.

Even before Sandy, the Bloomberg administration realized that it would need help from the federal government and new local institutions to better understand the challenges that climate change presents for the city. In 2007, the city asked the Federal Emergency Management Agency (FEMA) to update its maps of areas of the city vulnerable to flooding, which had not been updated since the maps were first released in 1983.[30] In 2008, the Bloomberg administration created a new local body, "modeled on the Intergovernmental Panel on Climate Change," to understand the risks that climate change poses for the city.[31] With funding from the Rockefeller Foundation,[32] it established the New York City Panel on Climate Change (NPCC) to assess the potential local impacts of climate change, and appointed as heads Cynthia Rosenzweig and William Solecki, two well-qualified academics who had led the 2001 federally funded assessment of climate risks to the New York region.[33]

Published in 2010, the New York City Panel's first report (NPCC 2010) provided "the first official climate change projections for New York City" for temperature increase, precipitation, and sea level rise.[34] NPCC 2010 predicted that New York City's climate might resemble those of "Raleigh, North Carolina or Norfolk, Virginia today" by the 2080s,[35] and highlighted the likelihood of "more frequent, intense, and longer" heat waves.[36] It projected increases in precipitation and highlighted the potential for "inland flooding," warning specifically of the risks of "increased street, basement, and sewer flooding,"[37] such as those that the city experienced in 2021 as a result of Hurricane Ida.[38] It also illustrated the uncertainty about the potentially grave threats that climate change presents for cities such as New York; for example, the panel offered two starkly different sets of projections of sea level rise by 2080, warning that sea levels might increase by as little as 12 to 23, or as much as 41 to 55, inches.[39] In addition, the Panel identified the risks that climate change presents to the city's energy, transportation, water supply, wastewater, drainage, solid waste, and communications infrastructure.[40]

Notwithstanding the growing awareness of the risks that the city faced before 2012, New York City undertook few tangible actions in this period to address these risks beyond acquiring more information about local risks to global warming. The city took some measures to address the risks of extreme heat, such as encouraging painting of roofs white to reduce temperatures in the city, and planting trees, which also had the immediate benefit of making the city more attractive.[41] But it did little to address the risks of coastal flooding. In fact, the city was increasing the potential for damage from such flooding by rezoning areas along the waterfront to allow for new housing (although some of the risks to new development were mitigated through construction standards for waterfront areas).[42] The city did not plan, let alone implement, a comprehensive program to reduce harm from coastal flooding, even though ideas for reducing such harm – such as storm surge barriers, nature-based measures, and retreat – were on policymakers' radar.[43] In the Assessment and Action Plan that DEP's Climate Change Program issued in 2008, the agency proclaimed that the time had come to shift "from analysis to action," but the agency did little to specifically adapt for climate change the water supply, wastewater, and stormwater infrastructure that it manages.[44] DEP appears to have only incorporated climate change projections into its planning and pursued some capital projects that would have the collateral benefit of mitigating climate risks to the city's water infrastructure.[45] Officials at DEP – and the Department of City Planning and other city agencies – seemed to think there was too much uncertainty about the extent and timing of climate risks to justify bold actions.[46] For example, although the subway system had nearly flooded multiple times in the decades before Sandy, neither the city nor the state-dominated agency that controls the subway did much to protect it against flooding until after it flooded during Sandy.[47]

The city's failure to heed the warnings to begin adapting to the risks of flooding and high heat should be put in the context of the paucity of funding available to city policymakers for adapting to climate change. Coastal protection infrastructure, such as storm surge barriers, is expensive to build and maintain.[48] Yet New York, like many other cities, had no dedicated stream of local revenues to pay for adaptation. Moreover, until 2020, local governments did not have much access to reliable federal funding to adapt proactively before disasters such as hurricanes.[49] Instead, they were mostly beholden to disaster-related federal funds, which could only be used to rebuild and increase resilience *after* disaster strikes. In combination, the lack of federal funding to adapt before disasters and the availability of federal assistance after hurricanes, fires, and other natural disasters likely disincentivized local officials from acting prophylactically. If the city had been able to invest in adaptation before Sandy, it is likely that the damage would have have been lessed as studies suggest that adapting in advance of disaster more than pays for itself by reducing the costs of disaster recovery.[50]

2012–2023: INITIAL STEPS TOWARD COASTAL PROTECTION

In February 2012, eight months before Sandy struck New York, four academics from Princeton and the Massachusetts Institute of Technology, including the prominent climate scientist and NPCC panelist Michael Oppenheimer, published an article about the potential for climate change to lead to massive flooding in New York City from more powerful hurricanes and other storms.[51] Amid its sophisticated projections and figures, the article bluntly warned that "NYC is now highly vulnerable to extreme hurricane-surge flooding."[52] Four years earlier, in 2008, DEP itself warned of the potential for amplified storm surge flooding as the climate warms.[53] On October 29, 2012, millions of New Yorkers experienced a version of the massive storm surge flooding that these policymakers and academics had predicted; indeed, provided with the horrible opportunity to see his "research come to life," Oppenheimer observed from the Hudson River as Sandy hit New York.[54] Although Sandy was no longer technically a hurricane when it arrived in New York, it produced a huge storm surge and flooded 17 percent of the land in the city, in part because it arrived close to the time of "a 'spring' tide, when the tide was at the very peak of its monthly cycle."[55] The flooding produced a cascade of effects: forty-four people died in the city, thousands of patients had to be evacuated from hospitals and nursing homes, subways flooded, almost two million people lost electricity, communications systems went down, and wastewater treatment plants stopped working, causing the city to discharge polluted water into surrounding waterways.[56] Sandy generated over $65 billion in damages in the U.S., making it the second costliest storm in the country as of 2013 (after Hurricane Katrina).[57]

Policymakers interpreted Sandy as an illustration of the risks that climate change presents for the city, although they were cautious about attributing Sandy itself to climate change.[58] The storm not only showed a generation of New Yorkers that projections of coastal flooding could actually come to pass but also that they could be experienced now, not in decades. In response, policymakers immediately redoubled their efforts to better understand the risks that climate change presented, especially the risks of coastal flooding. In January 2013, FEMA released interim flood maps – Advisory Base Flood Elevation maps – and six months later it issued Preliminary Work Maps (PWMs) that showed that the 100-year floodplain was an area 45 percent larger than in 1983 maps, inhabited by 400,000 people, comparable to the area flooded by Sandy.[59] The city government recalled the NPCC "on an emergency basis to update its projections to inform planning for rebuilding and resiliency post-Sandy."[60] Using FEMA's PWMs, and the panel's projections for local sea level rise, the NPCC created "a series of 'future flood maps'" that indicated that "[w]ith more than 2.5 feet of sea level rise, New York city's 100-year floodplain in the 2050s could be … 24 percent … of the city,"[61] an area inhabited by 800,000 people, approximately 10 percent of New York's population.[62]

The storm also highlighted the inequitable vulnerability within the city to coastal flooding.[63] Some boroughs were more affected by flooding than others.[64] Low income was associated with exposure to flooding, as were old age and to some degree race.[65] The storm underscored the particular vulnerability of the public housing stock owned by the New York City Housing Authority to flooding. Thirty-five sites owned by the Housing Authority, which housed over 60,000 people, "suffered major storm-related damage."[66] The inequitable distribution of vulnerability to climate change had not been a major theme in the pre-2012 assessments of the local climate risks, but it was increasingly recognized after the storm in relation not only to coastal flooding but also to other climate impacts, such as heat.[67]

Spurred by Sandy's devastating toll, the Bloomberg administration used its final year in office to lay the groundwork for the transition from climate risk analysis to action. The centerpiece of this effort was to establish a Special Initiative for Rebuilding and Resiliency (SIRR) to develop a plan to protect New York from climate risks.[68] Building on the NPCC's projections, in June 2013, the initiative produced a 445-page report with a ten-year plan that it estimated would cost almost $20 billion.[69] The report indicated that half that amount was already available to the city – $5.5 billion from the city's capital plan and the remaining $5 billion from the federal government – and was optimistic that the city would be able to secure an additional $5 billion primarily from the federal government, leaving a $4.5 billion gap.[70] As of 2022, the federal government had provided approximately $15 billion to the city after Sandy – $10 billion from FEMA and $4.2 billion from Housing and Urban Development Community Development Block Grant-Disaster Recovery grants.[71] However, as of 2022, the city had only spent $11 billion of the money it received.[72]

The SIRR laid out a multipronged approach to protecting the city against coastal storm surge flooding that has essentially guided city policy since Sandy.[73] First, the city would remain committed to developing its waterfront and not back away from the area. Second, the city would take steps to reduce damages from future coastal flooding and increase the city's ability to rebound from it. The city would implement design standards for new and substantially rebuilt buildings and other structures on the waterfront. In addition, the city would build neighborhood-specific coastal protection infrastructure and advocate that the federal Army Corps of Engineers construct such infrastructure.[74] Combining measures at the individual building level with neighborhood coastal protection projects would provide "multilayered defenses"[75] that reduce the likelihood of coastal flooding and increase the city's ability to bounce back when flooding occurred.

Commitment to the Waterfront

Remaining committed to the waterfront was a cornerstone of SIRR and the city has continued to allow new development in the waterfront since Sandy. "We are a coastal city – and we cannot, and will not, abandon our waterfront," Bloomberg proclaimed in his mayoral foreword to the report.[76] SIRR did not support retreating from the city's shoreline through governmental buyouts of private properties, and the city bought out very few properties after Sandy.[77] Only toward the end of the de Blasio administration did the city recognize that there are some waterfront areas that will not be habitable going forward and endorse the idea of a voluntary buyout program, a proposal that the next mayoral administration vowed in 2023 to carry forward on a limited scale.[78] Perhaps the best evidence of SIRR's commitment to waterfront development was its proposal to deal with flood risks to the South Street Seaport and Financial District neighborhoods in lower Manhattan by creating new land in the East River, and paying for the project by allowing residential and commercial development on the new land.[79] "Seaport City" has not been built, although the idea of creating new land in the East River was revived in 2021, this time with the thought that the new land would be devoted to public spaces.[80]

In the decade after Sandy, there was no indication in the city's land use policies that the city was interested in meaningfully retreating from the waterfront. In 2021, NYU's Furman Center found that of new multifamily housing built between 2010 and 2020, "18.2 percent of new market rate units and 13.6 percent of units targeted to low-income households were built in areas with a high risk of flooding over the next 100 years."[81] The city even rezoned some waterfront areas to allow for more development in the decade after Sandy.[82] In a small concession to climate change, though, it created five coastal risk districts between 2017 and 2021 to restrict new development in a few low-lying areas of Brooklyn, Queens, and Staten Island.[83] In 2021, the city issued a new plan for its waterfront that envisions more development on the waterfront. It supports new development in "most of NYC's coastal areas … at currently permitted residential densities" with "physical design improvements, flood retrofits, and sound waterfront asset management."[84] While it suggests that the city might limit new residential development in a few more low-lying coastal areas, the plan also indicates that the city might increase the allowable density in other areas of the waterfront.[85]

Reducing the Risks along the Waterfront

While continuing to allow new development along the waterfront, the city has implemented some of the SIRR's recommendations for building- and neighborhood-level protections to mitigate impacts of coastal flooding. With respect to the building-level protections, in 2014, the city amended the building code to include "new, significantly, higher standards for flood-resilient construction for [new and 'substantially modified'] buildings in the current 100-year floodplain."[86] The city also changed zoning laws to enable buildings in the 100-year – and later also the 500-year – floodplain to meet the higher construction standards without running afoul of zoning requirements, such as height limits.[87] However, few buildings in the city's existing 100-year floodplain comply with the updated construction standards since most of them predate the standards, and are not required to retrofit for resilience.[88] The city also took steps to increase the likelihood that newly built infrastructure will be resilient to climate risks[89] and used federal funding to improve the resiliency of some of the important infrastructure in the existing 100-year floodplain, such as hospitals.[90]

Less progress has been made to try to contain floodwaters along the city's shorelines. As mentioned earlier, SIRR recommended coastal protection infrastructure to protect large swaths of the city's coastline, in addition to building-level measures. A point of contention is whether such infrastructure should take the form of a small number of large storm surge barriers located far from the shore, or a series of discrete barriers combined with more nature-based solution closer to land. SIRR staked out a position in favor of a series of discrete neighborhood-specific projects, which seems to have remained the city's preferred approach in the years since.[91] SIRR squarely rejected what it described as the "'silver bullet' solution" of building a large storm surge barrier across New York Harbor from Sandy Hook, New Jersey to the Rockaway Peninsula in New York.[92] It warned that a large outer harbor barrier would be costly, complex, and take decades to build. It also might fail, as the Army Corps of Engineers' levees failed to protect New Orleans during Hurricane Katrina in 2005.[93] Instead of one or two large barriers, the report recommended the construction of a long list of "discrete" coastal protection infrastructure projects, including some local storm surge barriers and nature-based approaches such as wetlands and dune restoration, which would offer coastal communities a diversified portfolio of protections.[94] Through a modular approach to coastal protection, the city would be able to develop coastal protections incrementally.[95] The federal government – and to some extent the state – would be brought into the endeavor because the city would need funding from higher levels of government and because of federal and state jurisdiction over coastal areas.[96]

Unfortunately, building multiple discrete coastal protection projects proved more difficult than SIRR imagined. By 2021, none of the nine projects that the de Blasio administration classified as neighborhood coastal protection projects had been completed.[97] Indeed, only two were under construction that year (the East Side Coastal Resiliency project, which includes rebuilding East River Park on Manhattan's Lower East Side to protect against storm surge flooding, and the federal Army Corps' Rockaways Atlantic Shoreline Project in Far Rockaway, Queens, which combines a sea wall with beach restoration).[98]

A 2021 planning guidance document from the Mayor's Office of Climate Resiliency offered an explanation for the slow place that echoes the concerns among some environmentalists about the obstacles to building the new infrastructure necessary to adapt to, and limit, climate change: "The planning, design and construction of these [neighborhood coastal protection] projects can take up to ten years or more due to the many technical challenges, jurisdictional intersections, and robust community engagement that is required."[99] Designing and constructing neighborhood coastal protection projects is a novel task for the city, the guidance document explained, and city agencies were still learning how to address the challenge.[100] Constructing this "newer form of capital asset in the city" involved characterizing risks – including storm surge and tidal flooding – and designing technical responses to them while considering "social impacts" to city neighborhoods, working with multiple federal, state, and local agencies to satisfy their criteria (such as the benefit cost analysis requirement of FEMA and HUD for project funding), and engaging meaningfully with the public.[101] Furthermore, "[t]he implementation of [the] … first generation of projects created new opportunities for the City to engage with communities, and often challenged and stretched the City's existing engagement practices and resources."[102]

The development of the East Side Coastal Resiliency (ESCR) project put some of these challenges plainly into view. After Sandy, city officials identified the area along the East River by Chinatown and the Lower East Side as the first priority for building coastal protections that would ring southern Manhattan.[103] The area suffered massive flooding during Sandy and is densely populated, with thousands of low-income people living in large public housing buildings near the waterfront. It is also home to important infrastructure.[104] Moreover, the city owns of much of the land where the ESCR is located, which was supposed to help facilitate the construction project.[105]

The city secured $338 million of federal funding for the ESCR through the Rebuild by Design competition that the federal government initiated after Sandy to spur resilient rebuilding.[106] The initial designs for the ESCR came from architects participating in the Rebuild by Design competition who extensively engaged the public in developing their designs.[107] This plan featured a park along the East River that was designed to hold floodwaters. In 2018, after the first deputy mayor overseeing the project changed, the city abruptly altered the plan for the ESCR from the design that had been developed.[108] The design that the city imposed involved destroying the existing park and rebuilding it at a higher elevation on fill to minimize the likelihood of flooding.[109] According to *New York Times* architectural critic Michael Kimmelman, mayoral officials "had not raised insuperable objections during nearly five years of community consultation," but then "suddenly swapped the plan for what officials decided was a more technically sound one."[110] City officials explained that the innovative floodable park design was too complex to build and that the Parks Department would have difficulty managing it after construction because the department had no guaranteed budget for repairing the park after it flooded.[111]

Whatever the cause of the city government's sudden shift, the change in the design provoked an outcry among community members against the city, as well as divisions within the community. Some community members unsuccessfully sued to block the city's preferred design, while others supported moving forward notwithstanding the city's bungling because of the protection that the rebuilt park would offer against storm surge flooding.[112] While the infighting dragged on, the community remained just as vulnerable to flooding as it had been during Sandy.[113] NYU PhD sociology student Malcolm Araos, who followed the public engagement process on the ESCR for his dissertation, argues that those who supported going ahead with the city's plan tended to be people of color who are residents of the public housing buildings near the East River Park that suffered extensive damage from flooding during Sandy; the opponents tended to be white people who are more likely to live in market-rate housing and who are focused on the destruction of the existing park – and 1,000 trees – that the city's design entails.[114] The city council member for the area sided with advancing the project, and the park reconstruction project finally started in 2021.[115]

Notwithstanding all the attention that the ESCR has attracted, it – and the other waterfront resilience projects that are under construction in 2025[116] – will only protect narrow slices of New York City's 520-mile shoreline from coastal flooding. Moreover, most of the coastal areas to which the city has directed investments are in lower Manhattan, historically an important economic center, leaving the city's outer boroughs less protected.[117] Since the early twenty-first century, the city government has recognized that it needs funding and other assistance from the federal government to comprehensively address the risks of coastal flooding that the city faces.[118]

New York City is not alone in trying to externalize onto federal taxpayers some of the costs of protecting local residents. As indicated in Table 5.1, as of 2025, New York, Boston, Charleston, Miami, and other coastal cities (and states) are working with the Army Corps of Engineers to design coastal protection infrastructure that the Corps would build with contributions from subnational governments. These cities require the assistance of the Army Corps of Engineers if for no other reasons than the costs of comprehensive coastal protection, limited local expertise, and the limits on local legal authority to build in coastal waters.[119] It also might not be desirable for coastal cities to unilaterally address the flood risks that they face even if they could do so; large coastal protection infrastructure, such as storm surge barriers, will likely impact people living beyond any particular locality, potentially diverting water from one area to another. A single large barrier protecting parts of New York City might send water to neighboring counties in Long Island.[120] Coastal protection infrastructure also might affect regional development patterns if property values increase in protected areas and they gentrify.[121] Just as federal

TABLE 5.1 *Selected Army Corps projects to protect against climate change related coastal flooding*[122]

Geographic Area	Status of Project	Nonfederal Sponsors and Partners[123]
Boston, Massachusetts	*City of Boston Coastal Storm Risk Management Feasibility Study*: Feasibility study ongoing.[124]	Sponsor: City of Boston[125]
Charleston, South Carolina	*Charleston Peninsula Coastal Storm Risk Management Study*:[126] Congress has authorized the project but not yet appropriated funding for construction.[127]	Sponsor: City of Charleston[128]
Coastal Texas Project (Houston/Galveston)	*Coastal Texas Protection and Restoration Feasibility Study*:[129] Congress has authorized the project but not yet appropriated funding for construction.[130]	Sponsor: Texas General Land Office (for the feasibility study, ecosystem restoration, and beach nourishment);[131] Gulf Coast Protection District (for the Galveston Bay Storm Surge Barrier System)[132]
Miami-Dade Back Bay, Florida	*Miami-Dade Back Bay Coastal Storm Risk Management Feasibility Study*:[133] Congress has authorized the project but not yet appropriated funding for construction.[134]	Sponsor: Miami-Dade County[135]
New York/New Jersey	*NY & NJ Harbor & Tributaries Focus Area Feasibility Study (HATS)*:[136] Feasibility study is ongoing.[137]	Sponsors: New York State Department of Environmental Conservation, New Jersey Department of Environmental Protection Partners: New York State Department of State, New York City Mayor's Office of Climate and Environmental Justice[138]
Norfolk, Virginia	*Norfolk Coastal Storm Risk Management Project*: Congress has authorized the project.[139]	Sponsor: City of Norfolk[140]

regulation was necessary to address pollution that crossed local and state borders in the 1960s and 1970s, federal agencies such as the Army Corps with large geographic scope for action may be better positioned to design and build coastal protection infrastructure to avoid individual cities and states addressing their problems by exporting floodwaters to other areas.

The Army Corps' ongoing New York & New Jersey Harbor & Tributaries Focus Area Feasibility Study (HATS study) is identifying measures to protect the region against storm surge flooding.[141] The $52 billion option that the Army Corps identified in September 2022 as its preferred alternative harkens back to the modular approach that the city's SIRR report endorsed in 2013.[142] It encompasses building twelve storm surge barriers to protect parts of New York and New Jersey, including storm surge gates in Brooklyn for Newtown Creek and the Gowanus Canal that city policymakers have supported since at least SIRR.[143] Assuming the HATS study produces recommendations, there is no promise of Congressional funding for the study's recommendations. Congress would need to authorize the project and appropriate funds for it. The federal government would likely pay 65 percent of the construction costs, with the remainder funded by nonfederal governments (such as the states of New York and New Jersey, and possibly New York City).[144]

In addition to engaging a federal bureaucracy in protecting New York City and surrounding areas, the HATS Study seems to have galvanized robust citywide community advocacy on adaptation that has been unusual in the city, where city policymakers have typically defined the adaptation agenda in the early twenty-first century.[145] Community advocates appear to have four primary objections to the Corps' work leading up to the Corps' recommendation of the $52 billion alternative in 2022 and to this recommendation:[146] First, the Corps focused on designing infrastructure to address solely storm surge flooding, rather than developing infrastructure that would also mitigate other flood risks in the region, such as increased nuisance flooding due to sea level rise and rainfall flooding.[147] Second, the Corps' 2022 preferred alternative does not adequately protect environmental justice communities, such as the Bronx, "the poorest county in New York State."[148] Third, the Corps prioritizes engineering options, such as surge barriers, over nature-based solutions.[149] Fourth, the Corps did not engage adequately with community-based groups in designing coastal protection infrastructure that will have a major impact on the region.[150] Advocates and others make similar critiques of Army Corps coastal protection projects in other parts of the country as well.[151]

As mentioned earlier, in late 2023, the community-based advocates scored a major victory when they persuaded New York State to request that the Corps "overhaul the $52.6 billion storm surge protection plan proposed" by the Corps in 2022.[152] However, the impact of the community-based advocacy to which the Corps study has given rise on adaptation in New York City (and the metropolitan region in general) has yet to be determined. Will the advocacy transform into a grassroots movement to stop a Corps project that resembles familiar movements to thwart conventional infrastructure such as roads?[153] Advocates' comments suggest that their objections are to the Corps' approach to the study and its preferred alternative as of 2022, not to the idea of a Corps project to protect coastal areas.[154] This nuance raises the possibility that the advocacy might develop into a grassroots movement that could complement the top-down policymaker-driven impetus for coastal adaptation in the New York region, and provide additional momentum for governmental actions to help New York City address the serious flood risks that it faces from climate change.

CONCLUSION

Given the major benefits New York City would reap if it becomes more resilient to flooding, heat, and other impacts of global warming, the limited progress that city policymakers have made in adapting the city as of the early 2020s is striking. The city's limited adaptation actions before 2012 can be explained on the basis that city policymakers did not yet perceive adapting to climate change as in the city's economic interests. Policymakers were only beginning to understand the risks that the city faces from climate change. Much uncertainty remained about the character, magnitude, and timing of the risks, and the city did not have local or federal funding to do much about the risks. The city's lack of adaptation actions pre-Sandy emphasizes the need for the federal government to expand the availability of *proactive* federal funding and assistance for adaptation, so that adaptation does not become financially feasible for cities only after natural disasters strike, when the federal government injects disaster assistance. So that cities are not totally dependent on external funding for adaptation, cities also need to develop local sources of funding for it. Proactive investments in adaptation not only save lives, but also reduce the costs of dealing with disasters.

New York City had much more scope to adapt after Sandy, which made the risks of storm surge flooding highly visible and injected into the city substantial post-disaster federal appropriations. Yet still, the city's progress was slow in the decade after the storm.[155] By the end of 2021, the city had not completed any of its neighborhood coastal protection projects. The Army Corps' plans for more extensive coastal protections had not been formulated, let alone funded. Still today, in 2025, many people continue to live in the city's floodplain in buildings that have not been retrofitted to be more resilient, and the city continues to allow new development along much of its waterfront, albeit subject to higher construction standards.

Why does New York City remain so committed to developing its waterfront even though the city government knows that 24 percent of its land mass might be in the 100-year floodplain by the 2050s? New York City is by no means alone in continuing to develop its waterfront in the face of projected flood risks. Boston, Charleston, Miami, and other coastal cities are also allowing new development in flood-prone areas – and not seeking to relocate existing development to any significant extent – even though the local governments recognize the risks of flooding in the next several decades.[156]

Part of the explanation likely lies in continuing private demand for waterfront properties, which land developers seek to satisfy by building more housing along the shore.[157] Such demand may be inflated by the underpricing, at least until recently, of the premiums for federal flood insurance and homeowners' insurance relative to the risks from coastal storms and flooding.[158] Demand for waterfront properties – and their value – might decline as premiums for flood insurance increase as the National Flood Insurance Program implements its Risk Rating 2.0 system, and property and casualty insurers increase premiums for homeowners' insurance and withdraw from selling it in coastal areas, forcing people to turn to state-run insurers of last resort.[159] Another possibility is that coastal properties will remain attractive, but low- and middle-income people will be increasingly priced out of them, replaced by wealthy people who can afford to self-insure.[160]

Importantly, city governments also have their own economic incentives to satisfy demand for new waterfront development. New development generates property and other taxes, which are an important source of local government revenues.[161] Built out cities such as New York, Boston, and Charleston have limited space to develop, and reclaiming old industrial waterfronts has been a policy goal in leading cities for several decades.[162] Coastal cities such as New York also have housing affordability crises, which gives rise to an argument that waterfront land should be used to provide urgently needed housing, even if the housing may only be habitable for a few decades.[163] Cities are in effect gambling that the short-term benefits of continuing to add new development in waterfront areas will be worth the costs. Coastal cities may be hoping that these costs will arise far into the future, by which time cities might have new coastal protection infrastructure built with federal funds or other tools for mitigating the risks.[164]

The gamble at the local level is facilitated by federal policies that continue to enable city governments, developers, and landowners to externalize many of the costs of developing in floodplains. As mentioned earlier, federal flood insurance rates under the National Flood Insurance Program are rising, but rates for existing properties are still subsidized and increases are being phased in gradually.[165] Furthermore, only approximately a third of homeowners in floodplains pay for flood insurance, which limits the extent to which flood insurance discourages people from investing in floodplains.[166] Federal disaster assistance is available when floods occur, which limits the penalties that localities pay for failing to adapt.[167] Indeed, as New York's experience post-Sandy suggests, disasters may be one of the ways that cities obtain federal funding for adapting to climate change.[168] As discussed in Chapter 6, changes in federal policy may be necessary to encourage city policymakers to proactively focus on the costs of allowing new development in waterfront areas, and to steer such development to higher ground. As city policymakers attempt to externalize onto federal taxpayers through the Army Corps of Engineers some of the costs of coastal protection, the federal government should require local actors to bear more of the costs of local decisions that are increasing the need for federal funding for coastal protection.

6

An Urban Climate Change Agenda for the Early Twenty-First Century

INTRODUCTION

Earlier chapters of this book sought to understand why American cities have taken on the challenge of tackling climate change and how successful they have been in their efforts. In this final chapter, we turn our attention to the future. Building upon our assessment of American cities' incentives, successes, and failures to address environmental issues, we attempt to outline an agenda for them to pursue in the coming years. The chapter starts by charting an agenda for cities to adapt to climate change because we believe cities have the greatest incentives and levers to address this aspect of the climate challenge. It then turns to decarbonization. Throughout, we emphasize the need for higher levels of government to better support municipal efforts to tackle climate change and suggest ways for sympathetic lawmakers from higher levels of government to do so, especially at the federal level.[1]

The enormity of the challenges that climate change poses requires coordination between the federal government, the best-resourced level of government with the widest geographical scope of authority; large city governments, which are responsible for providing basic infrastructure and services to many Americans; and state governments, which are intermediaries between the federal government and cities and play an important role in coordinating action by multiple municipalities, especially smaller and poorer ones.[2] In short, climate change requires "a whole-of-government" approach involving all levels of government.[3] Even America's biggest city, New York, needs help.

Whether different levels of government will work together to address the multiple dimensions of climate change is a distinct question from whether they should do so. The federal government has not been consistently keen to marshal federal resources in the fight against climate change, particularly when Republican administrations are in control. Large cities also face headwinds that might leave them with fewer resources to address climate change than they had prior to the COVID pandemic. Some observers warn that large cities may be facing a structural change in their economies; the office-based economy on which postindustrial cities have relied may no longer be as dependable a source of property tax and other revenues and employment if remote work continues to limit demand for office space.[4] If the "urban doom loop" ensnares large cities, then, faced with diminished revenues and falling populations, they may neglect the environment, or narrow their focus to beautifying their local physical landscape to achieve the near-term goal of attracting new residents, tourists, and businesses.[5] Nonetheless, the need to adapt and limit climate change will loom large for a long time, no matter who holds office or what economic conditions exist over the next several years.

AN URBAN ADAPTATION AGENDA

Chapter 2 suggested that cities' environmental problems can be divided into two stylized paradigms: local public goods problems, and global public goods problems.[6] Cities' efforts to provide local public goods mainly benefit local residents, while cities' efforts to address global public goods mostly benefit people beyond city borders.

Adapting to climate change is closer to a local public goods problem, although some adaptation efforts could benefit regional or national, in addition to local, populations.[7] For example, if a city is able to manage coastal flooding near its shorelines, then fewer residents of these areas will need to relocate to other areas, which would relieve pressure on housing demand in municipalities further from the coast. In contrast, helping to limit climate change by reducing fossil fuel combustion benefits the world as a whole. While such reductions might generate local benefits – for example, particulate matter emissions might fall as GHG emissions decline because they are released in tandem – these local benefits will be incidental to the main goal of limiting planetary warming.

Adaptation is in some respects an extension of the longstanding efforts of local governments to protect their local populations, property, and infrastructure against physical risks. Cities have long struggled to deal with heat waves, and the same is true of hurricanes, flooding, fires, and human needs for drinking water.[8] In other respects, climate change presents novel local public goods problems for cities. It portends slow-onset structural shifts in physical phenomena, such as atmospheric temperatures and sea levels, which cities have assumed for generations are relatively stable or predictable, and on which they have based local land use decisions.[9] Moreover, the frequency and the severity of extreme events, such as hurricanes, heat waves, droughts, wildfires and storm surge, and rainfall flooding will also increase.[10]

Theoretically, cities should be strongly motivated to adapt to climate risks. Cities that fail to protect their populations from physical risks could pay high costs in terms of human misery – and lost economic activity.[11] Stated positively, cities that adapt stand to reap significant benefits from increasing the resilience of their populations and infrastructure to the higher temperatures, and increased flooding, drought, and wildfires that are accompanying global warming.

City governments have tools to assist in adaptation. They can deploy their authority over land use to limit, or increase the resilience of, new development in areas highly vulnerable to fires and flooding and expand development in areas less exposed to the risks of climate change. They build and maintain some of the infrastructure that needs to be upgraded to address some of the effects of global warming, such as drinking water, sewage and stormwater systems, and streets and sidewalks that can be resurfaced to reduce urban temperatures.[12] Local governments' knowledge of their cities is also useful since adaptation should be tailored to the specific physical risks that communities face.[13] These risks vary by city – drought in some places, coastal flooding in others, and so on – and even within cities, as some neighborhoods are hotter or more exposed to flooding than others.[14] Furthermore, adaptation measures will need to be adjusted to address the differential vulnerability of populations and neighborhoods within cities. Even when people in the city face essentially the same physical climate risks, such as smoke from wildfires drifting over the city, some people in the city will be more prone to suffer from the risks or have fewer resources to deal with them due to differences in income, race, preexisting health conditions, and other social and political factors.[15]

Notwithstanding the historical involvement of local governments in protecting people against physical risks, and the incentives for cities to safeguard their populations against climate change, adaptation presents a complex set of issues for large cities. There are many uncertainties about the character, magnitude, and timing of the effects of global warming in any given community. And even when projections are relatively clear, fiscally constrained cities will lack the resources and expertise to fully address the projected harms. Some forms of adaptation, such as the construction of novel forms of coastal protection infrastructure, are too technically complex and costly for even the largest cities to build on their own.[16] Moreover, adaptation likely needs to be coordinated across jurisdictional lines in some cases. It would be desirable to avoid one locality (or state) taking measures that harm others, for example by diverting floodwaters to other areas or imposing costs on other jurisdictions through failures to act, such as neglecting to reduce water consumption during droughts.[17]

Risk and Vulnerability Assessments

A starting point for local government efforts to adapt is an understanding of the physical climate risks that localities face, be they flooding from cloudbursts of rain, sea level rise, storm surges, drought, wildfires, heat, or other risks. As mentioned in Chapter 5, research for this book confirmed that ten of the twenty most populous cities had developed and published climate risk projections for their localities by 2020. However, we have little information about whether these projections are being updated sufficiently regularly to reflect advances in scientific understandings and remain useful for policymakers. Even New York City does not seem to have a dedicated mechanism to fund the work of the advisory panel that, under local law, is charged with periodically issuing projections of climate impacts for the city.[18] Moreover, there are many local governments in addition to the ten populous cities that have published projections that need accurate, regularly updated information about their exposure to climate risks. All of this emphasizes that the federal and state governments need to assist local governments in acquiring and updating information about the climate risks that they face.[19] In 2022, the National Oceanic and Atmospheric Administration launched an online portal to help communities analyze "their exposure to climate-related hazards, including drought, extreme heat, coastal and inland flooding, and wildfire."[20] While the portal was a good start, it too must be maintained, and local communities must have the resources to access it and derive exposure assessments from it for the portal to help address the information deficits at the local level about climate risks.[21] Some have suggested that the federal government create a National Climate Service, similar to the National Weather Service, to offer climate impact projections for localities at no cost.[22]

Beyond understanding the risks facing localities, local governments need to grasp the variegated vulnerability within their communities to climate risks to be able to help target limited government resources. Exposure to climate risks does not necessarily translate into vulnerability to these risks. As Professor Eric Klinenberg's analysis of the 1995 Chicago heat wave emphasized, there are individual risk factors for morbidity and mortality from heat, such as race, poverty, living alone, and age, as well as neighborhood-level factors, including an impoverished physical environment, reflected for example in "abandoned buildings, open spaces [and] commercial depletion."[23] Cities, states, and the federal government have started to map at the neighborhood level vulnerability to specific climate risks such as heat and flooding, or in some cases vulnerability to climate change generally.[24] Researchers also have started to score neighborhoods within cities based on their vulnerability to multiple hazards – the effects of climate change, displacement, and social-demographic factors.[25] Mapping and scoring efforts should be expanded and used to prioritize local government investments in increasing resilience, such as tree planting, cool roofs and cool pavements to reduce heat, and drainage or green infrastructure to lower flood risks, in urban areas.[26] By periodically updating maps of neighborhood vulnerability to climate impacts to take into account the effects of governmental adaption efforts and demographic changes, local governments might be able to track changes over time in which areas of the city are most vulnerable. Periodic updates also might provide data suggesting whether efforts to reduce neighborhood vulnerability to climate impacts are associated with displacement of low-income people and gentrification.[27]

Adaptation Actions

In addition to understanding the climate risks and vulnerabilities that their populations face, local governments need to act more aggressively to reduce these risks and vulnerabilities. Actually adapting to climate change is no easy matter for cities; adapting is not a one-time only event but rather a permanent and ongoing responsibility of cities that, as mentioned earlier, is an extension of the historic governmental function of safeguarding people and property against physical risks. In deciding what to do to adapt, and when to do it, cities are making decisions amid many uncertainties. These include uncertainties about the risks they face, and their magnitude, timing, and trajectory, which will depend on the trajectory of worldwide greenhouse gas emissions. Then there is the question of when cities should implement adaptation options. Climate risks will increase over time, but the costs of adapting might decline over time as more experience is gained adapting, suggesting there could be benefits to delay as well as disadvantages.

Cities will likely be making decisions about what adaptation actions to take, and when and how to take them, using their standard processes for determining operational and capital budgets, building physical infrastructure, and land use. However, they also might be called upon to use benefit-cost analysis to inform their choices more than is the norm at the local level, where benefit-cost analysis is not as commonly used as it is at the federal level.[28] Local governments seeking federal funding for climate adaptation already are familiar with applying benefit-cost analysis to adaptation efforts because federal agencies, such as the Army Corps of Engineers and the Federal Emergency Management Agency (FEMA), use benefit-cost analysis and benefit-cost ratios in their decision-making.[29] Greater use of benefit-cost analysis might help municipalities make decisions about adaptation under conditions of considerable uncertainty, while taking into account the overall benefits and costs of particular adaptation ideas for the community as a whole and for disadvantaged communities within urban areas.[30] However, greater use of benefit-cost analysis is unlikely to be a panacea for making the difficult decisions that large cities will face in the years to come. Benefit-cost analysis requires expertise to undertake that large cities likely lack in-house at the necessary scale. It is often criticized as biased toward protecting high-value properties and higher-income people and against low-income communities and communities of color, although the methods for valuing benefits could be altered to give greater weight to avoiding harms to low-income people in accordance with the principle of diminishing marginal utility of income.[31] Another complication with using benefit-cost analysis to make choices about which adaptation projects to pursue is that there are bound to be benefits (and costs) associated with certain adaptation actions that are hard to translate into monetary terms.[32] As a technocratic tool, benefit-cost analysis can conflict with the highly participatory approach to land use and decision-making in major American cities in the early twenty-first century.[33] Thus, even if benefit-cost analysis serves as an input into local decision-making about adaptation, it is unlikely to become the sole basis for making fundamental choices at the local level about how and when to adapt.

Setting to the side the question of how cities should decide which adaptation actions to take and when, we discuss two main categories of adaptation actions that cities are already starting to undertake as they begin to adapt. We start with actions that focus on increasing the resilience of urban populations, or building "social infrastructure."[34] Then we discuss actions that involve reshaping the city's physical environment, dividing the discussion into actions that involve upgrading and building physical infrastructure, and using legal and policy tools such as land use and building regulation.

Social Infrastructure

Some argue that governments should aim for "transformative climate adaptation" that addresses the "underlying" social, economic, and political factors that contribute to the higher vulnerability of certain communities to the effects of climate change, such as flooding and heat, rather than merely "end-point vulnerability."[35]

Large cities may be well placed to address some of the root causes of the greater vulnerability of certain people to the effects of global warming. Consider, for example, social isolation of senior citizens, which Klinenberg identified as an "individual-level risk factor[]" contributing to the high number of deaths in the 1995 Chicago heat wave.[36] Access to cooling technologies, such as air conditioning or heat pumps, and funding to pay for operating these technologies is important in a heat wave, and some local officials have taken steps to increase the access of low-income people to such technologies.[37] In addition, it is helpful for individuals living alone to be connected to other people who can check in on them and provide emergency help with groceries or medical needs. Local governments, working with community-based organizations, can help people form social connections and overcome individual isolation, and thereby save lives during emergencies and improve overall human well-being. In 2018, New York City established a pilot "Be a Buddy" program working with community-based organizations to have volunteers check in on vulnerable adults in neighborhoods highly vulnerable to heat; volunteers from the program then helped their buddies during the COVID pandemic.[38] More recently, New York City's public housing authority received funding from the federal Building Resilient Infrastructure and Communities (BRIC) program to establish "resilience hubs" where people can shelter from power outages, flooding, and heat.[39] Such hubs, which originated in Baltimore, are intended to be established in centers where vulnerable people are comfortable, and managed by community-based organizations.[40] During natural disasters, they might provide people with necessities, such as access to power, because they are supposed to have their own energy sources; at other times, the centers might foster social connections through community-led initiatives and services.

There may be other individual risk factors for climate harms that cities are well positioned to address, but it is also important to recall the limited fiscal capacity of even the largest U.S. cities, which constrains their ability to remedy long-standing inequalities in the distribution of income and wealth without financial assistance from the federal or state governments. Advocates for transformative climate adaptation have not settled on the bounds of the concept, but it potentially might encompass seeking to increase the incomes of low-income people since low income is a risk factor for harms from flooding and heat.[41] Early this century, cities made some efforts to boost the incomes of low-income people in light of concerns about growing economic inequality, for example through local minimum wage laws.[42] However, the longstanding view among experts on local government finance is that cities are likely not well positioned to significantly boost the incomes of low-income people on their own.[43] While cities where people want to locate may have some ability to address poverty, the conventional wisdom is that cities are constrained in their ability to redistribute income to low-income people by their position as relatively small units competing for mobile residents and businesses who will exit the jurisdiction if taxes and other costs exceed a certain tipping point.[44] As the U.S. jurisdiction with the largest geographical authority and fiscal base, the federal government is likely better positioned to address the root causes of poverty and other comparable risk factors for harms from climate change.[45]

Reshaping the Physical Landscape

In addition to building social resilience where they can, cities need to reshape aspects of their physical environment as they respond to the higher temperatures, and risks of flooding, drought, wildfires, and other events that climate change portends. Cities have various tools at their disposal to reshape this environment, including governmental investments in physical infrastructure, and regulatory requirements that private land and building owners adjust the spaces under their control.

PHYSICAL INFRASTRUCTURE Cities' infrastructure needs vary with the physical climate risks that they face, which will likely change over time as the planet warms. Many localities will need to upgrade – or build new – sewer, stormwater and drinking water infrastructure. Existing water infrastructure in both inland and coastal cities is at risk of being overwhelmed by sudden cloudbursts of rain, as illustrated by the failure of the aging drinking water infrastructure in Jackson, Mississippi, from a rainstorm in 2021.[46] Stormwater infrastructure might take the form of traditional gray infrastructure, such as pipes and holding tanks, or more novel forms of green infrastructure that absorb water without channeling it to pipes, such as rain gardens, green roofs, and sponge surfaces in playgrounds and other public spaces, or a hybrid of gray and green infrastructure.[47] Coastal cities that face greater risks of flooding due to sea level rise and more frequent and severe storms will also need a new class of costly coastal protection infrastructure, as discussed in Chapter 5. Similar to stormwater infrastructure, this coastal protection infrastructure could take the form of nature-based solutions, such as mangroves or wetlands, or hard infrastructure, such as storm surge barriers, or a combination of these approaches.[48]

Historically, local and state governments, rather than the federal government, have built infrastructure in the United States.[49] If this pattern holds as the country adapts to climate change, then cities will need additional funding from higher levels of government, especially the better-financed federal level, to upgrade existing, and build new, infrastructure in advance of climate change impacts. The findings of a survey that the New York State Comptroller's Office undertook in 2022 of local government plans for investments in climate-related infrastructure indicate the local need for funding from higher levels of government. The survey found that 48 percent of the costs of the investments that the ninety-five local government respondents planned in climate-related infrastructure between 2017 and 2026 – many of which concerned water infrastructure, such as wastewater treatment plants – would be paid by federal or state sources, with the localities covering the remaining 52 percent.[50]

Currently, cities are eligible to receive large amounts of federal funding for climate change adaptation only after experiencing a disaster, or contingent on a disaster declaration. Federal agencies such as the FEMA and the Department of Housing and Urban Development (HUD) provide significant assistance to communities to rebuild after disasters.[51] Recent disaster declarations enable localities to access federal funds to rebuild more resiliently.[52] Such declarations also enable localities to obtain federal "predisaster" funding to reduce damages from future disasters. FEMA's BRIC program is a "predisaster" competitive grant program for which cities can apply through their states, but the state must have had a disaster declaration in the previous seven years.[53]

Linking funding for adaptation to disasters likely discourages localities from adapting prophylactically to avoid a disaster. Tying federal funding to disasters means that localities are in effect rewarded with greater federal funding for experiencing a disaster.[54] The federal government would benefit from cities investing in adaptation prior to a disaster because predisaster investments reduce the costs of recovering from disasters, for which the federal government significantly pays under existing law.[55] Notably, there are precedents for disbursing funding for adaptation without the prerequisite of a federal disaster declaration, such as FEMA's Flood Mitigation Assistance (FMA) program.[56] It is a competitive grant program to reduce the harm to National Flood Insurance Program (NFIP)-insured buildings from future disasters, to which cities can apply through their state governments.[57]

In addition to decoupling to a greater extent funding for adaptation from disaster assistance, the federal government needs to boost the level of funding it provides to lower levels of government to adapt in advance of disasters. The Bipartisan Infrastructure Law (BIL) passed in 2021 increased federal funding for adaptation, but many local needs still remain unmet.[58] For example, demand outstripped the availability of funding for BRIC and FMA in the 2023 funding cycle. States, local governments, and other entities applied for almost $8 billion in funding for climate resilience from BRIC and FMA, while FEMA had only $1.8 billion to allocate under these programs.[59]

On top of boosting funding for anticipatory adaptation before disasters, the federal government should increase the use of formula funding for adaptation. Programs such as BRIC and the FMA allocate funding through competitive grants. Both large and small local governments likely would benefit from receiving more federal funding delivered predictably through formula funding programs, akin to the federal formula funding programs for transportation (assuming that the formula funding is additional to federal funding from competitive grant programs).[60] In 2022, on the tenth anniversary of Hurricane Sandy, New York City Mayor Eric Adams and Deputy Mayor Meera Joshi called for "federal formula" funding for climate resilience that would provide cities with a predictable source of funding for which they would not have to compete with other cities and states; they envisioned something akin to the formula funding that the federal government currently provides for "highways and transit."[61] The resilience infrastructure that the city requires, Adams explained, "involves significant long-term planning and needs regular and reliable resiliency funding."[62] Smaller municipalities that lack the resources to develop competitive grant applications might benefit even more than cities such as New York from dependable funding for resilience. Analysis shows that "[h]igh-capacity, larger cities tend to be the most successful at securing funding through the complicated and time-consuming BRIC application process."[63]

While cities require more, and differently structured, federal funding for adaptation than they currently receive, cities also should be developing their own revenue streams to help finance the construction and maintenance of local adaptation efforts, and the local components of federal and state cost shared programs. As the beneficiaries of adaptation efforts, cities should pay for at least some of them, assuming they can afford to do so.[64] In addition, the federal government risks driving up the costs of adaptation, and subsidizing local decisions that exacerbate climate risks and vulnerabilities, if it allows localities to fully externalize adaptation costs onto national taxpayers. Cities might levy "special assessments" or "climate resilience fees" and use the revenues to finance resilience or back bonds to fund resilience.[65] Fees might take the form of stormwater fees, levied on building owners based on factors such as their acreage of impervious surface area, or surcharges on the sales of property and casualty insurance policies.[66]

Even if the U.S. continues to rely on local and state governments to build most infrastructure, there will be some instances where it will be necessary to protect areas through federally constructed infrastructure. Some socially beneficial infrastructure may be too costly and complex for subnational governments to build, and it might be preferable to build on a regional or multistate scale to avoid one jurisdiction offloading floodwaters or other harms to other areas. As discussed in Chapter 5, the Army Corps of Engineers is currently studying building coastal protection infrastructure in cities facing serious risks of coastal flooding, such as Boston, Charleston, New York City, Miami, and Norfolk. The idea that the federal government would directly supply environmental infrastructure to benefit cities is not novel.[67] The

Army Corps has been building coastal and riverine infrastructure for many decades, and, in the twentieth century, the Bureau of Reclamation built vast systems that supply water for cities, such as the Colorado River water supply system.[68]

In light of the role that the Army Corps and other federal agencies may play in adapting to climate change, it seems worth considering whether these agencies' decision-making processes are well suited to designing and building coastal protection infrastructure that will fundamentally shape land use in some of the country's largest cities. While local governments may lack the funding to undertake costly adaptation measures, the Army Corps may lack the appropriate processes to design projects that address local desires (and earn Congressional authorization and funding).

In 2024, the Army Corps adopted potentially significant changes to the process that it uses to determine whether to build coastal protection infrastructure.[69] These changes could address some of the critiques of Corps' recent work to protect coastal cities.[70] These include criticisms that the Corps' methodology for valuing the benefits of Corps projects leads the agency to favor projects protecting wealthier areas, and thus leaves communities populated by low-income people and people of color under-protected;[71] that the Corps has a preference for gray infrastructure over nature-based solutions;[72] and that the Corps' process for designing coastal protection infrastructure in urban areas is ill-suited to easily developing project proposals that have the community support needed to receive Congressional authorization and appropriations.[73] If the Army Corps is going to be the federal agency charged with protecting some of the country's most populous cities against coastal flooding, then it needs to have the legislative and administrative framework to develop and execute plans that will protect against such flooding.

It also may be worth considering whether the federal government should create new agencies to build and manage infrastructure to address other risks from climate change than flooding. For example, are new federal agencies necessary to address risks from wildfires and heat? Or would it be preferable to expand the purview of existing agencies to address these and other climate risks?[74] There have also been proposals to create a Chief Resilience Officer at the federal level.[75]

LAND USE AND BUILDING REGULATION Local efforts to adapt to climate change should encompass regulatory measures in addition to infrastructure investments. Infrastructure might never be built, it might take many years to construct, and it might fail once constructed, as the levees failed in New Orleans in 2005 during Hurricane Katrina.[76] Moreover, there are market failures that justify regulations to reduce climate risks. While individuals have an incentive to protect themselves from disasters, such as flooding, they are unlikely to take the necessary actions to protect themselves and their neighbors, due to a lack of information about climate risks such as flooding, and limited access to capital.[77] At least until recently, climate risks were also not reflected in the costs of goods and services such as real estate, nor flood and property and casualty insurance.[78]

Local authority to regulate land use through zoning and other tools provides local governments with the authority to channel new development away from areas most prone to climate risks and spur new development in areas that are less prone to these hazards.[79] While limiting new development in less safe areas, cities might upzone areas to allow new and denser development in climate-safer neighborhoods, or provide density bonuses for new development in these areas, so that cities continue to have room to grow and people continue to have places to live.[80] To be sure, the latitude that cities have to channel new development will depend on local conditions – 70 percent of Charleston's land mass is currently in the 100-year floodplain, leaving it little room to which to channel new development to safer areas.[81] Both limiting new development in areas more prone to risks such as flooding and fires and allowing more development in less risk-prone areas are likely to be controversial. Landowners in climate-risky areas may fear that limiting development in their neighborhoods will reduce their property values by signaling the riskiness of the neighborhoods.[82] If the areas where development is limited due to climate risks, and where property values may fall as a result, are predominantly populated by low-income people of color, then limiting development might exacerbate the racial wealth gap and evoke comparisons to redlining.[83] Landowners and tenants in climate-safer areas may oppose new development for fear that it will change the character of their neighborhoods, by bringing more people, more traffic, and gentrification (if the climate-safer area currently is home to affordable housing). Cities might consider policy tools such as transferable development rights (TDR) programs to address the concerns of existing landowners in areas where new development is limited.[84] Under TDR programs, landowners burdened by development restrictions might receive "rights" which they could use themselves, or transfer to developers, to develop above existing allowable levels in neighborhoods less prone to climate risks. The rights would in effect compensate landowners for the limits on development in less safe areas and steer development toward less risky areas.[85]

Zoning is generally prospective in the sense that it affects new construction, and it does little to address the risks to buildings and infrastructure already built in areas that are subject to climate risks such as flooding and fires. Many commentators have argued that cities will eventually need to retreat from at least some of these areas, and there is an extensive literature on designing programs to buy out existing property owners from flood-prone areas.[86] Although some cities have established standing programs to buy out property owners from areas vulnerable to risks such as flooding, buying out property owners – and therefore retreat – has not yet been widely used as a strategy for adapting to climate change.[87] As the frequency and severity of coastal flooding and fires increase, buyouts might become a more salient local strategy for reducing vulnerability. However, additional federal funding for buyouts likely would be necessary to pursue this strategy on a large scale, and buyout programs would need to be carefully designed to avoid the inequities associated with the implementation of buyout program in some areas.[88] From a local perspective, buyouts are likely best considered as one of a number of tools, not a standalone panacea. They are not only costly, but to effectively reduce risks, buyouts should be comprehensive so that municipalities are not left continuing to provide services to a few remaining property owners. Moreover, cities are likely to resist buying out existing landowners and limiting uses of large areas of their land masses for as long as they can given the economic importance of land, which is a source of property taxes for local governments and a place to build the housing that is badly needed in many cities.

Complementing spatial regulation of land use to reduce climate vulnerability, local governments with authority over building codes might regulate at the building level. Cities with authority over building codes can require new buildings to be built to standards that provide greater protection against risks such as flooding, fires, and heat. For example, building codes might require "residential building cooling" in order to address heat risk.[89] Cities also might require existing buildings to retrofit to increase their resilience, for example by raising mechanical units to higher floors to reduce flood risks, or by upgrading to fire-resistant building materials.[90]

As mentioned in Chapter 5, local governments that are well aware of the risks of developing in waterfront areas are nonetheless continuing to allow such development, perhaps in part because they derive benefits from this development – such as the provision of new housing, and an expansion of their property tax base – and the federal government helps to address the downside risk through federal disaster assistance and subsidized flood insurance for existing properties.[91] To counter the risk that federal subsidies are facilitating lax local land use and building regulation, the federal government should consider bolstering the eligibility requirements for federal funding or potentially imposing deductibles that penalize lack of local adaptation.[92] When disbursing funds to communities that have suffered disasters, the federal government already imposes some requirements that communities rebuild resiliently, such as construction standards that require floodproofing.[93] The NFIP imposes some requirements on communities for individuals living within them to be able to buy federal flood insurance that could be strengthened, for example, by requiring that states or local governments mandate disclosure of flood risks when properties are sold.[94] Local governments also might be incentivized to develop adaptive land management practices by reducing the local cost shared portion of federally funded projects if the localities have policies that promote resilience (or increasing the local cost share if localities lack such policies).[95] The funds that the federal government provides cities offer it important levers for inducing adaptation at the local level. For instance, federal agencies might set resilient land use standards that cities must follow to avail themselves of federal funding. Doing so could help to mitigate the perverse incentives that *ex post* disaster assistance and federal flood insurance create.[96]

AN URBAN DECARBONIZATION AGENDA

As discussed in Chapter 4, stabilizing world temperatures is not an obvious policy goal for local governments to seriously take on board on their own, and it seems likely that cities will play a larger role in adapting to, rather than limiting, climate change.[97] Helping to limit climate change requires reducing fossil fuel combustion, which would require cities to impose upfront costs on local building owners and car and truck drivers, mainly for the benefit of the world as a whole. The efforts of any particular city might be cancelled out by the refusal or inability of other cities to require their residents to decarbonize. Moreover, regulating emissions in some but not all jurisdictions may merely redistribute the site of emissions, not reduce them, if carbon-intensive activities relocate from regulating to nonregulating jurisdictions.[98] Unlike with adaptation, city governments often lack important levers for reducing GHG emissions, such as control over electricity generation. As a result, city policymakers preoccupied with local economic prosperity have weak economic incentives to mandate aggressive decarbonization themselves. If the trajectory of New York City's decarbonization policies in the early twenty-first century is a guide, in the absence of mandates or subsidies from higher levels of government, cities will likely only impose costly regulations on local actors where community advocates apply concerted pressure on local officials and there are insiders within local government who favor such regulation. This type of pressure seems most likely to materialize when conservatives hostile to the climate agenda control the federal government and cities have active environmental groups and receptive local policymakers.[99] A healthy local economy may also be a prerequisite.

In an ideal world, the U.S. federal government, in coordination with national governments in other countries, would be taking the lead in decarbonizing the national economy.[100] The global scale of the problem is best suited to federal leadership in coordination with other countries.[101] Not only individual cities, but even states, within the U.S. are likely limited in the extent to which they can implement decarbonization policies without federal leadership; businesses and residents might exit states as well as cities that impose high costs on carbon emissions for U.S. jurisdictions with no or less stringent GHG reduction policies.[102] Decarbonizing also involves not only reducing GHG emissions by limiting fossil fuel combustion but also building out new renewable energy infrastructure on a massive scale to replace fossil fuel energy sources. This buildout will proceed more smoothly with federal government involvement. While some states are seeking to increase renewable energy generation and transmission within their borders, only the federal government likely has levers to facilitate large-scale expansions of interstate transmission of renewable energy.[103] The federal government also has the fiscal capacity to subsidize renewable energy generation on a significant scale to speed the energy transition, as the Inflation Reduction Act (IRA) demonstrated.[104]

If there were robust federal leadership of the energy transition, climate advocates would not need to press the multiplicity of states and cities to develop transformational regulations to decarbonize, though there would likely be an important role for states and local governments in achieving decarbonization.[105] Comprehensive federal regulation would require private and public actors to reduce GHG emissions across the board – from electricity, transportation, household appliances, waste, and other sources. For example, federal law might require cities to reduce the GHG emissions from their wastewater treatment plants and solid waste management systems to meet federal standards, similar to the reductions these plants are required to make in water pollution under the federal Clean Water Act.[106] Private actors might also pressure cities to respond to the signals that federal GHG regulation sends to reduce GHG emissions. For example, if there were a federal carbon price on transportation fuels that increased gasoline prices, the higher prices might induce drivers to shift more quickly to zero-emission vehicles, and possibly lead people to more highly value living close to mass transportation, which could lead to expansions of mass transit.[107] To make it easier to drive electric vehicles, local governments might reform zoning to allow publicly accessible chargers on privately owned spaces.[108] To facilitate denser urban living near mass transit, local governments might change zoning and other land use regulations, for example, by altering zoning to incentivize development in transit-rich areas.[109]

Unfortunately, the federal government is not comprehensively leading the energy transition, and there is no indication that it will start doing so anytime soon due political polarization about climate change. Under the Democratic presidential administration of Joseph Biden, the main thrust of the federal government's approach to limiting climate change was to financially incentivize decarbonization through tax credits,[110] and to a lesser extent grants and rebates, under the IRA and BIL.[111] This was a very different way of enlisting local governments (and states and private actors) in achieving environmental goals than predominates under the 1970s-era federal environmental statutes. Rather than requiring these actors to comply with minimum federal standards, often at their own expense, the IRA and BIL relied on financial carrots to change the cost-benefit calculus of climate action for cities (and other actors) to spur them to reduce GHG emissions.[112]

Congress has never legislatively required reductions in GHG emissions.[113] In lieu of that, the Environmental Protection Agency (EPA) has been regulating GHG emissions from new motor vehicles and new electric power plants under the decades-old Clean Air Act.[114] In 2024, the Biden administration finalized regulations under the Clean Air Act for greenhouse gas emissions from new motor vehicles, new and existing coal power plants, and new gas power plants that could significantly boost the sale of new electric cars and heavy trucks and reduce emissions from power plants.[115] However, as this book goes to press, the Biden-era regulations are imperiled in the second Trump administration.[116] The financial incentives for decarbonization in the IRA and BIL also may be repealed or scaled back through legislative changes or undermined through administrative actions.[117]

A Local Regulatory Agenda

As mentioned earlier, the federal government has been, at best, an inconsistent partner in decarbonizing the economy. Climate regulation in major cities and states provides a means of ensuring that the societal decarbonization project continues to advance, regardless of who is in power federally.[118] Moreover, climate regulation in large cities provides models for states and the federal government when they are amenable to decarbonization, and local regulation has proven to be an inspiration for federal and state policymakers committed to limiting climate change. For example, a number of the recommendations in New York State's scoping plan to decarbonize the state would impose statewide versions of building decarbonization policies already implemented in New York City, such as benchmarking and publicly disclosing building energy consumption, and a building performance standard.[119] Under the Biden administration, the federal government also adopted a building performance standard for its own buildings in 2022, after a small number of cities (and states) legislated such standards.[120] The scaling up of policies pioneered at the local level emphasizes the value of local regulation regardless of which party holds the presidency.

In designing a regulatory agenda, local governments should focus on those areas of the private sector over which they have the greatest control. Buildings stand out in this regard, and the pioneering building performance standards that Boston, New York City, Washington DC, and other leading cities have adopted show the potential for impactful local regulatory developments in this sphere. However, given the affordable housing crises in major cities such as New York, governments will need to be careful not to impose unfunded mandates that could drive up rents. At the same time, it is important to recognize that delays in decarbonizing private and publicly owned affordable housing could perpetuate inequalities in access to the health benefits of the energy transition insofar as reducing GHG emissions also lowers harmful conventional pollution.[121]

The local climate regulatory agenda should also be broadened beyond buildings to encompass land use regulation. Urban climate policymakers have not tended to focus on changing land use regulations as part of their efforts to reduce GHG emissions.[122] Land use is not a sector in the standard city inventory of sources of local GHG emissions, which tends to identify buildings and transportation as the main sources of city emissions.[123] But land use regulation influences urban GHG emissions, by setting the framework in which buildings exist and influencing (through choices between sprawl and density) the modes of transportation that people use (mass transit vs. the private car). Restrictive zoning that limits land use to single-family housing on large lots encourages sprawl, which is associated with higher GHG emissions than denser development due to increased car travel and larger houses that need to be cooled and heated.[124] Zoning that requires that particular uses provide a minimum number of parking spots increases GHG emissions by facilitating driving.[125] Zoning also may limit the places where renewable energy facilities, such as solar panels and wind turbines, and energy storage systems may be located.[126]

Indeed, there is considerable concern that local opposition to deploying renewable energy facilities and transmission lines, using land use and other regulations, will stall the buildout of renewable energy facilities needed to decarbonize electricity supplies and power electrified cars and homes.[127] In May 2023, Columbia Law School's Sabin Center released a report that found that "[i]n nearly every state, local governments have enacted laws and regulations to block or restrict renewable energy facilities, and/or local opposition has resulted in the delay or cancellation of particular projects."[128] Local opposition to the siting of renewable energy facilities once again underscores the structure of decarbonization: It imposes concentrated costs on local actors (in the case of solar and wind farms, consuming landscapes, destroying views, harming wildlife, etc.[129]), while mostly benefitting people outside the jurisdiction. Insofar as local governments are obstacles to building out renewable energy sources, states have the authority to limit the local role in permitting renewables, and expedite permitting processes, as some states have done.[130] Such state limitations may not be sufficient to address the full range of obstacles to constructing renewable facilities – federal action may be needed, for example, to expedite the siting of interstate electricity transmission lines and federal environmental review[131] – but it could be a start. Advocates can play a role in promoting openness at the local level to renewable facilities and urging state – and federal – action to address problematic local resistance to these facilities, while recognizing the concerns of environmental justice communities that they will be overburdened by such facilities.[132]

In addition to relaxing zoning and permitting regulations to enable the construction of renewable energy facilities, local governments should reconsider other aspects of land use regulation that are inconsistent with reducing GHG emissions, such as restrictive zoning that inhibits density. There are a host of changes that localities might consider, including upzoning urban areas to promote denser development; eliminating minimum parking requirements for land uses to encourage greater use of mass transit, walking, and biking; reallocating street space away from private cars to low-GHG modes of transportation (such as pedestrians and bicycles); and creating low-emission zones where drivers of high GHG-emitting vehicles would pay to drive.[133] Changes in land use likely will require political activism, as they almost certainly will encounter concentrated opposition from beneficiaries of the status quo, such as single-family homeowners and car drivers. Opposition from single-family homeowners has delayed and thwarted changes to promote greater development to address housing affordability crises and, in some instances, led to state preemption of local zoning authority.[134] It seems likely that promoting density and other land use changes in the name of limiting climate change will encounter similar opposition, and require political mobilization to overcome.[135] The "Yes in my backyard" (YIMBY) movement for relaxing zoning to spur new housing construction suggests that it is conceivable that local activism might emerge to support densifying new housing construction and building renewable energy facilities and transmission lines to support decarbonization, notwithstanding "not in my backyard" (NIMBY) opposition.[136]

Branching out still further from buildings, transportation, and land use, local governments also should consider expanding the agenda of local climate action by considering the GHG implications of local consumption of goods and services produced elsewhere but used within their borders. Large cities contribute to GHG emissions by importing goods and services produced elsewhere whose production processes are GHG intensive, such as construction materials and some foods.[137] Reducing local consumption of GHG-intensive goods and services could reduce GHG emissions, although perhaps not immediately because actors in other jurisdictions might buy the goods and services that one place is no longer importing. Down the line, changing local consumption patterns might reduce GHG emissions by helping to induce changes in norms, production processes, and the policies of higher levels of government with larger geographic jurisdictions.[138]

In 2023, New York City combined its standard geographic inventory, which emphasizes the city's contributions to climate change from buildings and transportation, with an inventory that estimates the emissions from the lifecycle of goods and services consumed, but not produced, by New York households. The "integrated inventory" showed that food was the third largest source of the city's emissions, accounting for 20% of emissions, with buildings still the top source (but accounting for 35% of emissions, rather than close to 70% under the geographic inventory) and transportation second (at 21%).[139] In announcing the results of the integrated inventory, the city committed to reducing GHG emissions from the food that the city government buys by 33% by 2030, and urged private and nonprofit actors to voluntarily reduce their emissions from food by 25% by 2030.[140] Since food emissions derive to a large extent from the production of meat and dairy products, reducing these emissions requires lowering the consumption of these foods and eating more plant-based foods.[141] Changes in the consumption of nonfood services and goods would also reduce the city's GHG emissions if they are viewed "holistically" as including emissions from goods and services imported into the city; "services" and "goods" were the fourth and fifth largest sources of the city's GHG emissions under the integrated inventory.[142] However, changing consumption patterns is complicated; the food that people eat is a matter of personal choice, influenced by religion and culture as well as the cost of food, and government leaders have understandably been reluctant to subject individual food choices to climate policy for fear of being attacked as taking away people's liberty to choose their food.[143] If any governments are willing to take onboard the challenge of encouraging people to eat climate-friendly diets, it may be municipal governments in large, deeply Democratic blue cities, such as the administration of Eric Adams, the sometime vegan (but fish eating) New York City mayor who wrote a book on how he changed his diet after he was diagnosed with Type 2 diabetes.[144]

CONCLUSION

While no city has the same problems or legal authority as another, this chapter seeks to outline a climate policy agenda for large American cities in the early twenty-first century and highlight the assistance that higher levels of government – in particular the federal government – should be providing cities.

As we suggested throughout this book, local governments, even well-resourced ones, often require prodding from community advocates to undertake ambitious climate actions. Such pressure is especially important to persuade local governments to adopt policies to decarbonize buildings and transportation in their borders, as these policies will impose upfront costs on local actors, and many of the benefits of reducing GHG emissions will be enjoyed beyond local borders. It is also vital for encouraging cities to adapt to global warming. Community advocates already have helped galvanize attention around risks such as extreme heat and flooding.[145] Yet, at least in New York City, community-based advocacy for adaptation efforts appears to have been less impactful than community pressure for the city government to take the lead in reducing GHG emissions from buildings.[146] As climate change accelerates, community-based coalitions of environmental and social justice groups applying pressure on the city government (as well as the state and the federal governments) will likely be crucial in encouraging cities to implement resilience policies. This century's environmental challenges require advocacy from civil society, and actions by all levels of government. In response, debates over which level of government is best positioned to act must give way to discussions about how each level of government can effectively complement the others – or step in when other governments are abdicating their responsibilities.

Coda

On February 8th, 1965, President Lyndon B. Johnson sent a special message to Congress on the "Conservation and Restoration of Natural Beauty."[1] The message decried the degraded state of the American environment, which Johnson feared was on the verge of being irreparably damaged, and called for federal action to reverse the trend.

In the opening paragraphs of his message, Johnson cast his ire on a narrow target: urbanization. "[O]ur people are crowding into cities and being cut off from nature," he complained. "Cities themselves reach out into the countryside, destroying streams and trees and meadows as they go."[2] To undo the degradation, Johnson called for the American people to "restore what has been destroyed and salvage the beauty and charm of our cities."[3] Among other things, salvaging cities would require developing more open spaces in urban areas and improving the quality of their parks.[4]

As the message went on, Johnson broadened his focus to include a wider range of environmental antagonists. In so doing, he made a claim that must have been startling at the time: Humankind had "altered the composition of the atmosphere on a global scale through … a steady increase in carbon dioxide from the burning of fossil fuels."[5] Later that year, the President's science advisory committee delivered a report that sounded the same alarm; they warned that the combustion of fossil fuels was causing an increase in atmospheric carbon dioxide and that this increase could lead to global warming.[6]

Sixty years after Johnson sent his message, the urban environment in many of America's cities is much improved. Leading American cities, such as Chicago and New York, have created new parks and are taking better care of the parks that they already had.[7] Air quality has improved as well. One no longer hears concerns that "three-fourths of the eight million people in the Los Angeles area are annoyed by severe eye irritation much of the year," which Johnson asserted to be the case in 1965.[8] At the urging of environmental justice organizations, cities have also made strides toward ensuring that environmental benefits and burdens are more equitably distributed among rich and poor urban inhabitants. Impressively, Johnson included "equal social access" to physical "beauty" among his ideals in the 1965 address.[9] For decades after Johnson's address, American cities made little notable progress to instantiate this ideal. But in the first two decades of the twenty-first century, things started to change. New York City's endeavor to redistribute solid waste away from low-income communities of color and to make sure that every resident lives within a ten-minute walk of a park are examples of cities' efforts to imbue equity concerns into environmental policy.

And yet, when it comes to climate change, remarkably little progress has been made. The country is not on track to meet President Biden's pledge to cut emissions to 50 percent below 2005 levels by 2030,[10] and President Trump, who was elected to a second term in late 2024, has promised to stymie what progress has been made.[11] Congress, for its part, has never legislated a comprehensive program to decarbonize the economy. The Inflation Reduction Act (IRA) of 2022 was a step forward, but it was also a concession to the federal government's inability; the IRA did not include any mandate to reduce emissions, and there are major questions about how effectively states and the market will respond to the incentives that the Act makes available, assuming they survive the second Trump presidency. And while some states have established their own GHG emission reduction targets, which could help pick up the federal government's slack, half of the states in the country have no such target on the books.[12]

All this leads us to the conclusion that environmentalists must look beyond the federal government – and even the states – for climate action. We think large cities are an important place to look. Although cities are constrained both legally and economically, they are able to build political consensus more easily than higher levels of government and are home to progressive organizations that want climate action. A number of these cities also face existential threats to their prosperity if they fail to adapt to climate change, which should be a powerful motivator for policymakers not only to adapt, but also to develop novel approaches to decarbonizing sectors over which cities have a degree of control, such as buildings.

Our goal in writing this book was to present a clear picture of cities' efforts to promote environmental improvement up to now, and their motivations for doing so, so that advocates and policymakers can effectively encourage cities to go even further. Given the enormity of the challenges facing the global environment, and strong headwinds blowing against the forces of progress, we cannot forsake any government's contribution, no matter how big or small.

Notes

INTRODUCTION

1. Phillip Lopate, *Waterfront: A Journey Around Manhattan* 15 (2004) ("By 1860 the port of New York was handling 52 percent of the nation's combined imports and exports."). Lopate explains that "the piers along the East River in Lower Manhattan remained the center of the city's shipping until the start of the twentieth century," when shipping moved to the Hudson River. *Id.* at 16. "In 1900, New York's shippers were still handling two-thirds of the nation's imports and one-third of its exports." *Id.* at 17. As late as 1950, New York was "still unloading and dispatching nearly a third of all foreign cargo." *Id.* As an aside, while working on this introduction, one of us (Wyman) came across Lopate's wonderful book and commends it to readers for the way in which it brings out the transformations in Manhattan's shoreline in the context of walking trips. *See also* Rutherford H. Platt, *The Humane Megacity: Transforming New York's Waterfront*, 51 *Environment* 46 (2009) (describing the history of the greenway that surrounds Manhattan).
2. *Playscape*, The Battery, www.thebattery.org/in-design/playscape (last visited Jan. 28, 2024). On the history of the Battery, see *History*, The Battery, www.thebattery.org/history/ (last visited Jan. 28, 2024); Roy Rosenzweig & Elizabeth Blackmar, The Park and the People: A History of Central Park 43–44 (1992); Dorceta E. Taylor, The Environment and the People in American Cities, 1600s–1900s: Disorder, Inequality, and Social Change 48, 122–23, 258 (2009).
3. *Playscape*, The Battery, *supra* note 2.
4. *Pier 26 Opening Invites Celebration and Ecological Exploration*, Hudson River Park (Sept. 30, 2020), https://hudsonriverpark.org/pier-26-opening/; *see also* Mark Joseph Jochim, *Henry Hudson and the Early History of Manhattan*, A Stamp a Day (Sept. 11, 2018), https://stampaday.wordpress.com/2018/09/11/henry-hudson-and-the-early-history-of-manhattan/.
5. Michael Kimmelman, *A New $260 Million Park Floats on the Hudson. It's a Charmer.*, N.Y. Times (May 20, 2021), www.nytimes.com/2021/05/20/arts/little-island-barry-diller.html; *see also id.* ("Little Island preens atop a bouquet of tulip-shaped columns, begging to be posted on Instagram."); *Pier History*, Little Island, https://littleisland.org/history/ (last visited July 11, 2024).
6. N.Y.C. Env't Prot., 2018 New York Harbor Water Quality Report 1 (2018). *See also* Eric Spitznagel, *Why New York Harbor Is the Cleanest It's Been in 110 Years*, N.Y. Post (Aug. 10, 2019), https://nypost.com/2019/08/10/why-new-york-harbor-is-the-cleanest-its-been-in-110-years/.

7. Dan Shapley, *Do People Swim in the Hudson River?*, RIVERKEEPER (June 29, 2021), www.riverkeeper.org/blogs/water-quality-blogs/do-people-swim-in-the-hudson-river/; Dan Shapley, *Will NYC Waters Ever Be Made Consistently Safe for Swimming?*, RIVERKEEPER (May 26, 2023), www.riverkeeper.org/blogs/water-quality-blogs/will-nyc-waters-ever-be-made-consistently-safe-for-swimming/. However, "most of the Hudson River" is still not suitable for swimming. N.Y.C. DEP'T CITY PLAN., NEW YORK CITY COMPREHENSIVE WATERFRONT PLAN 141 (2021), *available at* www.nyc.gov/assets/planning/download/pdf/plans-studies/comprehensive-waterfront-plan/nyc_comprehensive_waterfront_plan.pdf; Jesse McKinley, *Swimming the Lordly Hudson, All 315 Miles of It*, N.Y. TIMES (July 29, 2023), www.nytimes.com/2023/07/19/nyregion/hudson-river-swim-lewis-pugh.html. New York State advises that some people – though not "[w]omen under 50 and children under 15" – can eat a small amount of striped bass caught in the Hudson River in Lower Manhattan. N.Y. State, *Can You Eat that Striped Bass from the Hudson?*, N.Y. STATE DEP'T OF HEALTH, www.health.ny.gov/environmental/outdoors/fish/health_advisories/stripedbass.htm (last visited June 13, 2024); *see also* N.Y.C. DEP'T CITY PLAN., *supra*, at 225 (referring to New York State guidance on eating fish from NYC waters). During the twentieth century, General Electric "discharged PCBs into the Hudson River"; "[t]he Hudson River PCBs Superfund site includes the 200-mile stretch from Hudson Falls to the southern tip of Manhattan in New York City." Community Update, U.S. EPA, Lower Hudson River Sampling and Investigations to Begin this Spring (May 2023), www.epa.gov/system/files/documents/2023-05/English.pdf. On the continuing need to improve water quality in the water bodies surrounding New York City, see, for example, CITY OF N.Y., EJNYC: A STUDY OF THE ENVIRONMENTAL JUSTICE ISSUES IN NEW YORK CITY 135–137 (2024).
8. *Monitoring Our River's Improving Health*, HUDSON RIVER PARK, https://hudsonriverpark.org/the-park/parks-river-project/science/monitoring-our-rivers-improving-health/ (last visited June 13, 2024).
9. *See, e.g.*, Karen Zraick, *11 Million New Oysters in New York Harbor (But None for You to Eat)*, N.Y. TIMES (Dec. 10, 2021), www.nytimes.com/2021/12/10/nyregion/oysters-new-york-hudson-river.html; Andrew Revkin, *14-Foot Fish Spotted in River, Giving Hope to Vanished Giant's Return*, NAT'L GEOGRAPHIC (Mar. 7, 2019), www.nationalgeographic.com/environment/article/14-foot-atlantic-sturgeon-fish-hudson-river-endangered-species.
10. Jonathan Moens, *Growing Number of Whales Return to New York City Shores*, SCIENCELINE (Aug. 13, 2020), https://scienceline.org/2020/08/growing-number-of-whales-return-to-new-york-city-shores/.
11. Press Release, City of N.Y., Mayor Adams Breaks Ground on Battery Coastal Resilience to Protect Lower Manhattan from Sea Level Rise and Storm Surge, and Calls for Regular Federal Funding for Climate Infrastructure (May 6, 2024), www.nyc.gov/office-of-the-mayor/news/355-24/mayor-adams-breaks-ground-battery-coastal-resilience-protect-lower-manhattan-sea-level (announcing the Battery Coastal Resilience project to protect against sea level rise and storm surges and referring to the other projects under construction to address flood risks in lower Manhattan); CITY OF N.Y., PLANYC: A STRONGER, MORE RESILIENT NEW YORK 11, 13 (2013) (share of the city's land mass that flooded during Sandy).
12. Michael Kimmelman, *What Does It Mean to Save a Neighborhood?*, N.Y. TIMES (Dec. 2, 2021), www.nytimes.com/2021/12/02/us/hurricane-sandy-lower-manhattan-nyc.html; Rob Hotakainen, *In N.Y., Battling Climate Change Means Killing 1,000 Trees*, GREENWIRE (Dec. 22, 2021), www.eenews.net/articles/in-n-y-battling-climate-change-means-killing-1000-trees/.

13. City of N.Y., *Project Updates: Construction Project Areas for East Side Coastal Resiliency*, N.Y.C. E. SIDE COASTAL RESILIENCY PROJECT, www1.nyc.gov/site/escr/project-updates/project-updates.page (last visited June 11, 2024); Kimmelman, *supra* note 12; Malcolm Araos, *Democracy Underwater: Public Participation, Technical Expertise, and Climate Infrastructure Planning in New York City*, 52 THEORY & SOC'Y 1 (2021).
14. City of N.Y., *Brooklyn Bridge-Montgomery Coastal Resilience*, LOWER MANHATTAN COASTAL RESILIENCY PROJECT, www.nyc.gov/site/lmcr/progress/brooklyn-bridge-montgomery-coastal-resilience.page (last visited June 11, 2024).
15. City of N.Y., *The Battery Coastal Resilience*, LOWER MANHATTAN COASTAL RESILIENCY PROJECT, www.nyc.gov/site/lmcr/progress/battery-coastal-resilience.page (last visited June 11, 2024); Michael Gartland, *Battery Park to Get 5-Foot Lift to Protect against Rising Sea Levels, Climate Change*, N.Y. DAILY NEWS (May 6, 2024), www.nydailynews.com/2024/05/06/battery-park-to-get-5-foot-lift-to-protect-against-rising-sea-levels-climate-change/; N.Y. State, *Battery Park City Resiliency*, HUGH L. CAREY BATTERY PARK CITY AUTHORITY, https://bpca.ny.gov//nature-and-sustainability/resiliency/ (last visited June 11, 2024); *Wagner Park Will Close for Two Years Starting this Summer*, TRIBECA CITIZEN (Mar. 31, 2022), https://tribecacitizen.com/2022/03/31/wagner-park-will-close-for-two-years-starting-this-summer/.
16. Patrick McGeehan, *6 Years After Hurricane Sandy, Here's What They Came Up with: Really Big Sandbags*, N.Y. TIMES (May 5, 2019), www.nytimes.com/2019/05/05/nyregion/hurricane-sandy-manhattan-flooding.html; City of N.Y., *Interim Flood Protection Measure (IPFM)*, LOWER MANHATTAN COASTAL RESILIENCY, www.nyc.gov/site/lmcr/progress/interim-flood-protection-measure.page (last visited June 13, 2024).
17. *See, e.g.*, John R. Nolon, *In Praise of Parochialism: The Advent of Local Environmental Law*, 26 HARV. ENV'T L. REV. 365, 374–75 (2002); Katherine A. Trisolini, *All Hands on Deck: Local Governments and the Potential for Bidirectional Climate Change Regulation*, 62 STAN. L. REV. 669, 674–75 (2010). There are notable exceptions to the general scholarly tendency to neglect the role of cities in environmental law. *See generally, e.g.*, JOHN R. NOLON, PROTECTING THE ENVIRONMENT THROUGH LAND USE LAW: STANDING GROUND (2014); Sara C. Bronin, *Energy in the Ecopolis*, 45 ENV'T L. REP. 10514 (2015); Sarah Fox, *Home Rule in an Era of Local Environmental Regulation*, 44 ECOLOGY L.Q. 575 (2017); Trisolini, *supra*. For an argument that political science scholarship on local and state environmental policy is also under-developed, see Michael Jones, Elizabeth A. Shanahan & Lisa J. Hammer, *Environmental Policy*, *in* DONALD P. HAIDER-MARKEL ED., THE OXFORD HANDBOOK OF STATE AND LOCAL GOVERNMENT 778, 786, 788 (2014).
18. On California's leadership role in reducing conventional air pollution and, more recently, GHG emissions, from cars, see generally Ann E. Carlson, *The Trump Administration's Assault on California's Global Climate Leadership*, 112 AJIL UNBOUND 269 (2018); *see also generally* Ann E. Carlson, *Iterative Federalism and Climate Change*, 103 NW. U. L. REV. 1097 (2009).

    As Professor Michael Livermore has observed, "[i]n the United States, decentralization is often associated with federalism and devolution of authority to the states." Michael A. Livermore, *The Perils of Experimentation*, 126 YALE L.J. 636, 701 (2017) (citing Edward L. Rubin & Malcolm Feeley, *Federalism: Some Notes on a National Neurosis*, 41 UCLA L. REV. 903 (1994)).
19. *See, e.g.*, RICHARD J. LAZARUS, THE MAKING OF ENVIRONMENTAL LAW 249–50 (2004) (referring to states filling the void during the early years of the George W. Bush administration); Denise A. Grab & Michael A. Livermore, *Environmental Federalism*

in a Dark Time, 79 Ohio St. L.J. 667, 674–75 (2018) (describing the role of "Blue" states in making up for the federal leadership deficit in the first Trump administration). Richard Revesz is an exception. During the Clinton era, he published several articles underscoring the potential for state environmental regulation to develop alongside federal regulation. *See generally* Richard L. Revesz, *Rehabilitating Interstate Competition: Rethinking the 'Race-to-the-Bottom' Rationale for Federal Environmental Regulation*, 67 N.Y.U. L. Rev. 1210 (1992); Richard L. Revesz, *Federalism and Interstate Environmental Externalities*, 144 U. Pa. L. Rev. 2341 (1996); Richard L. Revesz, *The Race to the Bottom and Federalism Environmental Regulation: A Response to Critics*, 82 Minn. L. Rev. 535 (1997); Richard L. Revesz, *Federalism and Environmental Regulation: A Public Choice Analysis*, 115 Harv. L. Rev. 553 (2001); *see also* Trisolini, *supra* note 17.

20. Press Release, U.S. Census, Nation's Urban and Rural Populations Shift Following 2020 Census (Dec. 29, 2022), www.census.gov/newsroom/press-releases/2022/urban-rural-populations.html ("[U]rban areas … now account for 80.0% of the U.S. population …."); Einar H. Dyvik, *Share of Urban Population Worldwide in 2023, by Continent*, Statista (Jan.9, 2024), www.statista.com/statistics/270860/urbanization-by-continent/ ("In 2023, the degree of urbanization worldwide was at 57 percent.").
21. *Urban Climate Action Is Crucial to Bend the Emissions Curve*, U.N. Climate Change (Oct. 5, 2020), https://unfccc.int/news/urban-climate-action-is-crucial-to-bend-the-emissions-curve; Christopher Jones & Daniel M. Kammen, *Spatial Distribution of U.S. Household Carbon Footprints Reveals Suburbanization Undermines Greenhouse Gas Benefits of Urban Population Density*, 48 Env't Sci. Tech. 895, 900 (2013) ("Metropolitan statistical areas account for about 80% of the U.S. population and household carbon footprints."); *see also* Muhammad Luqman, Peter J. Rayner & Kevin R. Gurney, *On the Impact of Urbanisation on CO_2 Emissions*, 6 Urban Sustainability (2023), www.nature.com/articles/s42949-023-00084-2 ("In North America, the proportion [of GHG emissions coming from cities] reaches 80% depending upon the definition of emissions scope and urban boundary."). Ankit Mishra, *3 Key Measures U.S. Cities Can Adopt to Advance Net-Zero Initiatives*, Forbes (Feb. 19, 2024), www.forbes.com/sites/ankitmishra/2024/02/19/3-key-measures-us-cities-can-adopt-to-advance-net-zero-initiatives/ ("The New York Times reports that [U.S. cities] … are accountable for almost three-quarters of the nation's fossil-fuel generated carbon dioxide (CO_2) emissions.").
22. *Supporting Sustainable Cities*, Bloomberg Philanthropies, www.bloomberg.org/environment/supporting-sustainable-cities/ (last visited Jan. 28, 2024); *Environment*, The Kresge Found., https://kresge.org/our-work/environment/ (last visited Jan. 28, 2024).
23. About C40, C40 Cities, www.c40.org/about-c40/ (last visited June 13, 2024); C40 Cities, C40 Cities Membership, www.c40.org/wp-content/uploads/2023/04/C40-Cities-Membership-01_11_23.pdf (last updated May 2, 2024). For the list of C40 cities by region, see Our Cities, C40 Cities, www.c40.org/cities/ (last visited July 10, 2024).

    There is extensive literature on the networks that cities have joined to address climate change. *See generally, e.g.*, Kathryn Davidson et al., *A Decade of C40: Research Insights and Agendas for City Networks*, 10 Glob. Pol'y 697 (2019); Thi Minh Phuong Nguyen et al., *Understanding How City Networks Are Leveraging Climate Action: Experimentation Through C40*, 2 Urb. Transformations 1 (2020).
24. Rachel M. Krause & Christopher Hawkins, Implementing City Sustainability: Overcoming Administrative Silos to Achieve Functional Collective Action 29 (2021) (reporting results of the Smart and Sustainable Cities Survey that the authors implemented). On the Survey, see *id.* at 22–23.

25. BENJAMIN BARBER, COOL CITIES: URBAN SOVEREIGNTY AND THE FIX FOR GLOBAL WARMING (2017). Other works advancing similar arguments about the potential for cities to address climate change include DAVID MILLER, SOLVED: HOW THE WORLD'S GREAT CITIES ARE FIXING THE CLIMATE CRISIS (2020); DOUGLAS KELBAUGH, THE URBAN FIX: RESILIENT CITIES IN THE WAR AGAINST CLIMATE CHANGE, HEAT ISLANDS AND OVERPOPULATION (2019); JOAN FITZGERALD, GREENOVATION: URBAN LEADERSHIP ON CLIMATE CHANGE (2020); Rebecca Bratspies, *Protecting the Environment in an Era of Federal Retreat: The View from New York City*, 13 *FIU L. REV.* 5, 9–10 (2018) (emphasizing the potential for cities to protect the environment); Amy Turner, In a Devolving Legal and Political Landscape, Cities Are the Federal Government's Secret Weapon on Climate, Climate Law (July 5, 2024), https://blogs.law.columbia.edu/climatechange/2024/07/05/in-a-devolving-legal-and-political-landscape-cities-are-the-federal-governments-secret-weapon-on-climate/.
26. *Dr. Benjamin Barber*, GLOB. PARLIAMENT OF MAYORS, https://globalparliamentofmayors.org/dr-benjamin-barber/ (last visited Dec. 5, 2022). Barber recognized that cities would need more legal authority and resources from higher levels of government to fully realize their potential to reduce emissions.
27. BARBER, *supra* note 25, at 67.
28. Richard B. Stewart, *Pyramids of Sacrifice? Problems of Federalism in Mandating State Implementation of National Environmental Policy*, 86 YALE *L.J.* 1196 (1977). On Professor Stewart as the leading environmental law professor of his generation, see Brian Leiter, *In Memoriam: Richard B. Stewart*, BRIAN LEITER'S L. SCH. REPS. (Nov. 6, 2023), https://leiterlawschool.typepad.com/leiter/2023/11/in-memoriam-richard-b-stewart-1940-2023.html.
29. Stewart, *supra* note 28, at 1211–16.
30. Jonathan B. Wiener, *Think Globally, Act Globally: The Limits of Local Climate Policies*, 155 U. PA. L. REV. 1961, 1967 (2007).
31. MATTHEW EISENSON, OPPOSITION TO RENEWABLE ENERGY FACILITIES IN THE UNITED STATES (Sabin Center for Climate Change Law May 2023 ed.); Danielle Stokes, *Renewable Energy Federalism*, 106 *MINN. L. REV.* 1757 (2022); *State Preemption of Local Zoning Laws as Intersectional Climate Policy*, 135 HARV. L. REV. 1592 (2022); Steven Ferrey, *Flipped Constitutional Supremacy: Inferior Local Law Blocking Federal Policy*, 2023 *UTAH L. REV.* 65 (2023). For an example of opposition from tenants in Brooklyn, New York City to a battery storage project, *see, e.g.*, Erin Conlon, *Battery Storage and 315 Berry Street Could Help Us Meet Climate Goals. Tenants Have Concerns*, GREENPOINTERS (July 28, 2023), https://greenpointers.com/2023/07/28/battery-storage-at-315-berry-street-could-help-us-meet-climate-goals-tenants-have-concerns/.
32. *See generally* GERALD E. FRUG & DAVID J. BARRON, CITY BOUND: HOW STATES STIFLE URBAN INNOVATION (2013).
33. *See, e.g.*, ALAN ALTSHULER & DAVID LUBEROFF, MEGA-PROJECTS: THE CHANGING POLITICS OF URBAN PUBLIC INVESTMENT 72 (2003). In surveying theoretical scholarship on urban politics, Altshuler and Luberoff state that Clarence Stone "takes as his central premise (in common, to be sure, with nearly all other recent theorists of urban politics) that the central issue of local governance is economic development." *Id.*
34. *See generally* PAUL E. PETERSON, CITY LIMITS (1981).
35. As of 2024, environmental justice groups in New York City include WE ACT for Environmental Justice, founded in 1988, the New York City Environmental Justice Alliance, established in 1991, and UPROSE, founded in 1966. *Our Story*, WEACT, www.weact.org/whoweare/ourstory/ (last visited Jan. 28, 2024); *About Us*, N.Y.C. ENV'T JUST.

All., https://nyc-eja.org/about-us/ (last visited Jan. 28, 2024); *Who We Are*, UPROSE, www.uprose.org/mission (last visited Jan. 28, 2024). For a history of environmental justice campaigns in New York City, see Julie Sze, Noxious New York: The Racial Politics of Urban Health and Environmental Justice (2006).

36. *See Local Law* 97, NYC.gov, www.nyc.gov/site/sustainablebuildings/ll97/local-law-97.page (last visited Jan. 28, 2024).
37. *Cf.* Peterson, *supra* note 34, at 210 ("Economic limits shape not only urban policy but also the pattern of local politics."). *See also* Harvey Molotch, *The City as a Growth Machine: Toward a Political Economy of Place*, 82 Am. J. Socio. 309 (1976).
38. The federal government is providing $338 million, and New York City is paying the rest of the $1.45 billion cost of the East Side Coastal Resiliency project. City of N.Y., *Project Background*, N.Y.C. E. Side Coastal Resiliency Project, www1.nyc.gov/site/escr/about/project-background.page (last visited Jan. 28, 2024).
39. *See* Jonathan S. Masur, *Regulatory Oscillation*, 39 Yale J. on Reg. 743, 754 (2022) (noting how climate change is a global "collective action problem").
40. Helen Regan, *US vs. China: How the World's Two Biggest Emitters Stack Up on Climate*, CNN (Nov. 3, 2021), www.cnn.com/2021/10/28/world/china-us-climate-cop26-intl-hnk/index.html.
41. According to New York City's inventory of GHG emissions for 2022, the city emitted 53.7 million tons of $CO2_e$ in 2022. Mayor's Off. of Climate & Env't Just., City of N.Y., NYC Greenhouse Gas Inventories: Inventory of New York City Greenhouse Gas Emissions, https://climate.cityofnewyork.us/initiatives/nyc-greenhouse-gas-inventories/ (last visited July 3, 2024). That same year, total U.S. emissions were "6,343.2 [m]illion [m]etric [t]ons of CO_2 equivalent." U.S. Env't Prot. Agency, Sources of Greenhouse Gas Emissions, www.epa.gov/ghgemissions/sources-greenhouse-gas-emissions (last visited July 3, 2024) (total U.S. Greenhouse Gas Emissions by Economic Sector in 2022). *See also* Associated Press, *Study: Nearly 1 Percent of U.S. Greenhouse Gas Comes from New York City*, Fox News (Apr. 11, 2007), www.foxnews.com/story/study-nearly-1-percent-of-u-s-greenhouse-gas-comes-from-new-york-city (referring to New York City's 2007 greenhouse gas inventory).
42. City of N.Y., PlaNYC: Getting Sustainability Done 52 (2023) ("almost 70% of total citywide GHG emissions" are from buildings).
43. Inflation Reduction Act of 2022, Pub. L. No. 117–169, 136 Stat. 1818.
44. *See generally, e.g.*, Joe Aldy, Trying a Whole-of-Government Approach to Climate Change, Env't Forum (2021); Kathryn Urban, *A Whole-of-Government Approach to Climate Change: Assessing DoD's Role*, Am. Univ. (Mar. 1, 2022), www.american.edu/sis/centers/security-technology/whole-of-govt-approach-to-climate-change.cfm.
45. For a description of the Biden administration's efforts to organize the federal agencies in working groups to address specific climate risks (wildlife, drought, etc.) to better help communities, see David J. Hayes, Forging New Ground: Implementing a Climate Resilience Agenda Across the U.S. Federal Government (2022). The National Climate Adaptation and Resilience Strategy Act, introduced in the Senate in 2022 as S.3531, would build on the efforts of the Biden administration to organize the federal government to help promote resilience. S. 3531, 117th Cong. (2022). This draft law would require the appointment of a Chief Resilience Officer who would be charged with developing a "whole-of-government effort to build resilience," still meaning a whole-of-federal approach. *Id.* at § 2(b)(1)(B)(i). The bill does recognize the importance of "non-Federal partners" (including local governments) in adapting to climate change,

requiring, for example, that the National Climate Adaptation and Resilience Strategy that it mandates include "strategies for the Federal Government, in partnership with non-Federal partners." *Id.* at § 2(e)(1)(C). Still, this bill does not reflect much awareness of the need to rethink the relationship between the federal government and other levels of government to further resilience.

46. *U.S. Cities Factsheet*, U. MICH. CTR. FOR SUSTAINABLE SYS. (2023), https://css.umich.edu/publications/factsheets/built-environment/us-cities-factsheet (stating that 83 percent of Americans live in urban areas).
47. Environmental justice advocates in many places have focused on the disproportionate concentration of waste facilities in communities of color. *See* TAYLOR, *supra* note 2, at 498 ("African Americans, Native Americans, Latinos, and Asians have formed hundreds of environmental justice groups all over America. In addition to the traditional working-class issues discussed earlier [in the chapter], ethnic minority environmental groups focus on environmental inequalities, such as the disproportionate number of noxious industrial complexes, hazardous waste facilities, and pollution located in communities of people of color.").
48. Saul Steinberg, *View of the World from 9th Avenue* (illustration), *in* New Yorker, Mar. 29, 1976, cover.
49. *See, e.g.*, J. ERIC OLIVER, SHANG E. HA & ZACHARY CALLEN, LOCAL ELECTIONS AND THE POLITICS OF SMALL-SCALE DEMOCRACY 186, 200 (2012) (emphasizing that most Americans live in suburbs rather than cities with over 100,000 people, and that the "size, scope and bias" is "key to understanding ... local governance").
50. *See also* Bratspies, *supra* note 25, at 10 (mentioning that "the choices that New York City makes have the potential to shape the environmental behaviors of roughly 17% of the United States population" in focusing on the city's environmental initiatives during the first Trump administration). For a conceptual analysis of the different ways that climate policy is diffused among cities in Europe, see Kristine Kern, *Cities as Leaders in EU Multilevel Climate Governance: Embedded Upscaling of Local Experiments in Europe*, 28 ENV'T POL. 125 (2019). For a discussion of the literature on policy diffusion, and its limitations, see William Boyd, *The Poverty of Theory: Public Problems, Instrument Choice, and the Climate Emergency*, 46 COLUM. J. ENV'T L. 399, 445–448 (2021).
51. For example, in 1967, before the Environmental Protection Agency was created in 1970, the U.S. Public Health Service developed a system for ranking air pollution in metropolitan areas of the country. MATTHEW A. CRENSON, THE UN-POLITICS OF AIR POLLUTION: A STUDY OF NON-DECISIONMAKING IN THE CITIES 92 (1971). Also, the Public Health Service was involved in developing programs to regulate air pollution. *Id.* at 75–76 (referring to the Public Health Service's involvement in developing a regional program to control air pollution in Indiana). At the local level, health commissioners were involved in air pollution regulation in the mid twentieth century. *Id.* at 96–97. In the late nineteenth century, local medical societies in cities such as New York and Chicago took an interest in local water supply and sewage systems and garbage collection. JON C. TEAFORD, THE UNHERALDED TRIUMPH: CITY GOVERNMENT IN AMERICA, 1870–1900 at 211 (1984).
52. PETERSON, *supra* note 34, at 44. *See also* TAYLOR, *supra* note 2, at 31 (discussing framing of issues as environmental issues).
53. We are not alone in broadly defining what counts as the environment. Surveying literature on environmental justice, Julian Agyeman, David Schlosberg, Luke Craven, and Caitlin Mathews explain that "the environment in EJ terms has come to mean where we live, work, play, and, more recently, eat." Julian Agyeman et al., *Trends and*

Directions in Environmental Justice: From Inequity to Everyday Life, Community, and Just Sustainabilities, 41 ANN. REV. ENV'T & RES. 321, 332 (2016).

There is a related discussion of what it means to advance "sustainability," which is also often defined broadly to encompass "environmental, economic, and social" dimensions. Christopher V. Hawkins et al., *Making Meaningful Commitments: Accounting for Variation in Cities' Investments of Staff and Fiscal Resources to Sustainability*, 53 URB. STUD. 1902, 1904–1905 (2016).

54. On the varying meanings that individuals ascribe to the word city, see, for example, FRUG & BARRON, *supra* note 32, at 1 ("Lewis Mumford used to ask a very basic question: 'What is a city?' The answer depends one's angle of vision. For many people, the word 'city' is associated with images of density, so that only parts of the city seem citylike. Residents of Queens often talk about going to 'the city,' meaning Manhattan, even though they already live in the City of New York. The entire metropolitan region can also be experienced as one big city. Many residents of Boston's suburbs say they live in Boston even though they don't.").
55. *See, e.g.*, RICHARD BRIFFAULT & LAURIE REYNOLDS, CASES AND MATERIALS ON STATE AND LOCAL GOVERNMENT LAW 8 (8th ed. 2016) (noting "[t]here is not even a consistent terminology for local governments; different states include such diverse local units as parishes, borough, townships, as well as the more common forms of local government like county or city").
56. *See* U.S. CENSUS BUREAU, ANNUAL ESTIMATES OF THE RESIDENT POPULATION FOR INCORPORATED PLACES OF 50,000 OR MORE, RANKED BY JULY 1, 2022 POPULATION: APRIL 1, 2020 TO JULY 1, 2022 *available at* www.census.gov/data/tables/time-series/demo/popest/2020s-total-cities-and-towns.html#tables (last visited June 14, 2024) (listing the top twenty cities by population as of 2022, from highest to lowest as: New York City, Los Angeles, Chicago, Houston, Phoenix, Philadelphia, San Antonio, San Diego, Dallas, Austin, Jacksonville, San Jose, Fort Worth, Columbus, Charlotte, Indianapolis, San Francisco, Seattle, Denver, and Oklahoma City).
57. *See* MICHELLE WILDE ANDERSON, THE FIGHT TO SAVE THE TOWN 6 (2022) (emphasizing the growth in regional inequality since 1980 as "the wealthiest regions of the country have seen incomes increase faster than the modest gains elsewhere").

1 A BRIEF HISTORY OF CITIES IN ENVIRONMENTAL POLICY

1. *See, e.g.*, *Annual Report: Letter on Philanthropy*, BLOOMBERG PHILANTHROPIES, www.bloomberg.org/annualreport/annual-letter/ (last visited July 11, 2024); *State Preemption of Local Zoning Laws as Intersectional Climate Policy*, 135 HARV. L. REV. 1592 (2022); Sharon Jacobs & Dave Owen, *Community Energy Exit*, 73 DUKE L.J. (2023) (manuscript at 6, 36–40).
2. On the idea of a local public good, see Joseph E. Stiglitz, *The Theory of Local Public Goods Twenty-Five Years after Tiebout: A Perspective* 3–4 (Nat'l Bureau of Econ. Rsch., Working Paper No. 954, 1982):

> I am concerned here, however, with a class of public goods, which I shall refer to as local public goods, the benefits of which accrue only to those who belong to a particular group (which I shall call the community), and not to those who belong to other groups (communities) within the society. There is thus an element of 'privateness' in local public goods; while within the community the good is a pure public good, 'between' communities it acts like a private good. Those

outside the community receive no benefit. The concept is a natural one; the local public library in Princeton provides no benefits to the citizens of Houston, and conversely.

Public goods are usually considered to be nonrivalrous (one person's use of the good does not diminish the amount available for others) and nonexcludable (individuals cannot be prevented from enjoying the good). Julian Reiss, *Public Goods*, *in* THE STANFORD ENCYCLOPEDIA OF PHILOSOPHY (Edward N. Zalta ed., 2021).

3. On how states governed in the nineteenth century by delegating authority to local governments, see generally JON C. TEAFORD, *THE UNHERALDED TRIUMPH: CITY GOVERNMENT IN AMERICA, 1870–1900* (1984). *See also* DANIEL T. RODGERS, *ATLANTIC CROSSINGS: SOCIAL POLITICS IN A PROGRESSIVE AGE* 112–113 (1998) (In the late nineteenth century, progressives "on both sides of the Atlantic" focused on cities.).
4. *See, e.g.*, JAMES SALZMAN, *DRINKING WATER: A HISTORY* 59–62 (2012).
5. Professor David Schleicher refers to the "amazing amount of public infrastructure" constructed by local governments in the late nineteenth century, citing water supply infrastructure as an example. DAVID SCHLEICHER, *IN A BAD STATE: RESPONDING TO STATE AND LOCAL BUDGET CRISES* 54–55 (2023). *See also* JOSEPH D. KEARNEY & THOMAS W. MERRILL, *LAKEFRONT: PUBLIC TRUST AND PRIVATE RIGHTS IN CHICAGO* 171–176 (2021) (discussing the history of Chicago's drinking water supply system).
6. SALZMAN, *supra* note 4, at 61.
7. *Id.* at 58–59, 66, 68.
8. NELSON MANFRED BLAKE, *WATER FOR THE CITIES: A HISTORY OF THE URBAN WATER SUPPLY PROBLEM IN THE UNITED STATES* 138, 144 (1956).
9. *Id.* at 121–71. *See especially id.* at 135–42, 149–51, 163–67, 170.
10. JOEL A. TARR, *THE SEARCH FOR THE ULTIMATE SINK: URBAN POLLUTION IN HISTORICAL PERSPECTIVE* 114 (1996).
11. *Id.*
12. *Id.* at 115–17.
13. Katrina M. Wyman & Danielle Spiegel-Feld, *The Urban Environmental Renaissance*, 108 CAL. L. REV. 305, 306, 315 (2020).
14. *Id.* at 315.
15. DAVID STRADLING, *SMOKESTACKS AND PROGRESSIVES: ENVIRONMENTALISTS, ENGINEERS, AND AIR QUALITY IN AMERICA, 1881–1951* (1999). These ordinances were not particularly successful in reducing smoke in cities. The smoke from coal receded in cities after World War II, when urban dwellers transitioned to using natural gas and oil to heat homes, railroads electrified, and coal was used to power centralized power plants. *Id.* Concerns about other forms of air and water pollution emerged after World War II. *Id.*
16. There were multiple motivations for establishing Central Park, including emulating parks in leading European cities like London's Hyde Park; increasing the property values of privately owned lands surrounding the park; and lower down on the agenda, the human health benefits of parks for exercise and clean air. ROY ROSENZWEIG & ELIZABETH BLACKMAR, *THE PARK AND THE PEOPLE: A HISTORY OF CENTRAL PARK* 18, 23–36, 49, 54–55, 100, 214, 297, 301 (1992). *See also* DORCETA E. TAYLOR, *THE ENVIRONMENT AND THE PEOPLE IN AMERICAN CITIES, 1600S–1900S: DISORDER, INEQUALITY, AND SOCIAL CHANGE* 251–253 (2009).
17. ROSENZWEIG & BLACKMAR, *supra* note 16, at 1, 200–01; *see also* David Schuyler, *Parks in Urban America*, *in* OXFORD RESEARCH ENCYCLOPEDIA OF AMERICAN HISTORY (2015). Initially, Central Park was a city project, but conflict "between state Republicans and city Democrats" led New York State to appoint a board that chose the design for

the park and oversaw its building and management until 1870, when the City regained authority over the park. ROSENZWEIG & BLACKMAR, *supra* note 16, at 8. New York City acquired the land for Central Park, in part using eminent domain. *Id.* at 7, 59–66, 77–85, 91, 96, 150, 238.

18. DORCETA E. TAYLOR, *THE RISE OF THE AMERICAN CONSERVATION MOVEMENT: POWER, PRIVILEGE, AND ENVIRONMENTAL PROTECTION* 3, 297, 302, 321, 351 (2016).
19. Hadacheck v. Sebastian, 239 U.S. 394 (1915); Reinman v. Little Rock, 237 U.S. 171 (1915). *See also* Melanie Kiechle, *The Smell Detectives*, SCI. HIST. INST. (June 20, 2011), www.sciencehistory.org/distillations/the-smell-detectives (discussing bans on slaughterhouses locating in certain parts of the city established by the New York City Board of Health).
20. SONIA A. HIRT, *ZONED IN THE USA: THE ORIGINS AND IMPLICATIONS OF AMERICAN LAND-USE REGULATION* 134–141, 203 n.1 (2014); TAYLOR, *supra* note 16, at 380–404. Local governments implemented zoning rules using authority delegated to them under state law.
21. Village of Euclid v. Ambler Realty Co., 272 U.S. 365 (1926). *See also* TAYLOR, *supra* note 16, at 386 (New York City's 2016 zoning resolution separated "industrial and residential areas").
22. In 1917, the U.S. Supreme Court held in *Buchanan v. Warley* that a Louisville, Kentucky ordinance that restricted people to blocks where people of the same race were a majority was unconstitutional under the Fourteenth Amendment to the federal constitution. Buchanan v. Warley, 245 U.S. 60 (1917); *see also* TAYLOR, *supra* note 16, at 395–98 (describing the use of zoning to separate people of different races). Nonetheless, zoning was used extensively after 1917 to separate people based on race and income. Though expressly allocating land to people based on their race had been held to be unconstitutional, local governments separated people by race and income by reserving many areas of their localities for single-family homes. *See generally* RICHARD ROTHSTEIN, *THE COLOR OF LAW: A FORGOTTEN HISTORY OF HOW OUR GOVERNMENT SEGREGATED AMERICA* (2017); TAYLOR, *supra* note 16, at 381–82 (referring to the desires of the Fifth Avenue Association, which "helped to pass" New York City's 1916 zoning resolution, "to maintain the racial and class exclusivity" of the Avenue); HIRT, *supra* note 20, at 13, 161–73.
23. *See* MARTIN V. MELOSI, *GARBAGE IN THE CITIES: REFUSE, REFORM, AND THE ENVIRONMENT* 20–21 (2005) [hereinafter MELOSI, GARBAGE IN THE CITIES].
24. *Id.* at 17.
25. *See, e.g.*, SUELLEN HOY, *CHASING DIRT: THE AMERICAN PURSUIT OF CLEANLINESS* 76 (1995).
26. MELOSI, GARBAGE IN THE CITIES, *supra* note 23, at 17–18, 21.
27. *Id.* at 22–23.
28. HOY, *supra* note 25, at 74–76.
29. MELOSI, GARBAGE IN THE CITIES, *supra* note 23, at 28–32.
30. *Id.* at 51–63. *See also* TEAFORD, THE UNHERALDED TRIUMPH, *supra* note 3, at 232.
31. MELOSI, GARBAGE IN THE CITIES, *supra* note 23, at 24–25, 56, 63. *See also* HOY, *supra* note 25, at 83. Professor Lily Baum Pollans describes the approach that local governments implemented in the late nineteenth and early twentieth centuries for managing waste, by disposing of it, as "the first coherent American waste regime," and labels it the "Sanitary City regime." LILY BAUM POLLANS, *RESISTING GARBAGE: THE POLITICS OF WASTE MANAGEMENT IN AMERICAN CITIES* 19 (2021).
32. MELOSI, GARBAGE IN THE CITIES, *supra* note 23, at 190 ("By the mid-1960s, solid waste became a truly national issue. The Lyndon B. Johnson administration passed the first

federal regulations."); *see also* POLLANS, *supra* note 31, at 25 (the Solid Waste Disposal Act, passed in 1965, was "the first national solid waste law").

33. Ron Grossman, *Flashback: In the Battle against Cholera, A Creative City Engineer Raised Streets, Tunneled into the Lake and Reversed the River*, CHI. TRIB. (Jan. 29, 2021), www.chicagotribune.com/history/ct-opinion-flashback-cholera-chicago-sewers-20210129-da7e3juagrh5xdesn7umv5wbji-story.html.
34. KEARNEY & MERRILL, *supra* note 5, at 175; *see generally* MARTIN V. MELOSI, *THE SANITARY CITY: ENVIRONMENTAL SERVICES IN URBAN AMERICA FROM COLONIAL TIMES TO THE PRESENT* 55–56 (2008) [hereinafter MELOSI, THE SANITARY CITY].
35. KEARNEY & MERRILL, *supra* note 5, at 175–88.
36. *See generally* TAYLOR, *supra* note 16; MELOSI, GARBAGE IN THE CITIES, *supra* note 23.
37. TAYLOR, *supra* note 16, at 59.
38. *Id.*, at 275–76.
39. TARR, *supra* note 10, at 122–23.
40. MELOSI, THE SANITARY CITY, *supra* note 34, at 144. There was briefly a National Board of Health from the late 1870s until the 1880s. HOY, *supra* note 25, at 66–68.
41. JON C. TEAFORD, *THE RISE OF THE STATES: EVOLUTION OF AMERICAN STATE GOVERNMENT* 12, 20–21, 41, 50 (2002) [hereinafter TEAFORD, THE RISE OF THE STATES]. For example, while states were seeking to regulate local governments' disposal of sewage into waterways that crossed local borders, states were also assuming more responsibility for highways from local governments in the latter nineteenth and early twentieth centuries. *Id.* at 29–35.
42. Thanks to David Stradling for observing that the federal government was not seen as a problem solver in the nineteenth century in many domains.
43. TEAFORD, THE RISE OF THE STATES, *supra* note 41, at 124. Historian Jon Teaford underscores that the Great Depression of the 1930s marked a turning point in the role of local governments, as it visibly demonstrated the limitations of relying on local governments to provide necessary public services. *Id.* at 121–24, 128, 130. *See also* SCHLEICHER, *supra* note 5, at 61 (discussing the increase in the size of the federal government and its "share of public spending" during the Great Depression).
44. TEAFORD, THE RISE OF THE STATES, *supra* note 41, at 158–59.
45. *Id.* at 2, 158–59. However, there were already critiques from the left of the federal administrative state in the 1960s, such as from Ralph Nader. PAUL SABIN, *PUBLIC CITIZENS: THE ATTACK ON BIG GOVERNMENT AND THE REMAKING OF AMERICAN LIBERALISM* 76–86 (2021) [hereinafter SABIN, PUBLIC CITIZENS] (discussing the Nader task force reports on federal clean air and clean water regulation); *see also* JOHN C. ESPOSITO & LARRY J. SILVERMAN, *VANISHING AIR: THE RALPH NADER STUDY GROUP REPORT ON AIR POLLUTION* 185–187 (1970) (criticizing the federal National Air Pollution Control Administration for working closely with the auto and oil industries on research on air pollution). Teaford also indicates that the states were viewed more favorably as positive perceptions of the federal government waned in the 1970s. TEAFORD, THE RISE OF THE STATES, *supra* note 41, at 196.
46. Thanks to Professor Richard Lazarus for emphasizing the historical relationship between the federalization of environmental law and the Civil Rights Movement. For further discussion of the interplay between the two movements, *see* RICHARD J. LAZARUS, *THE MAKING OF ENVIRONMENTAL LAW* 92 (2004); Jedediah Purdy, *The Long Environmental Justice Movement*, 44 ECOLOGY L.Q. 809, 825–27 (2018); SABIN, PUBLIC CITIZENS, *supra* note 45, at 43–45, 48; Paul Sabin, *Environmental Law and the End of the New Deal Order*, 33 LAW & HIST. REV. 965, 973 (2015); ELIZABETH POPP BERMAN, *THINKING*

LIKE AN ECONOMIST: HOW EFFICIENCY REPLACED EQUALITY IN U.S. PUBLIC POLICY 157, 178 (2022); JAMES E. KRIER & EDMUND URSIN, *POLLUTION AND POLICY: A CASE ESSAY ON CALIFORNIA AND FEDERAL EXPERIENCE WITH MOTOR VEHICLE AIR POLLUTION*, 1940–1975, at 201 (1977) (quoting S. COMM. ON PUB. WORKS, NATIONAL AIR QUALITY STANDARDS ACT OF 1970, S. REP. NO. 91-1196, at 10–11 (1970)); *see also* Richard B. Stewart, *Pyramids of Sacrifice? Problems of Federalism in Mandating State Implementation of National Environmental Policy*, 86 YALE L.J. 1196, 1217–19 (1977) (discussing "moral ideals and the politics of sacrifice" and noting that the idea that humans owe duties to nature supports centralization).

47. WILLIAM BOYD, *THE SLAIN WOOD: PAPERMAKING AND ITS ENVIRONMENTAL CONSEQUENCES IN THE AMERICAN SOUTH* 169 (2015) (quoting PETER C. YEAGER, *THE LIMITS OF LAW: THE PUBLIC REGULATION OF PRIVATE POLLUTION* 130 (1991)). On Earth Day in April 1970, see *The History of Earth Day*, EARTHDAY.ORG, www.earthday.org/history/ (last visited Jan. 30, 2022).

48. In a 1963 Senate subcommittee report, Senator Muskie stated "Polluted air is not contained in a specific area but is carried from one political jurisdiction to another. It does not know State lines or city limits. Providing air of good quality to all of our people is a challenge and obligation for Government operations on all levels." S. REP. NO. 88-638 (1963) (excerpted in BOYD, *supra* note 47, at 177). *See also* LAZARUS, *supra* note 46; BOYD, *supra* note 47; Robert V. Percival, *Environmental Federalism: Historical Roots and Contemporary Models*, 54 MD. L. REV. 1141 (1995); Robert V. Percival, *Regulatory Evolution and the Future of Environmental Policy*, 1 U. CHI. LEGAL F. 159 (1997); RICHARD N. L. ANDREWS, *MANAGING THE ENVIRONMENT, MANAGING OURSELVES: A HISTORY OF AMERICAN ENVIRONMENTAL POLICY* 227–254 (1999).

49. Environmental problems were not the only problems that crossed state borders that eventually drew federal attention. Congress created a legislative framework in 1920 for licensing hydropower dams on waterbodies that crossed state borders and regulating the prices of hydropower sold across state boundaries, and in the 1930s, it created a framework for regulating the prices of natural gas and electricity sold across state borders, which the states are constitutionally unable to regulate. Shelley Welton, *The Bounds of Energy Law*, 62 B.C. L. REV. 2339, 2354–55 (2021).

50. KRIER & URSIN, *supra* note 46, at 173–75; SCOTT DEWEY, *DON'T BREATHE THE AIR: AIR POLLUTION AND U.S. ENVIRONMENTAL POLITICS, 1945–1970* 239–240 (2000). *See also, e.g.*, *Hearings before a Special Subcomm. on Air and Water Pollution of the Comm. on Pub. Works*, 89th Cong. 86 (Apr. 6, 1965) (references to "[t]ak[ing] action to abate interstate air pollution" were made during statements given at hearings on the Clean Air Act).

In 1967, partly at the urging of auto manufacturers who feared "chaos" if states were allowed to impose a multiplicity of emission standards and balkanize the car market, Congress expressly preempted states and local governments from establishing their own standards, creating an exception only for California to establish more stringent standards in light of its historical leadership in regulating car emissions and its distinct air pollution problems. Air Quality Act of 1967, Pub. L. No. 90–148, 81 Stat. 485, 501 (1967); KRIER & URSIN, *supra* note 46, at 181–83; *see also id.* at 2; David P. Currie, *Motor Vehicle Air Pollution: State Authority and Federal Pre-Emption*, 68 MICH. L. REV. 1083, 1087–90 (1970). California continues to enjoy the authority to establish vehicle emission standards, if granted a waiver by EPA. 42 U.S.C. §§ 7543(a)–(b) (2018). Other states can adopt the California standards. 42 U.S.C. § 7507 (2018). There is a strong economic rationale for avoiding a multiplicity of emission standards for a nationally marketed good such as cars. Uniform standards enable manufacturers to make a single product and thereby realize economies of scale that translate into lower prices for consumers. J. R. DeShazo & Jody Freeman, *Timing and Form of Federal Regulation: The Case of Climate Change*, 155 U. PA. L. REV. 1499, 1507–09 (2007); Stewart, *supra* note 46, at 1212.

51. DEWEY, *supra* note 50, at 158–60, 164; see also STRADLING, *supra* note 15, at 82 (describing the impact of coal smoke from New Jersey in New York Harbor, and failed efforts to have the federal government regulate the emissions in New Jersey).

52. DEWEY, *supra* note 50, at 158–72. However, New York State also may not have been particularly keen to stringently regulate its stationary sources of air pollution. ESPOSITO & SILVERMAN, *supra* note 45, at 135–41 (The New York-New Jersey Abatement Conference organized by the National Air Pollution Control Administration (NAPCA) in 1967–1968 led to improved regulation of sulfur oxides in New York and New Jersey, and New Jersey started regulating air pollution in 1967. New York State was less willing than New Jersey to consider strengthening state regulation of particulate matter emissions); *id.* at 172–73 (In 1969, the New York Air Quality Control Board was not willing to adopt as stringent standards for particulates and sulfur oxides as the NAPCA favored).

53. DEWEY, *supra* note 50, at 168; *see also* Jody Freeman, *The Uncomfortable Convergence of Energy and Environmental Law*, 41 HARV. ENV'T L. REV. 339, 396 n.254 (2017) (citing Bruce M. Kramer, *Transboundary Air Pollution and the Clean Air Act: An Historical Perspective*, 32 KAN. L. REV. 181 (1983)) (noting that the problem of interstate air pollution was one of the motivations for the federal Clean Air Act). *But see* DEWEY, *supra* note 50, at 169 (implying that there was opposition at the state level to federal regulation of air pollution in the late 1960s in describing an interstate compact that New York State, New Jersey, and Pennsylvania negotiated in 1967 to reduce air pollution as "motivated by a desire to forestall the impending possibility of more aggressive federal interference in the matter").

54. David Anderson, *Wagner Testifies on Air Pollution*, N.Y. TIMES (Feb. 19, 1964) (quoting Mayor Wagner).

55. *Id.* (quoting Mayor Wagner). Bolstering his argument for federal regulation further, Wagner asserted that due to strong westerly winds, "[the New York City metropolitan region is] the terminus of a 3,000 mile-long sewer of atmospheric filth starting as far away as California and growing like a dirty snowball all the way." *Id.*

56. DEWEY, *supra* note 50, at 158. *See also* ESPOSITO & SILVERMAN, *supra* note 45, at 112 (arguing for federal authority to order stationary sources to reduce air pollution partly because "even those few states seriously committed to abatement cannot deal effectively with pollution originating in another state").

57. Stewart, *supra* note 46, at 1212. Once the states assumed responsibility from localities for protecting waterways from pollution, some states did negotiate interstate compacts to control the pollution of shared watercourses. For example, Connecticut, New Jersey, and New York created the Tri-State Treaty Commission in 1931 to address the condition of New York Harbor. MELOSI, THE SANITARY CITY, *supra* note 34, at 144–45. But the interstate compacts that were negotiated were insufficient; while they prohibited discharges, they did not embody a wholesale plan to reduce "municipal and industrial pollution." *Id.* at 145. In other instances, cities went to court to stop others from dumping sewage into shared waters. *Id.* at 157. Congress also attempted to spur the states to negotiate interstate compacts to address interstate air pollution problems in the late 1960s. DEWEY, *supra* note 50, at 171. New York, New Jersey, and Pennsylvania unsuccessfully attempted to develop a Mid-Atlantic States Compact to address regional air pollution problems that might have also included Delaware and Connecticut. *Id.* at 168–72.

58. *See* MATTHEW A. CRENSON, *THE UN-POLITICS OF AIR POLLUTION: A STUDY OF NON-DECISIONMAKING IN THE CITIES* 5 (1971) (indicating that a leading federal air pollution

expert stated in testimony to Congress in 1966 that "cities' slowness to act [was] primarily the result of political and social obstacles, not technological difficulties").

59. ENRICO MORETTI, *THE NEW GEOGRAPHY OF JOBS* 19–21 (2012).
60. KRIER & URSIN, *supra* note 46, at 201; ESPOSITO & SILVERMAN, *supra* note 45, at 112.
61. ESPOSITO & SILVERMAN, *supra* note 45, at 82–83 (when Chicago granted the steel makers a variance from its air pollution ordinance in 1963, the order granting the variance "recited the economic importance of the steel industry to the city … as though the alternative was that the scores of furnaces, hearths, and sintering machines would have to be shut down, disassembled, and moved out of 'Chicagoland'"); *see also id.* at 297 (the owner of a paper mill in rural Maine threatened to reduce investment in the mill if the state adopted environmental regulation, a variation on the industry argument that a plant would close if a regulation were adopted).
62. William L. Andreen, *Of Fables and Federalism: A Re-examination of the Historical Rationale for Federal Environmental Regulation*, 42 ENV'T L. 627, 645 (2012) [hereinafter Andreen, *Of Fables and Federalism*]; Stewart, *supra* note 46, at 1212.
63. DEWEY, *supra* note 50, at 167. Andreen refers to threats from "industry leaders" in the 1960s to leave jurisdictions that strictly regulated water pollution for jurisdictions that took a laxer approach. William L. Andreen, *The Evolution of Water Pollution Control in the United States – State, Local, and Federal Efforts 1789–1972: Part I*, 22 STAN. ENV'T L.J. 145, 189 (2003).

    In addition to their desire to attract and retain industry, city governments also lacked an incentive to control pollution because they themselves were polluters. They discharged sewage into streams and contributed to air pollution by burning garbage at municipal incinerators and operating polluting buses for mass transit. MELOSI, THE SANITARY CITY, *supra* note 34, at 195; DEWEY, *supra* note 50, at 119, 121, 127.
64. KENNETH T. JACKSON, *CRABGRASS FRONTIER: THE SUBURBANIZATION OF THE UNITED STATES* 283 (1985).
65. *Id.* at 284–85. *See also id.* at 301; Gerald E. Frug, *The City as a Legal Concept*, 93 *HARV. L. REV.* 1057, 1064 (1980).
66. Frug, *supra* note 65, at 1064.
67. Andreen, *Of Fables and Federalism*, *supra* note 62, at 647 (citing Randall B. Ripley, Congress and Clean Air: The Issue of Enforcement, 1963, *in* CONGRESS & URBAN PROBLEMS 224, 226 (Frederic N. Cleaveland ed., 1969)). *See also* BOYD, *supra* note 47, at 176 (statistics about the limited spending on air pollution at the local and state levels in the early 1960s) (citing Jean J. Schuenenman, Air Pollution Problems and Control Problems in the United States (U.S. Dep't of Health, Educ., & Welfare, Pub. Health Serv., Cin., OH, Paper No. 62-84, Apr. 1962) *in Air Pollution: Hearings before a Subcomm. on Pub. Health and Safety of the H. Comm. on Interstate and Foreign Com.*, 88th Cong. 1, 48, 52–53 (1963)); ESPOSITO & SILVERMAN, *supra* note 45, at 230. The 1963 federal Clean Air Act significantly increased federal funding of state and local air pollution control programs and led to the creation of many more such programs. Andreen, *Of Fables and Federalism*, *supra* note 62, at 653–55.
68. DEWEY, *supra* note 50, at 133. In 1964–1965, the New York City Department of Air Pollution Control spent over a million dollars on air pollution control. In 1966, the year after John Lindsay was elected mayor, he signed a bill "to ban soft coal for heating, to forbid incinerators entirely in new buildings, and to require within three years 99 percent effective pollution controls on Con Ed and other users of bituminous coal." *Id.* at 131. *See also* E. Donald Elliott, Bruce A. Ackerman & John C. Millian, *Toward a Theory of Statutory Evolution: The Federalization of Environmental Law*, 1 *J.L. ECON. & ORG.* 313,

332 (1985). Despite some improvements, the city's air quality "in 1970 remained the worst in the country." Andreen, *Of Fables and Federalism*, *supra* note 62, at 657 n.284; *see also* DEWEY, *supra* note 50, at 131–34.

Ralph Nader's Study Group Report on Air Pollution, published in 1970, includes a revealing portrait of the dismal state of air pollution in New York City, which indicates that the City's Department of Air Resources then had a "budget of slightly over four million dollars and a staff of about 300" and was "the second largest agency of its kind in nation" after Los Angeles. ESPOSITO & SILVERMAN, *supra* note 45, at 207; *see also generally id.* at 203–23, 230. Given the tendency to overlook until recently the disproportionate burden of air pollution on low-income people and people of color, it is interesting that the Nader Study Group Report mentions the rising rates of asthma among poor people of color in New York. *Id.* at 204.

69. DEWEY, *supra* note 50, at 156 ("[B]y 1966 … New York City had the worst air of any American city due to its high concentrations of invisible emissions, particularly sulfur dioxide and carbon monoxide.").

70. *See, e.g.*, Andreen, *The Evolution of Water Pollution Control in the United* States, *supra* note 63, at 156–57, 199–200; Stewart, *supra* note 46; A. Dan Tarlock, *Environmental Law: Then and* Now, 32 WASH. *U. J. L. & POL'Y* 1, 23 (2010); ESPOSITO & SILVERMAN, *supra* note 45, at 112, 192; BOYD, *supra* note 47, at 176 (quoting testimony from 1963 Hearing of House Subcommittee on Public Health and Safety).

71. *See* JAMES M. FALLOWS, *THE WATER LORDS: RALPH NADER'S STUDY GROUP REPORT ON INDUSTRY AND ENVIRONMENTAL CRISIS IN SAVANNAH, GEORGIA* 200 (1971); LAZARUS, *supra* note 46, at 92; BOYD, *supra* note 47, at 153. By 1970, the federal government already had a track record of investing in research into pollution. *See, e.g.*, Andreen, *Of Fables and Federalism*, *supra* note 62, at 651–56. However, environmental advocates were also critical of the federal government's weak response to pollution problems before 1970 and sought to structure federal environmental laws, such as the 1970 Clean Water Act and the 1972 Clean Water Act, to limit the discretion of federal regulators and enable citizens to sue federal regulators to force action. *See, e.g.*, ESPOSITO & SILVERMAN, *supra* note 45, at vii–viii (foreword by Ralph Nader); *id.* at 304–09 (critiquing President Nixon's and Senator Muskie's proposals for new federal air pollution control legislation and endorsing ideas such as private rights of action to enable citizen lawsuits); SABIN, PUBLIC CITIZEN, *supra* note 45, at 76–86.

72. ESPOSITO & SILVERMAN, *supra* note 45, at 270 (referring to the argument that "national emission standards" would mean that "each company would be faced with identical requirements, and it would be impossible for industry to play one state against another"); *id.* at 271 (referring to the related argument that uniform national standards would mean that industries subject to stringent standards would not be disadvantaged vis-a-vis competitors located elsewhere in the nation).

73. CRENSON, *supra* note 58, at 72 (noting that U.S. Steel may have wanted East Chicago and Gary, Indiana to adopt local environmental regulations to avoid federal regulation because the company thought it would have less influence over federal lawmakers than local lawmakers); BOYD, *supra* note 47, at 150 ("During the debates over air and water pollution in the 1960s, pulp and paper representatives, along with their counterparts in other industries, mounted a well-orchestrated resistance to the push for stronger federal pollution control laws. 'States' rights' quickly emerged as one of the most common refrains in their arguments that pollution control should be left to state and local governments."); *id.* at 163–65 (describing opposition of pulp and paper industry leaders to federal water pollution control standards); *id.* at 175, 179 (describing opposition of the American Pulp

and Paper Association to federal regulation of air pollution in 1963 and 1967); ESPOSITO & SILVERMAN, *supra* note 45, at 271–72 (referring to industry opposition to a greater federal role in environmental policy, including national emission standards, in the debate leading up to the 1967 Air Quality Act).

74. LAZARUS, *supra* note 46, at 69 ("The average vote in favor of major federal environmental legislation during the 1970s was 76 to 5 in the Senate and 331 to 30 in the House, suggesting a broad bipartisan consensus."); *see also id.* at 75–79, 150–56; William L. Andreen, *The Evolution of Water Pollution Control in the United States – State, Local, and Federal Efforts, 1789–1972: Part II*, 22 STAN. ENV'T L.J. 215, 255–56 & n.264, 262–63 (2003). Professor Taylor describes polls showing high levels of public concern about air and water pollution in the early 1970s. "In 1970, 69 percent of the respondents [in a national poll were concerned] … about air pollution and 74 percent [were concerned] … about water pollution." TAYLOR, *supra* note 16, at 499.
75. City and state governments are subject to regulation under the Clean Water Act and Safe Drinking Water Act; states, but not cities, are regulated parties under the Clean Air Act.
76. LAZARUS, *supra* note 46, at 73–74.
77. Casswell F. Holloway et al., *Solving the CSO Conundrum: Green Infrastructure and the Unfulfilled Promise of Federal-Municipal Cooperation*, 38 HARV. ENV'T L. REV. 335, 345–48 (2014). *See also* SABIN, PUBLIC CITIZENS, *supra* note 45, at 100 ("Empowered by the Clean Air Act, Clean Water Act, and other legislation, the EPA directed much of its regulatory fire at local governments and private businesses. The agency forced municipalities like Detroit and Atlanta to install modern sewage treatment facilities costing hundreds of millions of dollars, and required cities to develop controversial transportation control plans to combat smog.").
78. Michael C. Finnegan, *New York City's Watershed Agreement: A Lesson in Sharing Responsibility*, 14 PACE ENV'T L. REV. 577, 613 n.209, 617–18 (1997); David W. Dunlap, *As a Plant Nears Completion, Croton Water Flows Again in New York City*, N.Y. TIMES (May 8, 2015), www.nytimes.com/2015/05/09/nyregion/croton-water-is-once-again-flowing-to-new-york.html.
79. Finnegan, *supra* note 78, at 625–44 (describing measures to which New York City committed in an agreement with upstate communities that was intended to enable the city to avoid a federal mandate to filter its drinking water).
80. *See, e.g.*, Brian Clark Howard, *Inside D.C.'s Massive Tunnel Project*, NAT'L GEOGRAPHIC (July 5, 2014), www.nationalgeographic.com/science/article/140703-combined-sewer-overflow-washington-storm-water-tunnel; *see also* Holloway et al., *supra* note 77, at 345–46.

    The federal Clean Air Act imposed responsibilities on states to develop state implementation plans to implement the National Ambient Air Quality Standards. New York City's government was involved in developing the state implementation plan for transportation, although the legal obligation to develop the plan applied to the state. U.S. EPA, TRANSPORTATION CONTROL STRATEGY DEVELOPMENT FOR NEW YORK METROPOLITAN AREA 1-1 TO 1-2 (1972).
81. Holloway et al., *supra* note 77, at 346–48.
82. *Id.* at 359–61, 367.
83. *See, e.g.*, Jim Rossi & Thomas Hutton, *Federal Preemption and Clean Energy Floors*, 91 N.C. L. REV. 1283, 1288 (2013); Alexandra B. Klass, *State Innovation and Preemption: Lessons from State Climate Change Efforts*, 41 LOY. L.A. L. REV. 1653, 1677 (2007).
84. *But see supra* note 50 (discussing California's authority to obtain a waiver to adopt more stringent emission standards for new cars that other states can adopt).

85. *See, e.g.*, 42 U.S.C. § 7416 (2018) (preserving the authority of state and local governments to more stringently regulate emissions). State laws may restrict the ability of local governments to exceed federal minimums.

2 AN ANALYTICAL FRAMEWORK

1. D.C. Code § 8-1772.21 (2022); Government of the District of Columbia, Department of Energy & Environment, Building Energy Performance Standards, https://doee.dc.gov/service/building-energy-performance-standards-beps (last visited June 21, 2024); Cliff Majersik, *What You Need to Know about the Bold New Building Laws in New York and D.C.*, GreenBiz (May 14, 2019), www.greenbiz.com/article/what-you-need-know-about-bold-new-building-laws-new-york-and-dc.
2. Institute for Market Transformation, *Snapshot of BPS Adoption Across the U.S.*, Building Performance Standards, www.imt.org/public-policy/building-performance-standards/ (last visited June 20, 2024) (identifying as of December 2023 Boston, Massachusetts; Cambridge, Massachusetts; Chula Vista, California; Denver, Colorado; Montgomery County, Maryland; New York, New York; Seattle, Washington; St. Louis, Missouri; Washington, D.C.; and the states of Colorado, Maryland, Oregon, and Washington); CBRE, *U.S. Building Performance Standards in 2023 and Beyond* (Oct. 20, 2023), www.cbre.com/insights/viewpoints/u-s-building-performance-standards-in-2023-and-beyond (identifying nine local and four state-enacted building performance standards).
3. Stefanos Chen & Winston Choi-Schagrin, *What's Holding Up New York's Climate Progress? Apartment Buildings.*, N.Y. Times (Mar. 10, 2023), www.nytimes.com/2023/03/10/nyregion/greenhouse-gas-law-nyc.html. To be sure, reductions in energy use to achieve an energy efficiency or greenhouse gas reduction target might produce energy cost savings over time, even if they initially require upfront investments.
4. Glen Oaks Vill. Owners, Inc. v. City of New York, 2023 NY Slip Op 33867 (N.Y. Sup. Ct. 2023) at 19 (quoting the plaintiffs' self-description); Steve Cuozzo, *Loony "Environmental" Mandates Will Kill NYC's Middle-Class Housing*, N.Y. Post (Mar. 12, 2023), https://nypost.com/2023/03/12/nycs-local-law-97-is-a-threat-to-affordable-housing/. Although the New York State Supreme Court dismissed the plaintiffs' claims, an intermediate appellate revived the plaintiffs' field preemption claim against New York City's building performance standard in May 2024. Glen Oaks Vill. Owners, Inc. v. City of New York, 227 A.D.3d 523 (N.Y. App. Div. 2024).
5. Cuozzo, *supra* note 4 (referring to statement of another cooperative complex in New York City that changing its heating systems to comply with the local law would require a special assessment or increases in maintenance fees). *See also* Carl Campanile, *NYC Pols Urge Albany to OK Tax Break for 'Green' Mandate that Could Cost Co-op, Condo Owners $20K*, N.Y. Post (Mar. 17, 2024), https://nypost.com/2024/03/17/us-news/nyc-pols-urge-albany-to-ok-tax-break-for-green-mandate-that-could-cost-co-op-condo-owners-20k/ (reporting that city council members are urging New York State to adopt a property tax abatement to help residential building owners defray the costs of the building upgrades needed to comply with New York City's building performance standard requiring reductions in greenhouse gas emissions). In 2019, the Urban Green Council estimated that implementing the building performance standard that New York City passed that year to reduce greenhouse gas emissions would cost $20 billion over ten years, assuming building owners used only retrofits to meet the requirements in the law. Urban Green Council, Retrofit Market Analysis (June 18, 2019), www.urbangreencouncil.org/wp-content/uploads/2022/11/2019.06.18-Urban-Green-Retrofit-Market-Analysis.pdf.

6. Washington D.C.'s 2018 and New York City's 2019 building performance standards were passed before the federal Inflation Reduction Act of 2022 increased subsidies for decarbonization, including building decarbonization.
7. Sarah Anzia, Local Interests: Politics, Policy, and the Interest Groups in US City Governments 140 (2022) (quoting J. Eric Oliver, Shang E. Ha & Zachary Callen, Local Elections and the Politics of Small-Scale Democracy 10 (2012)). *See also, e.g.*, Charles Tiebout, *A Pure Theory of Local Expenditures*, 64 J. Pol. Econ. 416 (1956); Harvey Molotch, *The City as a Growth Machine: Toward a Political Economy of Place*, 82 Am. J. Socio. 309 (1976); Paul E. Peterson, City Limits (1981); Edward Glaeser, Triumph of the City: How Our Greatest Invention Makes Us Richer, Smarter, Greener, Healthier, and Happier (2012); Matthew E. Kahn, Adapting to Climate Change: Markets and the Management of an Uncertain Future (2021). Anzia provides recent empirical evidence of the importance of economic development in local politics. Anzia, *supra*, at 99; *see also id.* at 164–65 (describing the International City/County Management Association 2014 Economic Development Survey).

Whether cities should focus on promoting local economic prosperity, or whether state and federal laws should be changed to enable city governments to focus less on promoting such prosperity, are distinct questions from the empirical reality that city governments focus on local economic prosperity. For arguments that cities should focus on more than economic development, see Richard Schragger, City Power: Urban Governance in a Global Age 249–55 (2016) (advocating for broad formal grants of power to cities and noting that they "have a significant role to play in producing public goods and ameliorating economic inequality"); Michelle Wilde Anderson, The Fight to Save the Town 22, 44, 243 (2022) (arguing that cities with "citywide poverty" should focus on investing in existing residents, not attracting new residents and businesses); Gerald E. Frug, *The City as a Legal Concept*, 93 *Harv. L. Rev.* 1057, 1149–52 (1980) (proposing a structural reorganization of power for cities to promote public ability to participate in societal decision-making); *see also* Felipe Ford Cole, *Unshackling Cities*, 90 *U. Chi. L. Rev.* 1365, 1371–77 (2023) (situating Professor Frug's arguments within the history of local government scholarship). For arguments for changing state and federal laws to enable cities to take on more roles, see, for example, Gerald E. Frug & David J. Barron, City Bound: How States Stifle Urban Innovation 141–43, 231–33 (2013); Peterson, *supra*, at 217–22.

We borrow the term "economic prosperity" from Professor Sarah Anzia. Anzia, *supra*, at 138–43. Anzia suggests it as a more neutral term for describing what local governments aspire to than economic development and growth. Not all communities aspire to economic growth; even if communities do not want growth, they are likely to want to maintain an economic base to fund services for existing residents. As used here, economic prosperity encompasses aspirations to maintain a stable economic base and aspirations for economic development and growth.

We are aware that there are many potential understandings of what constitutes economic development (or economic prosperity). On a broad understanding of these terms, they could encompass socioeconomic equality and environmental sustainability. Based on the responses of cities and counties to the 2014 Economic Development survey of the International City/County Management Association, Anzia suggests that local government officials seem to narrowly equate economic development with "strengthening the local economy and the tax base," in line "with Peterson's account of cities." *Id.* at 165. According to the survey, "[t]he most common priorities for municipal governments are jobs (92%), the tax base (95%), and quality of life (92%). Only 52% report prioritizing environmental sustainability in their economic development strategies, and an even smaller share prioritize social equity (31%)." *Id.*

8. Zoltan Hajnal, *The Context of Local Policymaking: Who or What Governs?*, *in* THE OXFORD HANDBOOK OF STATE AND LOCAL GOVERNMENT 513, 523–524 (Donald P. Haider-Markel ed., 2014) ("On average, localities spend 31 percent of their budgets on police and fire protection, parks and recreation, sewage and waste." However, there is considerable variation in local expenditures.)
9. Political scientists and academics from other disciplines have sought to use large data sets to quantitatively analyze what drives local governments to adopt climate and sustainability policies. This research identifies multiple factors as contributing to local government efforts to address climate change and promote sustainability. *See, e.g.*, Christopher V. Hawkins, Rachel M. Krause, Richard C. Feiock & Cali Curley, *Making Meaningful Commitments: Accounting for Variation in Cities' Investments of Staff and Fiscal Resources to Sustainability*, 53 *URB. STUD.* 1902, 1917 (2016) (finding that "local priorities, regional governance, and participation in a climate protection network … receive the strongest empirical support in accounting for variation among cities in resource commitments to sustainability"); William L. Swann & Aaron Deslatte, *What Do We Know about Urban Sustainability? A Research Synthesis and Nonparametric Assessment*, 56 *URB. STUD.* 1729, 1730 (2019) (finding that existing literature suggests four categories of reasons why local governments adopt sustainability policies: "democratic responsiveness; organizational capacity; environmental conditions, complexity and dynamism; and governance institutions;" empirical analysis of surveys of local officials indicates that "organizational capacity" is the best predictor of the adoption of local sustainability policies but different factors might account for the adoption of different types of sustainability policies); Armin Jeddi Yeganeh et al., *Determinants of Climate Change Policy Adoption: A Meta-Analysis*, 31 *URB. CLIMATE* 1, 13–14 (2020) (finding that meta-analysis of quantitative research on the factors driving U.S. local governments to adopt climate policies indicates that "adoption is primarily driven by internal factors, including the level of public support and the presence of dedicated sustainability staff"; "populated and dense cities, particularly where residents have higher education and … lean Democratic politically" also more frequently adopt climate policy); Christof Brandtner & David Suarez, *The Structure of City Action: Institutional Embeddedness and Sustainability Practice in U.S. Cities*, 51 AM. REV. PUB. ADMIN. 121, 122 (2021) (finding from survey data of U.S. municipalities that "[c]ities in innovative states and regions that embrace sustainability, cities characterized by organizational rationalization and [that] have memberships in professional associations, and cities that accommodate expansive nonprofit sectors are the most likely to tackle threats to the natural environment"). *See also* RACHEL M. KRAUSE & CHRISTOPHER HAWKINS, IMPLEMENTING CITY SUSTAINABILITY: OVERCOMING ADMINISTRATIVE SILOS TO ACHIEVE FUNCTIONAL COLLECTIVE ACTION 8–10 (2021) (summarizing empirical research on why cities adopt sustainability policies that attributes the adoption to "co-benefits" and "government supply and stakeholder demands").

   It is not clear to what extent existing quantitative research is capturing the actual drivers of local environmental policy, as opposed to factors that merely correlate with cities adopting environmental policy. Consider, for example, the findings that cities are more likely to adopt climate policy if they have sustainability offices or are members of professional associations. The factors that lead cities to establish such offices and join these associations may be the underlying explanations for the city's climate policies. The findings that Democratic leaning cities, and densely populated cities, are more likely to adopt climate policies also are question begging. Since turnout in local elections is usually low, it seems unlikely that the political leanings of city residents in national elections, or the number of residents, by themselves explain the adoption of local climate policies. *See* Anzia, *supra* note 7, at 160 ("In the local government context, there are many reasons to doubt that city officials would design policies with an eye toward representing the interests of all adult city residents. Low voter turnout and scarce media coverage are just two of them.").

In addition, it is not clear that the policies that researchers are using as evidence of local commitment represent meaningful commitments by local governments that impose costs on local actors. For example, as we discuss in Chapter 4, while localities have committed to reducing greenhouse gas emissions or undertaken inventories of greenhouse gas emissions, few local governments have imposed – let alone enforced – laws that will require costly investments by private actors in lowering emissions, such as the decarbonization of private buildings, which are often the city's largest source of greenhouse gas emissions. *See, e.g.*, Yeganeh et al., *supra*, at 4–6, tbl. 1 (2020) (identifying the dependent variables used in empirical studies).

For an impressive summary of the empirical political science literature on why cities adopt sustainability policies, see Krause & Hawkins, *supra*, at 8–10. This chapter's explanations of the drivers of local environmental policy are broadly consistent with the factors identified in Krause & Hawkins's literature survey, which we came upon in researching this book. Perhaps most relevant to the top-down and bottom-up interest explanations that we offer for the emergence of local environmental policy is Krause & Hawkins's use in summarizing the literature of "[a] political market framework, which presents policy decisions as the outcome of the exchange between government supply and stakeholder demands." *Id.* at 9. They use the idea that "demand" contributes to policy adoption to encompass advocacy by community groups, the essence of our "bottom-up" explanation for the emergence of local environmental policy. However, they also would seem to include advocacy by business groups as a demand-side factor, while in the framework in this chapter such advocacy, especially from large, established business groups, would count as a "top-down" explanation. *Id.* at 10 ("On the demand side, support from citizen and community interest groups is a primary factor that explains local involvement.... Community characteristics known to correlate with environmental support, such as a liberal political leaning and high education levels, are commonly employed proxies and consistently show positive impact on city efforts. When controlling for these general indicators of support, studies show that cities' commitments to sustainability are strongly linked to the advocacy of organized interests – such as environmental, neighborhood, or business groups – in the policy-making process.") (citations omitted). Krause & Hawkins suggest that the supply side factors influencing the adoption of local environmental policy concern "governmental capacity"; "high governmental capacity, in terms of both fiscal and human resources, is consistently found to be a key factor enabling cities to pursue climate and sustainability initiatives." *Id.* at 9. Our top-down explanation for local environmental policy focuses on the views of elites inside and outside city government, rather than the features of local government, such as the number of employees working on sustainability or whether the local government is a council-manager or mayor-council system (which are factors mentioned by Krause & Hawkins in discussing the influence of the supply side on policy adoption). *Id.* at 9–10. Since we focus on large U.S. cities, we generally assume a certain level of local government capacity, although we recognize that there are capacity differences among large cities.

Another precedent for thinking of urban policy as emerging from the top down and the bottom up is Vicki Been, Josiah Madar & Simon Thomas McDonell, *Urban Land-Use Regulation: Are Homevoters Overtaking the Growth Machine*, 11 J. Empirical Legal Stud. 227 (2014). This article empirically examines whether rezonings in early twenty-first century New York City during the Bloomberg administration reflected the "growth machine" theory of zoning, according to which it is driven by "concentrated interest groups, namely, developers, landowners, and their allies in government and civic life," or the homevoter theory of zoning, which argues zoning reflects the interests of homeowners. *Id.* at 231, 233. Our top-down interest group story focuses on the same groups as the "growth machine" theory. The interest groups that we envisage as partly giving rise to environmental policy from the bottom up are broader than homeowners. We also include climate activists, advocates for animals (such as birds), and other individuals.

10. Paul Peterson's *City Limits* provides the classic academic statement of the limited focus of local governments on economic development. "City politics is limited politics," he wrote in his short book, published in 1981. PETERSON, *supra* note 7, at 4.
11. *Id.* at 187–88 (discussing New York City's mid-1970s fiscal crisis). *City Limits* was published just a few years "after New York City's near-bankruptcy," which many regarded at the time that the book was published as a kind of morality lesson for city governments that strayed from focusing on economic development to engage in redistribution.FRUG & BARRON, *supra* note 7, at 16–17 (providing an intellectual history of Peterson's *City Limits* that relates his arguments to the declining fortunes of major cities, including New York City, in the 1960s and 1970s). Other discussions of Peterson's arguments in *City Limits* include JULIAN BRASH, BLOOMBERG'S NEW YORK: CLASS AND GOVERNANCE IN THE LUXURY CITY 134 (2011); ALAN ALTSHULER & DAVID LUBEROFF, MEGA-PROJECTS: THE CHANGING POLITICS OF URBAN PUBLIC INVESTMENT 57–62 (2003). For different perspectives on the history of New York City's fiscal crisis, see JACK NEWFIELD & PAUL DU BRUL, THE PERMANENT GOVERNMENT: WHO REALLY RULES NEW YORK? (1983); KIM PHILLIPS-FEIN, FEAR CITY: NEW YORK'S FISCAL CRISIS AND THE RISE OF AUSTERITY POLITICS (2017); DAVID SCHLEICHER, IN A BAD STATE: RESPONDING TO STATE AND LOCAL BUDGET CRISES 70–74 (2023).
12. *See* FRUG & BARRON, *supra* note 7, at 75–76; BRASH, *supra* note 11, at 135–36; SCHLEICHER, *supra* note 11, at 77; Rebecca Bratspies, *Protecting the Environment in an Era of Federal Retreat: The View from New York City*, 13 *FIU* L. REV. 5, 30–33 (2018); Cole, *supra* note 7, at 1416; *Best Practices: Achieving a Structurally Balanced Budget*, GOV'T FIN. OFFICERS ASS'N (Feb. 28, 2012), www.gfoa.org/materials/achieving-a-structurally-balanced-budget.

    On the overarching importance of state law in constraining cities, see generally FRUG & BARRON, *supra* note 7, at 3, 20; Nestor M. Davidson, *The Dilemma of Localism in an Era of Polarization*, 128 YALE L.J. 872 (2019); Erin Adele Scharff, *Hyper Preemption: A Reordering of the State-Local Relationship?*, 106 GEO. L.J. 1469 (2018); Richard Briffault, *The Challenge of the New Preemption*, 70 STAN. L. REV. 1995 (2018). One of the ways that state law constrains cities is by influencing the size of localities. Size affects local populations and the scope of the issues that local governments can address. *See, e.g.*, OLIVER ET AL., *supra* note 7, at 14–21.
13. FRUG & BARRON, *supra* note 7, at 69–73.
14. *See, e.g.*, Davidson, *supra* note 12; Scharff, *supra* note 12; Briffault, *supra* note 12. On the partisan divide, see, for example, Jowei Chen & Jonathan Rodden, *Unintentional Gerrymandering: Political Geography and Electoral Bias in Legislatures*, 8 Q.J. POL. SCI. 239 (2013).

    State preemption of local action in the environmental area is nothing new. It has long been the case that industries that are unsuccessful in blocking local environmental regulation will appeal to state lawmakers to preempt or weaken local environmental laws. In 1915, the state legislature in Alabama took away municipal authority to regulate smoke after lobbying by manufacturers in Birmingham who wanted to avoid another local effort to address air pollution. DAVID STRADLING, SMOKESTACKS AND PROGRESSIVES: ENVIRONMENTALISTS, ENGINEERS, AND AIR QUALITY IN AMERICA, 1881–1951, at 136 (1999). In more recent years, plastic bag manufacturers have asked state legislatures to overturn local regulations to limit the distribution of bags. *See, e.g.*, Scott Rodd, *Banning the Bans: State and Local Officials Clash over Plastic Bags*, STATELINE (Jan. 29, 2018), https://stateline.org/2018/01/29/banning-the-bans-state-and-local-officials-clash-over-plastic-bags/.

15. Molotch, *supra* note 7, at 320; PETERSON, *supra* note 7, at 26–29.

The paucity of local control over immigration policy was brought into sharp relief as we were working on this book when over 100,000 foreign migrants arrived in New York City starting in 2022, as the city was recovering from the impact of the COVID pandemic. Hurubie Meko, *What to Know about the Migrant Crisis in New York City*, N.Y. TIMES (Dec. 6, 2023), www.nytimes.com/article/nyc-migrant-crisis-explained.html.

16. *See* Katrina M. Wyman & Danielle Spiegel-Feld, *The Urban Environmental Renaissance*, 108 CAL. L. REV. 305, 350–58 (2020). *See also, e.g.*, Engine Mfrs. Ass'n v. S. Coast Air Quality Mgmt. Dist., 541 U.S. 246, 258 (2004) (stating "it appears likely that at least certain aspects of [local vehicle fleet rules] are pre-empted."); Cal. Rest. Ass'n v. City of Berkeley, 89 F.4th 1094, 1107 (9th Cir. 2024) (holding that federal law preempts a local ordinance prohibiting natural gas infrastructure in new buildings); Fla. Retail Fed'n, Inc. v. City of Coral Gables, 282 So. 3d 889, 896 (Fla. Dist. Ct. App. 2019) (holding that Florida state law preempts a local ordinance to ban the use of polystyrene food containers).

17. PETERSON, *supra* note 7; GLAESER, *supra* note 7; EDWARD GLAESER & DAVID CUTLER, SURVIVAL OF THE CITY: LIVING AND THRIVING IN AN AGE OF ISOLATION (2021); KAHN, *supra* note 7, at 12–13; ANZIA, *supra* note 7, at 82 (citing PETERSON, *supra* note 7).

18. PETERSON, *supra* note 7, at 29; GLAESER, *supra* note 7, at 59–61; KAHN, *supra* note 7, at 7; GLAESER & CUTLER, *supra* note 17, at 6–8.

19. ANZIA, *supra* note 7, at 142 (quoting OLIVER ET AL., *supra* note 7, at 10). *See also, e.g.*, Tiebout, *supra* note 7; Molotch, *supra* note 7; PETERSON, *supra* note 7; GLAESER, *supra* note 7; KAHN, *supra* note 7; Cole, *supra* note 7, at 1370. Anzia provides recent empirical evidence of the importance of economic development in local politics. ANZIA, *supra* note 7, at 99; *see also id.* at 164–65 (describing the International City/County Management Association 2014 Economic Development Survey).

20. DANIEL DOCTOROFF, GREATER THAN EVER: NEW YORK'S BIG COMEBACK 68 (2017).

21. *Id.*; *see also id.* at 112 (Doctoroff suggests that as deputy mayor he was "thinking of the city like a business"). For references in the scholarly literature on urban politics to the city as a "product" and population growth as a proxy for economic growth, see JOHN R. LOGAN & HARVEY MOLOTCH, URBAN FORTUNES: THE POLITICAL ECONOMY OF PLACE 41 (1987) ("Tiebout likened towns and cities to products – packages of benefits and costs from which consumers make their choices."); Molotch, *supra* note 7, at 310 ("The clearest indication of success at growth is a constantly rising urban-area population."). John Logan and Harvey Molotch, as well as Richard Schragger, critique the idea of thinking of the city as a product. LOGAN & MOLOTCH, *supra*, at 41 ("To think of whole towns and cities as 'products' and residents as 'shoppers' truly strains the market metaphor."); SCHRAGGER, *supra* note 7, at 19, 34, 259 (rejecting the idea of the city as a product and urging that a city be considered a "process").

22. DOCTOROFF, *supra* note 20, at 69–70.

23. On Doctoroff's background, see, for example, DOCTOROFF, *supra* note 20, at 2–4; BRASH, *supra* note 11, at 50–51.

24. *See, e.g.*, BRASH, *supra* note 11, at 112, 126, 129. *Id.* at 197 ("some progressive organizations criticized the Bloomberg administration's broad development agenda and the Hudson Yards plan from a specifically class-based point of view, arguing that it privileged the interests of wealthy New Yorkers over those of the middle class, the working class, and the poor").
25. *See* Tiebout, *supra* note 7. For an exploration of the benefits, and limits, of Tiebout's theory in explaining redistribution by local governments, see CLAYTON P. GILLETTE, LOCAL REDISTRIBUTION AND LOCAL DEMOCRACY 34–45 (2011).
26. For a theoretical argument that developers may advocate policies that are in their interests, as well as the interests of localities as a whole in economic development, see GILLETTE, *supra* note 25, at 77. Brash provides an example where the real estate industry and the city government in New York both favored a development project (redeveloping Hudson Yards on the far west side of Manhattan), but for different reasons. BRASH, *supra* note 11, at 200–02.
27. *See, e.g.*, LOGAN & MOLOTCH, *supra* note 21, at 62 ("The people who use their time and money to participate in local affairs are the ones who – in vast disproportion to their representation in the population – have the most to gain or lose in land-use decisions. Local business people are the major participants in urban politics … particularly business people in property investing, development, and real estate financing" (citations omitted)); Molotch, *supra* note 7, at 320 (discussing the "key ideological prop for the growth machine" that growth makes jobs, noting that "[t]his claim is aggressively promulgated by developers, builders, and chambers of commerce; it becomes a part of the statesman talk of editorialists and political officials."); Been, Madar & McDonell, *supra* note 9, at 233 (discussing the growth machine theory of zoning, according to which zoning policy is driven by "concentrated interest groups, namely, developers, landowners, and their allies in government and civic life"); Norman I. Fainstein & Susan S. Fainstein, *Regime Strategies, Communal Resistance, and Economic Forces*, *in* Susan S. Fainstein et al. eds., RESTRUCTURING THE CITY: THE POLITICAL ECONOMY OF URBAN DEVELOPMENT 245, 254 (1983) (discussing the aims of the state in urban redevelopment, and stating that "[b]usiness dominates the political system" and "the state aims to segment off the administrative apparatus of redevelopment from democratic representative mechanisms, to keep decision-making bottled up among a small circle of technocrats, developers, and elite public officials sharing common interests"); CLARENCE STONE, REGIME POLITICS: GOVERNING ATLANTA 1946–1988, at 220 (1989) (emphasizing the power of Atlanta's "downtown business elite" in local governance in the forty years after 1946 but arguing that the business elite is not ruling "in command-and-control fashion"); BRASH, *supra* note 11, at 11–12, 20 (arguing that postindustrialization and neoliberalism were "associated with the emergence of new elites" seeking to reshape cities in their interests, in particular a "'transnational capital class' (TCC) defined by its ownership of the globalized means of production" and a "professional-managerial class (PMC)" supporting it, and that the interests of New York City's "postindustrial elite" during the Bloomberg mayoralty did not always align with those of the city's heretofore-dominant "real estate interests").

For a helpful analysis of the literature on urban politics that brings out the role that many scholars attribute to elites in urban politics and scholarly understandings of who are elites in city politics, see ALTSHULER & LUBEROFF, *supra* note 11, at 49–75 (identifying five theories of urban politics), 248–269 (revisiting the theories). This chapter benefitted from the useful guide that Altshuler & Luberoff provide to the theories of urban politics of Fainstein & Fainstein, Logan & Molotch, Peterson, Stone and other scholars. *Id.* at 57–72. Pluralism competes with the view that urban politics are dominated by elites.

See, e.g. Edward V. Schneier, Antoinette Pole & Anthony Maniscalco, New York Politics: A Tale of Two States 98, 99 (3d ed. 2023); Altshuler & Luberoff, *supra* note 11, at 51–53; Hajnal, *supra* note 8, at 514–515.

28. *See* Newfield & Du Brul, *supra* note 11, at 63–64.
29. *Id.* at 64–65. On Du Brul, see Dennis Hevesi, *Paul Du Brul, Writer and Leader in Fight to Ban Lead Paint, Dies*, N.Y. Times (Dec. 20, 1987). On Newfield, see Douglas Martin, *Jack Newfield, Proud Muckraker, Dies*, N.Y. Times (Dec. 22, 2004).
30. Newfield & Du Brul, *supra* note 11, at 63–64. *See also id.* at 65 ("The apex of permanent institutional power is banking and finance."); *id* at 66 ("The next level of permanent power are the owners of New York's most valuable resource – the major landlords and developers.").
31. *Id.* at 76 ("The cornerstone of the permanent government is the Golden Triangle of politics-real estate-banking."). Newfield and Du Brul contrasted the city's "permanent government" with "the temporary government" of three of the city's mid-twentieth century mayors (Robert Wagner, Jr., John Lindsay, and Abe Beame). Nonetheless, they included some public officials within the permanent government. *See id.* at 64, 70. On the downfall of Robert Moses, see *id.* at 64, 140; Robert A. Caro, The Power Broker: Robert Moses and the Fall of New York 1138–44 (1974).
32. We draw the term the "Creative Class theory" from Alina Maria Pavelea et al., *Is the Creative Class a Game Changer in Cities? A Socioeconomic Study on Romania*, 13 Sustainability 5807 (2021). *See also* Edward L. Glaeser, *Review of Richard Florida's* The Rise of the Creative Class, 35 *Reg'l Sci. & Urb. Econ.* 593, 594 (2005) (using the term "'creative capital' theory of city growth"); Krause & Hawkins, *supra* note 9, at 9 (stating cities may implement sustainability policies to appeal to the Creative Class).

Globalization profoundly altered the political economy of American cities in the late twentieth century. *See, e.g.*, Terry Nichols Clark et al., *Amenities Drive Urban Growth*, 24 *J. Urb. Aff.* 493, 493 (2002). As trade liberalization and automation accelerated, the number of American manufacturing jobs decreased substantially, and the spread between the value of high- and low-skilled labor increased. Justin R. Pierce & Peter K. Schott, *The Surprisingly Swift Decline of U.S. Manufacturing Employment*, 106 Am. Econ. Rev. 1632, 1632 (2016); Susan Clarke & Richard Gaile, The Work of Cities 29 (1998).

Theorists use various terms to describe the class of workers that saw their fortunes rise during this period. Richard Florida calls them the "Creative Class." Richard Florida, The Rise of the Creative Class (2002). Florida distinguishes between the core *Super-Creative Core Class*, which he defines as including people working in "science and engineering, architecture and design, education, arts, music, and entertainment" and *Creative Professionals*, which include people working in "business and finance, law, healthcare, and related fields." *Id.* at 8. In reviewing Florida's book, *The Rise of the Creative Class*, Professor Edward Glaeser argued that Florida's "'creative class' theory of city growth" is a version of "the human capital theory of city growth," and therefore not especially novel. Glaeser, *supra*, at 594.

Susan Clarke and Gary Gaile speak of "knowledge-based economy" workers. Clarke & Gaile, *supra*, at 198. Robert Reich labels them "symbolic analysts." Robert B. Reich, The Work of Nations: Preparing Ourselves for 21st Century Capitalism 178 (1992).

These different theorists also identify slightly different occupations as comprising the sector to which they refer, including (but not limited to) those working in science, technology, entertainment, architecture, the arts, and sometimes finance, management consulting, and law. The common thread that runs throughout all these descriptions is that they describe a class of workers whose value derives from their human faculties and whose chief asset is their ideas. For the sake of simplicity, we borrow Richard Florida's term, the "Creative Class," to refer to the relevant sector of the workforce.

33. *See, e.g.*, Yeganeh et al., *supra* note 9, at 14 (noting how "previous studies have shown environmental protection and economic development are not mutually exclusive"); Hongtao Yi, Richard C. Feiock & Frances S. Berry, *Overcoming Collective Action Barriers to Energy Sustainability: A Longitudinal Study of Climate Protection Accord Adoption by Local Governments*, 79 Renewable & Sustainable Energy Rev. 339, 344 (2017) ("As predicted, population had a positive influence and economic development policies had a positive influence, suggesting climate protection policies compliment industrial development efforts.").
34. *See, e.g.*, John B. Osborne, *Cholera*, Encyc. Greater Phila., https://philadelphiaencyclopedia.org/essays/cholera/ (last visited July 11, 2024).
35. Martin V. Melosi, The Sanitary City: Environmental Services in Urban America from Colonial Times to the Present 12, 14, 26, 85, 114, 125 (2008).
36. Roy Rosenzweig & Elizabeth Blackmar, The Park and the People: A History of Central Park 48–49 (1992); Dorceta Taylor, The Environment and the People in American Cities, 1600s–1900s: Disorder, Inequality, and Social Change 253 (2009); Jon C. Teaford, The Unheralded Triumph: City Government in America, 1870–1900, at 206–07 (1984).

    The sellers of pollution control equipment, and environmentally cleaner products, also may advocate for local environmental protection measures. *See, e.g.*, Evolv-Electric Transportation, *NYC Council Hearing on Electric School Bus Bill 455-2018 December 17, 2018*, YouTube (Dec. 17, 2018), www.youtube.com/watch?v=qPab-aN7Q5A (showing testimony of electric school bus manufacturers for school bus electrification).
37. Notably, Peterson pointed to local governmental provision of "sewers" as a policy that would attract business; thus, in our terms he could be seen as recognizing the potential that certain forms of environmental protection would promote local prosperity. Peterson, *supra* note 7, at 28; *see also* Anzia, *supra* note 7, at 140 (quoting Peterson's examples of developmental policies, which include sewers). However, reflecting perhaps the conventional wisdom of the mid-twentieth century, when the deindustrialization of local economies was ongoing, Peterson saw local governments as likely to see lax approaches to the environment – rather than environmental protection – as in their local economic interests. He posited that local governments might seek to lure capital by "ignor[ing] various external costs of production, such as air pollution, water pollution, and the despoliation of trees, grass, and other features of the landscape." Peterson, *supra* note 7, at 28. He suggested the federal government (and perhaps states) were more likely to be better positioned to establish stringent environmental standards; they might have a better chance of resisting antiregulatory or deregulatory pressure from industries that would be reluctant to exit a nation (and perhaps a state). *Id.* at 170–71.
38. In 1967, Dr. John T. Middleton, director of the National Center for Air Pollution Control, told the Subcommittee on Air and Water Pollution of the Senate Committee on Public Works: "Perhaps the most important of the factors that tend to discourage standard setting at the State and local levels is that such action seems inevitable to bring one major function of the State or local government – the protection of public health and welfare – into direct conflict with another – that of ensuring economic growth." *Air Pollution – 1967 (Air Quality Act): Hearings before the Subcomm. on Air and Water Pollution of the S. Comm. on Pub. Works*, 90th Cong. 1153 (1967) (excerpted in William Boyd,

THE SLAIN WOOD: PAPERMAKING AND ITS ENVIRONMENTAL CONSEQUENCES IN THE AMERICAN SOUTH 178 (2015)). In explaining the reluctance of the Mayor of Gary, Indiana to introduce an air pollution ordinance in 1962, Matthew Crenson recounts that the Mayor said in a newspaper interview, "He did not feel that 'the city should be rushed into action that might prove unwise.' Gary's pollution problem presented difficulties that other cities did not face. To the Mayor, the most important of these difficulties was one that 'revolves around the fact that U.S. Steel plants here, which are major contributors to the city's economy, are also major contributors to its air pollution.' [Mayor] Chacharis said that he 'would not want to damage the steel company by imposing a too-stringent pollution ordinance.'" MATTHEW CRENSON, THE UN-POLITICS OF AIR POLLUTION 68 (1971); *see also* PETERSON, *supra* note 7, at 167–71 (discussing Crenson's work). The argument that local air pollution regulation would harm the local economy was not new when used in the 1950s and 1960s. Professor David Stradling recounts that steel manufacturers and other industries in Birmingham, Alabama, which competed with the steel industry in Pittsburgh, successfully weakened a local anti-smoke ordinance passed in 1912 by emphasizing "that rigorous smoke abatement would mean economic disaster for the city." STRADLING, *supra* note 14, at 133; *see also id.* at 131–37. Pollution control equipment can be expensive. For example, Professor William Boyd mentions that in "the early 1970s," federal pollution laws led to the pulp and paper industry allocating "more than 30 percent of all capital spending … to pollution abatement." BOYD, *supra*, at 151.

39. Drawing on political activity at the local level in the early twenty-first century, such as successful campaigns in some localities for living wage ordinances, scholarship recognizes the potential for local governments to engage in redistributive policies that Peterson considered ill-suited to the local level. *See, e.g.*, GILLETTE, *supra* note 25, at 9–12 (discussing living wage ordinances as within municipalities' legal authority where representative of local interests); SCHRAGGER, *supra* note 7, at 139–49 (discussing successful living wage ordinances as challenging the conventional view of local authority). *See* PETERSON, *supra* note 7, at 173 ("[B]road-scale redistributive policy proposals are inappropriately addressed to local governments.… [I]f a city-wide minimum wage is passed, it will drive business outside the city's boundaries.").
40. For related points, see ANZIA, *supra* note 7, at 141–42 (contrasting the literature emphasizing the power of developers and that emphasizing the power of homeowners and tenants, and raising questions about whether there has been a change over time in the power of the different interests); Katherine Levine Einstein, Maxwell Palmer & David M. Glick, *Who Participates in Local Government? Evidence from Meeting Minutes*, 17 *PERSP. ON POL.* 28, 29 (2018) (discussing local participation initiatives, such as zoning meeting participation, as redistributing influence to environmental interests).
41. MEREDITH BARGES & VIVECA MORRIS, BUILDING SAFER CITIES FOR BIRDS: HOW CITIES ARE LEADING THE WAY ON BIRD-FRIENDLY BUILDING POLICY 12 (2023). The legislation also was supported by leading members of the New York real estate industry. *Id.* at 17.
42. *Id.* at 15–17, 19.
43. For related discussion, see FRUG & BARRON, *supra* note 7, at 13 ("Cities may have more agency than some urban theorists suggest, but they are subject to state-imposed restrictions that limit their ability to take advantage of the discretion afforded them by prevailing economic and social conditions."); SCHRAGGER, *supra* note 7, at 18–43 (arguing that cities have some agency but that the degree of their agency should not be overstated); Richard Schragger, *The Perils of Land Use Deregulation*, 170 *U. PA. L. REV.* 127, 190–94

(2021) (describing land use regulation as offering cities a lever to achieve local redistributive goals); ANZIA, *supra* note 7 (offering evidence of the influence of interest groups in local politics).

The past several decades of scholarship emphasizing the constraints on local governments that Doctoroff so aptly captured in lay language might be regarded as a reaction to an earlier generation of scholarship that portrayed local governments as powerful entities able to redraw the landscape within their borders. PETERSON, *supra* note 7, at 4 (arguing that his emphasis on the limits of city power contrasts with "four literatures" that have "taken the city as a more or less autonomous decision-making unit").

44. Charles W. Tyler & Heather K. Gerken, *The Myth of the Laboratories of Democracy*, 122 COLUM. L. REV. 2187, 2199–2200 (2022). Tyler & Gerken focus on state lawmakers and executive agency officials, but their points also apply at the local level. Professor Sarah Anzia provides an important empirical analysis of the influence of interest groups in local governments. ANZIA, *supra* note 7.
45. *See also* GILLETTE, *supra* note 25, at 31–32 (referring to "the greater opportunities that local governance provides for participation in decision making about matters of public policy than more-centralized governments"). However, the accessibility of local governments does not mean that local policymakers will be equally receptive to everyone's views. *See, e.g.*, LILY BAUM POLLANS, RESISTING GARBAGE: THE POLITICS OF WASTE MANAGEMENT IN AMERICAN CITIES 84 (2021) (referring to a lack of inclusion "of all voices" at the local level in Seattle).
46. Noah Kazis, *American Unicameralism: The Structure of Local Legislatures*, 69 HASTINGS L.J. 1147, 1159, 1172 (2018). *See also* PETERSON, *supra* note 7, at 123; ANZIA, *supra* note 7, at 6. In the nineteenth century, there were U.S. cities with bicameral legislatures. TEAFORD, *supra* note 36, at 25, 41, 44, 116 (referring to Baltimore, Philadelphia, and St. Louis).
47. ANZIA, *supra* note 7, at 160 (low voter turnout in local elections); PETERSON, *supra* note 7, at 119 (same); OLIVER ET AL., *supra* note 7, at 55 ("Turnout in most local elections, particularly when they are nonconcurrent with state or national races, is usually below 25 percent of eligible voters and is often under 10 percent.") (citing Zoltan L. Hajnal & Paul G. Lewis, *Municipal Institutions and Voter Turnout in Local Elections*, 38 URB. AFF. REV. 645 (2003)); *id.* at 64–65 (discussing higher turnout when local elections are concurrent with federal elections); SCHLEICHER, *supra* note 11, at 170 ("The key elections in New York City or Wyoming are party primaries, rather than general elections. But turnout in primaries is very low, and the ballot does not indicate relevant information like which party faction a candidate is associated with…. Where elections are low-turnout and low-information, interest groups become more powerful."). *See also* Pete Sikora, *How #GasFreeNYC Won a Gas Ban in New York City*, https://docs.google.com/document/d/1TpU9nEW4Rni2h339jhir3U7r2SO1L_Jz8Y5lGlx7kNc/edit (last visited Feb. 23, 2024).

Anzia provides some empirical evidence that interest group activity in elections contributes to the election of candidates with views favorable to the active interest groups, though she emphasizes that elections are only one channel through which interest groups influence local policy. ANZIA, *supra* note 7, at 262–63; *see also, e.g.*, *id.* at 262 ("[I]n cities where environmental groups are more electorally active, the winning candidates are significantly less favorable to growth.").

48. Gillette emphasizes that in considering why local governments redistribute, it is valuable to consider why individuals who support redistribution would seek redistribution from local governments, as opposed to the federal or state governments. GILLETTE, *supra* note 25, at 83. As suggested in the body of the text, environmentalists might focus

on city governments because they perceive higher levels of government as less receptive to their policy preferences, for example when Republicans opposed to climate regulation control the White House.

In suggesting that local governments may have more political latitude to address climate change than higher levels of government because city voters tend to lean Democratic, we are not suggesting that cities address climate change more than higher levels of governments *because* urban voters are more Democratic. This would be a difficult argument to make because voter turnout in city elections tends to be low, suggesting that residents do not drive policy outcomes through voting. *See supra* note 47. Moreover, as discussed in Chapter 4, few city governments have implemented actions to limit climate change that would impose significant costs on local residents. Still, the dominant Democratic ethos in cities may grant local government officials more scope to think that they can take some actions to address climate change than higher levels of government, at least when those higher levels are controlled by Republicans.

49. In May of 2022, the news site Five Thirty Eight published a poll of Americans' political priorities. Geoffrey Skelley & Holly Fuong, *We Asked 2,000 Americans about Their Biggest Concern*, FIVETHIRTYEIGHT (May 17, 2022, 6:00 AM), https://fivethirtyeight.com/features/we-asked-2000-americans-about-their-biggest-concern-the-resounding-answer-inflation/. The pollsters had asked the respondents what issue or issues were most important to them. Looking at the sample as a whole, 16 percent of respondents stated that climate change was one of the most important problems facing the country. But there was a huge difference between the percentage of Democratic and Republican respondents on the question: 30 percent of Democrats stated that climate change was among the most important issues compared to only 6 percent of Republicans. Only two other issues – election fraud and immigration – showed such a large partisan divide. *Id.*

However, some commentators dispute that there is such a stark partisan divide over beliefs about climate change. *See* ANTHONY LEISEROWITZ ET AL., YALE U. & GEORGE MASON U., POLITICS & GLOBAL WARMING, APRIL 2022 (2022); Gregg Sparkman et al., *Americans Experience a False Social Reality by Underestimating Popular Climate Policy Support by Nearly Half*, 13 NATURE COMM. 1 (2022).

50. A recent study of partisan sorting between 1856 and 2016 found that "[g]eographic sorting within states is currently at a historic high." Ethan Kaplan et al., *Partisan Spatial Sorting in the United States: A Theoretical and Empirical Overview*, 211 J. OF PUB. ECON. 1, 2 (2022). Democratic voters tend to cluster in urban areas of their states, whereas Republicans dominate in rural areas. *See, e.g.*, Jacob Brown & Ryan D. Enos, *The Measurement of Partisan Sorting for 180 Million Voters*, 5 NATURE HUMAN BEHAV. 998 (2021).

51. On agglomeration economies and their implications for local policy, *see, e.g.*, Edward L. Glaeser, *Introduction, in* AGGLOMERATION ECONOMICS (2010); Glaeser, *supra* note 7, at 24–25; GILLETTE, *supra* note 25, at 96–102; FRUG & BARRON, *supra* note 7, at 160; David Schleicher, *Local Government Law's "Law and___" Problem*, 40 FORDHAM URB. L.J. 1951, 1952, 1959–64 (2013); SCHRAGGER, *supra* note 7, at 22–25; Schragger, *supra* note 43, at 200.

52. GLAESER & CUTLER, *supra* note 17, at 5 (referring to plagues as "the most terrible demons of density"); Daniel de Visé, *Two Million People Fled America's Big Cities from 2020 to 2022*, THE HILL (Apr. 12, 2023), https://thehill.com/homenews/3944865-two-million-people-fled-americas-big-cities-from-2020-to-2022/; Emily Badger, Robert Gebeloff & Josh Katz, *The Places Most Affected by Remote Workers' Moves around the Country*, N.Y. TIMES (June 17, 2023), www.nytimes.com/interactive/2023/06/17/upshot/17migration-patterns-movers.html.

53. *See, e.g.*, *OECD Policy Responses to Coronavirus (COVID-19): Cities Policy Responses*, OECD, www.oecd.org/coronavirus/policy-responses/cities-policy-responses-fd1053ff/

(last updated July 23, 2020) (stating "the urban premium will likely not turn into an urban penalty as agglomeration benefits continue to prevail"); *The Impact of Coronavirus on Cities: The Pros and Cons of Agglomeration Economies*, ORKESTRA (APR. 6, 2020), www.orkestra.deusto.es/en/about-orkestra/news-events/beyondcompetitiveness/1920-impact-coronavirus-cities-pros-cons-agglomeration-economies; Alan Berube & Eli Byerly-Duke, *Which Metro Areas Have Fared Better in the COVID-19 Rebound?*, BROOKINGS (June 16, 2022) www.brookings.edu/blog/the-avenue/2022/06/16/which-metro-areas-have-fared-better-in-the-covid-19-rebound/; Shauna Brail & Mark Kleinman, *Impacts and Implications for the Post-COVID City: The Case of Toronto*, 15 CAMBRIDGE J. REGIONS, ECON. & SOC'Y 495 (2022), https://doi.org/10.1093/cjres/rsac022 ("Post pandemic, these findings point to the expectation that the economic benefits of agglomeration, proximity and face-to-face contact will not disappear.").

54. *See also* GILLETTE, *supra* note 25.
55. On the meaning of local public goods, see Joseph E. Stiglitz, *The Theory of Local Public Goods Twenty-Five Years after Tiebout: A Perspective* 3–4 (Nat'l Bureau of Econ. Rsch., Working Paper No. 954, 1982):

> I am concerned here, however, with a class of public goods, which I shall refer to as *local* public goods, the benefits of which accrue only to those who belong to a particular group (which I shall call the community), and not to those who belong to other groups (communities) within the society. There is thus an element of 'privateness' in local public goods; while *within* the community the good is a pure public good, 'between' communities it acts like a private good. Those outside the community receive no benefit. The concept is a natural one; the local public library in Princeton provides no benefits to the citizens of Houston, and conversely.

Public goods are usually considered to be nonrivalrous (one person's use of the good does not diminish the amount available for others) and nonexcludable (individuals cannot be prevented from enjoying the good). Julian Reiss, *Public Goods, in* THE STANFORD ENCYCLOPEDIA OF PHILOSOPHY (Edward N. Zalta ed., 2021).

56. Professor Anzia alludes to the keen interest that many people have in their local environment when she argues that proposed land use changes attract opposition in part because they are visible to people. ANZIA, *supra* note 7, at 150–51.
57. *See, e.g.*, BRASH, *supra* note 11, at 192 (noting how Community Board 4 in New York City criticized the Bloomberg administration's plan for redeveloping Hudson Yards for emphasizing "large parks serving commercial areas rather than small neighborhood parks"). Chapter 3 discusses efforts to reduce the burdens of solid waste collection on low-income communities of color in New York City.
58. MELOSI, *supra* note 35, at 67. Melosi also mentions that "[t]he wealthiest sections of the city were not always the first to obtain new sewers, in large measure because they did not suffer the kinds of drainage problems found in slums or the neighborhoods of the poor." *Id. But see* NYC MAYOR'S OFFICE OF CLIMATE & ENVIRONMENTAL JUSTICE, EJNYC: A STUDY OF ENVIRONMENTAL JUSTICE ISSUES IN NEW YORK CITY 27 (2024) ("at first, the [Croton] Aqueduct and sewer served wealthy New Yorkers who had access to pipes and water hookups").
59. Complaint at para. 23, W. Harlem Env't Action, Inc. v. N.Y.C. Dep't of Env't Prot., No. 92-45133 (N.Y. Sup. Ct. June 22, 1992); Vernice D. Miller, *Planning, Power and Politics: A Case Study of the Land Use and Siting History of the North River Water Pollution Control Plant*, 21 FORDHAM URB. L.J. 707, 714–15, 720–21 (1994); *WE ACT Calls for Retrofitting of North River Waste Treatment Plant*, WE ACT, www.weact.org/es/2015/12/

we-act-calls-for-retrofitting-of-north-river-waste-treatment-plant/ (last visited Feb. 23, 2024); Michael Specter, *Harlem Groups File Suit to Fight Sewage Odors*, N.Y. TIMES (June 22, 1992), www.nytimes.com/1992/06/22/nyregion/harlem-groups-file-suit-to-fight-sewage-odors.html.

Historically and to this day, people of color and low-income people have borne the burden of facilities dealing with urban solid waste. In Chicago, garbage dumps were often located in immigrant neighborhoods. Jobs in urban waste management were often dangerous, and many of the people who took them in cities such as Chicago and San Francisco were immigrants. DAVID PELLOW, GARBAGE WARS: THE STRUGGLE FOR ENVIRONMENTAL JUSTICE IN CHICAGO 21, 35, 38–39 (2002). As discussed further in Chapter 3, many of the waste transfer stations to which New York City's garbage moves en route to landfills outside the city are concentrated in a small number of communities of color and low-income neighborhoods.

60. TAYLOR, *supra* note 36, at 59. On discrimination in the provision of water services based on race in the past and today, see COTY MONTAG, NAACP LEGAL DEF. AND EDUC. FUND, INC., WATER/COLOR: A STUDY OF RACE AND THE WATER AFFORDABILITY CRISIS IN AMERICA'S CITIES (2019), www.naacpldf.org/wp-content/uploads/Water_Report_FULL_5_31_19_FINAL_OPT.pdf; CALIFORNIA TASK FORCE TO STUDY AND DEVELOP REPARATION PROPOSALS FOR AFRICAN AMERICANS, INTERIM REPORT 255–56 (2022).

After New York City built a system to import clean water into the city in the mid-nineteenth century, poor people used "public wells and water hydrants" while the wealthy "paid for indoor plumbing and water." TAYLOR, *supra* note 36, at 200; *see also* MELOSI, *supra* note 35, at 23, 57, 59; GLAESER & CUTLER, *supra* note 17, at 80.

61. According to the Trust for Public Land's survey of the 100 most populated U.S. cities, "residents who identify as people of color have about the same and in some cases better 10-minute walk access compared to white residents." TRUST FOR PUBLIC LAND, 2021 CITY PARK FACTS: THE YEAR IN PARKS 2 (2021), www.tpl.org/2021-city-park-facts. However, "[t]he median city … has 30% less park space per person in neighborhoods of color relative to white neighborhoods." *Id.* In New York City, 99% of the population lives within a half mile (10 minute) walk from a park, but "residents in neighborhoods of color" have 33% less park space per person than people living in "white neighborhoods." *Id.* (Distribution of Park Space); *see also id.* (Walkable Park Access). In the twentieth century, Robert Moses famously built many parks in New York City, but of the "255 parks" he built in "the five boroughs, only one … was in Harlem." Miller, *supra* note 59, at 714 (citing CARO, *supra* note 31, at 510). Of the thirty-one parks that the Chicago Park District built in the 1940s and 1950s, "only two … were … in areas with more than a handful of Black residents at the time of construction." KEVIN LOUGHRAN, PARKS FOR PROFIT: SELLING NATURE IN THE CITY 51 (2022).

When Central Park was built in the nineteenth century, Black landowners and "poor whites" were displaced from land incorporated into the park. TAYLOR, *supra* note 36, at 275–76.

62. On the meaning of global public goods, see, for example, Inge Kaul, Pedro Conceição, Katell Le Goulven & Ronald U. Mendoza, *Why Do Global Public Goods Matter Today?*, *in* PROVIDING GLOBAL PUBLIC GOODS: MANAGING GLOBALIZATION 1, 3 (Inge Kaul, Pedro Conceição, Katell Le Goulven & Ronald U. Mendoza eds., 2003) ("Global public goods are public goods with benefits – or costs, in the case of such 'bads' as crime and violence – that extend across countries and regions, across rich and poor population groups, and even across generations.").

63. *See* Jonathan Rosenbloom, *Outsourced Emissions: Why Local Governments Should Track and Measure Consumption-Based Greenhouse Gases*, 92 U. COLO. L. REV. 451, 465–66 (2021) (describing the main sources of urban emissions according to standard local GHG inventories).
64. *See* Chapter 4.
65. For a similar point, see Richard B. Stewart, *Pyramids of Sacrifice? Problems of Federalism in Mandating State Implementation of National Environmental Policy*, 86 YALE L.J. 1196, 1213 (1977).
66. *See, e.g.*, BENJAMIN BARBER, COOL CITIES: URBAN SOVEREIGNTY AND THE FIX FOR GLOBAL WARMING (2017); DAVID MILLER, SOLVED: HOW THE WORLD'S GREAT CITIES ARE FIXING THE CLIMATE CRISIS (2020); *About C40*, C40 CITIES, www.c40.org/about-c40/ (last visited Feb. 23, 2024).
67. *See, e.g.*, Stewart, *supra* note 65; Jonathan H. Adler, *Jurisdictional Mismatch in Environmental Federalism*, 14 N.Y.U. ENV'T L.J. 130, 175 (2005) ("Global climate change policy is a prime example of increasing state activity where federal action would provide for a greater jurisdictional match."); Jonathan B. Wiener, *Think Globally, Act Globally: The Limits of Local Climate Policies*, 155 U. PA. L. REV. 1961, 1964 (2007) (discussing "policy problems with subnational state-level actions to reduce GHG emissions").
68. *See, e.g.*, BARBER, *supra* note 66.
69. Thus, we broadly agree with Elinor Ostrom, who emphasized that climate change is likely best addressed through actions at multiple scales, including the local level. Elinor Ostrom, *A Polycentric Approach for Coping with Climate Change* (World Bank, Background Paper to the 2010 World Development Report, Policy Research Working Paper No. 5095, 2009).
70. *See, e.g.*, Richard L. Revesz, *The Race to the Bottom and Federal Environmental Regulation: A Response to Critics*, 82 MINN. L. REV. 535, 536–37 (1997) ("Before responding to the arguments raised by my critics, I set forth briefly the main components of my approach to the analysis of the allocation of responsibility over environmental regulation between the federal government and the states.... My starting point is a rebuttable presumption in favor of decentralization.... This presumption for decentralization should be overcome, however, if there is a systemic evil in letting states decide the level of environmental protection that will apply within their jurisdictions."); Stewart, *supra* note 65, at 1211 ("Four structural factors hinder governmental provision of high environmental quality on a noncentralized basis and help to explain why resort to federal legislation is a necessary or appropriate complement to rising public concern with environmental quality."). Stewart contrasts centralization with decision-making at the state and local levels. *Id.* at 1211–1212.
71. Michael Jones, Elizabeth A. Shanahan & Lisa J. Hammer, *Environmental Policy*, *in* THE OXFORD HANDBOOK OF STATE AND LOCAL GOVERNMENT 778, 783 (Donald P. Haider-Markel ed., 2014) ("the debate regarding the merits of decentralization has not been resolved"); see also *id.* at 781–83 (describing the "centralization/decentralization debate in environmental policy").

3 LOCAL ENVIRONMENTAL PROTECTION IN NYC

1. JULIAN BRASH, *BLOOMBERG'S NEW YORK: CLASS AND GOVERNANCE IN THE LUXURY CITY* 42–43 (2011).
2. One of the authors, Spiegel-Feld, was in her senior year of high school in New York City when the planes hit and remembers countless conversations from the adults in her orbit about whether people and businesses would relocate from the city to the suburbs.

3. *Mayor Michael R. Bloomberg's State of the City Address*, N.Y. TIMES (Jan. 30, 2002), www.nytimes.com/2002/01/30/nyregion/mayor-michael-r-bloombergs-state-of-the-city-address.html; James Parrott, *New York City's Tale of Two Recessions*, 53 CHALLENGE 32, 38–39, 44 (2010); New York City Office of the Comptroller, William C. Thompson, Jr., Comptroller, XI Economic Notes (Sept. 2003), comptroller.nyc.gov/wp-content/uploads/documents/economic-notes-090203.pdf. *See also* BRASH, *supra* note 1, at 82 ("Mayor Bloomberg inherited a city economy radically destabilized by 9/11, the end of the 1990s stock market boom, and the onset of a national recession.").
4. BRASH, *supra* note 1, at 1, 50–51, 83–84.
5. *See generally* BRASH, *supra* note 1.

Mayor Bloomberg made no secret of the fact that he was engaged in a global competition for what he considered the world's "best and brightest." In his 2008 "State of the City" address, the mayor stated:

> We are in a competitive struggle. And the stakes couldn't be higher. Over the past year, I've seen cities from London to Paris to Shanghai, pushing the frontiers of progress. They are doing everything they can to attract the best and the brightest in every field: medicine; engineering; construction; and more. These cities are not putting up barriers; they're not looking inward or blaming someone else. They're not afraid of the new or the different, and we shouldn't be either. If we are, we won't have a future.

Mayor Bloomberg's 2008 State of the City Address, N.Y. TIMES (Jan. 17, 2008), www.nytimes.com/2008/01/17/nyregion/17stateofnyc.html.

6. *See, e.g.*, BRASH, *supra* note 1, at 140 (The Bloomberg administration's "luxury city strategy privileged the needs of high-valued-added companies (and their elite employees) for which the value of a New York location outweighed the cost, to the detriment of more cost-sensitive industries and residents.").
7. *Id.* at 140.

Major cities such as Boston and Washington, D.C. were well positioned to take advantage of the reordering of the labor markets that privileged the Creative Class because the creative sectors were already clustered in major cities. According to Richard Florida, by 2010, the Creative Class already accounted for "more than 40 percent of the workforce in eleven metros," including Boston, San Jose, and Washington, D.C. RICHARD FLORIDA, THE RISE OF THE CREATIVE CLASS REVISITED 206 (2012); *id.* at 207 (Table 11.1: Top Twenty Creative Class Metros, 2010); *see also* DANIEL L. DOCTOROFF, *GREATER THAN EVER: NEW YORK'S BIG COMEBACK* 114 (2017) (In 2002, industries such as finance, "media and advertising, higher education, and professional and business services … represented 24 percent of the employment and a disproportionate share of the economic output of the city."). Creative sectors have grown as a proportion of total employment in the decade since 2010; in New York City, for example, the technology sector grew "twice as fast as any other city sector" between 2012 and 2021. Cara Eisenpress, *There Are Now More Tech Jobs than Wall Street Jobs in New York City*, CRAINS N.Y. (July 18, 2022), www.crainsnewyork.com/technology/there-are-more-tech-jobs-wall-street-jobs-new-york-city.

8. BRASH, *supra* note 1, at 111–112; *see also*, FLORIDA, *supra* note 7, at 280–303 (quality of place is key for mobile individuals).
9. BRASH, *supra* note 1, at 122. *See also* KEVIN LOUGHRAN, *PARKS FOR PROFIT: SELLING NATURE IN THE CITY* 42 (2022) ("Bloomberg believed that civic amenities were an important piece of attracting the 'creative class' to cities, and he therefore sought to enhance all kinds of public spaces, including parks, bike lanes, promenades, and other

recreational features."). Cas Holloway, who was the commissioner for the Department of Environmental Protection under Bloomberg, made the connection between improving the local environment and economic growth quite clear in an article that he coauthored on the role of green infrastructure in municipal stormwater control strategies. Casswell F. Holloway et al., *Solving the CSO Conundrum Green Infrastructure and the Unfulfilled Promise of Federal-Municipal Cooperation*, 38 HARV. ENV'T L. REV. 335, 338 n.2 (2014) ("[C]ities are motivated by regional and, in some cases, global competition to attract citizens, cutting edge industries, etc. They recognize that environmental health – sometimes synonymous with livable cities – is necessary for economic health.").

On the attractions of urban areas to high-income earners, see, for example, EDITH S. BAKER, THE LURE OF BIG CITIES FOR THE HIGHLY EDUCATED, U.S. BUREAU OF LABOR STATISTICS, MONTHLY LABOR REVIEW (2016) (summarizing JEFFREY C. BRINKMAN, BIG CITIES AND THE HIGHLY EDUCATED?: WHAT'S THE CONNECTION?, BUSINESS REVIEW (Federal Reserve Bank of Philadelphia, Third Quarter 2015)), www.bls.gov/opub/mlr/2016/beyond-bls/the-lure-of-big-cities-for-the-highly-educated.htm; JEFFREY C. BRINKMAN, BUSINESS REVIEW, BIG CITIES AND THE HIGHLY EDUCATED: WHAT'S THE CONNECTION? (2015), *available at* www.philadelphiafed.org/-/media/frbp/assets/economy/articles/business-review/2015/q3/brq315_big_cities_and_the_highly_educated.pdf.

10. DOCTOROFF, *supra* note 7, at 330; Terry N. Clark et al., *Amenities Drive Urban Growth*, 24 J. Urb. Aff. 493, 499 (2002) ("Talented high-tech staff, who can locate where they choose, are often courted by cities that compete for them with public amenities. This is a reversal of *smokestack chasing*, which was the leading policy of US cities for decades"). *See also* RACHEL M. KRAUSE & CHRISTOPHER V. HAWKINS, *IMPLEMENTING CITY SUSTAINABILITY: OVERCOMING ADMINISTRATIVE SILOS TO ACHIEVE FUNCTIONAL COLLECTIVE* 9 (2021) (emphasizing the appeal of "environmental quality" to the "creative class").
11. BRASH, *supra* note 1, at 130; see also *id.* at 18; Susanna Schaller & Johannes Novy, *New York City's Waterfronts as Strategic Sites for Analyzing Neoliberalism and Its Contestations, in* TRANSFORMING URBAN WATERFRONTS: FIXITY AND FLOW 166, 170 (Gene Desfor et al. eds., 2010); JUAN GONZÁLEZ, *RECLAIMING GOTHAM: BILL DE BLASIO AND THE MOVEMENT TO END AMERICA'S TALE OF TWO CITIES* 105 (2017); Diane Cardwell, *Mayor Says New York Is Worth the Cost*, N.Y. TIMES (Jan. 8, 2003), www.nytimes.com/2003/01/08/nyregion/mayor-says-new-york-is-worth-the-cost.html.
12. DOCTOROFF, *supra* note 7, at 330. *See also* KRAUSE & HAWKINS, *supra* note 10, at 9 (emphasizing the appeal of "environmental quality" to the "creative class").
13. GONZÁLEZ, *supra* note 11, at 161–62, 164–68, 195. The Bloomberg administration's stop-and-frisk policy, under which the police stopped many more Black and Latino people than white people, was held unconstitutional, and many years later Bloomberg apologized for it just before his brief, unsuccessful campaign to be the Democratic party candidate for president in 2020. *Id.* at 169–70; Shane Goldmacher, *Michael Bloomberg Pushed 'Stop-and-Frisk' Policing. Now He's Apologizing*, N.Y. TIMES (Nov. 17, 2019), www.nytimes.com/2019/11/17/us/politics/michael-bloomberg-speech.html; Floyd v. City of New York, 959 F. Supp. 2d 540 (S.D.N.Y. 2013).
14. GONZÁLEZ, *supra* note 11, at 120 ("New York City's most desirable parks were suddenly transformed under Bloomberg into playgrounds for the city's wealthy"); *id.* at 148 (referring to Progressive council member Melissa Mark-Viverito's "challenging further privatization of parks by Mayor Bloomberg, especially when it came to Randall's Island"). *See also* Timothy Williams, *On Randalls Island, New Ball Fields via Deal with Elite Schools*, N.Y. TIMES (Feb. 10, 2007), www.nytimes.com/2007/02/10/nyregion/10randalls.html.

15. Bloomberg extended the permissible term limits to enable him to serve three rather than two terms. Sewell Chan & Jonathan P. Hicks, *Council Votes, 29 to 22, to Extend Term Limits*, N.Y. TIMES (Oct. 23, 2008), https://archive.nytimes.com/cityroom.blogs.nytimes.com/2008/10/23/council-to-debate-term-limits-change/; BRASH, *supra* note 1, at 263–66.
16. GONZÁLEZ, *supra* note 11.
17. *Id.* at 161 (quoting de Blasio); *see also* David W. Chen, *De Blasio, Announcing Mayoral Bid, Pledges to Help People City Hall Forgot*, N.Y. TIMES (Jan. 27, 2013), www.nytimes.com/2013/01/28/nyregion/bill-de-blasio-kicks-off-campaign-for-mayor.html.
18. GONZÁLEZ, *supra* note 11, at 3; *see also* Chen, *supra* note 17; Halley Potter, *Universal Pre-K: The First Challenge for NYC's Next Mayor?*, THE CENTURY FOUNDATION (Nov. 1, 2013), https://tcf.org/content/commentary/universal-pre-k-the-first-challenge-for-nycs-next-mayor/.
19. *See, e.g.*, CITY OF NEW YORK, *ONE NEW YORK: THE PLAN FOR A STRONG AND JUST CITY* 206 (2015) [hereinafter ONENYC 2015] ("*Parks and public space are essential to economic development*, civic engagement, and community revitalization, promoting interaction with neighbors, attracting visitors, and providing a venue for art and culture.") (emphasis added).
20. GONZÁLEZ, *supra* note 11, at 199; Dana Rubinstein, *Bloomberg Official Responds to de Blasio's Parks Criticism*, POLITICO (Oct. 7, 2014), www.politico.com/states/new-york/city-hall/story/2014/10/bloomberg-official-responds-to-de-blasios-parks-criticism-016403 [hereinafter Rubinstein, *Bloomberg Official Responds*]; Dana Rubinstein, *De Blasio Promises to Be the Un-Bloomberg on Parks*, POLITICO (Oct. 7, 2014), www.politico.com/states/new-york/city-hall/story/2014/10/de-blasio-promises-to-be-the-un-bloomberg-on-parks-017228 [hereinafter Rubinstein, *De Blasio Promises*].
21. *See, e.g.*, Mayor Bloomberg, *Mayor Michael Bloomberg's 2003 State of the City Address*, GOTHAM GAZETTE (Jan. 23, 2003), www.gothamgazette.com/government/1670-mayor-michael-bloombergs-2003-state-of-the-city-address (touting the decline in the city's infant mortality during Bloomberg's first year); *Mike Bloomberg*, Johns Hopkins Bloomberg School of Public Health, https://publichealth.jhu.edu/about/history/mike-bloomberg (last visited Feb. 9, 2024) (investing in the School of Hygiene and Public Health so as to double its size beginning in 1991); Tom Watkins, *Bloomberg: Nanny-in-Chief or Health Crusader?*, CNN (Mar. 24, 2013), www.cnn.com/2013/03/24/us/michael-bloomberg-profile/index.html ("Since taking office in 2002, Bloomberg has unleashed a tsunami of public health initiatives.").
22. *See, e.g.*, JULIE SZE, *NOXIOUS NEW YORK: THE RACIAL POLITICS OF URBAN HEALTH AND ENVIRONMENTAL JUSTICE* 133, 141 (2007).
23. New York City law defines environmental justice as follows: "The term 'environmental justice' means the fair treatment and meaningful involvement of all persons, regardless of race, color, national origin, or income, with respect to the development, implementation and enforcement of environmental laws, regulations, policies and activities and with respect to the distribution of environmental benefits. Fair treatment means that no group of people, including a racial, ethnic or socioeconomic group, should (i) bear a disproportionate share of the negative environmental consequences resulting from industrial, municipal and commercial operations or the execution of federal, state or local programs and policies or (ii) receive an inequitably low share of environmental benefits." N.Y.C., N.Y., ADMIN. CODE tit. III, Ch. 10, § 3-1001 ("environmental justice").
24. However, as discussed later, the equitable distribution of facilities for managing waste across the city was not achieved during the Bloomberg era.
25. Geraldine Sealey, *Is Recycling Worth the Trouble, Cost?*, ABC NEWS (Mar. 8, 2002), https://abcnews.go.com/US/story?id=91824; N.Y.C. INDEP. BUDGET OFF., REFUSE AND RECYCLING: COMPARING THE COSTS (2004).

26. City of N.Y., PlaNYC: A Greener, Greater New York 133–34 (2007) [hereinafter PlaNYC 2007].

Other leading cities also established specialized bureaucracies devoted to sustainability in the early twenty-first century, including Austin, Miami, and Philadelphia. *Office of Sustainability Accomplishments,* City of Austin Office of Sustainability, https://cdn.knightlab.com/libs/timeline3/latest/embed/index.html?source=1qM_G-jLiwoa6JubHaZSW6_dhUladSNLgKZAGI-lkg7Q (last visited July 10, 2024); *Office of Miami Sustainable Initiatives,* City of Miami, http://archive.miamigov.com/grants/sustainable.html (last visited July 10, 2024); Press Release, City of New York, Mayor de Blasio Appoints Nilda Mesa as Director of the New Office of Sustainability (Dec. 4, 2014), www1.nyc.gov/office-of-the-mayor/news/940-14/mayor-de-blasio-appoints-nilda-mesa-director-the-new-office-sustainability; Philadelphia, PA Exec. Order No. 1-07 § 3 (2007), *available at* www.phila.gov/media/20181101115156/Executive-Order-1-07.pdf.

For context, of the 504 cities with populations over 20,000 that responded to a 2015–2016 survey, 46 percent had "staff whose jobs are dedicated to sustainability." Krause & Hawkins, *supra* note 10, at 23, 29. Krause & Hawkins conclude that their "survey results … show that less than half of midsize to large cities in the United States have staff dedicated to their sustainability efforts." *Id.* at 41. Looking at the results from another perspective, close to half of U.S. cities do have dedicated sustainability staff.

27. Ben McGrath, *The Untouchable*, The New Yorker (Aug. 29, 2009), www.newyorker.com/magazine/2009/08/24/the-untouchable.
28. ICLEI-Local Governments for Sustainability USA in Association with the Mayor's Office of Long-Term Planning and Sustainability, City of New York, The Process Behind PlaNYC 19 (2010); *id.* at 13. *See also* PlaNYC 2007, *supra* note 26, at 3.
29. ICLEI-Local Governments For Sustainability, *supra* note 28, at 13 ("Led by the Deputy Mayor's Office, City agency staff analyzed citywide land-use and infrastructure issues comprehensively – for the first time in decades – in preparation for the 2012 Olympics bid.").
30. Doctoroff, *supra* note 7, at 9.
31. *Id.* at 9–11 ("[H]osting the Olympics could be the antidote to New York's development phobia."). *See also* Brash, *supra* note 1, at 165 (characterizing the bid for the Olympics as embodying elements supported by many different private and public elites in New York City); *id.* at 237, 243 (the Bloomberg administration used the bid for the Olympics "as a 'forcing mechanism' … [for various] development projects").
32. Doctoroff, *supra* note 7, at 26–27. Before Mayor Rudolph Giuliani left office at the end of 2001, he publicly supported the Olympics bid (in 2000) and the Department of City Planning (in 2001) released a plan for rezoning the far west side that was similar to the plan for the area of the bid proponents. Brash, *supra* note 1, at 152, 155. NYC2012, the private organization that organized the bid, "coordinate[d]" with the Department of City Planning under Giuliani as well. *Id.* at 152.
33. Doctoroff, *supra* note 7, at 66.
34. *Id.* at 268.
35. *See id.* at 274 ("At one of the pre-Olympic decision meetings, the City Planning Department brought in Joe Salvo, the head of its Population Division, to make a presentation. Salvo's series of PowerPoint slides told a compelling story: the virtuous cycle of the successful city was taking hold. Crime was down; housing starts, particularly in the outer boroughs, were up; and newcomers were pouring in much faster than people were leaving, at an accelerating rate. The result was that population was growing more quickly

than we had anticipated. In fact, he predicted the city would have a startling 9 million people by 2030 [up from 8.1 million when we took office]."). *See also* PLANYC 2007, *supra* note 26, at 4, 6; Katherine Bagley & Maria Gallucci, *Bloomberg's Hidden Legacy*, INSIDE CLIMATE NEWS (Nov. 18, 2013), https://insideclimatenews.org/news/18112013/bloombergs-hidden-legacy-climate-change-and-future-new-york-city-part-1/ (indicating that predictions of population growth provided an impetus for what became PlaNYC).

36. DOCTOROFF, *supra* note 7, at 319.
37. *London Plan 2004*, LONDON.GOV.UK (Feb. 2004), www.london.gov.uk/programmes-strategies/planning/london-plan/past-versions-and-alterations-london-plan/london-plan-2004; *Congestion Charge in London*, POLITICS.CO.UK, www.politics.co.uk/reference/congestion-charge/ (last visited July 10, 2024).
38. DOCTOROFF, *supra* note 7, at 322.
39. In 2004, the New York City Energy Policy Task Force concluded that "New York City has adequate electricity resources today, but only by a slim margin."N.Y.C. ENERGY POL'Y TASK FORCE, NEW YORK CITY ENERGY POLICY: AN ELECTRICITY RESOURCES ROADMAP 9 (2004).
40. Interview with Laurie Kerr, Former Senior Pol'y Advisor, Off. of Long-Term Plan. & Sustainability, N.Y.C. Off. of the Mayor (Oct. 2022). On Kerr's role, see ICLEI-LOCAL GOVERNMENTS FOR SUSTAINABILITY, *supra* note 28, at 12, 48.
41. On the launch of PlaNYC, see Thomas J. Lueck, *Bloomberg Draws a Blueprint for a Greener City*, N.Y. TIMES (Apr. 23, 2007), www.nytimes.com/2007/04/23/nyregion/23mayor.html.
42. *Mayor Michael R. Bloomberg's State of the City Address*, *supra* note 3 ("New York has more than 500 miles of shoreline, yet much of our waterfront is inaccessible and neglected. We must bring new life to the waterfront.").
43. *Id.* The idea of creating a recreational path around Manhattan did not originate with the Bloomberg administration; for example, it was included in the city's first comprehensive waterfront plan, issued in 1992. DEP'T OF CITY PLAN., CITY OF NEW YORK, NEW YORK CITY COMPREHENSIVE WATERFRONT PLAN: RECLAIMING THE CITY'S EDGE v (1992) [hereinafter N.Y.C. WATERFRONT PLAN 1992]. *See also* Rutherford H. Platt, *The Humane Megacity: Transforming New York's Waterfront*, 51 ENVIRONMENT 46 (2009) (describing the history of the greenway that surrounds Manhattan).
44. Anne Schwartz, *Trends Transforming America's Urban Parks*, GOTHAM GAZETTE (July 31, 2012), www.gothamgazette.com/article//20050523/200/1424. ("In his keynote speech, Mayor Bloomberg also stressed the economic growth that flows from investing in urban parks. Speaking from a stage decorated to look like a pocket park – with the ubiquitous green portable café tables and chairs, a bench flanked by greenery, and a bicycle – he noted the attraction of good city parks to everyone from a young person starting a career to a family raising children in the city to a business leader deciding where to locate. 'In a tough economy, we know it's important to keep investing in what makes a city inviting to businesses and new residents,' he said. 'The time to make the investment is tough times. The city walked away from its future during the 70s. We did not do that this time.'")

   Cities in other countries are also using greening as a tool to attract elite inhabitants. Shanghai, for example, has launched an aggressive program to expand recreational green space around the city and relocate heavily polluting industries outside the city's borders. According to Shanghai-based urban studies professor Harry den Hartog, one of the goals of these efforts is actually to "create a comfortable living environment for a selective upper middle class." Harry den Hartog, *Shanghai's Strive to Excel in Climate Change Adaptation and Low-Carbon Promises: A Model to Follow?*, *in* GLOBAL SUSTAINABLE

CITIES: CITY GOVERNMENTS AND OUR ENVIRONMENTAL FUTURE 291, 301–02 (Danielle Spiegel-Feld, Katrina Miriam Wyman, & John J. Coughlin eds., 2023).

45. *See, e.g.*, LOUGHRAN, *supra* note 9, at 40–46 (indicating that "Bloomberg was sold" on the High Line after its proponents demonstrated its economic benefits to the city, including higher property tax revenues). Some of those who advocated for the construction of Central Park in the 1800s did so thinking it would increase the value of surrounding land. ROY ROSENZWEIG & ELIZABETH BLACKMAR, *THE PARK AND THE PEOPLE: A HISTORY OF CENTRAL PARK* 30–34 (1992).

46. *See, e.g.*, Press Release, City of N.Y., Mayor Bloomberg Discusses New Parks and Destinations that Are a Part of the Remaking of the City's Waterfront in Weekly Radio Address (Aug. 19, 2012), www.nyc.gov/office-of-the-mayor/news/300-12/mayor-bloomberg-new-parks-destinations-are-a-of-remaking-the-city-s (discussing waterfront parks and their benefits, including their ability to "attract visitors to stimulate the local economy and create jobs").

    In a 2002 article published in the *Journal of Urban Affairs*, the sociologist Terry Clark and colleagues argued that globalization transformed city economies from production based to consumption based and made attracting visitors "big business for local officials" who built new amenities, including parks, to lure tourists. Clark et al., *supra* note 10, at 495; *see also* GERALD E. FRUG & DAVID J. BARRON, *CITY BOUND: HOW STATES STIFLE URBAN INNOVATION* ch. 8 (2008). Clark et al. note that tourism in Chicago increased tremendously during the 1990s – from 32 million visitors in 1993 to 42.9 million visitors in 1997 – and "entertainment," which city officials describe as including tourism, conventions, restaurants, hotels and related economic activities, became Chicago's biggest industry. Clark et al., *supra* note 10, at 504. This boost in Chicago's tourism corresponded with a major investment in urban greening; Clark et al. report that during the 1990s, the Chicago Lakefront was largely rebuilt, the city planted around one million new trees, and it became a national leader in brownfield redevelopment. Correlation does not equal causation, but the correlation here is striking.

47. Mayor Bloomberg, *supra* note 21.

    On the value of parks in terms of tourism, see, for example, THE TRUST FOR PUBLIC LAND, MEASURING THE ECONOMIC VALUE OF A CITY PARK SYSTEM 3–4 (2009); JOHN L. CROMPTON, *MEASURING THE ECONOMIC IMPACT OF PARK AND RECREATION SERVICES* 11–15 (National Recreation and Park Association, 2010).

    On the dramatic decline in manufacturing jobs in New York City during the second half of the twentieth century, see DOCTOROFF, *supra* note 7, at 73 ("In 1961, there were 847,000 manufacturing jobs in New York City. By 2002, manufacturing employees had fallen to 140,000.").

    According to the New York State Department of Labor Statistics, the average salary of a worker in the tourism industry is lower than the average wage in the city as a whole, and 60 percent of employees in this sector do not have a bachelor's degree.OFFICE OF THE N.Y. STATE COMPTROLLER, THE TOURISM INDUSTRY IN NEW YORK CITY: REIGNITING THE RETURN (2021), www.osc.state.ny.us/files/reports/osdc/pdf/report-2-2022.pdf. Forty-five percent of these employees are immigrants, which is also higher than the citywide average. *Id.* In other words, tourism has become an essential source of blue-collar work in America's biggest city. Tourism employment in New York City increased in importance in the New York City economy after Bloomberg left office, growing at a faster pace than total private sector jobs in the decade between 2009 and the 2019 pandemic. *Id.*

48. PLANYC 2007, *supra* note 26, at 30 ("Case Study: New York City's Three Great Ages of Parks Development"); *see also id.* at 29 ("Over the last five years, the City has added more

than 300 acres of new parkland, much of it by reclaiming stretches of the waterfront that were abandoned by industry decades ago"); *id.* at 31 (the city set "in motion over the last five years the creation of nearly 2,700 acres of parkland – the largest expansion of our system since the New Deal"); City of N.Y., PlaNYC: A Greater, Greener New York: Update April 2011 at 34 (2011) [hereinafter PlaNYC 2011 Update]. New York City's 2021 Comprehensive Waterfront Plan emphasizes the transformation of the waterfront into many parks in recent decades, maintaining that "[t]oday, NYC's waterfront consists of a green network of parks and open spaces that spans all five boroughs and rivals that of any global coastal city." City of N.Y., New York City Comprehensive Waterfront Plan 110 (2021) [hereinafter N.Y.C. Waterfront Plan 2021].

49. PlaNYC 2007, *supra* note 26, at 30.

The administration in which a park opened in whole or in part should not necessarily be credited with creating and building the park; the history of the park may long predate the administration, and New York State, the federal government, and private actors also may have had significant roles in the establishment of a park in New York City. *See infra* notes 54 and 57.

50. PlaNYC 2007, *supra* note 26, at 30. The plan expressly mentioned the importance of addressing inequitable access to parks "[i]n the interest of … environmental justice." *Id.*

51. PlaNYC 2007, *supra* note 26, at 31.

52. Data compiled by Adalene Minelli and Sara Savarani for this book from NYC's Open Data about Parks Properties indicates that between 2002 and 2013, the city parks department acquired 426.98 acres of land. NYC Open Data, Parks Properties, https://nycopendata.socrata.com/Recreation/Parks-Properties/enfh-gkve/about_data (last visited Jan. 9, 2024). Acquired for these purposes means "designated under NYC Parks' jurisdiction." NYC Open Data, User Guide, Parks Properties, https://docs.google.com/document/d/1NExNJF5YKIDo40OopiofHainRuGG3Pz_jKSrMujPsPk/edit (last updated June 29, 2019).

53. Rubinstein, *Bloomberg Official Responds*, *supra* note 20. *See* OneNYC 2015, *supra* note 19, at 206 (implying that "79.5 percent" of "New Yorkers [are] living within walking distance to a park" in establishing a goal to increase that share to "85 percent by 2030"); N.Y.C. Mayor's Office of Climate & Environmental Justice, *EJNYC: A Study of Environmental Justice Issues in New York City* 63 (2024) [hereinafter EJNYC] ("As of July 2023, almost 85 percent of New Yorkers are within walking distance of a park").

54. Since zoning changes made in 1993, the city has required that "public waterfront open spaces … be constructed as a condition of redevelopment of most commercial and higher-density residential waterfront sites." N.Y.C. Waterfront Plan 2021, *supra* note 48, at 124–25; *see also* N.Y.C. Waterfront Plan 1992, *supra* note 43, at 162–66 (outlining proposal for waterfront public access areas and waterfront access plans); Katherine Flynn, *Private Money, Public Space*, AIA Architect (Oct. 1, 2018), www.architectmagazine.com/aia-architect/aiafuture/private-money-public-space_o (describing the history of Domino Park in Brooklyn).

55. Data compiled by Adalene Minelli and Sara Savarani for this book from NYC's Open Data about Parks Properties indicates that between 2002 and 2021, the city parks department acquired 682.67 acres of land, of which 500.55 acres was on the waterfront (73.3 percent). NYC Open Data, Parks Properties, *supra* note 52. Acquired for these purposes means "designated under NYC Parks' jurisdiction." NYC Open Data, User Guide, *supra* note 52.

56. The political scientist Boris Vormann argues that the waterfront "served as a particularly strong backdrop for deindustrialization processes and imaginaries of a better future, because

its increasing state of dereliction in the 1960s and 1970s came to be regarded as a symbol of a broken Fordist system, upon which a more sustainable urban fortune could be built." Boris Vormann, *Towards an Infrastructural Critique of Urban Change: Obsolescence and Changing Perceptions of New York City's Waterfront*, 19 CITY 356, 357 (2015). On Portland, Oregon's revitalization of its South Waterfront District, which included restoring salmon habitat, and its relationship to the city's efforts to nurture the knowledge economy, see Chris Hagerman, *Shaping Neighborhoods and Nature: Urban Political Ecologies of Urban Waterfront Development in Portland, Oregon*, 24 CITIES 285, 289, 293 (2007).

57. *See, e.g.*, Jane Margolies, *How Hudson River Park Helped Revitalize Manhattan's West Side*, N.Y. TIMES (Sept. 19, 2023), www.nytimes.com/2023/09/19/business/hudson-river-park-development-manhattan.html (plans for Hudson River Park "emerged in the 1980s and 1990s"). The city's first comprehensive waterfront plan, issued in 1992, recommended the creation of new waterfront parks to help reconnect the city to the waterfront. N.Y.C. WATERFRONT PLAN 1992, *supra* note 43, at 51. The Regional Plan Association's Third Regional Plan for the New York-New Jersey-Connecticut Metropolitan Area, issued in 1996, recommended establishing new parks in formerly industrial areas of the waterfront. ROBERT D. YARO & TONY HISS, REG'L PLAN ASS'N, A REGION AT RISK: THE THIRD REGIONAL PLAN FOR THE NEW YORK–NEW JERSEY–CONNECTICUT METROPOLITAN AREA 108 (1996), https://s3.us-east-1.amazonaws.com/rpa-org/pdfs/RPA-Plan3-A-Region-at-Risk-S150OPT.pdf. It also mentioned existing citizen and government initiatives to establish Hudson River Park and Brooklyn Bridge Park, among others. *Id. See also* Platt, *supra* note 43 (describing the history of proposals to create greenways surrounding Manhattan).
58. Schaller & Novy, *supra* note 11, at 167, 171.
59. *Id.* at 168; *see also* PLANYC 2007, *supra* note 26, at 17, 22; SZE, *supra* note 22, at 128 (referring to the decline of the Red Hook waterfront in Brooklyn in the 1950s and linking it to containerization); Vormann, *supra* note 56.

    Many waterfront areas came to house locally undesirable land uses such as waste sites and hazardous manufacturing sites. Schaller & Novy, *supra* note 11, at 167, 171.
60. Schaller & Novy, *supra* note 11, at 168 ("[t]he 1972 federal mandate to clean the country's waterways and improve sewage treatment practices reduced pollution levels, and living and playing by the water's edge once again became conceivable."). On the impacts of the Clean Water Act, see also Robert B. Semple, Jr., *This Environmental Law Made Half of America's Fresh Waters Swimmable and Fishable*, N.Y. TIMES (Oct. 26, 2022), www.nytimes.com/2022/10/26/opinion/environment/clean-water-act-sackett-epa.html; Jim Dwyer, *Remembering a City Where the Smog Could Kill*, N.Y. TIMES (Feb. 28, 2017), www.nytimes.com/2017/02/28/nyregion/new-york-city-smog.html.
61. Schaller & Novy, *supra* note 11, at 167, 171.
62. *Id.* at 169 (citing Elizabeth O'Brien, *N.Y.C.'s Riverfront Revival: City Pledges $36M for Waterfront Development Bond Buyer*, BOND BUYER (July 5, 2005)).
63. This table provides examples of parks of five or more acres opened between 2002 and 2021; it does not purport to offer a comprehensive list of parks of this size opened in the city in this period. Data for this table was collected using NYC Open Data, as well as a list of state and federal parks maintained by NYC Parks, and other sources. NYC Open Data, *Parks Properties* (last updated Jan. 9, 2024), https://nycopendata.socrata.com/Recreation/Parks-Properties/enfh-gkve; *Other Parks in New York City*, N.Y.C. PARKS, www.nycgovparks.org/park-features/other-parks-in-nyc (last visited July 10, 2024) (listing federal and state parks in NYC). The table identifies the year a park was opened, or the year the first part of the park was opened to the public when a park was or is being built in stages. Grace Soutter provided research that was helpful in understanding the scale of park development in the city.

64. *Barretto Point Park*, N.Y.C. PARKS, www.nycgovparks.org/parks/X307 (last visited July 10, 2024).
65. *Barretto Point Park:* Highlights, N.Y.C. PARKS, www.nycgovparks.org/parks/X307/highlights/19772 (last visited July 10, 2024).
66. *Bridge Park*, N.Y.C. PARKS, www.nycgovparks.org/parks/X094 (last visited July 10, 2024).
67. Press Release, N.Y.C. Parks, NYC Parks Cuts the Ribbon on Bridge Park's Renovated Waterfront (May 28, 2015), www.nycgovparks.org/parks/X094/pressrelease/21314.
68. *Concrete Plant Park*, N.Y.C. PARKS, www.nycgovparks.org/parks/concrete-plant-park (last visited July 10, 2024).
69. *Id.*
70. *Locust Point Marina*, N.Y.C. PARKS, www.nycgovparks.org/parks/locust-point-marina (last visited July 10, 2024).
71. *Locust Point Marina*, A GREAT BIG CITY, https://agreatbigcity.com/parks/locust-point-marina (last visited July 10, 2024).
72. *Mill Pond Park*, N.Y.C. PARKS, www.nycgovparks.org/parks/mill-pond-park/ (last visited July 10, 2024).
73. *Id.*
74. *Brooklyn Bridge Park*, N.Y.C. PARKS, www.nycgovparks.org/parks/brooklyn-bridge-park (last visited July 10, 2024).
75. A *Look at 10 of the New Parks of the Past 50 Years*, *infra* note 120.
76. *Bush Terminal Park*, N.Y.C. PARKS, www.nycgovparks.org/parks/bush-terminal-park (last visited July 10, 2024).
77. A *Look at 10 of the New Parks of the Past 50 Years*, *infra* note 120.
78. *Bushwick Inlet Park*, N.Y.C. PARKS, www.nycgovparks.org/parks/bushwick-inlet-park (last visited July 10, 2024).
79. *Bushwick Inlet Park Goes Green*, N.Y.C. PARKS (Oct. 23, 2013), www.nycgovparks.org/parks/bushwick-inlet-park/dailyplant/23019.
80. *Domino Park*, www.dominopark.com/ (last visited June 15, 2024); *Domino Park*, AIA N.Y., www.aiany.org/architecture/featured-projects/view/domino-park/ (last visited June 15, 2024).
81. *About Domino Park*, *infra* note 120.
82. *Marsha P. Johnson State Park (East River State Park)*, N.Y. STATE PARKS, RECREATION & HISTORIC PRESERVATION, www.parks.ny.gov/parks/155/details.aspx (last visited July 10, 2024).
83. Press Release, Rachel Gordon, N.Y. State Parks, Recreation & Historic Preservation, Playground at East River State Park Opens (Apr. 29, 2010), https://parks.ny.gov/newsroom/press-releases/release.aspx?r=785.
84. *WNYC Transmitter Park*, N.Y.C. PARKS, www.nycgovparks.org/parks/transmitter-park (last visited July 10, 2024).
85. *Id.*
86. Governors Island is technically part of New York County (Manhattan) even though it is closer to Brooklyn. *Governors Island*, www.govisland.com/ (last visited July 10, 2024). Note that this site indicates the Island is 172 acres.
87. *Governors Island: Basic Information*, NAT'L PARK SERV., www.nps.gov/gois/planyourvisit/basicinfo.htm (last visited July 10, 2024).
88. *The History of Governors Island*, GOVERNORS ISLAND, www.govisland.com/history (last visited July 10, 2024) (referring to 2005 as "the first year the Island was open to the public").
89. *Plan Your Visit*, HUDSON RIVER PARK, https://hudsonriverpark.org/visit/plan-your-visit/ (last visited July 10, 2024).

90. *Waterfront Timeline*, *infra* note 117 (noting the year the first section of the park opened to the public). The park has been built over time. Sam Roberts, *After 29 Years of Delays, a River Park Takes Shape*, N.Y. Times (May 16, 2006), www.nytimes.com/2006/05/16/nyregion/16westway.html.
91. *Experience Southpoint Park*, N.Y. State: Roosevelt Island Operating Corp., https://rioc.ny.gov/350/Experience-Southpoint-Park (last visited July 10, 2024).
92. Nick Garber, *Roosevelt Island Opens Southpoint Park Renovation: See It*, Patch (Dec. 6, 2021), https://patch.com/new-york/upper-east-side-nyc/roosevelt-island-opens-southpoint-park-renovation-see-it (noting Southpoint Park first opened in 2011).
93. *The High Line*, N.Y.C. Parks, www.nycgovparks.org/parks/the-high-line (last visited July 10, 2024).
94. *History*, *infra* note 118.
95. *Elmhurst Park*, N.Y.C. Parks, www.nycgovparks.org/parks/elmhurst-park/ (last visited July 10, 2024).
96. *Id.*
97. *Hunter's Point South Park*, N.Y.C. Parks, www.nycgovparks.org/parks/hunters-point-south-park/ (last visited July 10, 2024).
98. *A Look at 10 of the New Parks of the Past 50 Years*, *infra* note 120.
99. *Park at Beach 108 Street*, N.Y.C. Parks, www.nycgovparks.org/parks/park-at-beach-108-street (last visited July 10, 2024).
100. *Park at Beach 108 Street*, A Great Big City, https://agreatbigcity.com/parks/park-at-beach-108-street (last visited July 10, 2024).
101. *Sunset Cove Park*, N.Y.C. Parks, www.nycgovparks.org/parks/sunset-cove-park (last visited July 10, 2024).
102. *Id.* (date when the park was restored and reopened after being closed for a decade).
103. *Brookfield Park*, N.Y.C. Parks, www.nycgovparks.org/parks/brookfield-park (last visited July 10, 2024).
104. *A Look at 10 of the New Parks of the Past 50 Years*, *infra* note 120.
105. *Fairview Park*, N.Y.C. Parks, www.nycgovparks.org/parks/fairview-park (last visited July 10, 2024).
106. Giavanni Alves, *Nearly 20 Years and More than $20 Million Later, Fairview Park Finally Opens on South Shore*, N.Y.C. Council (June 2, 2021), https://council.nyc.gov/joseph-borelli/2021/06/03/nearly-20-years-and-more-than-20-million-later-fairview-park-finally-opens-on-south-shore/.
107. *Freshkills Park*, *infra* note 122. Note that "most of the site remains closed to the public." *Freshkills Park*, N.Y.C. Parks, www.nycgovparks.org/parks/freshkills-park (last visited July 10, 2024).
108. Freshkills Park: Landfill-to-Park Timeline, https://timeline.freshkillspark.org (last visited July 10, 2024) (noting the opening of "the first complete park project," Schmul Park, in 2012).
109. *Goodhue Park*, N.Y.C. Parks, www.nycgovparks.org/parks/goodhue-park (last visited July 10, 2024).
110. Michael Sedon, *Goodhue Park, New York City's Newest, Now Open for Staten Islanders*, SILive (Apr. 24, 2013), www.silive.com/news/2013/04/goodhue_park_on_the_north_shor.html
111. *Heritage Park*, N.Y.C. Parks, www.nycgovparks.org/parks/R160 (last visited July 10, 2024).
112. *Ribbon-Cutting Celebration Held at Staten Island's Heritage Park*, Trust for Pub. Land (Oct. 27, 2014), www.tpl.org/media-room/ribbon-cutting-celebration-held-staten-islands-heritage-park.

113. *Old Place Creek Park*, N.Y.C. Parks, www.nycgovparks.org/parks/old-place-creek-park (last visited July 10, 2024).
114. *Old Place Creek Is New Again*, N.Y. 1 News (Oct. 20, 2016), https://spectrumlocalnews.com/nys/buffalo/news/2016/10/19/old-place-creek-is-new-again.
115. *Richmond Terrace Park History*, N.Y.C. Parks, www.nycgovparks.org/parks/richmond-terrace-wetlands/history (last visited July 10, 2024).
116. *Id.*
117. *Waterfront Timeline*, Hudson River Park, https://hudsonriverpark.org/timeline-of-waterfront-history/ (last visited July 10, 2024) (noting the year the first section of the park opened to the public); *Ways to Support*, Hudson River Park, https://hudsonriverpark.org/get-involved/support/ (last visited July 11, 2024). Hudson River Park was established by a state law, the Hudson River Park Act, which creates a trust to govern the park; of the twelve voting members of the trust, the governor and the mayor appoint five each, and the Manhattan borough president appoints two. Hudson River Park Act, § 5.2(c), 1998 N.Y. Sess. Laws ch. 592 (McKinney). On the history of the park, which has been built gradually over the past twenty-five years, and the connections between the park and the ill-fated Westway project, see William W. Buzbee, Fighting Westway: Environmental Law, Citizen Activism, and the Regulatory War that Transformed New York City 216–19 (2014); Margolies, *supra* note 57; Platt, *supra* note 43, at 55. Federal money provided to New York State after the city and state abandoned Westway helped to pay for the construction of the road that borders Hudson River Park, and bike and walking paths. Buzbee, *supra*, at 216–17.

    The city, state, and federal governments and private sources provide funding for new construction; the Hudson River Park Trust is intended to pay for the maintenance of the park without city or state funding under the Hudson River Park Act. *Hudson River Park Trust*, Hudson River Park, https://hudsonriverpark.org/about-us/hudson-river-park-trust (last visited July 10, 2024). Hudson River Park Act § 2 (Legislative Findings and Intent).
118. *History*, High Line, www.thehighline.org/history (last visited July 10, 2024) (noting the year the first section opened to the public). *See also* Joshua David & Robert Hammond, High Line: The Inside Story of New York City's Park in the Sky (2011). New York City contributed substantially to the cost of building the High Line, but the Friends of the High Line raises funds to pay for maintenance of the park. Press Release, City of N.Y., Mayor Bloomberg, Speaker Quinn and Friends of the High Line Break Ground on the Third and Final Section of the High Line at the Rail Yards (Sept. 20, 2012), www.nyc.gov/office-of-the-mayor/news/331-12/mayor-bloomberg-speaker-quinn-friends-the-high-line-break-ground-the-third-final#/12; *About*, High Line, www.thehighline.org/about/ (last visited July 10, 2024); Loughran, *supra* note 9, at 47; Kate Ascher & Sabrina Uffer, The High Line Effect, Council on Tall Buildings & Urban Habitat 2015 Conference 224, 227 (2015), *available at* https://global.ctbuh.org/resources/papers/download/2463-the-high-line-effect.pdf.

    For supportive and critical versions of the history of the High Line and its impacts, see, respectively, Doctoroff, *supra* note 7, at 171–80, 276–77, 313–14 and Loughran, *supra* note 9, at 31–49.
119. *The Curious Garden* opens with a grim description of the Lower West Side prior to the High Line's creation: "There once was a city without gardens or trees or greenery of any kind. Most people spent their time indoors. As you can imagine, it was a very dreary

place." PETER BROWN, THE CURIOUS GARDEN (2009). Then, a young boy named Liam discovers a fledgling garden up on an abandoned railroad and helps the plants there to grow. With time, the garden flourishes, spreading across the whole railway, and eventually leads more gardens to sprout throughout the city, turning the once gray, sad city into a happy, green place. *Id.*

120. *A Look at 10 of the New Parks of the Past 50 Years*, N.Y.C. PARKS, www.nycgovparks.org/highlights/10-of-the-new-parks-of-the-past-50-years (last visited June 15, 2024); Mary Frost, *Brooklyn Bridge Park Celebrates Nearly 5 Million Visitors in 2023*, BROOKLYN DAILY EAGLE (Nov. 30, 2023) (visitors included "both locals and tourists"); *Brooklyn Bridge Park Tours and Activities*, EXPEDIA, www.expedia.com/Brooklyn-Bridge-Park-Brooklyn-Heights.d6247487.Vacation-Attraction (last visited July 11, 2024) (advertising the park as a tourist destination). Community members advocated for the creation of Brooklyn Bridge Park on the piers near Brooklyn Heights after the Port Authority indicated it would sell the land to a developer; in 2002, the city and the state bought the area from the Port Authority and funded the construction of the park. The park, which is now owned by the city, is maintained with funds from development in the park, which pays payments in lieu of taxes. *See generally* Liz Robbins, *The Battle of Brooklyn Bridge Park*, N.Y. TIMES (Aug. 1, 2014), www.nytimes.com/2014/08/03/nyregion/the-battle-of-the-brooklyn-bridge-park.html; DOCTOROFF, *supra* note 7, at 184, 192–93, 279–80; Brooklyn Bridge Park Legal Def. Fund v. N.Y. State Urb. Dev. Corp., 825 N.Y.S. 2d 347, 353, 355 (Sup. Ct. 2006), *aff'd*, 50 A.D.3d 1029 (N.Y. App. Div. 2008), *appeal denied*, 10 N.Y.3d 714 (2008). *See also* PLANYC 2011 UPDATE, *supra* note 48, at 38 (describing Brooklyn Bridge Park as "the most significant major park to be built in that borough since Prospect Park was built 135 years ago"). Domino Park opened on the Brooklyn waterfront in 2018. *About Domino Park*, DOMINO PARK, www.dominopark.com (last visited July 10, 2024). On Domino Park, see Katharine Schwab, *Can NYC's Next Big Park Recapture the Magic of the High Line?*, FAST CO. (June 7, 2018), www.fastcompany.com/90174744/can-nycs-next-big-park-recapture-the-magic-of-the-high-line; Flynn, *supra* note 54; Jared Green, *Domino Park: Privately-Owned Public Infrastructure*, THE DIRT (Jan. 27, 2022), https://dirt.asla.org/2022/01/27/domino-park-privately-managed-publicly-owned-coastal-infrastructure/.

121. Hilary Howard, *A Wildlife Oasis Opens atop a Notorious Former Dump*, N.Y. TIMES (Oct. 15, 2023), www.nytimes.com/interactive/2023/10/15/nyregion/freshkills-park-opens.html. The planning process for the park began in 2003. *2003: Draft Master Plan Announcement*, FRESHKILLS PARK (Sept. 1, 2003), https://timeline.freshkillspark.org/2003/09/draft-master-plan-announcement/. In 2012, the city opened "the first complete park project" to the public. *2012: Schmul Park Reopens*, FRESHKILLS PARK (Oct. 4, 2012), https://timeline.freshkillspark.org/2012/10/schmul-park-reopens/.

122. *Freshkills Park*, N.Y.C. PARKS, www.nycgovparks.org/park-features/freshkills-park/about-the-site (last visited July 10, 2024).

123. Our list of the twenty most populous cities is based on 2022 population estimates from the U.S. Census Bureau. *See* U.S. CENSUS BUREAU, ANNUAL ESTIMATES OF THE RESIDENT POPULATION FOR INCORPORATED PLACES OF 50,000 OR MORE, RANKED BY JULY 1, 2022 POPULATION: APRIL 1, 2020 TO JULY 1, 2022 *available at* www.census.gov/data/tables/time-series/demo/popest/2020s-total-cities-and-towns.html#tables (last visited June 14, 2024) (listing the top twenty cities by population as of 2022, from highest to lowest as: New York City, Los Angeles, Chicago, Houston, Phoenix, Philadelphia, San Antonio, San Diego, Dallas, Austin, Jacksonville, San Jose, Fort Worth, Columbus, Charlotte, Indianapolis, San Francisco, Seattle, Denver, and Oklahoma City).

124. For discussion of postindustrial parks in Chicago and Houston, see LOUGHRAN, *supra* note 9; JOSEPH D. KEARNEY & THOMAS W. MERRILL, *LAKEFRONT: PUBLIC TRUST AND PRIVATE RIGHTS IN CHICAGO* (2021).
125. Data from 2014 City Park Facts Data Tables and 2022 City Park Facts Data Tables, available at Trust for Public Land, *Park Data Downloads* www.tpl.org/parkserve/downloads (last visited July 11, 2024). It is not clear whether the 2014 data includes acreage devoted to water bodies; the 2022 data clearly excludes such acreage. In addition, there is a discrepancy in the park acreage for Houston in 2014; the data summary indicates 49,497 acres.
126. PLANYC 2007, *supra* note 26, at 129; *NYC Parks Celebrates One Millionth Tree with Bronx Community Members*, N.Y.C. PARKS (Nov. 24, 2015), www.nycgovparks.org/parks/joyce-kilmer-park/dailyplant/23507.
127. PLANYC 2007, *supra* note 26, at 14. *See also id.* at 41 ("As our need for space grows while our supply of land remains fixed, we must use our existing stock of land more efficiently. Brownfields represent one of our greatest opportunities.").
128. PLANYC 2007, *supra* note 26, at 18 (Rent-Burdened Households in New York City).
129. DOCTOROFF, *supra* note 7, at 73–74.
130. PLANYC 2007, *supra* note 26, at 21; ONENYC 2015, *supra* note 19, at 70, 74–75.
131. DOCTOROFF, *supra* note 7, at 75 ("Over twelve years, the Bloomberg Administration would propose 140 separate rezoning actions. To put it another way, we would rezone 40 percent of the entire city! Only two of the Bloomberg Administration's proposals would be defeated."); *see also Amanda M. Burden*, BLOOMBERG ASSOCIATES, https://associates.bloomberg.org/team/amanda-m-burden/ (last visited July 11, 2024) ("As Commissioner, she spearheaded the largest planning effort in the city since 1961, initiating comprehensive rezoning plans for 124 neighborhoods – almost 40% of the city – and catalyzing significant new housing opportunities in diverse communities throughout New York City's five boroughs.").

The Bloomberg rezonings included rezonings to facilitate commercial development, and downzonings and "contextual rezonings" of residential areas to limit new development in response to neighborhood pressure to preserve neighborhood character. *See generally* Vicki Been, Josiah Madar, & Simon Thomas McDonell, *Urban Land-Use Regulation: Are Homeowners Overtaking the Growth Machine*, 11 J. EMPIRICAL LEGAL STUD. 227 (2014); *see also* PLANYC 2007, *supra* note 26, at 21 (map showing publicly initiated rezonings between 2002 and 2007 indicates a considerable amount of land was being rezoned to "promote[] neighborhood preservation"); Amy Armstrong, Vicki Been, Josiah Madar, & Simon McDonnell, FURMAN CTR. FOR REAL EST. & URB. POL'Y, *POLICY BRIEF: HOW HAVE RECENT REZONINGS AFFECTED THE CITY'S ABILITY TO GROW?* 8 (2010) ("the net effect of … [the city's rezoning of 'almost 18% of the City's total lot area' in 2003-07] was to increase the City's total residential development capacity 'on paper' by about 1.7%").With the passage of time, some observers criticize the Bloomberg administration's approach to zoning for reducing development in many areas of the city and contributing to the city's housing affordability crisis in the 2020s. Nick Garber, *Bloomberg Housing Policy Faces Harsh Reassessment as Shortage Worsens*, CRAIN'S N.Y. BUS. (Apr. 8, 2024).
132. PLANYC 2007, *supra* note 26, at 41–42. The city does not actually know how much land in its borders is contaminated. LUIS INARAJA VERA, *N.Y.U. FURMAN CTR., POLICY BRIEF, MAKING DIRTY LAND CLEAN: AN ANALYSIS OF NEW YORK CITY'S VOLUNTARY CLEANUP PROGRAM* 14 (2018), https://furmancenter.org/files/Analysis_of_NYC_Voluntary_Cleanup_Program.pdf (citing PLANYC 2007, *supra* note 26, at 43).

133. "Brownfields are properties with actual or potential environmental contamination that could complicate expansion or redevelopment activities on the site." INARAJA VERA, *supra* note 132, at 2 (citation omitted). See also Comprehensive Environmental Response, Compensation, and Liability Act, 42 U.S.C. § 9601(39)(A) (defining "brownfield site").
   On the city program, see PLANYC 2007, *supra* note 26, at 44; PLANYC 2011 UPDATE, *supra* note 48, at 50–57; ONENYC 2015, *supra* note 19, at 194–95; INARAJA VERA, *supra* note 132, at 3; DOCTOROFF, *supra* note 7, at 76, 78.
134. INARAJA VERA, *supra* note 132, at 5, 12–14; *see also* ONENYC 2015, *supra* note 19, at 196–97; *Voluntary Cleanup*, N.Y.C. OFF. OF ENV'T REMEDIATION, www.nyc.gov/site/oer/remediation/voluntary-cleanup.page (last visited July 11, 2024).
   In 1993, Chicago established a program to remediate brownfields in the city to enable them to be redeveloped. Under the Chicago Brownfields Initiative, the city government acquires the contaminated properties, cleans them up, and transfers them for development. Jessica Higgins, Note, *Evaluating the Chicago Brownfields Initiative: The Effects of City-Initiated Brownfield Redevelopment on Surrounding Communities*, 3 NW. J.L. & SOC. POL'Y 240 (2008).
135. INARAJA VERA, *supra* note 132, at 7–8.
136. *Id.* at 8; N.Y.U. FURMAN CTR., STATE OF NEW YORK CITY'S HOUSING AND NEIGHBORHOODS IN 2015, at 6 (2016), *available at* https://furmancenter.org/research/sonychan/2015-report.
137. On the relationship between the brownfields that are cleaned up and development, *see also* N.Y.C. WATERFRONT PLAN 2021, *supra* note 48, at 192; EJNYC, *supra* note 53, at 8, 18.
138. Press Release, Env't Prot. Agency, EPA Awards $9.35 Million to New York to Improve Air Quality (Nov. 12, 2019), www.epa.gov/newsreleases/epa-awards-935-million-new-york-improve-air-quality; Dwyer, *supra* note 60.
   Research indicates that in the U.S. generally, the Clean Air Act had significant impacts on air quality within a few years of its passage. *See, e.g.*, Adam Isen et al., *Every Breath You Take – Every Dollar You'll Make: Long-Term Consequences of the Clean Air Act of 1970*, 125 *J.* POL. ECON. 848, 851 (2017). The magnitude of improvements in air quality increased as time went on. *See, e.g.*, J. Vernon Henderson, *Effects of Air Quality Regulation*, 86 AM. ECON. REV. 789, 790 (1996).
139. *See, e.g.*, Juan Moreno-Cruz, *Understanding the Industrial Contribution to Pollution Offers Opportunities to Further Improve Air Quality in the United States*, 116 PNAS 19768 (2019).
140. PLANYC 2007, *supra* note 26, at 119 (New York City not in compliance with ambient air quality standards for ozone and PM2.5); *New York Nonattainment/Maintenance Status for Each County by Year for All Criteria Pollutants*, U.S. ENV'T. PROT. AGENCY, www3.epa.gov/airquality/greenbook/anayo_ny.html (last visited June 15, 2024) (nonattainment in year 2024 for ozone levels in Bronx, Kings, New York, Queens, and Richmond Counties).
141. PLANYC 2007, *supra* note 26, at 121; *see also id.* at 89.
142. *Id.* at 89, 123; Katrina M. Wyman & Danielle Spiegel-Feld, *The Urban Environmental Renaissance*, 108 CAL. L. REV. 305, 359–60 (2020); Rebecca Bratspies, *Protecting the Environment in an Era of Federal Retreat: The View from New York City*, 13 *FIU* L. REV. 5, 31–32 (2018); BRASH, *supra* note 1, at 260.
143. PLANYC 2007, *supra* note 26, at 88–89, 91, 122.
144. Winnie Hu & Anna Ley, *New York City Welcomes Congestion Pricing with Fanfare and Complaints*, N.Y. TIMES (Jan. 5, 2025), https://www.nytimes.com/2025/01/05/nyregion/nyc-congestion-pricing-tolls.html; N.Y. Veh. & Traf. Law §§ 1701-1706.

145. *Hearing on Local Law No. 43 before the Comm. on Env't Prot.*, at 12 (May 28, 2010) (testimony of Daniel Kass, Deputy Comm'r for Env't Health, Dep't of Health & Mental Hygiene) [hereainafter Kass Testimony]. *See also* PLANYC 2007, *supra* note 26, at 129, 155; PLANYC 2011 UPDATE, *supra* note 48, at 124; EJNYC, *supra* note 53, at 80 (describing the New York City Community Air Survey as "the largest ongoing urban air monitoring program in the United States").
146. PLANYC 2007, *supra* note 26, at 129.
147. Kass Testimony, *supra* note 145, at 13.
148. *Id.* at 14–15.
149. *Id.* at 19 (testimony of Cas Holloway, Comm'r, Dep't of Env't Prot.).
150. Lyuou Zhang et al., *Evaluating the Impact of the Clean Heat Program on Air Pollution Levels in New York City*, 129 ENV'T HEALTH PERSPS. 127701 (2021); *see also* Diana Hernandez, *Clean Heat: A Technical Response to a Policy Innovation*, 18 CITYSCAPE 277 (2016). Kevin Cromar, who is an associate professor of environmental medicine at New York University's Grossman School of Medicine, and Jason Schwartz, who is legal director at the Institute for Policy Integrity at New York University's School of Law, were instrumental in developing the data that built the scientific case for phasing out residual fuel oils. *See* KEVIN R. CROMAR & JASON A. SCHWARTZ, *INST. FOR POL'Y INTEGRITY, RESIDUAL RISKS: THE UNSEEN COSTS OF USING DIRTY OIL IN NEW YORK CITY'S BOILERS* (Jan. 2010), *available at* https://policyintegrity.org/files/publications/ResidualRisks.pdf. Data collected by the Environmental Defense Fund and the Urban Green Council also played a role. *See* ENVIRONMENTAL DEFENSE FUND & URBAN GREEN COUNCIL, *THE BOTTOM OF THE BARREL: HOW THE DIRTIEST HEATING OIL POLLUTES OUR AIR AND HARMS OUR HEALTH* (Dec. 2009), *available at* www.edf.org/sites/default/files/10085_EDF_Heating_Oil_Report.pdf.
151. N.Y.C. Dep't of Health & Mental Hygiene, 88 EPI DATA BRIEF 2 (2017), www1.nyc.gov/assets/doh/downloads/pdf/epi/databrief88.pdf. Admittedly, the majority of areas that had the worst air pollution prior to the Clean Heat Program were in Manhattan and this is still the case today. Komal Shukla et al., *Zip Code Level Estimation of Air Quality and Health Risk Due to Particulate Matter Pollution in New York City*, 56 ENV'T SCI. & TECH. 7119 (2022). As such, one could argue that the program reduced air pollution in wealthy areas the most. But all boroughs saw local sulfur dioxide levels fall following implementation of the Clean Heat program. N.Y.C. Dep't of Health & Mental Hygiene, *supra*; EJNYC, *supra* note 53, at 75. And given that low-income populations in New York City appear to be more vulnerable to the impacts of air pollution than higher-income areas, the health benefits may actually have been greatest in lower-income areas. *See, e.g.*, Shukla et al., *supra*, at Fig. 4 (predicting that some areas of the Bronx will be among the NYC neighborhoods to experience the greatest reduction in avoidable deaths and asthma-related hospital visits if fuel oil #4 is eliminated from commercial and residential buildings, even though they will not be among the areas to see the greatest change in PM 2.5 concentrations as a result of the phase out). *See also id.* at 7120 ("NYC is demographically and geographically diverse with about 192 (fused in some cases to facilitate stable health rate estimates) Zip Code Tabulation Areas (ZCTAs) … Health and monetary co-benefits from pollution reduction vary among ZCTAs because of these distinct population characteristics"); EJNYC, *supra* note 53, at 77 ("Generally, the neighborhoods that experience the greatest levels of pollution are not the neighborhoods that suffer the most pollution-attributable health outcomes. Adverse health outcomes related to pollution are concentrated in low-income communities and communities of color, particularly Black and Hispanic or Latino communities.").

152. *See also Hearing on Int. No. 886 and Int. No. 359 Before the N.Y. Council Comm. on Env't Prot.* 3 (Jan. 28, 2016) (testimony of Nilda Mesa, Director, Mayor's Off. of Sustainability) ("[O]ur Clean Heat programs will reduce emissions most in high income neighborhoods, yet the largest share of health benefits will occur in low income neighborhoods. In NYC, unlike other cities or nationwide, we do not observe consistent differences in levels of fine particulate matter (PM2.5) by neighborhood poverty, but there are strong differences in PM2.5-attributable health events due to underlying neighborhood susceptibility. This is why it's so important to consider poverty levels along with environmental pollution sources when pursuing environmental justice.").
153. *See* Boston, Mass., Regulations for the Control of Atmospheric Pollution, Reg. 2 (2019), *available at* www.boston.gov/sites/default/files/embed/a/air_pollution_regs.pdf; N.Y.C., N.Y., Local Law of 2010 No. 43 (2010); N.Y.C. Dep't of Env't Prot., Rules Governing the Emissions from the Use of #4 and #6 Fuel Oil in Heat and Hot Water Boilers and Burners (2011); Katie Pyzyk, *Philly Mayor Signs Law to Boost Big Building Efficiency, Phase out Dirty Fuel*, SMARTCITIESDIVE (Dec. 12, 2019), www.smartcitiesdive.com/news/philly-mayor-signs-laws-to-boost-big-building-efficiency-phase-out-dirty-f/568931/.
154. On the distinction between upstream and downstream regulation, see Wyman & Spiegel-Feld, *supra* note 142, at 340 and the sources cited therein.
    Although the federal government often regulates pollution upstream, for example by regulating power plants and industrial facilities and establishing pollution standards for manufactured products, local governments also may have some ability to regulate upstream. For example, cities that own electric utilities might be able to control emissions from the power sector. *See* Shelley Welton, *Public Energy*, 92 N.Y.U. L. REV. 267, 272, 290 (2017); Alexandra B. Klass & Rebecca Wilton, *Local Power*, 75 VAND. L. REV. 93, 100–01, 104, 114, 118–19, 143 (2022). Even if a city does not own an electric utility, it might be able to influence the emissions and other affairs of a utility serving its residents through the terms of the franchise agreement between the city and the utility. Klass & Wilton, *supra*, at 116, 137–40, 145, 154.
155. NEW YORKERS FOR DE BLASIO, ONE NEW YORK, RISING TOGETHER 2 (2013).
156. *Id.*
157. GONZÁLEZ, *supra* note 11, at 3 (citing JAMES PARROT, N.Y. FISCAL POL'Y INST., *BRIEFING ON MAYOR DE BLASIO'S PRELIMINARY FY 2016 NYC BUDGET: ADDRESSING NEEDS AND BUDGETING CAUTIOUSLY AS THE RECOVERY PROGRESSES* 24 (2015)).
158. Mayor de Blasio's first Housing Plan illustrates the pervasive concerns about housing unaffordability. THE CITY OF NEW YORK, MAYOR BILL DE BLASIO, HOUSING NEW YORK, A FIVE-BOROUGH, TEN-YEAR PLAN 5 (2014), www1.nyc.gov/assets/buildings/pdf/housing_plan.pdf. In considering the prevalence of rent burdened households, it is worth keeping in mind that only approximately 31 percent of New York households own their homes (as of 2021). N.Y.C. DEP'T OF HOUSING PRESERVATION & DEV., 2021 NEW YORK CITY HOUSING AND VACANCY SURVEY SELECTED INITIAL FINDINGS 9 (2022), www1.nyc.gov/assets/hpd/downloads/pdfs/services/2021-nychvs-selected-initial-findings.pdf.
159. *See, e.g.*, ONE NEW YORK, RISING TOGETHER, *supra* note 155, at 52–56, 69–72. Notwithstanding de Blasio's emphasis on addressing income inequality – and racial inequalities manifest in Bloomberg-era policies such as stop-and-frisk – the term "environmental justice" did not appear once in his platform. In the platform, de Blasio promised to "implement the" 2006 solid waste plan "including opening the 91st Street Marine Transfer Station." *Id.* at 56.
160. Chapters 4 and 5 consider de Blasio's impact on local policies to limit and adapt to climate change.

161. Mayor de Blasio's support for Amazon building a second headquarters in New York is an example of his interest in promoting economic development. After Amazon reversed its decision to establish such a headquarters following criticisms from progressive Democrats, de Blasio stuck by his support for the ill-fated attempt to attract Amazon to New York, while criticizing Amazon for withdrawing. CNN reported that de Blasio told Meet the Press, "'I am representing 8.6 million people, and a clear majority of those believe we need more fairness in our economy. But of course, we need jobs, we need growth, we need revenue,' said the mayor, who called himself a progressive. 'Progressives can do both.'" Jill Disis, *New York Mayor Says Amazon Headquarters Debacle Was 'An Abuse of Corporate Power'*, CNN (Feb. 17, 2019), www.cnn.com/2019/02/17/tech/bill-de-blasio-amazon-hq2/index.html.
162. *NYC Recession Blog*, CITIZENS' BUDGET COMM. N.Y. 1 (Feb. 26, 2019), https://cbcny.org/sites/default/files/media/files/Recession%20Feb26.pdf; Lydia Polgreen, *Study Confirms 9/11 Impact on New York City Economy*, N.Y. TIMES (June 30, 2004), www.nytimes.com/2004/06/30/nyregion/study-confirms-9-11-impact-on-new-york-city-economy.html.
163. Jason Bram, *How Did New York City's Economy Weather the Pandemic?*, LIBERTY ST. ECON. (Apr. 13, 2023), https://libertystreeteconomics.newyorkfed.org/2023/04/how-did-new-york-citys-economy-weather-the-pandemic/.
164. *Fiscal 2018–2022 Financial Plan Overview*, N.Y.C. COUNCIL, https://council.nyc.gov/budget/fy18-22_financial_plan_overview/ (last visited Feb. 14, 2024); Emma G. Fitzsimmons, *De Blasio's Costly Legacy: The Biggest City Work Force Ever*, N.Y. TIMES (Dec. 31, 2021), www.nytimes.com/2021/12/31/nyregion/de-blasio-budget-unions-nyc.html.
165. ONENYC 2015, *supra* note 19, at 14 ("The explicit addition of equity is critical, because a widening opportunity gap threatens the city's future."). *See also* Samar Khurshid, *De Blasio's Record on Jobs and the Economy*, GOTHAM GAZETTE (Oct. 24, 2017), www.gothamgazette.com/city/7270-de-blasio-s-record-on-jobs-and-the-economy (discussing de Blasio's focus on inequality).
166. Signifying the newfound focus on equity as a priority on par with economic growth, the de Blasio administration changed the name of the city's sustainability plan from "PlaNYC" to "OneNYC" to convey its commitment to bridging divides in the city. *See, e.g.*, ONENYC 2015, *supra* note 19, at 5 ("We have made equity an explicit guiding principle – a lens through which we view all of our planning, policymaking, and governing."). OneNYC is organized around four principles: "growth, equity, sustainability, and resiliency[,]" and the four major sections of OneNYC are devoted to each principle, respectively. *Id.* at 5–6. *See also* Jarrett Murphy, *On the Environment, De Blasio Defied Expectations with Bold Goals, but Now Must Deliver*, CITYLIMITS (Nov. 2, 2017), https://citylimits.org/2017/11/02/on-the-environment-de-blasio-defied-expectations-with-bold-goals-but-now-must-deliver/ ("like everything in the de Blasio administration, achievements under OneNYC are viewed through an 'equity lens'").

    The de Blasio administration's first iteration of OneNYC, released in 2015, featured a full-page box titled "Environmental Justice" that listed various areas in which the administration was committed to addressing environmental inequities.
167. Rachel Holliday Smith, *Skylines and Streetscapes: How New York City Physically Changed in de Blasio Era*, THE CITY (Dec. 19, 2021), www.thecity.nyc/2021/12/29/skylines-and-streetscapes-how-new-york-city-physically-changed-in-de-blasio-era/; *see also* CITY OF N.Y., ONENYC 2050: BUILDING A STRONG AND FAIR CITY 26 (2019), https://climate.cityofnewyork.us/wp-content/uploads/2022/10/OneNYC-2050-Summary.pdf.
168. Stefanos Chen, *The People vs. Big Development*, N.Y. TIMES (last updated Sept. 10, 2021), www.nytimes.com/2020/02/07/realestate/the-people-vs-big-development.html;

Mihir Zaveri, *Plan to Bring More Housing to SoHo Is Approved*, N.Y. TIMES (Dec. 15, 2021), www.nytimes.com/2021/12/15/nyregion/soho-rezoning-vote.html.

169. Lachlan Hyatt, *"We Really Changed the Structure of Housing Production": Vicki Been on the de Blasio Administration's Affordable Housing Record & What Comes Next*, GOTHAM GAZETTE (Jan. 28, 2022), www.gothamgazette.com/city/11041-vicki-been-challenges-opportunities-in-affordable-housing-development-policy-de-blasio.

170. ONENYC 2015, *supra* note 19, at 194 ("Brownfield cleanup and redevelopment represents one of our best opportunities to engage communities and reclaim land for development in the city.").

171. *Id.*; *see also id.* at 197 ("Over the next four years, we will double the number of place-based community brownfield planning areas by designating twenty new neighborhoods and focusing our incentives to help them better identify strategic brownfield properties and implement community development projects."); EJNYC, *supra* note 53, at 180 (describing the "Place-Based Community Brownfield Planning" program and indicating that it has existed since 2005).

On the connection between cleaning up brownfields and environmental justice, *see, e.g.*, Lincoln L. Davies, Note, *Working toward a Common Goal? Three Case Studies of Brownfields Redevelopment in Environmental Justice Communities*, 18 STAN. ENV'T L.J. 285 (1999).

172. ONENYC 2015, *supra* note 19, at 206. The full sentence is: "Parks and public space are essential to economic development, civic engagement, and community revitalization, promoting interaction with neighbors, attracting visitors, and providing a venue for art and culture." *Id.* This is not the only reference to the economic benefits of parks in the plan. On the same page, it states: "Beautiful parks and public spaces improve quality of life, attracting residents and businesses to New York City." *Id.*

For an example of a de Blasio era investment in a premier public space in Manhattan, see Dana Rubinstein, *De Blasio Signals Possible Shift in Parks Strategy*, POLITICO (Apr. 25, 2017), www.ny4p.org/news/politico-de-blasio-parks-strategy (reporting that the city planned to spend $100 million to reduce a gap in the Manhattan Waterfront Greenway, while noting that de Blasio had built fewer acres of parks than Bloomberg).

173. Data compiled by Adalene Minelli and Sara Savarani for this book from NYC's Open Data about Parks Properties indicates that, during the Bloomberg administration, between 2002 and 2013, the city parks department acquired 426.98 acres of land, of which 263.75 acres was on the waterfront (almost 62 percent). During the de Blasio administration, between 2014 and 2021, the city parks department acquired 255.69 acres, of which 236.79 acres was on the waterfront (almost 93 percent). NYC Open Data, Parks Properties, *supra* note 52. Acquired for these purposes means "designated under NYC Parks' jurisdiction." NYC Open Data, User Guide, *supra* note 52.

174. *Community Parks Initiative*, N.Y.C. PARKS, www.nycgovparks.org/about/framework-for-an-equitable-future/community-parks-initiative (last visited Feb. 19, 2024). *See also* N.Y.C. PARKS, *NYC PARKS: FRAMEWORK FOR AN EQUITABLE FUTURE* 9 (2014) (referring to the Community Parks Initiative as "NYC Parks' leading effort to comprehensively invest in New York City's under-resourced communities"); Lisa W. Foderaro, *Correction Seen After Years of Disinvestment in Neighborhood Parks*, N.Y. TIMES (Oct. 7, 2014), www.nytimes.com/2014/10/08/nyregion/correction-seen-after-years-of-disinvestment-in-neighborhood-parks.html; ONENYC 2015, *supra* note 19, at 208 (describing the de Blasio administration's commitment to increasing "the utility of parks and public space in under-resourced and growing neighborhoods" and referring to the Community Parks Initiative); Press Release, First Day of Spring: Mayor de Blasio Opens

Five Newly Improved Parks Across All Five Boroughs in One Day (Mar. 20, 2018), www.nyc.gov/office-of-the-mayor/news/145-18/first-day-spring-mayor-de-blasio-opens-five-newly-improved-parks-across-all-five-boroughs-in.

In a report published in 2021, the last year of the de Blasio administration, the city indicated that "[b]etween 2014 and the pandemic, the City has … targeted $318 million in a community parks initiative to rebuild 67 parks that had seen little or no investment in the prior two decades in growing, lower-income neighborhoods." CITY OF N.Y. DEP'T OF HOUS. PRES. & DEV., WHERE WE LIVE NYC: FAIR HOUSING TOGETHER 28 (2020), www1.nyc.gov/assets/hpd/downloads/pdfs/wwl-plan.pdf [hereinafter WHERE WE LIVE NYC].

175. ONENYC 2015, *supra* note 19, at 208.

176. MELISSA CHECKER, THE SUSTAINABILITY MYTH: ENVIRONMENTAL GENTRIFICATION AND THE POLITICS OF JUSTICE (2020); LOUGHRAN, *supra* note 9; KENNETH GOULD & TAMMY LEWIS, GREEN GENTRIFICATION: URBAN SUSTAINABILITY AND THE STRUGGLE FOR ENVIRONMENTAL JUSTICE (2017); Laura Kusisto, *New York City's Parks Grow with Private Funds*, WALL ST. J. (July 7, 2013) ("Mr. Bloomberg's approach has been controversial. Community groups have complained it creates a disparity between parks in wealthy neighborhoods and those in poorer places."); Tom Angotti, *On the Waterfront*, THE INDYPENDENT (Nov. 19, 2012), https://indypendent.org/2012/11/on-the-waterfront/ (criticizing Bloomberg's legacy development projects on the waterfront). For a synthesis of various critiques of the green growth agenda, and evidence that green growth rhetoric and high costs of living are correlated, see Melissa Garcia-Lamarca et al., *Urban Boosterism and City Affordability: For Whom Is the 'Branded' Green City?*, 58 URB. STUD. 90 (2019).

177. LOUGHRAN, *supra* note 9, at 93. As Loughran mentions, the idea of creating parks to boost property values is not novel; increasing the value of privately owned land was one of the motivations for establishing Central Park. *Id.* at 92.

Loughran also criticizes cities' increasing reliance on private groups such as the Friends of the High Line to manage and fund marquee parks. He argues that it widens the spread between the quality of green space that the elite and other urban residents enjoy and contributes to these parks being elite preserves that benefit the wealthy and private developers. *Id.* at 93, 179.

178. Press Release, New York City Parks, Mayor Bloomberg Cuts Ribbon on $7.2 Million Barretto Point Park in the South Bronx (Oct. 3, 2006), www.nycgovparks.org/news/press-releases?id=20262. According to a *New York Times* story reporting the launch of de Blasio's Community Parks Initiative, "$80 million of the $130 million in the new plan was allotted specifically to neighborhood parks in Mr. Bloomberg's preliminary 2015 budget, released shortly before he left office." Foderaro, *supra* note 174. *See also* Rubinstein, *Bloomberg Official Responds to de Blasio's Parks Criticism*, *supra* note 20; Michael Kimmelman, *Mayor de Blasio's Plan for Parks Needs to Grow*, N.Y. TIMES (Oct. 28, 2014), www.nytimes.com/2014/10/29/arts/design/mayor-de-blasios-plan-for-parks-needs-to-grow.html; Rubinstein, *De Blasio Promises*, *supra* note 20.

Notably, the Bloomberg administration's original PlaNYC, released in 2007, quantified the differential access to parks across city neighborhoods and aimed to address this inequity, "in the interest of public health and environmental justice." PLANYC 2007, *supra* note 26, at 30. It aimed "to ensure that nearly every New Yorker lives within a 10-minute walk of a park by 2030." *Id.* at 31. *See also* PLANYC 2011 UPDATE, *supra* note 48, at 34 ("over two million New Yorkers still live more than a 10-minute walk from [a park]"); Christina D. Rosan, *Can PlaNYC Make New York City "Greener and Greater" for Everyone?: Sustainability Planning and the Promise of Environmental Justice*, 17: 9 LOCAL ENVIRONMENT 959, 968 (2012) (arguing that the planning process for PlaNYC included environmental justice advocates and addressed some of the priorities of environmental justice groups, and "noting that PlaNYC 2030 explicitly uses the term 'environmental justice' seven times while other sustainability plans in large US cities do not mention the term").

179. According to the Trust for Public Land's survey of the 100 most populated U.S. cities, "residents who identify as people of color have about the same and in some cases better 10-minute walk access compared to white residents." TRUST FOR PUBLIC LAND, 2021 CITY PARK FACTS: THE YEAR IN PARKS 2 (May 2021). However, "[o]n average, among the 100 cities, residents of neighborhoods where most people identify as Black, Hispanic and Latinx, Indigenous and Native American, or Asian American and Pacific Islander have access to 44 percent less park space per person than do residents in neighborhoods that are predominantly white. This disparity is most significant in Hispanic/Latinx neighborhoods, where residents have access to 54% less park acreage per person than those in white neighborhoods." *Id.* In New York City, 99 percent of the population lives within a half mile (10 minutes) walk from a park, but "[r]esidents in neighborhoods of color" have 33 percent less park space per person than people living in "white neighborhoods." *Trust for Public Land, 2021 City Park Facts Data Tables, Acreage Park System Highlights* (Distribution of Park Space & Walkable Park Access), available at www.tpl.org/park-data-downloads (last visited June 15, 2024); *see also* EJNYC, *supra* note 53, at 7 ("New York City has made great progress toward its goals of increasing access to parks and open space, however, there remains a gap in park density: the average amount of accessible park space is 9 acres per 1,000 residents in EJ [Environmental Justice] Areas and 11 acres per 1,000 residents in non-EJ Areas, amounting to a 19 percent deficit for residents in EJ Areas."). In the twentieth century, Robert Moses famously built many parks in New York City, but of the "255 parks" he built in "the five boroughs, … only one … was in Harlem." Vernice D. Miller, *Planning, Power and Politics: A Case Study of the Land Use and Siting History of the North River Water Pollution Control Plant*, 21 *FORDHAM URB. L.J.* 707, 714 & 714 n.44 (1994) (citing ROBERT CARO, THE POWER BROKER: ROBERT MOSES AND THE FALL OF NEW YORK 510 (1974)).

180. Indeed, the New York City Environmental Justice Alliance warned that the choice to allocate funding under the Community Parks Initiative to "growing neighborhoods" "could mean that park investments under this program would reward rapidly gentrifying communities with increased park investments, thereby creating a wicked loop where gentrifying communities attract a disproportionate share of park investments, which in turn spurs even more displacement." N.Y.C. ENV'T JUST. ALL., *NYC CLIMATE JUSTICE AGENDA: STRENGTHENING THE MAYOR'S ONENYC PLAN* 26 (2016).

As Professor Sarah Fox explains, "The exact parameters of gentrification have been notoriously difficult to define…. Broadly speaking, however, gentrification refers to changes in a neighborhood that occur as 'higher-income groups move into low-income areas, potentially altering the cultural and financial landscape of the original neighborhood.'" Sarah Fox, *Environmental Gentrification*, 90 U. COLO. L. REV. 803, 805 (2019) (quoting U.S. DEP'T OF HOUS. & URB. DEV., ENSURING EQUITABLE NEIGHBORHOOD CHANGE: GENTRIFICATION PRESSURES ON HOUSING AFFORDABILITY 1 (2016), www.huduser.gov/portal/sites/default/files/pdf/Insights-Ensuring-Equitable-Growth.pdf).

181. CHECKER, *supra* note 176, at 13. *See also* ENVIRONMENTAL JUSTICE INTERAGENCY WORKING GROUP, *NEW YORK CITY'S ENVIRONMENTAL JUSTICE FOR ALL REPORT:*

Scope of Work 13 (2021) ("Some community members and advocates have expressed concerns that the provision of environmental benefits, which aim to improve the physical environment and quality of life for New Yorkers, may contribute to displacement and neighborhood change.").

Sometimes the amenities that give rise to concern are not physical green space, such as new parks, but "gray" infrastructure that is merely associated with sustainability. For example, in 2017, when the de Blasio administration announced plans to add a protected bike lane to Sunset Park, a formerly industrial part of Brooklyn, community activists objected to the idea out of concern that it would bring in a wave of wealthier residents. Caroline Spivack, *Sunset Parkers Clash over Fourth Avenue Bike Lane*, Brooklyn Paper (May 18, 2017), www.brooklynpaper.com/sunset-parkers-clash-over-fourth-avenue-bike-lane/ ("'Cyclists are thought of as rolling gentrification through our community,' said Sunset Parker Elizabeth Yeampierre, the head of local activist group Uprose. 'And when they show up, whether it's in Red Hook or Bushwick, it's the end of our time.'").

182. Chen, *supra* note 168. *See also* Isabelle Anguelovski & James J.T. Connolly, *Introduction: Positioning Urban Green Injustices*, *in* The Green City and Social Injustice: 21 Tales from North America and Europe 1, 9 (Isabelle Anguelovski & James J.T. Connolly eds., 2022) (discussing general trends in displacement of low-income residents of color after green infrastructure projects are built).

183. *See generally* Vicki Been, Ingrid Gould Ellen & Katherine O'Regan, Furman Ctr., Supply Skepticism: Housing Supply and Affordability (2018); Vicki Been, Ingrid Gould Ellen & Katherine O'Regan, Supply Skepticism Revisited (NYU Law & Economics Research Paper, 2023), https://papers.ssrn.com/sol3/papers.cfm?abstract_id=4629628#.

A 2016 report by NYU's Furman Center found that fifteen of twenty-two sub-borough areas that were classified as "low income" in 1990 were "gentrifying" by 2014. N.Y.U. Furman Ctr., *supra* note 136, at 5–6. Williamsburg-Greenpoint, one of the neighborhoods that Checker highlights and that was rezoned in the Bloomberg administration to facilitate more development, experienced the highest rent increases of any sub-borough area between 1990 and 2010–2014. *Id.* The Furman Center report equates "gentrification" with "rapid rent growth in low-income neighborhoods." *Id.* at 4. Compare Gould & Lewis, *supra* note 176, at 9 ("Brooklyn's rising rents and home prices are outpacing the rest of the city. From 2004 to 2014, median home prices rose 44 percent in Brooklyn but only 30 percent in Manhattan. Median rents from 2012 to 2015 rose 26 percent in Brooklyn and only 13 percent in Manhattan."). On the rezoning of Williamsburg-Greenpoint during the Bloomberg administration, see Diane Cardwell, *City Is Backing Makeover for Decaying Brooklyn Waterfront*, N.Y. Times (May 3, 2005), www.nytimes.com/2005/05/03/nyregion/city-is-backing-makeover-for-decaying-brooklyn-waterfront.html.

184. Gould & Lewis, *supra* note 176; Seung Kyum Kim & Longfeng Wu, *Do the Characteristics of New Green Space Contribute to Gentrification?*, 59 Urb. Stud. 360 (2022); Isabelle Anguelovski et al., *Green Gentrification in European and North American Cities*, 13 Nature Commc'ns 3816 (2022); Jessica Quinton et al., *How Well Do We Know Green Gentrification? A Systematic Review of the Methods*, 46 Progress in Hum. Geography 960 (2022); Alisha Yee Chan et al., *Displacement of Racially and Ethnically Minoritized Groups after the Installation of Stormwater Control Measures (i.e., Green Infrastructure): A Case Study of Washington, DC*, 18 Int'l J. Env't Rsch. & Pub. Health 10054 (2021).

185. Galia Shokry, James J.T. Connolly & Isabelle Anguelovski, *Understanding Climate Gentrification and Shifting Landscapes of Protection and Vulnerability in Green Resilient Philadelphia*, 31 URB. CLIMATE 100539, at 12 (2020) (green resilient infrastructure might be both a "cause and consequence [of] gentrification"); Trina Hamilton & Winifred Curran, *From "Five Angry Women" to "Kick-Ass Community": Gentrification and Environmental Activism in Brooklyn and Beyond*, 50 URB. STUD. 1557, 1561 (2013) (discussing "gentrifier-enhanced environmental activism," in which "gentrifiers" join long-standing local activists to fight for environmental improvements, such as the clean-up of Newtown Creek in Brooklyn, New York).

186. *See* ENV'T JUST. INTERAGENCY WORKING GRP., *NEW YORK CITY'S ENVIRONMENTAL JUSTICE FOR ALL REPORT: SCOPE OF WORK* 13 (2021) ("Understanding, measuring, and preventing displacement (whether associated with environmental benefits or not) requires broad policies on housing affordability, workforce development, and more equitable incomes[.]"); Emilia Oscilowicz, Sarka Hajtmarova, & Isabelle Anguelovski, *Enacting Just Urban Green Futures: Promising Policy and Planning Tools and Regulations for Europe and North America*, *in* THE GREEN CITY AND SOCIAL INJUSTICE: 21 TALES FROM NORTH AMERICA AND EUROPE 295 (Isabelle Anguelovski & James J.T. Connolly eds., 2022) (identifying policy options).

Some argue that investments in low-income neighborhoods and communities of color should be "just green enough." Michael Maciag, *New York City Gentrification Maps and Data*, GOVERNING (Jan. 29, 2015), *available at* www.governing.com/archive/new-york-gentrification-maps-demographic-data.html; Winifred Curran & Trina Hamilton, *Just Green Enough: Contesting Environmental Gentrification in Greenpoint, Brooklyn*, 17 LOCAL ENV'T 1027, 1028 (2012) ("The 'just green enough' strategy organises for cleanup and green space aimed at the existing working-class population and industrial land users, not at new development."); Alessandro Rigolon et al., *More than "Just Green Enough": Helping Park Professionals Achieve Equitable Greening and Limit Environmental Gentrification*, 38 J. PARK & RECREATION ADMIN. 29, 33 (2020) (arguing that the "just green enough" approach favors the creation of small, rather than iconic, public spaces, but not fewer public spaces, in historically disadvantaged communities and that this approach also can include creating new affordable housing). It is important to note that there are some environmental justice advocates who are actively seeking more greenery in communities of color and low-income neighborhoods; for example, WE ACT for Environmental Justice listed "Trees in Northern Manhattan" as one of its advocacy priorities for 2023 in their "2023 Policy Agenda." WE ACT FOR ENVIRONMENTAL JUSTICE, 2023 POLICY AGENDA, CAMPAIGNS AND INITIATIVES 8 (2023).

187. *See, e.g.*, Rebecca Bratspies, *"Underburdened" Communities*, 110 CALIF. L. REV. 1933, 1940–42, 1956–57 (2022); Peggy M. Shepard, *Issues of Community Empowerment*, 21 FORDHAM URB. L.J. 739, 739–40 (1994). In New York City, not only waste facilities, but other kinds of polluting facilities, such as highways, bus depots, and power plants, are located in or near communities of color and low-income neighborhoods. EJNYC, *supra* note 53, at 30–34.

188. *See generally* SZE, *supra* note 22, at Ch. 4.

189. Bratspies, *supra* note 187, at 1960 (The "focus" of New York City's 2006 Solid Waste Management Plan "on equity was a direct result of advocacy from grassroots environmental justice organizations that tirelessly documented the many ways the current system placed undue burdens on New York's low-income communities of color."); *id.* at 1960 n.173 ("Probably no single person did more to make this plan a reality than Eddie Bautista, the leader of NYC-EJA [New York City Environmental Justice Alliance].") (citations omitted).

Other early environmental justice campaigns in New York City are described in SZE, *supra* note 22. These include the campaign led by West Harlem Environmental Act, Inc. (WE ACT) to persuade the Metropolitan Transportation Authority (MTA), which operates the largest public bus fleet in North America, to replace its diesel buses with less polluting buses. Northern Manhattan houses a disproportionate number of the boroughs' bus depots, and WE ACT argued that the buses exacerbated rates of asthma in the area, which were already among the highest in the United States. Peggy Shepard, *Breathe at Your Own Risk: Transit Justice in West Harlem*, 12 *RACE, POVERTY & ENV'T* 51 (Winter 2005/2006); SZE, *supra* note 22, at 91–108; WE ACT for Env't Just., Press Release, WE ACT Files Title VI Complaint against MTA (Nov. 15, 2000), www.weact.org/2000/11/we-act-files-title-vi-complaint-against-mta/; *Dirty Diesel Campaign*, WE ACT, www.weact.org/campaigns/dirty-diesel-campaign/ (last visited Feb. 21, 2024). In the late 1990s, there was a similar campaign by environmental justice groups in coalition with others to get the Massachusetts Bay Transit Authority to replace its diesel buses with compressed natural gas buses. Julian Agyeman et al., *Trends and Directions in Environmental Justice: From Inequity to Everyday Life, Community, and Just Sustainabilities*, 41 Ann. Rev. Env't & Res. 321, 326 (2016) (citing JULIAN AGYEMAN, SUSTAINABLE COMMUNITIES AND THE CHALLENGE OF ENVIRONMENTAL JUSTICE (2005)).

190. Owing to the high cost of incineration, and the air pollution that it creates, city officials fell out of love with large-scale incineration fairly quickly during the 1930s and 1940s. MARTIN V. MELOSI, *FRESH KILLS: A HISTORY OF CONSUMING AND DISCARDING IN NEW YORK CITY* 146–48 (2020). New York City stopped incinerating garbage in 1994. Eric Lipton, *City Seeks Ideas as Trash Costs Dwarf Estimate*, N.Y. TIMES (Dec. 2, 2003), www.nytimes.com/2003/12/02/nyregion/city-seeks-ideas-as-trash-costs-dwarf-estimate.html.

There was a period of time when New York City externalized a substantial share of the environmental costs of its trash by simply dumping it into the ocean, where it would wash onto the shores of New Jersey and Long Island. Bowing to pressure from neighboring jurisdictions, in 1930, New York City announced its intention to phase out ocean dumping and rely on incineration instead. MELOSI, *supra*, at 138. But the city was still engaged in ocean dumping when the Supreme Court put an end to that practice in a unanimous opinion in the 1931 case *State of New Jersey v. City of New York*, 283 U.S. 473 (1931).

191. MELOSI, *supra* note 190, at 16.

192. Since the 1950s, the city has collected residential trash and private haulers have collected commercial trash; Fresh Kills took residential and commercial trash. N.Y.C. DEP'T OF SANITATION, FINAL COMPREHENSIVE SOLID WASTE MANAGEMENT PLAN: EXECUTIVE SUMMARY at ES-8 (2006), https://dsny.cityofnewyork.us/wp-content/uploads/2017/12/about_swmp_exec_summary_0815.pdf [hereinafter N.Y.C. DEP'T OF SANITATION, FINAL COMPREHENSIVE SOLID WASTE MANAGEMENT PLAN]. *See also* SZE, *supra* note 22, at 113 (indicating that Fresh Kills "primarily" received "residential trash" but that commercial trash also was taken by barge to Fresh Kills before the city increased tipping fees for commercial trash in the late 1980s). On the division of responsibility for collecting residential and commercial trash in New York, and the historical involvement of the Mafia in the collection of commercial trash until the 1990s, see *id.* at 120. On the volume of trash that Fresh Kills received, *see, e.g.*, Robert Sullivan, *How the World's Garbage Dump Evolved into a Green Oasis*, N.Y. TIMES (Aug. 14, 2020), www.nytimes.com/2020/08/14/nyregion/freshkills-garbage-dump-nyc.html ("no less than 150 million tons of garbage had been dumped at Fresh Kills").

193. SZE, *supra* note 22, at 113.
194. MELOSI, *supra* note 190, at 20.
195. SZE, *supra* note 22, at 112. In the 2020 presidential election, for example, Donald Trump received approximately 62 percent of the vote. James Yates, *Election 2020: A Look at How Staten Island Voted*, SILIVE.COM (Nov. 4, 2020), www.silive.com/politics/2020/11/election-2020-live-results-for-staten-island-races-including-congress-and-president.html. In 1948, the year Fresh Kills opened, a majority of Staten Islanders voted for Republican Thomas Dewey over Democrat Harry Truman. Tom Wrobleski, *Not Always Red: Staten Island's Presidential Votes, 1856 to 2012*, SILIVE.COM (Nov. 5, 2016), www.silive.com/opinion/columns/2016/11/how_staten_island_voted_for_pr.html.
196. In FRESH KILLS, Martin Melosi quotes William O'Dwyer, New York City's mayor from 1946 to 1950, as stating, "[t]he voting strength of various localities, or lack of it, too often was the final determining factor as to where garbage was to be dumped, and Staten Island, sparsely populated and with little voting strength, became one of the likely spots." MELOSI, *supra* note 190, at 168.
197. Barbara Warren, Taking Out the Trash: A New Direction for New York City's Waste 2 (Organization of Waterfront Neighborhoods & Consumer Policy Institute/Consumers Union, 2000), https://advocacy.consumerreports.org/wp-content/uploads/2013/03/trash-report.pdf.
198. Sze, *supra* note 22, at 113; ERIC. A. GOLDSTEIN & MARK IZEMAN, *THE NEW YORK ENVIRONMENT BOOK* 4 (1990); *see also* N.Y.C. DEP'T OF SANITATION, FINAL COMPREHENSIVE SOLID WASTE MANAGEMENT PLAN, *supra* note 192, at ES-8.
199. SZE, *supra* note 22, at 113–14.
200. Affidavit of Eddie Bautista at ¶¶ 6–7, Nat'l Waste & Recycling Ass'n v. City of N.Y., No. 101686/2018 (N.Y. Sup. Ct. 2019) [hereinafter Bautista Affidavit], *available at* www.nylpi.org/wp-content/uploads/2019/04/Affidavit-of-Eddie-Bautista-Executed-PDFA.pdf (last visited July 11, 2024); SZE, *supra* note 22, at 114 ("Many of the garbage environmental justice activists became involved in the issue since the late 1980s because of the growing waste transfer station problem that emerged when tipping fees at Fresh Kills increased for private carters."); BARUCH COLL. OF PUB. AFF., CASE STUDY 1: SOLID WASTE MANAGEMENT AND ENVIRONMENTAL JUSTICE: BUILDING AND SUSTAINING COALITIONS 5–6 (2011).
201. MELOSI, *supra* note 190, at 396.
202. *Id.* at 418.
203. Giuliani was reelected as mayor for a second term in 1997. Justin Oppmann, *Giuliani Wins with Ease*, CNN (Nov. 4, 1997), http://edition.cnn.com/SPECIALS/1997/elections/mayor/; *Giuliani Won't Run for Third Term*, N.Y. TIMES (OCT. 3, 2001), www.nytimes.com/2001/10/03/nyregion/giuliani-wont-run-for-third-term-2001100392613094035.html.
204. MELOSI, *supra* note 190, at 410; BARUCH COLL. OF PUB. AFF., *supra* note 200, at 2; *see also* SZE, *supra* note 22, at 123 (discussing the concentration of the waste management industry into a few large companies in the U.S. and the growing dispersal of solid waste in the U.S., with more states, including New York State, exporting garbage to other states in the U.S.). In the 1980s, there was a "garbage crisis" in the United States as local landfills closed. LILY BAUM POLLANS, *RESISTING GARBAGE: THE POLITICS OF WASTE MANAGEMENT IN AMERICAN CITIES* 33 (2021).
205. Bautista affidavit, *supra* note 200, at ¶ 15 ("These 15-ton capacity trucks would pick up the trash and take it to a land-based transfer station. The waste was then exported by an 18-wheel tractor trailer that has a capacity of approximately 25 tons. Thousands of diesel truck trips were coming in and out of these communities each week.").

206. Bautista affidavit, *supra* note 200, at ¶ 14; *see also* N.Y.C. DEP'T OF SANITATION, FINAL COMPREHENSIVE SOLID WASTE MANAGEMENT PLAN, *supra* note 192, at ES-8; BARUCH COLL. OF PUB. AFF., *supra* note 200, at 5.
207. SZE, *supra* note 22, at 113. The three most affected communities were "Williamsburg/Greenpoint, … Sunset Park/Red Hook in Brooklyn, and the South Bronx. More than half of the fifty-four private waste transfer stations (for putrescible, or smelly, garbage and construction and demolition debris) are located in just two neighborhoods: South Bronx with thirteen and Williamsburg/Greenpoint with seventeen facilities …. In 2004, according to information from the DOS [Department of Sanitation] compiled by New York Lawyers for the Public Interest, these two neighborhoods handled 73 percent of the city's putrescible and construction and debris waste." *Id.* at 113–14.

    On high asthma rates, *see, e.g.*, BARUCH COLL. OF PUB. AFF., *supra* note 200, at 4 ("South Bronx had one of the highest asthma rates in the world."); Eddie Bautista, *Garbage Wars: The Struggle for Waterfront Justice*, 3 *J. COMMUNITY ADVOCACY & ACTIVISM* 17, 20 (1998) (referring to high rates of asthma in Williamsburg/Greenpoint and South Bronx). On the concerns with high asthma rates in environmental justice communities in New York City, see generally SZE, *supra* note 22; CH Siddique Humayan, *The Mystery of Asthma*, BROOKLYN INK (Nov. 6, 2013), http://brooklynink.org/2013/11/06/53132-the-mystery-of-asthma/ ("There are few places in the world with higher rates of asthma than Red Hook, where one in four people struggle to breath."); N.Y.C. CHILDHOOD ASTHMA INITIATIVE, ASTHMA FACTS: SECOND EDITION (2003), www.nyc.gov/assets/doh/downloads/pdf/asthma/facts.pdf.
208. MELOSI, *supra* note 190, at 453.
209. N.Y.C. DEP'T OF SANITATION, FINAL COMPREHENSIVE SOLID WASTE MANAGEMENT PLAN, *supra* note 192.
210. Bautista, *supra* note 207, at 22 ("in January 1997 the New York City Environmental Justice Alliance; New York Lawyers for the Public Interest; and the Consumer Policy Institute helped bring together community-based environmental and civic groups to form the Organization of Waterfront Neighborhoods (OWN)"); MELOSI, *supra* note 190, at 436–37; Warren, *supra* note 197, at 2–3; BARUCH COLL. OF PUB. AFF., *supra* note 200, at 6 (indicating OWN was established in 1997). *But see* SZE, *supra* note 22, at 115 (indicating OWN was founded in 1996).
211. SZE, *supra* note 22, at 116 ("Borough equity or self-sufficiency is the idea that each borough should handle its own waste."); Bautista affidavit, *supra* note 200, at ¶ 16 (OWN "began to advocate for the use of the already existing but dormant MTS's [marine transfer stations] to be renovated and utilized again."). The locations to which New York City's garbage was exported outside the city for landfilling or incineration also could be historically marginalized communities, further compounding the environmental injustice of the city's approach to solid waste management. SZE, *supra* note 22, at 130–31.
212. SZE, *supra* note 22, at 116.
213. *Id.*
214. *Id.* ("The biggest barrier to this concept [of borough equity] is Manhattan, which is the richest borough and generates 40 percent of the city's commercial waste, all of which is handled through Brooklyn, Bronx, and Queens."). *See also* N.Y.C. DEP'T OF SANITATION, FINAL COMPREHENSIVE SOLID WASTE MANAGEMENT PLAN, *supra* note 192, at ES-10 ("over 40 percent of the City's commercial waste originates [in Manhattan] but [there are] no private putrescible transfer stations" therein). In 2006, when the city council approved the solid waste management plan, the Department of Sanitation was trucking the residential waste it collected in Manhattan to New Jersey.

Council of the City of N.Y., *Report of the Infrastructure Division, Committee on Sanitation and Solid Waste Management* 11–13 (July 19, 2006).

215. Bautista affidavit, *supra* note 200, at ¶ 22 ("In 2006, I left my position at NYLPI [New York Lawyers for the Public Interest] to go work directly at the Mayor's office; I joined the Bloomberg administration as the Director of City Legislative Affairs. My role was largely based on getting the Solid Waste Management Plan passed by the Council – that's what I got brought in for, though it was never quite said."). Bautista remained in the Bloomberg administration until 2010, when he joined New York City Environmental Justice Alliance. *Id.* at ¶ 28. Bautista also worked on other issues than the solid waste management plan while in the mayor's office. *Eddie Bautista,* N.Y.C. Env't Just. All., https://nyc-eja.org/about-us/eddie-bautista-executive-director/ (last visited Feb. 23, 2024). On Bautista's role in founding OWN, see Baruch Coll. of Pub. Aff., *supra* note 200, at 6 (referring to Bautista as a cofounder of OWN and indicating OWN was established in 1997).

Under the New York State Environmental Conservation Law, the city must prepare a solid waste management plan. N.Y. Env't Conserv. Law § 27-0107 (McKinney); Residents for Sane Trash Sols., Inc. v. U.S. Army Corps of Eng'rs, 31 F. Supp. 3d 571, 578 (S.D.N.Y. 2014). In 2004, the Bloomberg administration published a proposed solid waste management plan. The New York State Department of Environmental Conservation approved the city's plan in 2006, after the city council voted that year to submit the plan to the state. Gracie Point Comm. Council ex. rel. Ard v. N.Y. State Dep't of Env't Conservation, 936 N.Y.S. 2d 342, 345 (2011); *Residents for Sane Trash Sols.*, 31 F. Supp. 3d at 579.

216. Bautista affidavit, *supra* note 200, at ¶ 24 ("[T]he Mayor was clear, he wanted this plan because of environmental justice and equity. Back in 2001 and 2002, his own framing of the waste plan was as an equity, environmental justice, and public health goal."). Bautista's affidavit was submitted by New York Lawyers for Public Interest in conjunction with an amicus brief that it filed when elements of the waste industry unsuccessfully challenged a 2018 waste equity law. Affirmation of Melissa Iachan, Senior Staff Attorney, Env't Just. Program, New York Lawyers for Public Interest, in Support of Motion for Leave to File an Amicus Brief with Attached Statement of Interest, Memorandum of Law, and Affidavit in Opposition to the Verified Petition and In Support of the Motion to Dismiss the Complaint at ¶ 1, Nat'l Waste & Recycling Assoc. v. City of N.Y., Index No. 101686/2018 (N.Y. Sup. Ct.) (Apr. 1, 2019); *In re* Nat'l Waste & Recycling Ctr. v. City of N.Y., 189 A.D.3d 582 (N.Y. App. Div. 2020), *aff'g* No. 101686/2018, 2019 WL 4899040 (N.Y. Sup. Ct. Oct. 4, 2019).

217. N.Y.C. Dep't of Sanitation, Final Comprehensive Solid Waste Management Plan, *supra* note 192. *See also* Baruch Coll. of Pub. Aff., *supra* note 200, at 7.

A number of environmental groups played roles in the adoption of the 2006 solid waste management plan and in defending key elements of it. These include OWN, New York City Environmental Justice Alliance, New York City Lawyers for the Public Interest, OUTRAGE, UPROSE, the Natural Resources Defense Council, the Environmental Defense Fund, and the League of Conservation Voters. *See, e.g.*, Baruch Coll. of Pub. Aff., *supra* note 200, at 4, 6.

218. Bratspies, *supra* note 187, at 1960–63; Mallory Szczepanski, *An Exclusive Look at the 91st Street Marine Transfer Station in New York,* Waste360 (May 23, 2019), www.waste360.com/transfer-stations/exclusive-look-91st-street-marine-transfer-station-new-york. In 2005, the city council voted against the construction of the East 91st marine transfer

station at the site of an old marine transfer station used from roughly 1940 to 1999 but Mayor Bloomberg vetoed the city council decision, and the council "did not override" his veto. *Residents for Sane Trash Sols.*, 31 F. Supp. 3d at 579. For court cases challenging the construction of the marine transfer station at East 91st Street, see *Residents for Sane Trash Sols.*, 31 F. Supp. 3d at 579–84, 599.

219. Recycling had been on the city's agenda as an approach for dealing with waste for decades before 2006. *See, e.g.*, Sze, *supra* note 22, at 137. ("Local Law 19, passed in 1989, required that 25 percent of the city's waste be recycled by 1994.")

However, recycling is not a panacea. It is also associated with environmental injustice, for example, if recyclables are processed or disposed of in environmental justice communities. *Id.* at 138–39. *See also* David Naguib Pellow, Garbage Wars: The Struggle for Environmental Justice in Chicago 157 (2002) ([Recycling] "is often a source of significant social and environmental inequalities confronting workers and communities of color.").

220. Bratspies, *supra* note 187, at 1957–58 ("New York City's overburdened communities … [t]hrough fierce and persistent public advocacy, … convinced the New York City Department of Sanitation (DSNY) to enact a new Solid Waste Management Plan in 2006."); OneNYC 2015, *supra* note 19, at 177 ("The 2006 adoption of the City's comprehensive Solid Waste Management Plan (SWMP) was a landmark achievement of long-term waste planning and environmental justice. The plan was championed by grassroots environmental justice organizations, who long advocated for the City to switch from a truck-based waste export system that overburdened low-income communities to an equitable network of marine and rail transfer stations located in all five boroughs.").

221. The term is borrowed from the title of a chapter in Sze's book, Noxious New York. Sze, *supra* note 22.

222. N.Y.C. Dep't of Sanitation, Final Comprehensive Solid Waste Management Plan, *supra* note 192, at ES-7; City of New York, Comprehensive Solid Waste Management Plan 4–10 to 4–11 (2006), www.nyc.gov/assets/dsny/downloads/resources/reports/solid-waste-management/2006-swmp/swmp-comprehensive-report-2006.pdf. *See also* City Council, Transcript of the Minutes of the Committee on Sanitation and Solid Waste Management 18–20 (July 19, 2006) (exchange between Council Member David Yassky and Robert Orlan, Deputy Commissioner for Legal Affairs in the Department of Sanitation, where Orlan states that the plan commits the city to trying to reduce the "transfer station capacity" in the four most affected areas voluntarily, and that the city agrees to support a bill mandating reductions in tonnage if voluntary efforts fail by April 2007); *see also id.* at 32–34 (the exchange between Council Member Charles Barron & John Doherty, Commissioner, Department of Sanitation); *id.* at 43–47, 54–56 (Council Member David Yassky's failed effort to amend the plan).

223. *New Coalition Challenges Mayoral Candidates on Environmental & Economic Sustainability*, Transform Don't Trash NYC (Oct. 2, 2013), https://transformdonttrashnyc.org/press/new-coalition-challenges-mayoral-candidates-on-environmental-economic-sustainabilty/ ("A new coalition of labor, environmental justice, community and other advocates convened on the steps of City Hall to launch a new campaign to tackle the problems in the commercial solid waste industry."); *see also* Bratspies, *supra* note 187, at 1959 ("Community leaders from overburdened communities continued to pressure for change under the banner of the Transform Don't Trash Coalition."). In the de Blasio era, the communities which hosted the most private waste transfer stations were "low-income communities and communities of color in

the South Bronx, North Brooklyn, Sunset Park, and Southeast Queens[.]" ALL. FOR A GREATER N.Y., TRANSFORM DON'T TRASH NYC: HOW TO INCREASE GOOD JOBS, RECYCLING, AND JUSTICE IN THE COMMERCIAL WASTE INDUSTRY 9 (2013), https://transformdonttrashnyc.org/wp-content/uploads/2015/02/TransformDontTrashNYC_Report_FINAL_LoRes_1151.pdf.

224. *New Coalition Challenges*, *supra* note 223; *Transform Don't Trash NYC Coalition Launches to Clean Up Commercial Waste*, TRANSFORM DON'T TRASH NYC (Oct. 13, 2013), https://transformdonttrashnyc.org/press/transform-dont-trash-nyc-coalition-launches-to-clean-up-commercial-waste/; ALL. FOR A GREATER N.Y., TRANSFORM DON'T TRASH NYC, *supra* note 223; Kiera Feldman, *Trashed: Inside the Deadly World of Private Waste Collection*, PROPUBLICA (Jan. 4, 2018), www.propublica.org/article/trashed-inside-the-deadly-world-of-private-garbage-collection. In 2014, the Citizens Budget Commission also recommended a franchise system for collecting commercial waste. CITIZENS BUDGET COMM'N, GETTING THE FISCAL WASTE OUT OF SOLID WASTE COLLECTION IN NEW YORK CITY (Sept. 23, 2014) https://cbcny.org/research/getting-fiscal-waste-out-solid-waste-collection-new-york-city; Carol Kellermann, *A Chore We Must Do: Over-Hauling Private Waste Management in New York City*, GOTHAM GAZETTE (Aug. 1, 2019), www.gothamgazette.com/public-safety/130-opinion/8706-a-chore-we-must-do-over-hauling-private-waste-management.

225. *New Coalition Challenges*, *supra* note 223.

226. *New Yorkers Cheer Signing of Commercial Sanitation Reform Bill*, TRANSFORM DON'T TRASH NYC (Nov. 20, 2019), https://transformdonttrashnyc.org/press/new-yorkers-cheer-signing-of-commercial-sanitation-reform-bill/; New *York City Council Introduces Legislation to Overhaul the Private Carting Industry*, TRANSFORM DON'T TRASH NYC (May 29, 2019), https://transformdonttrashnyc.org/press/new-york-city-council-introduces-legislation-to-overhaul-the-private-carting-industry/; *Community-Labor-Environmental Coalition Praises de Blasio Plan to Reform Commercial Sanitation*, TRANSFORM DON'T TRASH NYC (Aug. 17, 2016), https://transformdonttrashnyc.org/press/community-labor-environmental-coalition-praises-de-blasio-plan-to-reform-commercial-sanitation/.

227. *New Yorkers Rally for Passage of Commercial Waste Zones Bill Ahead of City Council Vote*, TRANSFORM DON'T TRASH NYC (Oct. 30, 2019), https://transformdonttrashnyc.org/press/new-yorkers-rally-for-passage-of-commercial-waste-zones-bill-ahead-of-city-council-vote/; *New Yorkers Cheer Signing of Commercial Sanitation Reform Bill*, *supra* note 226; *NYC Council Passes Commercial Waste Zones!*, N.Y.C. ENV'T JUST. ALL. (Oct. 2019), https://campaign.r20.constantcontact.com/render?m=1103489391006&ca=97e46802-a62e-433d-a059-6b012d2e6d1c.

228. *Commercial Waste Zones Plan*, N.Y.C. DEP'T OF SANITATION, www.nyc.gov/site/dsny/resources/reports/commercial-waste-zones-plan.page (last visited Mar. 8, 2024). N.Y.C., N.Y., LOCAL LAW NO. 199: COMMERCIAL WASTE ZONES, tit. 16-B, § 16-1002 (2019) ("For each area designated as a commercial waste zone pursuant to section 16-1001, the department shall be authorized to select and to enter into agreements with no more than three awardees per zone."). In addition, the Department is "authorized to select and enter into agreements with" up to five "awardees" to collect "containerized commercial waste from any commercial establishment within the city." *Id.*

229. *Hearing Before the N.Y.C. Council Comm. on Sanitation & Solid Waste Mgmt.*, at 23–25 (June 19, 2018) (testimony of Kathryn Garcia, Comm'r, N.Y.C Dep't of Sanitation) (Commercial waste zones for the "private waste hauling industry" "will … dramatically reduce truck traffic associated with this industry by 60 percent or more…. This

initiative will improve the quality of life for New Yorkers living and working across the city, but these benefits will be particularly felt in the neighborhoods with the highest concentrations of transfer stations[,] … the exact communities we are discussing today."); N.Y.C. Dep't of Sanitation, Commercial Waste Zones: A Plan to Reform, Reroute, and Revitalize Private Carting in New York City 7 (2018), www.nyc.gov/assets/dsny/downloads/resources/reports/cwz-implimentation-plan/cwz-implementation-plan.pdf [hereinafter Commercial Waste Zones Plan] (truck traffic from "commercial waste collection" will be reduced by 60 percent while "labor standards" will be strengthened and "customer service" will be retained). *But see* N.Y.C. Dep't of Sanitation, NYC Commercial Waste Zone Program: Final Generic Environmental Impact Statement at S-9 (2019) [hereinafter Environmental Impact Statement] ("the proposed action is expected to reduce citywide commercial carter truck [vehicle miles travelled] by approximately 50 percent from the No Action condition, and by 47 to 60 percent within the case study areas.")

The current system means that multiple companies, each one using a different truck, sometimes pick up trash from businesses on the same street because they contract with a different carter. N.Y.C. Dep't of Sanitation & N.Y.C. Bus. Integrity Comm'n, Private Carting Study 1 (2016); www.nyc.gov/assets/dsny/site/resources/reports/commercial-waste-zones-plan; Feldman, *supra* note 224.

230. Feldman, *supra* note 224. *See also* Environmental Impact Statement, *supra* note 229, at 14–21.

The Environmental Impact Statement for the Commercial Waste Zones law identifies the neighborhoods where waste transfer facilities are clustered as "certain overburdened districts of Brooklyn, the Bronx, and Queens with disproportionate numbers of waste transfer stations." *Id.* at 1–13. *See also* Bratspies, *supra* note 187, at 1956–57, 1959.

231. Commercial Waste Zones Plan, *supra* note 229, at 47; Press Release, City of N.Y., Mayor de Blasio Signs Landmark Legislation to Reform Commercial Waste Collection Industry (Nov. 20, 2019), www.nyc.gov/office-of-the-mayor/news/556-19/mayor-de-blasio-signs-landmark-legislation-reform-commercial-waste-collection-industry; Feldman, *supra* note 224.

232. Local Law 199 states that "Since 2010, private waste collection trucks have killed dozens of people on New York City streets." N.Y.C., N.Y., Local Law No. 199, § 1 (2019) (Legislative Purpose).

233. In 2013, the council passed a law to reduce emissions from the vehicles used by private carters, Local Law 145. *Local Law 145 of 2013: Vehicle Emission Law*, N.Y.C. Bus. Integrity Comm'n, www.nyc.gov/site/bic/industries/vehicle-emissions-law.page (last visited Feb. 24, 2024). In 2018, the council passed a "waste equity law," N.Y.C., N.Y., Local Law No. 152 (2018). Bautista affidavit, *supra* note 200, at ¶¶ 29–37; *see also* Melosi, *supra* note 190, at 534. When the law was passed, three low-income communities of color in North Brooklyn, Southeast Queens, and the South Bronx processed "about two-thirds of" the city's garbage, notwithstanding the 2006 solid waste management plan. *Hearing on Int. No. 157-B, Waste Equity before the N.Y.C. Council Comm. on Sanitation and Solid Waste Mgmt.* (June 19, 2018) (testimony of Melissa Iachan, Senior Staff Attorney, N.Y. Lawyers for the Pub. Interest, Inc.); *see also Committee on Sanitation and Solid Waste Management, City Council, Transcript of the Minutes of the Committee on Sanitation and Solid Waste Management* 29 (June 19, 2018) (exchange between Antonio Reynoso, chair, and Kathryn Garcia, Commissioner, Dep't of Sanitation). The law requires reductions in the amount of waste that transfer stations in the overburdened areas are permitted to receive, and caps the share of the city's waste

that any particular city district can be permitted to receive to avoid the creation of new overburdened areas. Notably, although the waste equity law is historic in mandating reductions in overburdened communities, it may have only "modest" effects on truck traffic in these areas, according to Eric Goldstein, a long-time advocate for reforming the city's approach to waste and New York City Environment Director at the Natural Resources Defense Council. *Id.* at 124–26. The law focused on reducing *permitted* capacity at waste transfer stations, and the transfer stations' permitted capacity exceeded their actual processing when the law was passed.

234. Press Release, N.Y.C. Department of Sanitation, As of Today, First NYC Commercial Waste Zone Fully Implemented (Jan. 2, 2025), https://www.nyc.gov/site/dsny/news/25-001/as-today-first-nyc-commercial-waste-zone-fully-implemented#:~:text=As%20of%20Today%2C%20First%20NYC%20Commercial%20Waste%20Zone%20Fully%20Implemented,-January%202%2C%202025&text=The%20New%20York%20City%20Department,Zone%20is%20now%20fully%20operational. On the history of the law's implementation, see Julianne Cuba, *Exclusive: Adams Administration Has Delayed Commercial Waste Reform That's Required by Law*, StreetsBlogNYC (Jan. 27, 2023), https://nyc.streetsblog.org/2023/01/27/exclusive-adams-administration-has-delayed-commercial-waste-reform-thats-required-by-law; Sophia Chang, *Long Overdue Reform of NYC Private Trash Collection Hits Another Road Bump*, Gothamist (Sept. 14, 2023), https://gothamist.com/news/long-overdue-reform-of-nyc-private-trash-collection-hits-another-speed-bump; Cole Rosengren, *New York City Awards Historic Commercial Waste Zone Contracts Ahead of September Transition*, WasteDive (Jan. 30, 2024), www.wastedive.com/news/new-york-commercial-waste-zone-contract-award-dsny-adams/705960/.

235. On the destinations for New York City's garbage, see Justin Davidson, *Voyage of the Gross*, Curbed (Aug. 12, 2022), www.curbed.com/2022/08/nyc-trash-landfill-incineration-recycling-compost-voyage-gross.html.

There are efforts to reduce the amount of garbage that the city produces. In 2023, the administration of Mayor Eric Adams began phasing in universal curbside collection of organics and the city council legislated such collection, initiatives that may increase the rate at which organics are diverted from the waste that the city sends to landfills. Press Release, City of N.Y., Mayor Adams Announces Roadmap for Nation's Largest Compost Collection Program, Including Achieving Decades-Long Goal of Providing Curbside Service to Every New York City Resident (Feb. 1, 2023), www.nyc.gov/office-of-the-mayor/news/084-23/mayor-adams-roadmap-nation-s-largest-compost-collection-program-including-achieving#/0; Jacob Wallace, *New York City Zero Waste Package, Including Mandatory Residential Organics Program, Becomes Law*, WasteDive (July 10, 2023), www.wastedive.com/news/new-york-city-mandatory-organics-collection-law-eric-adams/685977/; Liam Quigley, *Composting Is Universal in NYC. But Is Anyone Participating?*, The Gothamist (Feb. 14, 2025), https://gothamist.com/news/composting-is-universal-in-nyc-but-is-anyone-participating.

In the 2010s and early 2020s a number of U.S. cities, including New York City, have passed laws to reduce polysterene and single-use plastics. In 2013, the New York City Council passed a law banning polystyrene containers, which are all but impossible to recycle. N.Y.C., N.Y., Local Law No. 142 (2013). In 2016, the Council passed a law requiring stores charge a fee for plastic bags, which comprise 2 or 3 percent of the city's waste (New York State later preempted the local law before passing its own plastic bag ban). N.Y.C., N.Y., Local Law No. 63 (2016). In 2021, the Council passed a measure prohibiting establishments from giving out plastic straws unless a customer specifically requests them. N.Y.C., N.Y., Local Law No. 64 (2021). For an analysis of different local approaches to reducing disposable plastic bags, see Tatiana Homonoff, Lee-Sien Kao, Javiera Selmon, & Christina Seybolt, *Skipping the Bag: The Unintended Consequences of Disposable Bag Regulation*, 41 J. POL'Y ANALYSIS & LAND MGMT. 226 (2022). On the framing of waste as a problem of disposal versus a "extraction-manufacturing-consumption-waste chain," see POLLANS, *supra* note 204, at 103.

236. *See* Rebecca Bratspies, *Decarceration with Decarbonization:* Renewable Rikers *and the Transition to Clean Power*, 13 SAN DIEGO J. CLIMATE & ENERGY L. 1, 18 (2022) (referring to the laws as "groundbreaking") [hereinafter Bratspies 2022]; Bratspies, *supra* note 142, at 26–30 (providing background on the city's environmental justice laws and emphasizing that the local interest in environmental justice was partly a response to the retreat from federal interest in addressing environmental injustices during the first Trump administration). As Bratspies 2022 mentions, the press release that Mayor de Blasio's office issued when he signed the laws quotes him as stating that they "recognize the historic injustices that have disproportionately fallen on low-income residents and communities of color – the burden of pollution and the effects of climate change – and offer a different path forward." Press Release, City of New York, Mayor de Blasio Signs Legislation to Better Promote Environmental Justice through the Work of City Agencies (Apr. 25, 2017), www.nyc.gov/office-of-the-mayor/news/262-17/mayor-de-blasio-signs-legislation-better-promote-environmental-justice-the-work-city.

237. N.Y.C., N.Y., ADMIN. CODE tit. 3, ch. 10, § 3-1001 (defining "environmental justice," "low-income community," "low-income population," and "minority community"); *see also id.* ("The term 'environmental justice area' means a low-income community located in the city or a minority community located in the city.... The term 'low-income community' means a census block group, or contiguous area with multiple census block groups, having a low-income population equal to or greater than 23.59 percent of the total population of such block group or groups, or such other percentage as may be determined by the New York state department of environmental conservation in the course of setting parameters for the location of potential environmental justice areas within the state of New York and made publicly available on the website of such department.... The term 'low-income population' means a population having an annual income that is less than the poverty threshold established by the United States census bureau.... The term 'minority community' means a census block group, or contiguous area with multiple census block groups, having a minority population equal to or greater than 51.1 percent of the total population of such block group or groups, or such other percentage as may be determined by the New York state department of environmental conservation in the course of setting parameters for the location of potential environmental justice areas within the state of New York and made publicly available on the website of such department.... The term 'minority population' means a population that is identified or recognized by the United States census bureau as Hispanic, African-American or Black, Asian and Pacific Islander or American Indian.").

238. *Id.* at § 3-1003.

239. *Environmental Justice*, N.Y.C. MAYOR'S OFF. OF CLIMATE & ENV'T JUST., https://climate.cityofnewyork.us/topic/environmental-justice/ (last visited July 10, 2024). On the history of WE ACT, see Shepard, *supra* note 187, at 739, 751–54.

One of the laws, Intro 886, was originally proposed by the African American Environmentalist Association, and introduced in the early 2000s by then-council member Charles Barron, whose wife, Inez Barron, introduced the bill that passed. Press Release, *supra* note 236. *See also Hearing on Int. No. 886 Environmental Justice Law, Int. No. 359 Environmental Justice Study before the N.Y.C. Council Comm. on Env't Prot.* (Jan. 28, 2016) (testimony of Norris McDonald, President, African American Environmentalist Association) ("I drafted the Environmental Justice Bill for Councilman Charles Barron in 2003 and Councilmember Barron introduced the bill (Int. No. 404) in 2004 with seven cosponsors. After meeting with Councilwoman Inez Barron in 2014 to request re-introduction of the legislation and after much review and revisions by the Committee on Environmental Protection, Councilwoman Barron introduced the legislation that we are considering today."). The Environmental Protection Committee's legislative counsel Samara Swanston also was credited for her work on the environmental justice legislation. *See Hearing on Int. No. 886 Environmental Justice Law, Int. No. 359 Environmental Justice Study before the N.Y.C. Council Comm. on Env't Prot.* 16 (Jan. 28, 2016) (statement of Council Member Donovan Richards, standing in for Council Member Inez Barron).

240. Norris McDonald, President of the African American Environmentalist Association, recommended that the legislation include "a citizen lawsuit provision to allow potential victims of environmental race discrimination to enforce the EJA and the regulations promulgated thereunder," and that it enable "citizens, and DEP [Department of Environmental Protection] at the request of citizens, to obtain injunctions to prevent construction and operation of discriminatory polluting facilities and operations that violate the EJA violations," among other changes. *Hearing on Int. No. 886 Env't Justice Law, Int. No. 359 Environmental Justice Study before the N.Y.C. Council Comm. on Env't Prot.* (Jan. 28, 2016) (testimony of Norris McDonald, President, African American Environmentalist Association).

241. EJNYC, *supra* note 53, at 9; N.Y.C., N.Y., ADMIN. CODE tit. 3, Ch. 10, § 3-1003 & § 3-1007. The mandated mapping tool was released in April 2024 along with the study. The online mapping tool was due in 2018 under N.Y.C., N.Y., ADMIN. CODE tit. 3, Ch. 10, § 3-1007. The 2024 report used New York State's classification of Disadvantaged Communities in the city pursuant to the 2019 New York State Climate Leadership and Community Protection Act, but included recommendations for changes to the State's "disadvantaged communities criteria" that would increase the share of such communities in New York City. EJNYC, *supra* note 53, at 40–41, 47–51.

242. N.Y. Climate Leadership and Community Protection Act of 2019, N.Y. ENV'T CONSERV. LAW § 75-0117 (McKinney 2024) ("disadvantaged communities shall receive no less than thirty-five percent of the overall benefits of spending on clean energy and energy efficiency programs, projects or investments"); *id.* at § 75-0111 (directing the "climate justice working group" to "establish criteria" for the identification of disadvantaged communities "for the purposes of co-pollutant reductions, greenhouse gas emissions reductions, regulatory impact statements, and the allocation of [related] investments"); Tackling the Climate Crisis at Home and Abroad, Exec. Order No. 14,008 §§ 219, 222–23, 86 Fed. Reg. 7619, 7629, 7631–32 (Jan. 27, 2021) (establishing environmental justice as a policy for federal agencies and directing agencies to take specified actions for implementing this policy); *Justice40: A Whole-of-Government Initiative*, WHITE HOUSE, www.whitehouse.gov/environmentaljustice/justice40/ (last visited Feb. 24, 2024); EJNYC, *supra* note 53, at 12 (describing "the increasing prevalence of EJ action at the state and federal level"); *id.* at 223–28 (describing environmental justice initiatives in various cities and states).

243. ICLEI-LOCAL GOVERNMENTS FOR SUSTAINABILITY, *supra* note 28, at 15 (Mayoral Support).

244. *Deal Reached to Transform Commercial Waste Collection to Protect Workers, Communities, and Environment*, TRANSFORM DON'T TRASH NYC (Oct. 10, 2019), https://transformdonttrashnyc.org/press/deal-reached-to-transform-commercial-waste-collection-to-protect-workers-communities-and-environment/.
245. PLANYC 2007, *supra* note 26, at 121 ("Through these strategies, we will accelerate air quality improvements so that every New Yorker can depend on the promise that they are breathing the cleanest air of any big city in America.").
246. On the intransigence on the part of State legislators that blocked Bloomberg's congestion pricing proposal, see *supra* note 142 and accompanying text. The Bloomberg administration's efforts to require and then incentivize the privately owned yellow taxis that the city government licenses to use less-emitting vehicles were held by the courts to be preempted by federal law. *Metro. Taxicab Bd. of Trade v. City of N.Y.*, 2008 WL 4866021 (S.D.N.Y. 2008); *Metro. Taxicab Bd. of Trade v. City of N.Y.*, 615 F.3d 152 (2d Cir. 2010), *cert. denied* 562 U.S. 1264 (2011). For background on the efforts to change the taxi fleet to reduce local sources of air pollution in the city, see PLANYC 2007, *supra* note 26, at 123–24; PLANYC 2011 UPDATE, *supra* note 48, at 127. On federal regulation of new motor vehicle emissions and fuel economy, see Clean Air Act § 209(a), 42 U.S.C. § 7543(a); Energy Policy and Conservation Act (EPCA), 49 U.S.C. § 32919(a).
247. *See supra* notes 117 and 120.
248. For an assessment of de Blasio's accomplishments as he finished his second term as mayor which suggests that he accomplished less to reduce inequality generally, see Emma G. Fitzsimmons & Jeffery C. Mays, *Is New York Still a 'Tale of Two Cities'?*, N.Y. TIMES (Dec. 22, 2021), www.nytimes.com/2021/12/22/nyregion/de-blasio-legacy-inequality.html. For a contrasting perspective, see Sally Goldenberg, *De Blasio Became NYC Mayor with High Hopes, Leaves with Confounding Record*, POLITICO (Dec. 30, 2021), www.politico.com/states/new-york/city-hall/story/2021/12/30/de-blasios-legacy-how-the-operative-failed-at-politics-while-tackling-inequality-1403157 (quoting economist James Parrott as crediting de Blasio for reductions in inequality during his time as mayor). *See also* Elizabeth Kim, *Did de Blasio Make a Dent in the 'Tale of Two Cities'? A New Analysis of NYC Income Inequality Makes a Case*, GOTHAMIST (Nov. 30, 2021), https://gothamist.com/news/did-de-blasio-make-a-dent-in-the-tale-of-two-cities-a-new-analysis-of-nyc-income-equality-makes-a-case (discussing data which show "the clearest evidence so far that income inequality began to shrink under Mayor de Blasio").
249. For a related point, see WHERE WE LIVE NYC, *supra* note 174, at 15 ("The fair housing challenges that New York City faces today are rooted in the nation's history of slavery and racist laws, policies and customs that have shaped the city's built and social environments for centuries.").
250. *See* FRUG & BARRON, *supra* note 46 (emphasizing that state law constraints on cities channel cities toward certain economic development strategies, such as striving to be a global or a tourist city).
251. *See id.*; PAUL E. PETERSON, CITY LIMITS 29 (1981); *see also* Jasper Rubin, *San Francisco's Waterfront in the Age of Neoliberalism*, *in* TRANSFORMING URBAN WATERFRONT, FIXITY AND FLOW 144 (Gene Desfor et al. eds., 2011) (arguing that local governments not only face strong incentives to pursue pro-growth policies in order to provide a source of local revenue, but they may effectively be forced to do so in order to satisfy the credit agencies that rate their bonds).
252. ONENYC 2015, *supra* note 19, at 206.

4 DECARBONIZATION EFFORTS IN NYC

1. Many scholars have treated local (and other subnational) efforts to reduce GHG emissions as "a puzzle." Daniel A. Farber, Yuichiro Tsuji & Shiyuan Jing, *Thinking Globally, Acting Locally: Lessons from the U.S., Japan, and China*, 82 OHIO ST. L.J. 953, 956 (2021); *see also* Jonathan B. Wiener, *Think Globally, Act Globally: The Limits of Local Climate Policies*, 155 U. PA. L. REV. 1961, 1965–67 (2007); Richard B. Stewart, *States and Cities as Actors in Global Climate Regulation: Unitary vs. Plural Architectures*, 50 ARIZ. L. REV. 681, 690 (2008); Kirsten Engel, *State and Local Climate Change Initiatives: What Is Motivating State and Local Governments to Address a Global Problem and What Does This Say about Federalism and Environmental Law*, 38 URB. LAW. 1015, 1016, 1023 (2006). Some scholars have even argued that local governments "have a disincentive to pursue climate protection because its costs are local but the benefits of GHG reduction are shared globally." Rachel M. Krause, Hongtao Yi & Richard C. Feiock, *Applying Policy Termination Theory to the Abandonment of Climate Protection Initiatives by U.S. Local Governments*, 44 POL'Y STUD. J. 176, 180–81 (2016). Of course, many activities that produce GHG emissions also emit local air pollutants, and so the reduction of GHG emissions can produce perceptible co-benefits; making buildings more energy efficient so that they burn less oil for heat is an example of an action that produces both GHG benefits and local air pollutant benefits. But other types of GHG reducing activities – for example, reducing the amount of climate-warning refrigerant that leaks from air conditioners and heat pumps – do not impact local air quality perceptibly.

   Professor Sara Hughes identifies five explanations for why cities have acted to address climate change: "opportunities for leadership;" "entrepreneurial cities and city branding;" "capturing local co-benefits;" "responsibility to address a threat;" and "responding to (in) action at other levels of government." SARA HUGHES, REPOWERING CITIES: GOVERNING CLIMATE CHANGE MITIGATION IN NEW YORK CITY, LOS ANGELES, AND TORONTO 32–39 (2019). Accurately reflecting the state of the literature, Hughes does not focus on the influence of local interest groups in large progressive American cities as a factor, a point that we stress based on what we learned from researching the history of climate legislation New York City adopted in 2019 and 2021.
2. *See, e.g.*, Yael R. Lifshitz, *Energy Cities: The Case of London*, *in* GLOBAL SUSTAINABLE CITIES: CITY GOVERNMENTS AND OUR ENVIRONMENTAL FUTURE 193, 205–06 (Danielle Spiegel-Feld, Katrina Miriam Wyman & John J. Coughlin eds., 2023) (discussing some of the regulatory hurdles involved with reducing emissions through distributed electricity generation "given the way that electric grids are regulated" in London).
3. *See* Katherine A. Trisolini, *All Hands on Deck: Local Governments and the Potential for Bidirectional Climate Change Regulation*, 62 STAN. L. REV. 669, 674 (2010); Peter John Marcotullio et al., *The Geography of Global Urban Greenhouse Gas Emissions: An Exploratory Analysis*, 121 CLIMATIC CHANGE 621, 623 (2013); Danielle Spiegel-Feld & Katrina M. Wyman, *Building Better Building Performance Standards*, 52 ENV'T L. REP. 10268, 10269 (2022).
4. *Sources of Greenhouse Gas Emissions*, ENV'T PROT. AGENCY, www.epa.gov/ghgemissions/sources-greenhouse-gas-emissions (last visited Mar. 29, 2024).
5. *See, e.g.*, Gilbert E. Metcalf, *Designing a Carbon Tax to Reduce U.S. Greenhouse Gas Emissions*, 3 REV. ENV'T ECON. & POL'Y 63 (2009) (outlining benefits of a carbon tax); IMF, *How to Mitigate Climate Change*, Fiscal Monitor, at viii (Oct. 2019) (arguing that a carbon tax would be the "most powerful and efficient" mitigation strategy); Erin Adele Scharff, *Green Fees: The Challenge of Pricing Externalities under State Law*, 97 NEB. L. REV. 168, 180–81 (2018) (describing limitations on local taxing authority in addressing environmental

externalities). *But see* Ysabelle Kempe, *Tax on Gas-Powered Large Buildings Will Go to Voters in Berkeley, California*, SMART CITIES DIVE (June 10, 2024), www.smartcitiesdive.com/news/tax-buildings-natural-gas-decarbonization-electrification-berkeley-ca-ballot-measure/718394/ (voters in Berkeley will vote on whether to tax large buildings using gas based on consumption and methane leaks from the gas).

6. SAM MARKOLF ET AL., *BROOKINGS INST., PLEDGES AND PROGRESS: STEPS TOWARD GREENHOUSE GAS EMISSION REDUCTIONS IN THE 100 LARGEST CITIES ACROSS THE UNITED STATES* 2 (2020).

   The Brookings report "identif[ied] the 100 most populous cities in the United States based on 2017 estimates from the U.S. Census Bureau." *Id.* at 8. In contrast, our list of the twenty most populous cities is based on 2022 population estimates from the U.S. Census Bureau. *See* U.S. CENSUS BUREAU, ANNUAL ESTIMATES OF THE RESIDENT POPULATION FOR INCORPORATED PLACES OF 50,000 OR MORE, RANKED BY JULY 1, 2022 POPULATION: APRIL 1, 2020 TO JULY 1, 2022 *available at* www.census.gov/data/tables/time-series/demo/popest/2020s-total-cities-and-towns.html#tables (last visited June 14, 2024) (listing the top twenty cities by population as of 2022, from highest to lowest as: New York City, Los Angeles, Chicago, Houston, Phoenix, Philadelphia, San Antonio, San Diego, Dallas, Austin, Jacksonville, San Jose, Fort Worth, Columbus, Charlotte, Indianapolis, San Francisco, Seattle, Denver, and Oklahoma City). As a result, there is some variation in the cities examined. There are seven cities that we looked at as among the top twenty that were not included in the Brookings report: Charlotte, Dallas, Fort Worth, Houston, Jacksonville, Oklahoma City, and San Jose.

7. *See infra* note 12 and accompanying text. Our list of the twenty most populous cities is based on 2022 population estimates from the U.S. Census Bureau; *see supra* note 6.

   Fort Worth, Jacksonville, and Oklahoma City are the three cities among the top twenty most populous cities in the U.S. that did not have a GHG reduction target as of 2020, assuming, as this chapter does, that signing the Mayors Climate Protection Agreement is not counted as adopting a GHG reduction target. *See infra* note 12. The Agreement, which mayors started signing in 2005, merely committed cities to "[s]trive to meet or beat the Kyoto Protocol target in their own communities." *Mayors Climate Protection Agreement*, THE UNITED STATES CONFERENCE OF MAYORS, www.usmayors.org/programs/mayors-climate-protection-center/ (last visited Mar. 29, 2024). If signing the Agreement is counted as adopting a GHG reduction target, then Oklahoma City is the only city among the twenty most populous to not have a target. Oklahoma City's first sustainability plan, *adaptokc*, published in 2020, includes a plan to establish a GHG inventory and update it every five years. CITY OF OKLA. CITY PLAN. DEP'T, ADAPTOKC: ADAPTING FOR A HEALTHY FUTURE 110 (2020).

   Surveying a body of scholarship, Krause et al. report that "[t]hese studies generally find that cities with larger, more educated and liberal populations, higher capacity governments, and economies that put less stress on the environment are more likely to engage on [climate protection]." Krause et al., *supra* note 1, at 181. Krause and Hawkins provide suggestive evidence that small size correlates with lesser likelihood to address GHG emissions. They report that "almost 45 percent" of the 504 cities with populations exceeding 20,000 that responded to a "Smart and Sustainable Cities Survey" in 2015–2016 considered "climate change mitigation or adaptation … low or nonexistent priorities." RACHEL M. KRAUSE & Christopher V. Hawkins, *Implementing City Sustainability: Overcoming Administrative Silos to Achieve Functional Collective Action* 22–23, 25–26 (2021). Out of these 504 cities, 57 percent had completed inventories of local government GHG emissions, and 47 percent had inventories of community-wide GHG emissions, which are more complicated to undertake because they measure emissions throughout the jurisdiction, not just from city operations. *Id.* at 28–29.

8. Markolf et al., *supra* note 6, at 16 ("Of the 45 cities with GHG reduction targets and corresponding baseline GHG inventories, 32 have conducted at least one additional GHG inventory. The remaining 13 cities do not appear to have any publicly available GHG inventories for the years subsequent to the establishment of their climate action plan (and corresponding baseline emissions."). The study authors found that, "[b]ased on their most recent GHG inventory data, 26 of the 32 cities that had at least one additional inventory since 2010 experienced a decrease in emissions compared to their baseline emission levels, while six cities experienced an increase." *Id.* at 4. The study also concluded that "[o]verall, about two-thirds of cities are currently lagging their targeted emission levels." *Id.* at 18–19, Figure 5. Note, however, that the Brookings data does not have a common starting year or comparison year for cities. This definition of "lagging" is based on data that looks at the most recent GHG inventory and assesses how close a city is to achieving its target, by estimating what the target would require of the city by way of emissions reductions in the year of the most recent inventory, assuming a linear decrease in emissions over time. For example, Austin's baseline year is 2015, and the year of the most recent GHG inventory for assessing its progress is 2016. In contrast, Chicago's baseline year is 1990 and the most recent inventory being used by Brookings to assess is 2015. *Id.* at 17, Figure 4.

   A 2021 study by Bloomberg Associates focused on the reasons why cities are lagging in implementing climate actions. Bloomberg Assoc., Global Covenant of Mayors for Climate & Energy and World Resources Institute, Accelerating Climate Action in Cities: Research Findings and Recommendations 2 (2021) ("While nearly two-thirds of cities surveyed had climate action plans or started to pilot projects … only 22% reported implementing projects at scale."). *See also* Joseph Kane, Adie Tomer, Caroline George & Jamal Russell Black, Brookings Inst., Not According to Plan: Exploring Gaps in City Climate Planning and the Need for Regional Action (2022) (analyzing why cities are failing to meet GHG reduction targets in climate action plans).
9. Of the thirteen cities that we count as in the top twenty that are also in the Brookings report, eleven had more than one inventory, which is important for assessing the city's progress in reducing its emissions (Austin, Chicago, Columbus, Denver, Los Angeles, New York City, Philadelphia, Phoenix, San Diego, San Francisco, and Seattle). Markolf et al., *supra* note 6, at 17, Figure 4. Of the eleven, seven of the cities (roughly 64 percent, close to two-thirds) were lagging in achieving their emissions targets, based on the Brookings' estimate of where the cities should be if the cities were on track (Chicago, Columbus, New York City, Philadelphia, Phoenix, San Francisco, and Seattle). *Id*, at 18, Figure 5. One of the eleven was on target to meeting its target (Denver) and three were over-performing relative to their targets (Austin, Los Angeles, and San Diego). *Id.*
10. Markolf et al., *supra* note 6, at 18 Figure 5.
11. Jonathan D. Rosenbloom, *Outsourced Emissions: Why Local Governments Should Track and Measure Consumption-Based Greenhouse Gases*, 92 U. Colo. L. Rev. 451, 465 (2021) ("A typical Sector-based Inventory lists 'stationary energy' as the large majority of GHGs, with 'residential buildings' and 'commercial and institutional buildings and facilities' being the largest sector-based emissions."). On the sources of New York City's greenhouse gas emissions, see *NYC Greenhouse Gas Inventories*, NYC Mayor's Off. Climate & Env't Just., https://climate.cityofnewyork.us/initiatives/nyc-greenhouse-gas-inventories/ (last visited Mar. 29, 2024). *See also* PlaNYC 2007, *infra* note 12, at 135 (69 percent of NYC's GHG emissions come from buildings); City of N.Y., PlaNYC: Getting Sustainability Done 52 (2023) [hereinafter PlaNYC 2023] ("almost 70% of total citywide GHG emissions" are from buildings).

12. Data collected by determining the year that a GHG target was first established in each city and charting how many targets were established in each given year. This graph does not reflect whether a city stopped having a GHG reduction target after establishing one and does not reflect whether a city increased or reduced the stringency of its GHG reduction target after adopting its first target. Note that this graph also includes the first publicly available GHG reduction target that a city established, whether for city operations or community emissions. Where there is no other available data, we used the year of the first climate action plan for the city. The graph does not count signing the U.S. Mayors Climate Protection Agreement as adopting a GHG reduction goal; the Agreement, which mayors started signing in 2005, merely committed cities to "[s]trive to meet or beat the Kyoto Protocol target in their own communities." U.S. CONF. OF MAYORS, *Mayors Climate Protection Center, Mayors Climate Protection Agreement*, www.usmayors.org/programs/mayors-climate-protection-center/ (last visited July 11, 2024).

See AUSTIN, TEX., RES. NO. 20070215-023 (2007) (setting greenhouse gas reduction goals in 2007); CHARLOTTE, N.C., *SUSTAINABLE AND RESILIENT CHARLOTTE BY 2050 RESOLUTION* (2018) (setting a goal to reduce greenhouse gas emissions in 2018); CHI., ILL., *CHICAGO CLIMATE ACTION PLAN* 9 (2008), www.chicago.gov/city/en/progs/env/climateaction.html (showing a timeline of Chicago's climate activities, including joining the Chicago Climate Exchange in 2003 to reduce greenhouse gas emissions by 6 percent by 2010); *City of Columbus Climate Action Plan*, CITY OF COLUMBUS, www.columbus.gov/sustainable/cap/ (last visited Mar. 29, 2024) ("In February 2020, Mayor Ginther announced a bold and ambitious goal for the Columbus community to be carbon neutral by 2050."); CITY OF DALL., MEMORANDUM, GREENHOUSE GAS EMISSIONS 12, 15 (2009), www3.dallascityhall.com/committee_briefings/briefings0809/TEC_GreenhouseGasEmissions_081109.pdf (outlining initiatives to reduce Dallas greenhouse gas emissions 7 percent below 1990 levels by 2012); CITY & CNTY. OF DENVER, 80 X 50 CLIMATE GOAL: STAKEHOLDER REPORT (2017) ("In 2007, Denver established its first GHG emission reduction goal with the 2007 Climate Action Plan."); Kristin Musulin, *Houston Unveils First Climate Action Plan*, UTILITYDIVE (Apr. 25, 2020), www.utilitydive.com/news/houston-unveils-first-climate-action-plan/576752/ (noting Houston's 2020 plan to reduce greenhouse gas emissions); INDIANAPOLIS, IND., CITY-COUNTY SPEC. RES. NO. 10 (2017) (requiring Indianapolis to produce a climate action plan in 2017); CITY OF L.A., GREEN LA: AN ACTION PLAN TO LEAD THE NATION IN FIGHTING GLOBAL WARMING (2007) (establishing GHG emissions reduction goals for Los Angeles in 2007); CITY OF N.Y., PLANYC: A GREENER, GREATER NEW YORK (2007) [hereinafter PLANYC 2007] (establishing GHG emissions reduction goals for New York City in 2007); CITY OF PHX., CLIMATE ACTION PLAN FOR GOVERNMENT OPERATIONS (2009) ("In December 2008, the City Council adopted a goal to: Reduce emissions from city operations to 5 percent below the 2005 levels by 2015."); CITY OF PHILA., LOCAL ACTION PLAN FOR CLIMATE CHANGE 3 (2007) ("In 1999 the City committed to a goal to reduce Philadelphia greenhouse gases to 10 percent below 1990 levels by 2010."); CITY OF SAN ANTONIO, SA CLIMATE READY: A PATHWAY FOR CLIMATE ACTION & ADAPTATION (2019) (detailing San Antonio's 2019 goal to reduce greenhouse gas emissions); *Overview: SD Sustainability*, CITY OF SAN DIEGO, www.sandiego.gov/sustainability/overview (last visited May 7, 2024) ("In 2015, the City Council approved San Diego's Climate Action Plan, which calls for the City to cut half of all greenhouse gas (GHG) emissions by 2035."); S.F., CA., RES. NO. 158–02 (2002) (setting greenhouse gas reduction goals for San Francisco in 2002); CITY OF SAN JOSE, GREEN VISION 2011 ANNUAL REPORT 3 (2012), www3.sanjoseca

.gov/clerk/Agenda/20120320/20120320_0303att.pdf (noting a Greenhouse Gas Reduction Strategy adopted in November 2011); SEATTLE, WASH., RES. NO. 30316 (2001) (adopting greenhouse gas emission reduction goals for Seattle in 2001).

Oklahoma City does not appear to have established a GHG reduction target. *See Air Quality*, CITY OF OKLAHOMA CITY, www.okc.gov/departments/planning/programs/sustainability/adaptokc/air-quality (last visited May 7, 2024) (noting that Oklahoma City's efforts to establish a GHG target are still in progress). Similarly, Fort Worth and Jacksonville, despite joining the U.S. Mayors Climate Protection Agreement in 2007, have both stalled in producing meaningful climate action plans; they are also counted as not having a GHG reduction target in this chapter. *See* Julie Ryan, *North Texas Cities Combating Climate Change from the Bottom Up*, GREENSOURCEDFW (Feb. 9, 2018), https://greensourcedfw.org/articles/north-texas-cities-combating-climate-change; ACEEE, 2021 CITY CLEAN ENERGY SCORECARD: FORT WORTH, TX (2021); Haley Samsel, *Fort Worth Remains One of Few Major Cities without a Climate Action Plan. Where Does It Go from Here?*, FORT WORTH REP. (Aug. 17, 2023), https://fortworthreport.org/2023/08/17/fort-worth-remains-one-of-few-major-cities-without-a-climate-action-plan-where-does-it-go-from-here/; Owen Holmes, *Better Late than Never: Peyton Commits to Fight Global Warming*, FOLIO WEEKLY (July 19, 2007); Sydney Boles et al., *What Jacksonville Can Learn from Nashville about Fighting Climate Change*, WUSF (May 30, 2021), https://wusfnews.wusf.usf.edu/environment/2021-05-30/what-jacksonville-can-learn-from-nashville-about-fighting-climate-change. As of this writing, Jacksonville, however, is developing GHG reduction goals as part of its "Resilient Jacksonville" program. CITY OF JACKSONVILLE, RESILIENT JACKSONVILLE 188 (Oct. 2023).

13. PLANYC 2007, *supra* note 12, at 132–33. *See also* PLANYC 2023, *supra* note 11, at 12 (NYC's Climate Milestones).
14. *See generally* HUGHES, *supra* note 1, at 35–37 (discussing the importance of the co-benefits that localities may experience in acting to reduce GHG emissions as a factor driving local actions).
15. *See, e.g.*, Natalie Wong, *NYC Landlords Bracing for Millions in Fines with New Climate Law*, BLOOMBERG (Jan. 19, 2023), www.bloomberg.com/news/articles/2023-01-19/nyc-landlords-bracing-for-millions-in-fines-with-new-climate-law; Carl Campanile, *NYC Co-op Owners, Covering Over 800K Apartments, Rebel against Massive Climate Law Costing Millions*, N.Y. POST (Apr. 30, 2023), https://nypost.com/2023/04/30/co-op-owners-rebel-against-massive-nyc-climate-law-costing-millions/.
16. DANIELLE SPIEGEL-FELD ET AL., CARBON TRADING FOR NEW YORK CITY'S BUILDING SECTOR: REPORT OF THE LOCAL LAW 97 CARBON TRADING STUDY GROUP TO THE NEW YORK CITY MAYOR'S OFFICE OF CLIMATE & SUSTAINABILITY 63 tbl. 8 (2021).
17. PLANYC 2007, *supra* note 12, at 11–13 (laying out goals for NYC in 2030, including a 30 percent emissions reduction).
18. *Id.* ("Collectively these initiatives address the greatest challenge of all: global warming.").
19. N.Y.C. ENERGY POL'Y TASK FORCE, NEW YORK CITY ENERGY POLICY: AN ELECTRICITY RESOURCES ROADMAP 9 (2004), www.nyc.gov/html/om/pdf/energy_task_force.pdf.
20. *Id.*
21. CONG. RSCH. SERV., RL33302, ENERGY POLICY ACT OF 2005: SUMMARY AND ANALYSIS OF THE ENACTED PROVISIONS 1–2 (2006).
22. *Benchmarking Preconsidered Introductory: Water & Energy Disclosure: Transcript of the Minutes on Int. No. 476-A before the N.Y.C. Council Comm. on Env't Prot.* (June 27, 2008) (testimony of Rohit Aggarwala, Director, Mayor's Off. of Long-Term Plan. &

Sustainability). *See also* PLANYC 2007, *supra* note 12, at 13 ("To reduce demand [for energy], we will target our largest energy consumers – institutional buildings, commercial and industrial buildings, and multi-family residential buildings – and accelerate efficiency upgrades through a system of incentives, mandates, and challenges. Demand reductions will help all New Yorkers by lowering energy prices.").

23. *See* PLANYC 2007, *supra* note 12, at 134.
24. According to PlaNYC, "With almost 600 miles of coastline and over half a million New Yorkers living within our current flood plain, this change is especially dangerous to New York.... According to one estimate, a Category 2 hurricane would inflict more damage on New York than any other American city except Miami." PLANYC 2007, *supra* note 12, at 8.
25. ICLEI-LOCAL GOV'TS FOR SUSTAINABILITY USA & MAYOR'S OFF. LONG-TERM PLAN. & SUSTAINABILITY, CITY OF N.Y., THE PROCESS BEHIND PLANYC 20 (2010) ("The process to develop this target involved an analysis of the emissions reduction potential of various strategies, such as transit oriented development, citywide building retrofits, and clean energy, along with researching targets of other large cities around the world.").

    New York City's 30 percent reduction target by 2030 was more ambitious than targets established by some other cities in the late 1990s and early 2000s. *See, e.g.*, CITY OF PHILA., LOCAL ACTION PLAN FOR CLIMATE CHANGE i (2007), https://uccrnna.org/wp-content/uploads/2017/06/13_Philadelphia_2007_Local-Action-Plan-for-Climate-Change.pdf ("In 1999 the City committed to a goal to reduce Philadelphia greenhouse gases to 10 percent below 1990 levels by 2010."); MAYOR'S GREENPRINT DENVER ADVISORY COUNCIL, CITY OF DENVER CLIMATE ACTION PLAN 3 (2007), www.austintexas.gov/sites/default/files/files/Sustainability/Climate/Denver_Greenprint.pdf ("In 2005, Mayor Hickenlooper established Denver's initial greenhouse gas reduction goal: by 2012 Denver will reduce its emissions of greenhouse gases by 10 percent per capita relative to 1990 levels."); S.F. DEPT. OF ENV'T, CLIMATE ACTION PLAN FOR SAN FRANCISCO: LOCAL ACTIONS TO REDUCE GREENHOUSE GAS EMISSIONS ES-1 (2004), www.sfenvironment.org/media/5089 ("In 2002, the San Francisco Board of Supervisors passed the Greenhouse Gas Emissions Reduction Resolution, committing the City and County of San Francisco to a greenhouse gas emissions reductions goal of 20% below 1990 levels by the year 2012."). *But see* CITY OF BOS., CLIMATE: *Change*; THE CITY OF BOSTON'S CLIMATE ACTION PLAN 2 (2007) (noting that in April 2007, the mayor of Boston signed an executive order committing Boston to reducing its GHG emissions by 80 percent by 2050); CHI., ILL., CHICAGO CLIMATE ACTION PLAN 11 (2008), www.chicago.gov/city/en/progs/env/climateaction.html ("Chicago's goal is to reach an 80 percent reduction in greenhouse gas emissions from 1990 levels by 2050").
26. *See, e.g.*, PLANYC 2007, *supra* note 12, at 11, 140; Editorial Board, *OneNYC Needs More Data, Fewer Slogans*, OBSERVER (Apr. 29, 2015), https://observer.com/2015/04/onenyc-needs-more-data-fewer-slogans/ ("[PlaNYC] was data-heavy, examining trends about water supply and quality, energy usage and air pollution, land use, housing and transportation. It made recommendations to make New York a more livable and sustainable city; and it set measurable goals.").
27. MAYOR'S OFF. OF LONG-TERM PLAN. & SUSTAINABILITY, CITY OF N.Y., PLANYC: INVENTORY OF NEW YORK CITY GREENHOUSE GAS EMISSIONS (2007), https://climate.cityofnewyork.us/wp-content/uploads/2022/10/greenhousegas_2007.pdf [hereinafter N.Y.C. GHG INVENTORY 2007]. Shortly thereafter, the city council passed a law that codified the requirement to publish periodic updates to the inventory and

established a mandate – not just a target – to reduce citywide emissions by 30 percent below 2005 levels by 2030. N.Y.C, N.Y., LOCAL LAW NO. 22 (2008); N.Y.C. Admin. Code § 23–803.a, 805.

ICLEI, along with the World Resources Institute (WRI) and C40 Cities Climate Leadership Group (C40), created what is now the standard protocol used by local governments to track their GHG emissions. WEE KEAN FONG ET AL., GLOBAL PROTOCOL FOR COMMUNITY-SCALE GREENHOUSE GAS INVENTORIES: AN ACCOUNTING AND REPORTING STANDARD FOR CITIES (2020), https://ghgprotocol.org/sites/default/files/standards/GPC_Full_MASTER_RW_v7.pdf. The development of the protocol began in 2011 between C40 and ICLEI; WRI joined the partnership in 2012. JOLENE LIN, GOVERNING CLIMATE CHANGE: GLOBAL CITIES AND TRANSNATIONAL LAWMAKING 121–22 (2018).

28. The figure is populated based on the following data: AL ARMENDARIZ ET AL., AUSTIN COMMUNITY CLIMATE PLAN 12 (2015) ("The Office of Sustainability completed the most recent community-wide greenhouse gas inventory in 2010 following the U.S. Community GHG Protocol developed by the International Council for Local Environmental Initiatives (ICLEI).") counted as (2010); CHARLOTTE, STRATEGIC ENERGY ACTION PLAN 4 (2018) (citing 2015 Baseline GHG Emissions) (2018); CTR. FOR NEIGHBORHOOD TECH., CHICAGO'S GREENHOUSE GAS EMISSIONS: AN INVENTORY, FORECAST AND MITIGATION ANALYSIS FOR CHICAGO AND THE METROPOLITAN REGION 6 (2008) (citing Chicago's GHG Emissions 2000 and 2005) (2008); CITY OF COLUMBUS, The Columbus Green Community Plan: Green Memo III, at 14 (2015) (Baseline: Community Wide Total GHG in 2013) (2015); GREEN DALL., CITY OF DALLAS GREENHOUSE GAS EMISSIONS INVENTORY (2010) (charting the 2005 Community Wide Greenhouse Gas Emissions) (2010); CITY & CNTY. OF DENVER, CO 2005 GREENHOUSE GAS INVENTORY (2005) (2005); HOUS., 2007 COMMUNITY GREENHOUSE GAS (GHG) EMISSIONS INVENTORY (2009) (2009); METRO. DEV. COMM'N, THRIVE INDIANAPOLIS (2019) ("The City completes its first community-wide greenhouse gas emissions inventory and climate vulnerability assessment [in 2018]") (2019); L. A. REG'L COLLABORATIVE, LA COUNTY GHG INVENTORIES FOR CITIES IN LA COUNTY (2010) (2010); CITY OF N.Y., INVENTORY OF NEW YORK CITY GREENHOUSE GAS EMISSIONS (2007) (2007); PHILA., LOCAL ACTION PLAN FOR CLIMATE CHANGE 23 (2007) (includes completed 2006 inventory) (2007); PHX., 2012 COMMUNITY GREENHOUSE GAS EMISSIONS REPORT 2 (2017) (2017); SAN ANTONIO, 2014 GREENHOUSE GAS EMISSIONS INVENTORY (2016) (2016); CITY OF SAN DIEGO, CITY OF SAN DIEGO CLIMATE ACTION PLAN 19 (2015) (2010 Community-Wide Emissions Inventory) (2015); S.F. ENV'T, SAN FRANCISCO CLIMATE ACTION STRATEGY (2013 Update) ("GHG inventory methodologies have developed substantially since the first San Francisco community-wide inventory was compiled in 2004.") (2004); CITY OF SAN JOSE, GREENHOUSE GAS REDUCTIONS STRATEGY FOR THE CITY OF SAN JOSE (2011) (2000–2008 Average Emissions) (2011); *Global Warming Initiative – Seattle, WA*, INST. FOR LOCAL SELF-RELIANCE, https://ilsr.org/rule/climate-change/2533-2/ (last visited May 7, 2024) ("In April 2002 the city of Seattle completed a greenhouse gas inventory, the first step towards meeting their goals for greenhouse gas reductions") (2002). Note that data is based on the earliest publicly available report located. *See supra* note 6 for the list of the top twenty most populous cities.

29. The following three paragraphs draw from Danielle Spiegel-Feld, *Reducing Greenhouse Gas Emissions from Buildings in New York City: An Evolving Regime*, *in* GLOBAL SUSTAINABLE CITIES: CITY GOVERNMENTS AND OUR ENVIRONMENTAL FUTURE 259 (Danielle Spiegel-Feld, Katrina Miriam Wyman, & John J. Coughlin eds., 2023).

30. On the connection between the suite of Greener, Greater Buildings laws and PlaNYC, see PLANYC 2007, *supra* note 12, at 134–35, and *Benchmarking Preconsidered Introductory:*

Water & Energy Disclosure: Hearing on Int. No. 476-A before the N.Y.C. Council Comm. on Env't Prot. (June 27, 2008) (testimony of Rohit Aggarwala, Dir., Mayor's Off. of Long-Term Plan. & Sustainability).

31. For example, in Boston, Chicago, New York, Philadelphia, and Washington, D.C., buildings account for over 70 percent of local GHG emissions. *See* City of Bos., Greenhouse Gas Emissions Inventory 2005–2021 at 38 (2022), www.boston.gov/sites/default/files/file/2024/01/2005-2021%20City%20of%20Boston%20Greenhouse%20Gas%20Emissions%20Inventory.pdf; Press Release, Chi. Off. of the Mayor, Mayor Lightfoot Announces a Building Decarbonization Working Group (June 2, 2021), www.chicago.gov/city/en/depts/mayor/press_room/press_releases/2021/june/DecarbonizationWorkingGroup.html; *Climate Mobilization Act*, N.Y. City Council, https://council.nyc.gov/data/green/ (last visited Apr. 1, 2024); Helena Rudoff, *Philadelphia's 2019 Greenhouse Gas Inventory Reports 20% Reduction in Emissions Since 2006*, City of Phila. (Apr. 21, 2022), www.phila.gov/2022-04-21-philadelphias-2019-greenhouse-gas-inventory-reports-20-reduction-in-emissions-since-2006/; *Greenhouse Gas Inventories*, D.C. Dep't of Energy & Env't, https://doee.dc.gov/service/greenhouse-gas-inventories (last visited Apr. 1, 2024). PlaNYC (from 2007) refers to buildings accounting for 69 percent of New York City's emissions. PlaNYC 2007, *supra* note 12, at 135.
32. *See* Danielle Spiegel-Feld, *Frontiers in Regulating Building Emissions: An Agenda for Cities*, 47 Wm. & Mary Env't L. & Pol'y Rev. 103, 107–08 (2022).
33. *Metro. Taxicab Bd. of Trade v. City of* N.Y., 2008 WL 4866021 (S.D.N.Y. 2008); *Metro. Taxicab Bd. of Trade v. City of New York*, 615 F.3d 152, 158 (2d Cir. 2010).
34. Katrina M. Wyman & Danielle Spiegel-Feld, *The Urban Environmental Renaissance*, 108 Cal. L. Rev. 305, 360 (2020).
35. Retro-commissioning essentially requires buildings to tune-up the existing HVAC systems, and it typically does not require owners to invest in new systems. *Retro-commissioning*, N.Y. State Energy Res. & Dev. Auth., www.nyserda.ny.gov/PutEnergyToWork/Energy-Technology-and-Solutions/Building-Operations-and-Performance/Retro-Commissioning (last accessed Apr. 1, 2024).
36. N.Y.C, N.Y., Local Law No. 88 § 1 (2019) ("[M]ost large buildings have one master meter for electricity that measures building-wide usage, as opposed to separate meters that provide such information on a per tenant basis.").
37. N.Y.C. Mayor's Off. of Long-Term Plan. & Sustainability, Overview of the Greener, Greater Buildings Plan 2 (2014) [hereinafter Overview of the GGBP].
38. N.Y.C. Council, Meeting Minutes, Comm. On Env't Prot. (June 26, 2009) (testimony of Rohit Aggarwala). Other local governments have also presented decarbonization as an industrial strategy that will build new industries within their borders. *See, e.g.*, City of L.A., Green LA: An Action Plan to Lead the Nation in Fighting Global Warming 3 (2007); *see also* Hughes, *supra* note 1, at 25 (also referring to the 2007 Los Angeles climate action plan). Officials in California, which has been a leader among states in decarbonization efforts, have also suggested that addressing climate change would produce economic benefits. Stewart, *supra* note 1, at 691.
39. Overview of the GGBP, *supra* note 37, at 1. As initially adopted, Local Law 84 applied to buildings with more than 50,000 square feet; it was subsequently amended to cover buildings with greater than 25,000 square feet as well.
40. *About Benchmarking in New York City*, Urb. Green https://metered.urbangreencouncil.org/site/about#. (last visited Apr. 1, 2024) ("In 2009, as part of a suit[e] of energy efficiency laws called the Greener, Greater Buildings Plan, New York passed Local Law 84 (LL84) – one of the earliest benchmarking laws in the country and the first to be implemented.").

41. *See infra* note 50.
42. Emily Stewart, *How Mike Bloomberg Made His Billions: A Computer System You've Probably Never Seen*, Vox (Dec. 11, 2019), www.vox.com/2020-presidential-election/2019/12/11/21005008/michael-bloomberg-terminal-net-worth-2020.
43. N.Y.C. Glob. Partners, Best Practice: NYC Greener, Greater Buildings Plan (2010) ("Benchmarking provides the basis for empowering building owners to take steps towards minimizing energy use and maximizing the economic benefits of energy conservation.").
44. *Benchmarking Preconsidered Introductory: Water & Energy Disclosure: Hearing on Int. No. 476-A before the N.Y.C. Council Comm. on Env't Prot.* (June 27, 2008) (testimony of Russell Unger).
45. *Id.*
46. Mireya Navarro, *Bloomberg Drops an Effort to Cut Building Energy Use*, N.Y. Times (Dec. 4, 2009), www.nytimes.com/2009/12/05/science/earth/05bloomberg.html. Section 1 of Intro. 967 in 2009 would have required buildings to implement energy efficiency measures that would pay back in seven years or less. Intro. 967 became Local Law 87, which requires audits, and minimal retro-commissioning.
47. *Mayor Bloomberg's 2008 State of the City Address*, N.Y. Times (Jan. 17, 2008), www.nytimes.com/2008/01/17/nyregion/17stateofnyc.html.
48. *Mayors from 10 Major Cities Unite to cut Climate Pollution from Buildings*, NRDC (Jan. 29, 2014), www.nrdc.org/media/2014/140129-0.
49. *See infra* note 50.
50. Figure 4.3 is populated by data from the following table:

City	Benchmarking Law	Building Audit Law
Austin	2008	2008
Charlotte	None	None
Chicago	2013	None
Columbus	2020	None
Dallas	None	None
Denver	2016	None
Fort Worth	None	None
Houston	2022	None
Indianapolis	2021	None
Jacksonville	None	None
Los Angeles	2016	2016
New York	2009	2009
Oklahoma City	None	None
Phoenix	None	None
Philadelphia	2012	2019
San Antonio	None	None
San Diego	2019	2019
San Francisco	2011	2011
San Jose	2018	2018
Seattle	2010	2016

The data on the benchmarking laws comes from: Inst. for Mkt. Transformation, Comparison of U.S. Commercial Building Energy Benchmarking and

TRANSPARENCY POLICIES (2022). *See also* AUSTIN, TEX., CITY CODE §§ 6–7 (2008); CHI., ILL., MUN. CODE ch. 18–14 (2017); COLUMBUS, OHIO, CODE OF ORDINANCES tit. 41, ch. 4117 (2020); DENVER, COLO., REV. MUN. CODE chs. 4, 10 (2016); Press Release, Houston Mayor's Office of Resilience and Sustainability, Mayor Sylvester Turner Signs Sweeping Decarbonization Policy for City Buildings (Apr. 22, 2022) (for city-owned and operated buildings); INDIANAPOLIS, IND., REV. CODE tit. 3, ch. 710 (2021); L.A., CAL., MUN. CODE DIV. 97 §§ 91.9701–91.9712 (2016); N.Y.C, N.Y., ADMIN CODE tit. 28, art. 309 (2009); PHILA., PA., CODE § 9-3402 (2012); SAN DIEGO, CAL., MUN. CODE. ch. 14 art. 12 div. 1 (2019); S.F., CAL., ENV'T CODE ch. 20, § 2000–09 (2011);SAN JOSE, CAL., MUN. CODE tit. 17, ch. 17.85 §§ 200, 300, 410, 420, 510, 520, 540 (2018); SEATTLE, WASH., MUN. CODE tit. 22 ch. 22.920 (2010).

The data on the audit laws comes from: INST. FOR MKT. TRANSFORMATION, COMPARISON OF U.S. BUILDING AUDIT, TUNE-UPS, AND RETROCOMMISSIONING POLICIES (2021). *See also* AUSTIN, TEX., CITY CODE §§ 6–7 (2008); L.A., CAL., MUN. CODE div. 97 §§ 91.9701–91.9712 (2016); N.Y.C, N.Y., ADMIN. CODE tit. 28 ch. 3 art. 308 (2009); PHILA., PA., CODE § 9-3404 (2019) (auditing is alternative compliance method); SAN DIEGO, CAL., MUN. CODE ch. 14 art. 12 div. 1 (2019); S.F., CAL., ENV'T CODE CH. 20 § 2000–09 (2011); SAN JOSE, CAL., MUN. CODE tit. 17 ch. 17.85 §§ 200, 300, 410, 420, 510, 520. 540 (2018); SEATTLE, WASH., MUN. CODE tit. 22 ch. 22.920 (2016) (Seattle) (auditing is alternative compliance method).

In 2023, Charlotte launched a voluntary benchmarking program. Press Release, City of Charlotte, City of Charlotte Launches New Program to Cut Energy Use (Apr. 20, 2023), www.charlottenc.gov/CS-Prep/City-News/City-of-Charlotte-Launches-New-Program-to-Cut-Energy-Use. The state of Arizona blocked Phoenix from adopting a benchmarking law. Henry Grabar, *Phoenix Has Beef with Arizona*, SLATE (Sept. 19, 2016), https://slate.com/business/2016/09/phoenix-mayor-greg-stanton-is-fed-up-with-arizona-pre-empting-his-citys-laws.html. Note that the development of an ordinance regarding benchmarking was in progress in San Antonio, Texas, as of 2022. *See* Press Release, Greater San Antonio Chamber of Commerce, Chamber Informs Members of City's Energy Benchmarking Program (Sept. 28, 2022), www.sachamber.org/news/2022/09/28/chamber-news/chamber-informs-members-of-city-s-energy-benchmarking-program/.

51. CITY OF N.Y., MAYOR'S OFF. OF LONG-TERM PLAN. & SUSTAINABILITY, ONE CITY: BUILT TO LAST 6–7 (2014) [hereinafter ONE CITY: BUILT TO LAST].
52. URB. GREEN COUNCIL, NEW YORK CITY'S ENERGY AND WATER USE 2014 AND 2015 REPORT 3, 5 (2017) (referring to reduction in source energy use).
53. Karen Palmer & Margaret Walls, *Does Information Provision Shrink the Energy Efficiency Gap? A Cross-City Comparison of Commercial Building Benchmarking and Disclosure Laws* 3, 12–15 (Res. for the Future, Disc. Paper RFF DP 15–12, 2015).
54. Constantine E. Kontokosta, Danielle Spiegel-Feld & Sokratis Papadopoulos, *The Impact of Mandatory Energy Audits on Building Energy Use*, 5 NATURE ENERGY 309 (2020).
55. CITY OF N.Y., NEW YORK CITY'S PATHWAYS TO DEEP CARBON REDUCTIONS 5, 12 (2013) (stating that the rationale for a deep, "80 by 50" decarbonization target was to help limit the rise in global temperature and "prevent 'dangerous anthropogenic interference with the climate system,'" and also mentioning "the opportunity to integrate carbon reduction and climate resiliency objectives" including improving resiliency against storms like Sandy).
56. Daniel Aldana Cohen, *New York City as "Fortress of Solitude" after Hurricane Sandy: A Relational Sociology of Extreme Weather's Relationship to Climate Politics*, 30 ENV'T POL. 687, 697 (2021).
57. NEW YORK CITY'S PATHWAYS TO DEEP CARBON REDUCTIONS, *supra* note 55, at 46.

58. Clare Foran, *Donald Trump and the Triumph of Climate-Change Denial*, THE ATLANTIC (Dec. 25, 2016), www.theatlantic.com/politics/archive/2016/12/donald-trump-climate-change-skeptic-denial/510359/; Dylan Matthews, *Donald Trump Has Tweeted Climate Change Skepticism 115 Times. Here's All of It*, VOX (June 1, 2017), www.vox.com/policy-and-politics/2017/6/1/15726472/trump-tweets-global-warming-paris-climate-agreement.
59. Press Release, White House, President Trump Announces U.S. Withdrawal from the Paris Climate Accord (June 1, 2017), https://trumpwhitehouse.archives.gov/articles/president-trump-announces-u-s-withdrawal-paris-climate-accord/.
60. Robbie Gramer & Dan De Luce, *In Closed-Door Climate Showdown, It's Jared and Ivanka vs. Bannon and Pruitt*, FP (May 8, 2017), https://foreignpolicy.com/2017/05/08/in-closed-door-climate-showdown-its-jared-and-ivanka-vs-bannon-and-pruitt-climate-change-trump-paris-agreement/; Marie Risalvato, *US Climate Action Network Members React to Trump Paris Announcement*, U.S. CLIMATE ACTION NETWORK (June 1, 2017), www.usclimatenetwork.org/us_climate_action_network_members_react_to_trump_paris_announcement.
61. CITY OF N.Y., *Transcript: Mayor de Blasio Delivers Remarks on NYC Ferry's New South Brooklyn Route* (May 31, 2017), www.nyc.gov/office-of-the-mayor/news/378-17/transcript-mayor-de-blasio-delivers-remarks-nyc-ferry-s-new-south-brooklyn-route. On May 31, 2017, *The New York Times* published an article reporting that there were indications that Trump would announce that he would withdraw the U.S. from the Paris Agreement. Michael D. Shear & Coral Davenport, *World Awaits Trump Decision on U.S. Future in Paris Accord*, N.Y. TIMES (May 31, 2017), www.nytimes.com/2017/05/31/climate/trump-quits-paris-climate-accord.html.
62. CITY OF N.Y., *supra* note 61.
63. Julian Borger, *Bush Kills Global Warming Treaty*, THE GUARDIAN (Mar. 29, 2001), www.theguardian.com/environment/2001/mar/29/globalwarming.usnews.
64. On the twenty most populous cities, see *supra* note 6. Of the twenty cities, the following cities signed the Mayors Climate Protection Agreement: Austin, Charlotte, Chicago, Columbus, Dallas, Denver, Fort Worth, Indianapolis, Jacksonville, Los Angeles, New York City, Philadelphia, Phoenix, San Antonio, San Diego, San Francisco, San Jose, and Seattle. *Mayors Climate Protection Center*, U.S. CONFERENCE OF MAYORS, www.usmayors.org/programs/mayors-climate-protection-center/ (last visited Apr. 4, 2024). Houston and Oklahoma City were not signatories. *Id.*

    The Mayors Climate Protection Agreement was an initiative of the U.S. Conference of Mayors, which represents cities with 30,000 inhabitants or more. *About the Conference*, U.S. CONFERENCE OF MAYORS, www.usmayors.org/the-conference/about/ (last visited Apr. 5, 2024). The Mayors Climate Protection Agreement was unanimously passed by the U.S. Conference of Mayors on June 13, 2005. *See* Press Release, City of Bloomington, Ind., Mayor Signs Climate Protection Agreement (Apr. 21, 2006), https://bloomington.in.gov/news/2006/04/21/2438. By the end of 2009, 1,017 U.S. cities had signed the Mayors Climate Protection Agreement. Jonathan Hiskes. *America's Greenest Mayor, Laid Off and Looking On*, GRIST (Dec. 4, 2009), https://grist.org/article/2009-12-03-greenest-mayor-greg-nickels-seattle/. For useful context that underscores the limited reach of the cities that signed the Mayors Climate Protection Agreement, see Hari Osofsky, *The Geography of Solving Global Environmental Problems*, 58 N.Y.L. SCH. L. REV. 777, 784–85 (2014) (The "1,054 mayors" who signed the agreement "represent only about 5% of U.S. cities and 28% of the total U.S. population. The vast majority of cities and people are not participating in the mayors agreement.")
65. *See* Krause et al., *supra* note 1, at 177 ("ICLEI membership … facilitates the implementation of GHG abatement planning and action. Between 2006 and 2010, there was a

nearly sixfold increase in the number of municipalities pursing climate protection via ICLEI. Its membership peaked in 2010 with nearly 700 local governments, 565 of which were cities and towns." (citation omitted)). New York City has participated in ICLEI's Cities for Climate Protection Program and has been a member of ICLEI since 1999. N.Y.C. GHG INVENTORY 2007, *supra* note 27, at 6; *City of New York*, NY, ICLEI, https://iclei.org/network_city/city-of-new-york-ny/ (last visited Apr. 5, 2024). On the history of ICLEI, which created "the first global programme supporting cities in pursuing climate action" in 1993, see LIN, *supra* note 27, at 109; *see also* Krause et al., *supra* note 1, at 180–83 (discussing, inter alia, history of ICLEI, U.S. cities' changing involvement with ICLEI, characteristics of U.S. cities participating in ICLEI, and the opposition of the Tea Party Movement to ICLEI). On the distinction between ICLEI and the Mayors Climate Protection Agreement, see Krause et al., *supra* note 1, at 177, 180.

66. On the history of C40, see LIN, *supra* note 27, at 105–26. *See also* MICHELE ACUTO, GLOBAL CITIES, GOVERNANCE AND DIPLOMACY: THE URBAN LINK 103–4, 113–14 (2013) (New York City was chair of the C40 starting in 2010, and New York City and Los Angeles were members of the Steering Committee as of 2012).

67. Bloomberg Philanthropies helped to organize the effort. *America is All In*, BLOOMBERG PHILANTHROPIES, www.bloomberg.org/environment/supporting-sustainable-cities/america-is-all-in/ (last visited Apr. 9, 2024); *Who's In*, AMERICA IS ALL IN, www.americaisallin.com/whos-in (last visited Dec. 15, 2022) (noting 343 local governments as constituencies). The seventeen of the twenty most populous cities listed are: Austin, Charlotte, Chicago, Columbus, Dallas, Denver, Houston, Indianapolis, Los Angeles, New York City, Philadelphia, Phoenix, San Antonio, San Diego, San Francisco, San Jose, and Seattle. Fort Worth, Jacksonville, and Oklahoma City are not members.

68. Political theorist Benjamin Barber provided a rationale for city action in the face of federal inaction on climate change. BENJAMIN R. BARBER, COOL CITIES: URBAN SOVEREIGNTY AND THE FIX FOR GLOBAL WARMING 10 (2017) (cities have been forced to take on the climate crisis because "national leaders have defaulted in dealing with the big issues of an interdependent world … [including] climate change"). In the waning days of the George W. Bush administration, the political scientist Miranda Schreurs offered a similar explanation for American cities' leadership on climate. In her words, American cities had taken up the cause of climate change in response to the federal government's "failure … to play a strong leadership role on climate change politics." Miranda A. Schreurs, *From the Bottom Up: Local and Subnational Climate Change Politics*, 17 *J.* ENV'T *&* DEV. 343, 350 (2008).

69. Climate politics became a partisan issue in the early 1990s, after the failure of President Clinton's proposed BTU Tax. *See* MATTO MILDENBERGER, CARBON CAPTURED: HOW BUSINESS AND LABOR CONTROL CLIMATE POLITICS 123 (2020).

As of 2025, there is little evidence that the partisan divide over climate change is abating. In May of 2022, the news site Five Thirty Eight published a poll of Americans' political priorities. Geoffrey Skelley & Holly Fuong, *We Asked 2,000 Americans about Their Biggest Concern*, FIVETHIRTYEIGHT (May 17, 2022), https://fivethirtyeight.com/features/we-asked-2000-americans-about-their-biggest-concern-the-resounding-answer-inflation/. The pollsters had asked the respondents what issue or issues were most important to them. Looking at the sample as a whole, 16 percent of respondents stated that climate change was one of the most important problems facing the country. *Id.* But there was a huge difference between the percentage of Democratic and Republican respondents on the question: 30 percent of Democrats stated that climate change was among the most important issues compared to only 6 percent of Republicans. *Id.* Only two other issues – election fraud and immigration – showed such a large partisan divide. The vote tally for the Inflation

Reduction Act (IRA) passed in 2022 underscores the ongoing partisan divide over climate: not a single Republican senator voted for the IRA, which was passed through a budget reconciliation process that allowed Senate Democrats to bypass the filibuster. *See* Maxine Joselow, *Why the Inflation Reduction Act Passed the Senate but Cap-and-Trade Didn't*, WASH. POST (Aug. 10, 2022), www.washingtonpost.com/politics/2022/08/10/why-inflation-reduction-act-passed-senate-cap-and-trade-didnt/. However, there is polling data indicating broad support for specific climate policies, which raises questions about the extent of the partisan divide on climate change among the voting public. *See* ANTHONY LEISEROWITZ ET AL., YALE U. & GEORGE MASON U., POLITICS & GLOBAL WARMING, APRIL 2022 (2022) (finding that while more Democrats than Republicans consider climate change an urgent priority, a majority of poll respondents support an energy transition away from fossil fuels and funding to support renewable energy development); Gregg Sparkman, Nathan Geiger & Elke Weber, *Americans Experience a False Social Reality by Underestimating Popular Climate Policy Support by Nearly Half*, 13 NATURE COMM. 1 (2022).

On the clustering of Democratic voters in urban areas of their states, and Republican dominance in rural areas, see, for example, Jacob Brown & Ryan D. Enos, *The Measurement of Partisan Sorting for 180 Million Voters*, 5 NATURE HUM. BEHAV. 998, 998 (2021) ("A large proportion of voters live with virtually no exposure to voters from the other party in their residential environment."); *see also* Nate Silver, *The Senate's Rural Skew Makes It Very Hard for Democrats to Win the Supreme Court*, FIVETHIRTYEIGHT (Sept. 20, 2020), https://fivethirtyeight.com/features/the-senates-rural-skew-makes-it-very-hard-for-democrats-to-win-the-supreme-court/ ("[T]he Senate is an enormous problem for Democrats given the current political coalitions, in which Democrats are dominant in cities while Republicans triumph in rural areas.").

70. This graph shows the number of the top twenty most populous U.S. cities in ICLEI and C40 by year. Data in Figure 4.4 is populated by the following table.

City	Date Joined ICELI	Dated Joined C40
Austin	1993	2006
Charlotte	nonmember	nonmember
Chicago	1992	2005
Columbus	date not listed	nonmember
Dallas	2017	nonmember
Denver	1992	nonmember
Fort Worth	2023	nonmember
Houston	date not listed	2006
Indianapolis	2023	nonmember
Jacksonville	nonmember	nonmember
Los Angeles	date not listed	2006
New York	1999	2005
Oklahoma City	nonmember	nonmember
Philadelphia	2007	2005
Phoenix	nonmember	2020
San Antonio	2020	nonmember
San Diego	2023	nonmember
San Francisco	date not listed	2005
San Jose	2018	nonmember
Seattle	1999	2006

The data in the table is sourced from *ICLEI Members*, ICLEI, https://iclei.org/iclei-members/ (last visited Apr. 9, 2024) (listing the members and the year they became a member); *Our Cities*, C40 CITIES, www.c40.org/cities/ (last visited Apr. 9, 2024) (listing the members and the year they became a member). Note that four cities – Columbus, Houston, Los Angeles, and San Francisco – are not included in this figure for ICLEI, as ICLEI does not identify what year they joined. The graph also does not account for cities leaving ICLEI or C40 after joining; once a city joins ICLEI or C40, it is counted as in the organization. Krause et al. indicate that the number of U.S. municipalities that were members of ICLEI increased in the 2000s, peaked in 2010 at almost 700 and then declined precipitously. *See* Krause et al., *supra* note 1, at 181. *See also* KRAUSE & HAWKINS, *supra* note 7, at 7 Figure 1.2 (graph of number of municipal members in select climate and sustainability networks, 2000–2017).

71. *Hottest Summer Ever for New York City*, DAILY BEAST (Apr. 24, 2017), www.thedailybeast.com/cheats/2010/09/01/hottest-summer-ever-for-new-york-city. On the climate impacts felt throughout the country in the summer of 2017, see Rebecca Bratspies, *Protecting the Environment in an Era of Federal Retreat: The View from New York City*, 13 FIU L. REV. 5, 12–13 (2018).
72. William Neuman, *De Blasio Vows to Cut Emissions in New York's Larger Buildings*, N.Y. TIMES (Sept. 14, 2017), www.nytimes.com/2017/09/14/nyregion/de-blasio-mayor-environment-buildings-emissions.html; Samar Kurshid, *Mapping the Mayoral: Where De Blasio and Malliotakis Each Did Well*, GOTHAM GAZETTE (Nov. 10, 2017), www.gothamgazette.com/city/7313-mapping-the-mayoral-where-de-blasio-and-malliotakis-each-did-well.
73. Portions of the remainder of this chapter draw from Danielle Spiegel-Feld, *Reducing Greenhouse Gas Emissions from Buildings in New York City: An Evolving Regime, in* GLOBAL SUSTAINABLE CITIES: CITY GOVERNMENTS AND OUR ENVIRONMENTAL FUTURE 259, 263 (Danielle Spiegel-Feld, Katrina Miriam Wyman & John J. Coughlin eds., 2023).
74. N.Y.C., Off. of the Mayor, Transcript: Mayor de Blasio Announces NYC Will Be First City to Mandate that Existing Buildings Dramatically Cut Greenhouse Gas Emissions (Sept. 14, 2017), www.nyc.gov/office-of-the-mayor/news/589-17/transcript-mayor-de-blasio-nyc-will-be-first-city-mandate-existing-buildings. Later in the fall, council member Costa Constantinides introduced Intro 1745 which established mandatory targets for buildings. N.Y.C., N.Y., INTRO. 1745 (2017). On Intro 1745, see Bratspies, *supra* note 71, at 20–21.
75. N.Y.C., Off. of the Mayor, *supra* note 74. Notably, there were no members of the city council standing with de Blasio when he made his announcement, and the chair of the council's environmental protection committee, Costa Constantinides, who ultimately oversaw the complex process of drafting of the law mandating building emissions reductions, was reported in *The New York Times* as "taken aback" that the mayor had come out so soon for mandates before a bill had been drafted. Neuman, *supra* note 72.
76. Minutes of the City Council Meeting of April 18, 2019, at 1503.
77. The following paragraphs expand on material previously published in a condensed form in Katrina Wyman, *Building Efficiency*, 40 ENV'T FORUM (2023).
78. *See* N.Y.C., N.Y., INTRO. 967 § 1 (2009) (draft bill with § 28-308.3 requiring buildings to implement energy efficiency measures that would pay back in seven years or less); Navarro, *supra* note 46 (reporting that Bloomberg had wanted mandatory targets). On the idea that administration officials revived the ideas of mandates in the waning days of the administration, see Cohen, *supra* note 56, at 11 ("Without fanfare, on the

last day of Bloomberg's administration [31 December 2013], the Mayor's Office of Long-Term Planning and Sustainability uploaded a report … [which] outlined an 80% cut in GHG emissions by 2050, a significant acceleration of the original PlaNYC's target, largely through increased building retrofits.") (citing to City of N.Y., New York City's Pathways to Deep Carbon Reductions 46 (2013)).

79. One City: Built to Last, *supra* note 51, at 10. *See also* Matt Flegenheimer, *De Blasio Orders a Greener City, Setting Goals for Energy Efficiency of Buildings*, N.Y. Times (Sept. 20, 2014), www.nytimes.com/2014/09/21/nyregion/new-york-city-plans-major-energy-efficiency-improvements-in-its-buildings.html.

    In December 2014, the NYC council passed legislation increasing the goal for reducing citywide emissions from 30 percent by 2030, to an 80 percent reduction by 2050. N.Y.C, N.Y., Local Law No. 66, Intro 78–2014, (2014).

80. *John Lee*, LinkedIn, www.linkedin.com/in/john-lee-87771636/ (last visited Apr. 9, 2024); *Dan Zarrilli*, LinkedIn, www.linkedin.com/in/danielzarrilli/ (last visited Apr. 9, 2024).

81. *Costa Constantinides*, LinkedIn, www.linkedin.com/in/costa-constantinides-abbb554 (last visited Apr. 9, 2024).

    Constantinides had personal reasons for working hard to pass a law to remove fossil fuels from buildings. Removing them would not only reduce GHG emissions and help the climate, but also reduce local air pollution and therefore prevent more children from getting asthma, which afflicted his own son. Costa Constantinides, *From Asthma Alley to Renewable Row: Transform This Stretch of Queens*, Daily News (Jan. 16, 2022), www.nydailynews.com/opinion/ny-oped-20220116-ucjx47uc7felbl2wfwxbwzw2fq-story.html.

82. For other scholarship emphasizing the influence of interest groups in local government policy, see Sarah F. Anzia, Local Interests: Politics, Policy, and Interest Groups in US City Governments (2022). For a study finding that environmental advocacy groups have influenced city commitments to sustainability, see Kent E. Portney & Jeffrey M. Berry, *The Impact of Local Environmental Advocacy Groups on City Sustainability Policies and Programs*, 44 Pol'y Stud. J. 196 (2016).

83. Melissa Davey, Adam Vaughan & Amanda Holpuch, *People's Climate March: Thousands Demand Action around the World*, The Guardian (Sept. 21, 2014), www.theguardian.com/environment/live/2014/sep/21/peoples-climate-march-live. *See also Built to Last*, City of New York, www1.nyc.gov/site/builttolast/index.page (last visited Apr. 9, 2024) (announcing publication of *One City: Built to Last*, which established the 80 × 50 goal, on September 21, 2014).

    The People's Climate March, which occurred ahead of a UN climate summit in New York, was hailed as the "biggest ever call-to-action on climate change." Davey, Vaughan & Holpuch, *supra*.

84. *See* Cohen, *supra* note 56, at 14 ("The massive Sept. 21st, 2014 People's Climate March set the developments [towards LL97] in motion.").

85. ALIGN, Climate Works for All: A Platform for Reducing Emissions, Protecting Our Communities, and Creating Good Jobs for New Yorkers 10 (2015). *See Climate Works for All*, ALIGN, https://alignny.org/campaign/climate-works-for-all/ (last visited Apr. 9, 2024) ("After the 2014 People's Climate March, community groups, environmental justice organizations, labor unions and other allied advocates joined together to form the Climate Works For All coalition.").

86. *See, e.g.*, ALIGN, Climate Works for All, *supra* note 85, at 3, 10–11; *Climate Works for All*, ALIGN, https://alignny.org/campaign/climate-works-for-all/ (last visited Apr. 10, 2024).

In uniting environmental, social, racial, and economic objectives, the coalition reflects long-standing concerns of environmental justice organizations in the United States, which have been broader than the concerns of the established, mainstream environmental groups. *See* Julian Agyeman, David Schlosberg, Luke Craven & Caitlin Matthews, *Trends and Directions in Environmental Justice: From Inequity to Everyday Life, Community, and Just Sustainabilities*, 41 ANN. REV. OF ENV'T & RES. 321, 325–26 (2016). *See also* Dorceta E. Taylor, *The Rise of the Environmental Justice Paradigm: Injustice Framing and the Social Construction of Environmental Discourses*, 43 AM. BEHAV. SCI. 508, 556–59 (2000).

87. Sensing the growing momentum behind mandates, mayoral staff deployed experts to flesh out an operational approach for reducing emissions from buildings. In 2015, the Mayor's Office of Sustainability "established a technical working group … comprised of real estate interests, designers and advocates to establish methods of cutting building emissions" in New York City. David Giambusso, *Trump's Paris Withdrawal Sparks New Push for Energy Mandates in Buildings*, POLITICO (June 19, 2017), https://subscriber.politicopro.com/article/2017/06/09/trump-paris-withdrawal-sparks-new-push-for-energy-mandates-in-buildings-112653. The Technical Working Group produced a report in 2016. CITY OF N.Y., TECHNICAL WORKING GROUP, ONE CITY BUILT TO LAST TECHNICAL WORKING GROUP REPORT: TRANSFORMING NEW YORK CITY BUILDINGS FOR A LOW-CARBON FUTURE (2016), https://climate.cityofnewyork.us/wp-content/uploads/2022/10/TWGreport_04212016.pdf.
88. Giambusso, *supra* note 87; *City Council Members Call on de Blasio to Implement Stronger Energy Efficiency Standards*, CITY & STATE (June 8, 2017), www.cityandstateny.com/politics/2017/06/city-council-members-call-on-de-blasio-to-implement-stronger-energy-efficiency-standards/180549/.
89. CITY & STATE, *supra* note 88.
90. ALIGN, THE TRUMP FAMILY'S DIRTY BUILDINGS: A MAJOR CLIMATE THREAT TO NYC 4 (2017).
91. Statement by Pete Sikora, Dir., Climate & Inequality Campaigns, Cmtys. For Change (Oct. 12, 2022).
92. Press Release, ALIGN, Leading Advocate for Greater Energy Efficiency at New York City's Large Buildings Responds to Mayor de Blasio's Announcement (Sept. 14, 2017), https://alignny.org/press/leading-advocate-for-greater-energy-efficiency-at-new-york-citys-large-buildingsresponds-to-mayor-de-blasios-announcement-today/; *The Only Way to Meet NYC's Climate Targets: A Whole Building Approach to Emissions*, ALIGN (Oct. 30, 2017), https://alignny.org/resource/9748/.
93. *The Only Way to Meet NYC's Climate Targets: A Whole Building Approach to Emissions*, ALIGN, *supra* note 92 (stating in linked untitled document that energy efficiency mandates should "[p]rotect rent-regulated housing to prevent displacement").
94. URBAN GREEN COUNCIL, BLUEPRINT FOR EFFICIENCY 4, 6–7 (2018). On Urban Green Council, see URBAN GREEN COUNCIL, *Who We Are*, www.urbangreencouncil.org/who-we-are/ (last visited Apr. 10, 2024).
95. Shane Goldmacher & Jonathan Martin, *Alexandria Ocasio-Cortez Defeats Joseph Crowley in Major Democratic House Upset*, N.Y. TIMES (June 26, 2018), www.nytimes.com/2018/06/26/nyregion/joseph-crowley-ocasio-cortez-democratic-primary.html. After she won her House seat in the general election, Ocasio-Cortez urged Speaker Nancy Pelosi to introduce a resolution calling for a Green New Deal to decarbonize the country. David Roberts, *Alexandria Ocasio-Cortez Is Already Pressuring Nancy Pelosi on Climate Change*, VOX (Nov. 15, 2018), www.vox.com/energy-and-environment/2018/11/14/18094452/alexandria-ocasio-cortez-nancy-pelosi-protest-climate-change-2020.

96. Vivian Wang, *Democrats Take Control of New York Senate for First Time in Decade*, N.Y. TIMES (Nov. 7, 2018), www.nytimes.com/2018/11/07/nyregion/democrat-ny-senate.html. In the September primaries for state offices, progressives had defeated six moderate Democratic state senators who had caucused with Republicans. Jen Kirby, *The Primary Defeat of New York's "Independent Democrats," Explained*, VOX (Sept. 14, 2018), www.vox.com/policy-and-politics/2018/9/14/17859200/idc-new-york-primaries-democrats-biaggi-klein.
97. *Transcript of the Minutes of the Committee on Environmental Protection*, N.Y. City Council at 65 (Dec. 4, 2018) (spoken testimony of Pete Sikora).
98. *Id.*
99. Pete Sikora, *How #GasFreeNYC Won a Gas Ban in New York City*, N.Y. COMMUNITIES FOR CHANGE (Jan. 2022), *available at* https://docs.google.com/document/d/1TpU9nEW4Rni2h339jhir3U7r2SO1L_Jz8Y5lGlx7kNc/. Sikora refers briefly to "the campaign that won passage of NYC Local Law 97 as a model" for the campaign to ban natural gas combustion in new buildings, which occurred after the passage of Local Law 97. He also indicates that Local Law 97 "was the culmination of a multi-year, winning grassroots campaign." *See also id.* ("We flipped the usual script, where climate action can be perceived as well-intentioned, but also out of touch or even elitist. We made this fight more compelling through a multi-racial, justice-oriented coalition led by groups based in working class Black/Latino communities. We highlighted that a gas ban would create jobs and cut air pollution, especially in low-income communities of color."); *see also id.* ("In a deep blue place like New York – and really virtually any city – climate action is popular. Almost nobody defends fossil fuels because Republicans are marginalized."). On the demographics of New York City, see *Quick Facts: New York City*, U.S. CENSUS BUREAU, www.census.gov/quickfacts/newyorkcitynewyork (last visited Apr. 10, 2024).
100. Sikora, *supra* note 99.
101. *See, e.g.*, Rachel Holliday Smith, *Turnout in NYC's Primary Was Tragically Low – Again. Here Are 6 Experts' Ideas on How to Fix That*, THE CITY (Aug. 24, 2022), www.thecity.nyc/2022/8/24/23320921/turnout-new-york-primary-low-voting-rights (noting that New York was "a city with years of notoriously low voting rates under its belt"); Nolan Hicks, *Less Than 1/4 of NYC Voters Cast Ballots in Election That Saw All Seats Up for Grabs*, NEW YORK POST (Nov. 3, 2021), https://nypost.com/2021/11/03/less-than-1-4-of-nyc-voted-in-2021-election-despite-all-seats-up-for-grabs/ ("Turnout in New York City's municipal elections continued its years-long flat line … with no more than 1.2 million votes cast – a turnout rate no better than 24 percent, …. It's in line with the previous abysmal turnouts posted in every mayoral election since 2005."); Frederick P. Schaffer, *Low Voter Turnout in NYC Elections Is a Problem, and It Can Be Solved*, GOTHAM GAZETTE (Jan. 12, 2022), www.gothamgazette.com/130-opinion/11004-low-voter-turnout-nyc-elections-problem-can-solve (noting that, because of low turnout both in the 2021 New York City general election and the 2021 Democratic primary, and because "registered Democrats constitute roughly 70% of all registered voters" in New York City, "virtually all city offices, including all three citywide offices, were filled based on the votes of 17.5% of registered voters; the winner in a citywide race might thus have received as little as 9% of the votes of all registered voters").

Sikora's theory that interest groups can prompt the adoption of local environmental policy is consistent with the findings of academics that interest groups influence local policy under certain conditions. ANZIA, *supra* note 82. For a study finding that environmental advocacy groups have influenced city commitments to sustainability, see Portney & Berry, *supra* note 82.

102. ALIGN, Climate Works for All, *supra* note 85 (identifying as authors ALIGN, New York City Environmental Justice Alliance, New York City Central Labor Council, BlueGreen Alliance, American Federation of Labor and the Congress of Industrial Organizations); *Hearing on Intro. 1253 before the* N.Y.C. *Council Comm. On Env't Prot.* (Dec. 4, 2018) (written testimony of Rachel Rivera, Cynthia Norris, Pete Sikora, N.Y. Cmtys. for Change) (identifying New York Communities for Change as "a member of the Climate Works for All coalition"); *id.* (testimony of Annel Hernandez, N.Y.C. Env't Justice Alliance) (identifying the New York City Environmental Justice Alliance as a cofounder of "the Climate Works for All coalition with [ALIGN] and the NYC Central Labor Council"); *id.* (testimony of Jon Forster, Co-Chair, DC37 Climate Justice Comm) ("We have been working with CW4A Coalition on this Legislation for 3 years."); *id.* (Dec. 4, 2018) (written testimony of Aditi Varshneya, Cmty. Organizer, WE ACT for Env't Justice) (identifying WE ACT as a member of the coalition); Climate Works for All, Constructing a Greener New York, Building By Building (2019), www.nyclimateworks.org/_files/ugd/f10969_53e457d2f3fd46d588fc226fe6b244b2.pdf (noting document prepared for Climate Works for All by NY Working Families, ALIGN NY, NYCC). *See also about Us*, District Council 37, www.dc37.net/about/whoweare/ (last visited Apr. 16, 2024) (identifying DC 37 as "the largest public employee union in New York City").

103. On the history of the Natural Resources Defense Council, see Paul Sabin, Public Citizens: The Attack on Big Government and the Remaking of American Liberalism 44–45, 127 (2021).

The divisions among environmentalists over Local Law 97 persist as the city grapples with implementing the law. NRDC, the League of Conservation Voters and the Urban Green Council supported the rules that the city promulgated at the end of 2023 that provide building owners with a path to delay meeting the first set of GHG reduction targets if they submit building decarbonization plans, while "Food & Water Watch, New York Communities for Change, TREEage, and New York Public Interest Research Group" opposed the rules. Ben Brachfeld, *Local Law 97: Environmentalists Split as Adams Administration Rolls Out Finalized Rules for Landmark Climate Law*, amNY (Dec. 18, 2023), www.amny.com/environment/final-rules-local-law-97-adams-environmentalists/.

104. *Hearing on Intro. 1253 before the* N.Y.C. *Council Comm. on Env't Prot.* 101–102, 105, 108 (Dec. 4, 2018) (joint testimony of REBNY, NRDC, and 32BJ).

On 32BJ's approach to Local Law 97, see Noah Berman, *Powerful Head of Building Workers Union Takes on Critics, Explains Positions*, Gotham Gazette (June 13, 2019), www.gothamgazette.com/state/8594-powerful-figueroa-building-workers-union-32bj-takes-on-critics.

It is not unusual for unions to align with their employers in debates about environmental regulation; costly regulations could affect the bottom lines of employers and their employees. *See, e.g.*, John C. Esposito & Larry J. Silverman, Ralph Nader's Study Group Report on Air Pollution – Vanishing Air 279 (1970) (maintaining that coal companies and the United Mine Workers of America funded the same lobby group to oppose environmental regulation); William Boyd, The Slain Wood: Papermaking and Its Environmental Consequences in the American South 210 (2015) (describing the opposition of labor unions to environmental regulations in the pulp and paper industry).

105. Not referring specifically to the groups' New York City offices, historian Paul Sabin observes that public interest environmental groups such as NRDC and the

Environmental Defense Fund (EDF) that were founded in the late 1960s and early 1970s moved "away from a more movement-centered approach to social change. They embraced professional expertise, elite knowledge production, and inside-the-Beltway strategies, rather than mass protests and political action." SABIN, *supra* note 103, at 103. NRDC and EDF established "membership programs" but primarily to help with litigation and funding. *Id.* at 105, 127.

106. *Hearing on Intro. 1253 Before the N.Y.C. Council Comm. On Env't Prot.* (Dec. 4, 2018) (written testimony of Carl Hum, Real Estate Board of N.Y.).
107. *Id.* ("REBNY shares other concerns, in particular, the bill's exclusion of buildings with at least one rent-regulated unit which effectively means that over a third of GHG emissions from buildings over 25,000 sf will not be addressed."). *See also* William Neuman, *Big Buildings Hurt the Climate. New York City Hopes to Change That*, N.Y. TIMES (Apr. 17, 2019) ("Real estate industry executives say that while they support reducing emissions, they believe too many types of buildings were given exemptions, placing an undue burden for reducing the city's greenhouse gas output on the remaining buildings.").
108. *See, e.g., Hearing on Intro. 1253 before the N.Y.C. Council Comm. On Env't Prot.* (Dec. 4, 2018) (written testimony of Brett Thomason, ALIGN); *id.* (written testimony of Rachel Rivera, Cynthia Norris, Pete Sikora, N.Y. Cmtys. for Change).
109. Neuman, *supra* note 107.
110. *Hearing on Intro. 1253 Before the N.Y.C. Council Comm. On Env't Prot.* 106–07 (Dec. 4, 2018) (testimony of David Cohen); *id.* at 109–10 (testimony of Lindsay Robbins). On NRDC's reasons for opposing the exemption from the caps of rent-regulated buildings, *see id.* (written testimony of Donna De Costanzo, Dir., Eastern Region, Climate and Clean Energy Program, Natural Res. Def. Council) ("We join others in voicing concern about the bill's blanket exemption of buildings with a least one rent-regulated unit. The City will not be able to achieve its greenhouse gas reduction goals with this exclusion. The exemption directly contradicts the conclusion made by the Mayor's Technical Working Group and reiterated by the Urban Green 80 × 50 Buildings Partnership report that in order to achieve citywide GHG reductions of 40 percent by 2030, buildings of all types and sizes must participate. With this exemption, the majority of the burden of meeting our emissions reduction goals from buildings will rest upon less than 40% of New York City's total building stock – and over a third of the GHG emissions that come from buildings over 25,000 square feet will not be addressed. It is also important that these buildings and tenants get the benefits of energy efficiency. These are the buildings that often need energy efficiency upgrades the most and these are the tenants that would benefit most from lower energy and operating costs, and better functioning apartments.") NRDC supported requiring that rent-regulated buildings implement "low-cost prescriptive measures" as had been recommended by the Urban Green Council's 80 x 50 Buildings Partnership. *Id.*

    The New York League of Conservation Voters took a similar position to NRDC on the importance of including rent-regulated buildings and similarly supported requiring these buildings to implement low-cost prescriptive measures. *Id.* (written testimony of Adriana Espinoza, N.Y.C. Program Dir., N.Y. League of Conservation Voters).
111. N.Y.C, N.Y., LOCAL LAW NO. 97 §§ 5–6 (2019) (amending N.Y.C., N.Y., ADMIN CODE to add§§ 28–320 and 28–321). After New York State passed amendments to rent regulation in 2019 that protected tenants against rent increases for capital improvements, the city council amended Local Law 97 to circumscribe the buildings excluded from the caps to buildings "in which more than 35% of dwelling units" are rent stabilized. N.Y.C, N.Y., LOCAL LAW NO. 116 § 1 (2020).

112. *Hearing on Intro. 1253 before the N.Y.C. Council Comm. On Env't Prot.* 106–07 (Dec. 4, 2018) (written testimony of Donna De Costanzo, Dir., Eastern Region, Climate and Clean Energy Program, Natural Res. Def. Council); *id.* (written testimony of Brett Thomason, ALIGN); *id* (written testimony of Pete Sikora, N.Y. Cmtys. for Change). While not subject to the emissions caps, buildings with large numbers of rent-regulated units are instead required to implement a limited number of prescriptive upgrades such as "[r]epairing all heating system leaks" and "[i]nsulating pipes for heating and/or hot water." N.Y.C., N.Y., Admin. Code § 28-321.2.2.

The compromise provision requiring that rent-regulated buildings implement a list of prescribed measures is consistent with the recommendation in the Urban Green Council's 2018 consensus report "Blueprint for Efficiency" that rent-stabilized apartment buildings be required to implement "low-cost, energy-saving measures" that would not trigger rent increases under New York State rent regulation law, "instead of the percent reductions applicable to other sectors." Urban Green Council, *supra* note 94, at 16. In their testimony in December 2018 to the City Council Environmental Protection Committee, NRDC and 32BJ expressed support for requiring these low-cost prescriptive measures until the advisory board created by the law could come up with another approach to including the rent-stabilized apartment stock. *Hearing on Intro. 1253 Before the N.Y.C. Council Comm. On Env't Prot.* (Dec. 4, 2018) (written testimony of Donna De Costanzo, Dir., Eastern Region, Climate & Clean Energy Program, Natural Res. Def. Council); *id.* (written testimony of David Cohen, Pol. Manager, SEIU 32BJ). *See also id.* (testimony of John Mandyck, CEO, Urb. Green Council). ALIGN – and fellow Climate Works for All coalition members New York Communities for Change and the New York City Environmental Justice Alliance – also expressed support in their testimony for such prescriptive measures as an interim approach until state rent regulation laws were amended to protect tenants against rent hikes to offset the costs of decarbonizing buildings. *Id.* (Dec. 4, 2018) (written testimony of Brett Thomason, ALIGN); *id.* (Dec. 4, 2018) (written testimony of Rachel Rivera, Cynthia Norris, Pete Sikora, N.Y. Cmtys. for Change); *id.* (written testimony of Annel Hernandez, N.Y.C. Env't Justice All.).

113. In addition to the passage of Local Law 97 in New York City in 2019, another indication of the waning political power of major property owners that year was the passage of new tenant protection laws at the State level, which significantly increased protections for tenants in rent-regulated and market-rate housing in New York City and other parts of the State. *See generally* Housing Stability and Tenant Protection Act, S.B. 6458, 2019–20 Reg. Sess. (N.Y. 2019).

114. The presence of a large number of environmental interest groups in New York City is broadly consistent with the recent findings of political scientist Sarah Anzia on interest group activity at the local level. Anzia's surveys of city officials found that "environmental groups average between 'slightly' and 'somewhat' active." Anzia, *supra* note 82, at 94. However, Anzia's empirical findings that interest groups in general (not specifically environmental groups) are more active in larger cities imply, by extension, that environmental groups should be more active in New York than in other cities. She concludes that "[l]arger cities and cities that make policy on a larger number of issues have significantly more interest group activity, as do cities with more Democratic and liberal residents." *Id.* at 73. *See also id.* at 106 ("Democratic presidential vote is also positively associated with greater activity by … environmental groups…. It may be that some groups, such as environmental groups, are more active in Democratic places because Democrats tend to have more pro-environment policy views.").

115. N.Y.C., N.Y., ADMIN CODE § 28-320.1. As noted earlier, buildings with large numbers of rent-regulated units are instead required to implement a limited number of prescriptive upgrades such as "[r]epairing all heating system leaks" and "[i]nsulating pipes for heating and/or hot water." N.Y.C., N.Y., ADMIN. CODE § 28-321.2.2. *See also supra* note 112.
116. N.Y.C., N.Y., ADMIN. CODE § 28-320.2.1 ("The mayor shall appoint one architect, one engineer, *one building owner or manager*, one public utility industry representative, *one environmental justice representative*, one business sector representative, one residential tenant representative, and *one environmental advocacy organization representative*. The speaker shall appoint one architect, one stationary engineer, one construction trades representative, one green energy industry representative, one residential tenant representative, *one environmental justice organization representative, one environmental advocacy representative* and one not for profit organization representative.") (emphasis added).
117. Notably, environmental justice concerns have continued to be prominent in local climate politics since Mayor de Blasio left office. With respect to LL97, environmental justice advocates, joined with mainstream environmental advocates, were influential in steering city officials away from permitting emissions trading under the law, which real estate interests had once hoped would be allowed. Ciara Long, *NYC Could Soften Local Law 97's Controversial Fine Structure*, BISNOW (Apr. 14, 2022), www.bisnow.com/new-york/news/sustainability/nyc-city-council-hints-at-flexibility-on-local-law-97-compliance-112619; *Hearing on Intro. 1253 before the N.Y.C. Council Comm. On Env't Prot.* (Dec. 4, 2018) (written testimony of Carl Hum, Real Estate Board of N.Y.). More generally, the office that catalyzed discussions around LL97, which was once called the Mayor's Office of Sustainability, was renamed the "Mayor's Office of Climate and Environmental Justice" at the start of 2022 under Mayor Eric Adams. The 2024 assessment of the New York City Panel on Climate Change centered equity more than any previous assessment of the panel, embedding equity into the assessment and the workings of the panel. Deborah Balk, Christian Braneon, Robin Leichenko, Richard Moss & Joel Towers, NPCC4: *Climate Risk and Equity – Advancing Knowledge toward a Sustainable Future: Introduction*. 2024 ANNALS N.Y. ACAD. SCIS. 4–5 (2024), https://climateassessment.nyc/assessment/sample-assessment-mollis-amet-cras-ullamcorper-sem-nibh-sollicitudin-amet-etiam/. For brief discussion of the increasing prominence of equity in local climate policy, *see, e.g.*, Sheila R. Foster, Ana Baptista, Khai Hoan Nguyen, Jack Tchen, Marco Tedesco & Robin Leichenko, *Advancing Climate Justice in Climate Adaptation Strategies for New York City*, *in* N.Y.C. PANEL ON CLIMATE CHANGE 4TH ASSESSMENT 5–14 (2024), https://climateassessment.nyc/assessment/advancing-climate-justice-in-climate-adaptation-strategies-for-new-york-city/.
118. On the incorporation into federal policy of economic ideas, such as cap and trade approaches to regulating pollution, *see generally* ELIZABETH POPP BERMAN, THINKING LIKE AN ECONOMIST: HOW EFFICIENCY REPLACED EQUALITY IN U.S. PUBLIC POLICY (2022).

While Local Law 97 itself does not permit buildings to trade responsibility for reducing GHG emissions, in 2024, the city government created by regulation a fund that will use money raised from allowing buildings to pay to offset their emissions to decarbonize affordable housing. This offset program will facilitate the trading of responsibility for emissions reductions from buildings with caps to affordable housing buildings. Press Release, City of New York, Mayor Adams Launches New Program to Help Affordable Housing Projects Go Green, Save Green (Sept. 26, 2024), https://www.nyc.gov/

office-of-the-mayor/news/719-24/mayor-adams-launches-new-program-help-affordable-housing-projects-go-green-save-green; New York City, N.Y., Rules, Tit. 1, § 103-14 (e) (Affordable Housing Reinvestment Fund).

119. In late 2022, the city's Department of Buildings promulgated regulations for implementing Local Law 97 that specify the "emissions factors" for different "property types." N.Y.C. Dep't of Buildings, Final Rule – Procedures for Reporting on and Complying with Annual Greenhouse Gas Emissions for Certain Buildings 2, 8–14 (2022), *available at* https://a856-cityrecord.nyc.gov/RequestDetail?RequestId=20221213011.
120. N.Y.C., N.Y., Admin Code § 28-320.6.
121. N.Y.C. Dep't of Buildings, *supra* note 119, at 23–24.
122. *See id.* at 8–14.
123. N.Y.C., N.Y., Admin Code § 28-320.3.6.1.
124. Mariana Simões, *Office Buildings Could Evade Energy Upgrades via "Giant Loophole" in NYC's Climate Law, Environmentalists Warn*, CityLimits (Feb. 21, 2023), https://citylimits.org/2023/02/21/office-buildings-could-evade-energy-upgrades-via-giant-loophole-in-nycs-climate-law-environmentalists-warn/.

Since the passage of Local Law 97, the city government has imposed regulatory limitations on the use of renewable energy credits to comply with the law's emissions caps. New York City, N.Y., Rules, Tit. 1, § 103-14 (e)(1)(i) (renewable credits can be used to offset emissions only from grid-supplied electricity); § 103-14 (i)(2)(iv)(a) (owner filing building decarbonization plan cannot use renewable energy credits for 2024-2029 compliance period).

Notably, WE ACT's testimony to the City Council Environmental Protection Committee in December 2018 warned "against the inclusion of renewable energy credits as a method of alternative compliance. RECs do not improve local environmental health, support a thriving local economy, or even sufficiently move the needle on carbon reduction." *Hearing on Intro. 1253 before the N.Y.C. Council Comm. On Env't Prot.* (Dec. 4, 2018) (written testimony of Aditi Varshneya, Cmty. Organizer, WE ACT for Env't Justice).

125. Institute for Market Transformation, *Snapshot of BPS Adoption across the U.S.*, Building Performance Standards, www.imt.org/public-policy/building-performance-standards/ (last visited June 20, 2024) (identifying as of December 2023 Boston, Massachusetts; Cambridge, Massachusetts; Chula Vista, California; Denver, Colorado; Montgomery County, Maryland; New York, New York; Seattle, Washington; St. Louis, Missouri; Washington, D.C.; and the states of Colorado, Maryland, Oregon, Washington). *See, e.g.*, N.Y.C, N.Y., Local Law No. 97 (2019), *codified at* N.Y.C., N.Y., Charter § 651; N.Y.C., N.Y., Admin. Code §§ 24-802(e), 24-803(a)–(b), 28-320, 28-321; Bos., Mass., Ordinance Amending City of Boston Code, Building Energy Reporting and Disclosure (BERDO 2.0), ch. VII, §§ 7-2.1 to 7-2.2, (2021); Denver, Colo., Council Bill 21–1310 (2021); St. Louis, Mo., Building Energy Performance Standards (BEPS), Ordinance 71132 (Apr. 20, 2020); Wash., D.C., CleanEnergy D.C. Omnibus Amendment Act of 2018, D.C. Law 22–257 (2019); Chula Vista, Cal., Ordinance 3498 (2021); Seattle, Wa., Ordinance 126959, An Ordinance Relating To Regulating Greenhouse Gas Emissions In Larger Existing Nonresidential & Multifamily Buildings (Dec. 12, 2023). New York State is proposing to establish a state-wide energy efficiency-based building performance standard for large existing commercial and residential buildings. N.Y. State Climate Action Council, Scoping Plan: Full Report 188–89 (2022), https://climate.ny.gov/resources/scoping-plan/.

As of May 2024, there is litigation challenging the building performance standards in Denver and Colorado as preempted by the federal Energy Policy and Conservation Act. *See* Daniel Carpenter-Gold, *The Tortured Arguments Department: Corporate Landlords' Flimsy Challenge to Colorado Green-Building Policies*, PUB. HEALTH L. CTR. AT MITCHELL-HAMLINE SCH. OF L. (May 2, 2024), www.publichealthlawcenter.org/commentary/240502/5/2/24-tortured-arguments-department-corporate-landlords-flimsy-challenge; Complaint, Colorado Landlord Ass'n v. Ryan, Case No. 1:24-cv-01093 (D. Colo. Apr. 22, 2024).

126. *Mark Chambers*, LINKEDIN, www.linkedin.com/in/mark-chambers-ra-71793854/ (last visited Apr. 19, 2024).
127. Press Release, White House, Fact Sheet: Biden-Harris Administration Launches Coalition of States and Local Governments to Strengthen Building Performance Standards (Jan. 21, 2022), www.whitehouse.gov/briefing-room/statements-releases/2022/01/21/fact-sheet-biden-harris-administration-launches-coalition-of-states-and-local-governments-to-strengthen-building-performance-standards/.
128. Press Release, White House, Fact Sheet: Biden-Harris Administration Announces First-Ever Federal Building Performance Standard, Catalyzes American Innovation to Lower Energy Costs, Save Taxpayer Dollars, and Cut Emissions (Dec. 7, 2022), www.whitehouse.gov/briefing-room/statements-releases/2022/12/07/fact-sheet-biden-harris-administration-announces-first-ever-federal-building-performance-standard-catalyzes-american-innovation-to-lower-energy-costs-save-taxpayer-dollars-and-cut-emissions.
129. *See* Spiegel-Feld & Wyman, *supra* note 3, at 10271–72.
130. *See* Simões, *supra* note 124.
131. *See, e.g.*, Joseph G. Allen, Parichehr Salimifard & Jonathan Buonocore, *Want to Phase Out Fossil Fuels? We Must Fundamentally Change Our Buildings*, WASH. POST (Sept. 26, 2022), www.washingtonpost.com/opinions/2022/09/26/climate-carbon-fossil-fuel-energy-efficiency/.
132. On the growing incorporation of equity into local climate planning over time, see Claudia V. Diezmartínez & Anne G. Short Gianotti, *US Cities Increasingly Integrate Justice into Climate Planning and Create Policy Tools for Climate Justice*, 13 NATURE COMMC'NS 5763 (2022).
133. BOS., MASS., BUILDING ENERGY REPORTING & DISCLOSURE ORDINANCE (BERDO) § 7-2.2(g). Washington, D.C. also has a provision in its Clean Energy Omnibus Act that requires that at least 30 percent of the funds go in part toward benefitting low-income residents. D.C. CODE § 8-1774.10(c)(12)(A)(i) (2024).
134. BOS., MASS. CODE § 7-2.2(g); Emily Barkdoll, *Boston Passes Equitable Building Performance Standard*, NAT. RES. DEF. COUNCIL (Sept. 22, 2021), www.nrdc.org/experts/emily-barkdoll/boston-passes-equitable-building-performance-standard.
135. Benjamin Storrow, *Cities Look to Natural Gas Bans to Curb Carbon Emissions*, SCI. AM. (Nov. 25, 2019), www.scientificamerican.com/article/cities-look-to-natural-gas-bans-to-curb-carbon-emissions/ (noting a shift in local climate action "toward the carbon footprint associated with heating and cooling buildings," and noting the "newest trend in the local fight against climate change: bans on natural gas hookups in new buildings").
136. *See, e.g.*, BERKELEY, CAL., ORDINANCE 7672-NS § 1 ("It is the intent of the council to eliminate obsolete natural gas infrastructure and associated greenhouse gas emissions in new buildings where all-electric infrastructure can be most practicably integrated, thereby reducing the environmental and health hazards produced by the consumption and transportation of natural gas.").

137. N.Y.C, N.Y., LOCAL LAW NO. 154 § 28-506.1 (2021); Emilie Raguso, *Berkeley First City in California to Ban Natural Gas in New Buildings*, BERKELEYSIDE (July 17, 2019), www.berkeleyside.org/2019/07/17/natural-gas-pipes-now-banned-in-new-berkeley-buildings-with-some-exceptions.
138. Sikora, *supra* note 99.
139. Rebecca Leber, *The Gas Industry Is Losing Its Most Valuable Customer: Blue States*, VOX (May 4, 2023), www.vox.com/climate/2023/5/4/23711062/new-york-gas-stove-furnace-ban-new-buildings; Anna Phillips, *A Fight Brewing in Oregon Could Decide How We Heat Our Homes and Cook*, WASH. POST (Apr. 21, 2023), www.washingtonpost.com/climate-environment/2023/04/21/natural-gas-industry-oregon-ban/.
140. Brad Plumer & Hiroko Tabuchi, *How Politics Are Determining What Stove You Use*, N.Y. TIMES (Dec. 16, 2021), www.nytimes.com/2021/12/16/climate/gas-stoves-climate-change.html; *see also* NATHANIEL R. MATTISON, GUARINI CTR. ON ENV'T, ENERGY & LAND USE LAW, BEYOND GAS BANS: ALTERNATIVE PATHWAYS TO REDUCE BUILDING EMISSIONS IN LIGHT OF STATE PREEMPTION LAWS 2 (2022), https://guarinicenter.org/document/beyond-gas-bans/.
141. *California Rest. Ass'n v. City of Berkeley*, 89 F.4th 1094 (9th Cir. 2024), *amending and superseding* 65 F.4th 1045 (9th Cir. 2023); Cecilia Nowell, *Berkeley's First-in-the-nation Natural Gas Ban Is Dead. But Is the Battle Over?*, THE GUARDIAN (Apr. 9, 2024), www.theguardian.com/environment/2024/apr/09/berkeley-natural-gas-ban-lawsuit-repeal.
142. Liam Stack, *New York to Ban Natural Gas, Including Stoves, in New Buildings*, N.Y. TIMES (Apr. 28, 2023), www.nytimes.com/2023/04/28/nyregion/gas-stove-ban-ny.html; David Iaconangelo, *N.Y. Set to Pass First Statewide Gas-Ban Law*, GREENWIRE (Apr. 28, 2023), https://subscriber.politicopro.com/article/eenews/2023/04/28/n-y-set-to-pass-first-statewide-gas-ban-law-00094437; *New York State to Ban Fossil Fuels in New Buildings: State Law Banning New Oil, Gas Hookups is First in Nation*, FOOD & WATER WATCH (May 2, 2023), www.foodandwaterwatch.org/2023/05/02/new-york-state-to-ban-fossil-fuels-in-new-buildings/; Anna Phillips, *N.Y. Ditches Gas Stoves, Fossil Fuels in New Buildings in First Statewide Ban in U.S.*, WASH. POST (May 3, 2023), www.washingtonpost.com/climate-environment/2023/05/03/newyork-gas-ban-climate-change/.
143. *Mulhern Gas Co., Inc. v. Rodriguez*, No. 1:23-cv-1267 (N.D.N.Y. Oct. 12, 2023) (litigation challenging N.Y. State gas ban); *Ass'n of Cont. Plumbers of the City of New York, Inc., v. City of New York*, No. 1:2023-cv-11292 (S.D.N.Y. Dec. 29, 2023) (litigation challenging N.Y.C. gas ban); Mariana Simões, *Efforts to Block Gas Bans across the Nation Are Growing. Will It Work in New York?*, CITYLIMITS (Nov. 29, 2023), https://citylimits.org/2023/11/29/efforts-to-block-gas-bans-across-the-nation-are-growing-will-it-work-in-new-york/; Ysabelle Kempe, *Legal Threats to City, State Natural Gas Bans: A Timeline*, SMARTCITIESDIVE (Jan. 2, 2024, updated Mar. 27, 2024), www.smartcitiesdive.com/news/biggest-gas-ban-new-building-electrification-news-2023-timeline/702944/; Ben Elgin, *The Surprising Force Stalling Climate Progress: California Restaurants*, BLOOMBERG (May 13, 2024), www.bloomberg.com/news/features/2024-05-13/california-restaurants-are-a-surprising-force-stalling-climate-progress.
144. Thomas J. Lueck, *Bloomberg Draws a Blueprint for a Greener City*, N.Y. TIMES (Apr. 23, 2007), www.nytimes.com/2007/04/23/nyregion/23mayor.html.
145. *See, e.g.*, *GDP of the New York Metro Area from 2001 to 2021*, STATISTA (Jan. 2, 2023), www.statista.com/statistics/183815/gdp-of-the-new-york-metro-area/; Press Release, Thomas P. DiNapoli, N.Y.S. Comptroller, New York City Economy Continues to Set Records: City Added 820,000 Jobs from 2009 to 2018 (Apr. 17, 2019), www.osc.state.ny.us/press/releases/2019/04/new-york-city-economy-continues-set-records.

146. Jeffrey P. Cohen, Felix L. Friedt & Jackson P. Lautier, *The Impact of the Coronavirus Pandemic on New York City Real Estate: First Evidence*, 62 J. Reg. Sci. 858, 859 (2022).
147. Editorial, *Where Are the Big Ideas for New York City?*, N.Y. Times (Aug. 5, 2023), www.nytimes.com/2023/08/05/opinion/new-york-city-immigration-housing.html; Eric Feldman, *Delinquency Rate for City Office Buildings Skyrocketing*, Spectrum News NY1 (Mar. 5, 2024), https://ny1.com/nyc/manhattan/news/2024/03/05/the-delinquency-rate-for-city-office-buildings-is-skyrocketing; Emma G. Fitzsimmons & Jeffery C. Mays, *Is New York City Back? Not for Everyone*, N.Y. Times (Mar. 5, 2024), www.nytimes.com/2024/03/05/nyregion/nyc-economy-comeback.html; Alan Rappeport, *Cities Face Cutbacks as Commercial Real Estate Prices Tumble*, N.Y. Times (Mar. 15, 2024), www.nytimes.com/2024/03/14/business/commercial-real-estate-tax-revenue.html; Winnie Hu & Stefanos Chen, *New York City's Population Shrinks by 78,000, According to Census Data*, N.Y. Times (Mar. 14, 2024), www.nytimes.com/2024/03/14/nyregion/nyc-population-decline.html; Carl Campanile & Craig McCarthy, *NYC Homeless Shelter Population Surges 53% during Migrant Crisis: Mayor's Report*, N.Y. Post (Jan. 30, 2024), https://nypost.com/2024/01/30/metro/nyc-homeless-shelter-population-surges-53-amid-migrant-crisis-mayors-report/; Patrick Spauster, Adrian Nesta & Emma Whitford, *NYC Shelter Count*, CityLimits, https://citylimits.org/nyc-shelter-count/ (last visited Feb. 17, 2025) (NYC Dept. of Homeless Services (DHS) Shelter Population, Daily)
148. There are countervailing economic interests at play as well: by the end of 2021, the energy efficiency sector in New York State, which focuses on building energy retrofits, had still not fully recovered the jobs that were lost during the COVID-19 pandemic. N.Y. State Energy Rsch. & Dev. Auth., New York Clean Energy Industry Report 20 (2022), *available at* www.nyserda.ny.gov/About/Publications/New-York-Clean-Energy-Industry-Report. Weakening LL97 would presumably deal a blow to this sector by reducing demand for retrofits.
149. Stefanos Chen & Winston Choi-Schagrin, *What's Holding Up New York's Climate Progress? Apartment Buildings*, N.Y. Times (Mar. 10, 2023), www.nytimes.com/2023/03/10/nyregion/greenhouse-gas-law-nyc.html ("[M]onths before compliance begins, a mix of real estate interest groups are lobbying to delay the process or carve out exemptions, claiming that the requirements are too burdensome for residential boards with limited funding"); Steve Cuozzo, *Loony 'Environmental' Mandates Will Kill NYC's Middle-Class Housing*, N.Y. Post (Mar. 12, 2023), https://nypost.com/2023/03/12/nycs-local-law-97-is-a-threat-to-affordable-housing/ ("The loony law spells financial ruin for many of the city's 3,700 co-op and condo buildings, which are home to 800,000 apartments."); Campanile, *supra* note 15 ("Homeowners for a stronger New York is battling the terms of the city's Climate Mobilization Emissions Law of 2019 – Local Law 97 – by next year while backing state legislation introduced by state Assemblyman Ed Braunstein (D-Queens) and Sen. Kevin Parker (D-Brooklyn) to require the city to provide property tax breaks to help alleviate the costs."); Justin Brannan, Opinion, *Albany Must Ease the Shift to Greener Buildings*, N.Y. Daily News (Mar. 19, 2024), www.nydailynews.com/2024/03/19/albany-must-ease-the-shift-to-greener-buildings/ (urging the state legislature to pass property tax abatements for property owners that reduce GHG emissions). Some of the owners of residential and commercial properties subject to the emissions caps in the law brought a Hail Mary legal challenge to Local Law 97 on preemption and other grounds that was dismissed in October 2023. Glen Oaks Village Owners, Inc. v. City of New York, No. 154327/2022, 2023 WL 7130782, at *7, (N.Y. Sup. Ct. Oct. 27, 2023). However, in May

2024, an intermediate state appellate court resurrected the plaintiffs' claim that Local Law 97 is field preempted by the state's Climate Leadership and Community Protection Act. Glen Oaks Vill. Owners, Inc. v. City of New York, 227 A.D.3d 523 (N.Y. App. Div. 1st 2024); Nish Amarnath, *Legal Battle over NYC's Building Emissions Law Resurfaces in Appellate Court*, Smart Cities Dive (May 20, 2024), www.smartcitiesdive.com/news/nyc-building-emissions-law-appellate-court-decision/716606/.

A 2021 study that Spiegel-Feld and Wyman helped to author anticipated that residential buildings would have greater difficulty complying with the emissions caps in Local Law 97 than commercial buildings. Since commercial buildings are more electrified than residential buildings, the emissions of commercial buildings will decline more without them doing anything if New York State achieves its goals of decarbonizing grid-supplied electricity. Spiegel-Feld et al., *supra* note 16, at 10.

See also Dillon Brown, *Boston Energy Ordinance Will Create Difficult and Costly Compliance Challenges for City's Condo Associations*, Marcus Errico Emmer & Brooks, P.C. (Dec. 14, 2022), www.meeb.com/marcus-errico-emmer-brooks-newsletter/newsletter/boston-energy-ordinance ("[M]ost condominium association boards and managers are just beginning to understand how big, how challenging and how expensive it is going to be to comply.").

150. Mariana Simões, *After Criticism, City Staffs Up Local Law 97 Enforcement*, CityLimits (Mar. 13, 2024), https://citylimits.org/2024/03/13/after-criticism-city-staffs-up-local-law-97-enforcement/; New York City, N.Y., Rules, Tit. 1, § 103-14.

151. Samantha Maldonado, *Building Owners Could Get Two More Years to Comply with Impending Climate Law*, The City (Sept. 12, 2023), www.thecity.nyc/2023/9/12/23870862/local-law-97-climate-change-fines-delay; Rosemary Misdary, *Mayor Adams Wants to Soften Enforcement of Climate Law That Aims to Reduce Building Emissions*, Gothamist (Sept. 12, 2023), https://gothamist.com/news/adams-wants-to-soften-enforcement-of-landmark-climate-law-that-aims-to-reduce-building-emissions; Brachfeld, *supra* note 103; N.Y. City Dep't of Buildings, Notice of Adoption of Rule (Dec. 12, 2023), www.nyc.gov/assets/buildings/pdf/LL88_LL97.pdf (establishing penalties for non-compliance and rules for mediated resolutions).

152. Ben Brachfeld, *State Court Revives Suit to Overturn Local Law 97 on Appeal, Potentially Imperiling Landmark Climate Law*, amNY (May 28, 2024), www.amny.com/environment/state-court-revives-local-law-97-lawsuit-climate/. *See* N.Y.C., N.Y., Intro. No. 772 (2024). In September 2023, council member Linda Lee introduced the same bill, then known as Intro. No. 1197, which at the time was sponsored by 21 council members including Lee. N.Y.C., N.Y., Intro. No. 1197; *Bill Seeks to Put Off Local Law 97 Enforcement by a Decade*, Habitat (Oct. 2, 2023), www.habitatmag.com/Publication-Content/Green-Ideas/2023/2023-October/Bill-Seeks-to-Put-Off-Local-Law-97-Enforcement-by-a-Decade; *Hearing Transcript*, N.Y. City Council Stated Meeting (Sept. 28, 2023).

153. Interview with Cas Holloway (Oct. 19, 2022) (conducted by Danielle Spiegel-Feld).

5 ADAPTING TO CLIMATE CHANGE IN NYC

1. The Intergovernmental Panel on Climate Change defines "adaptation" as, "[i]n *human systems*, the process of adjustment to actual or expected *climate* and its effects, in order to moderate harm or exploit beneficial opportunities. In natural systems, the process of adjustment to actual climate and its effects; human intervention may facilitate adjustment

to expected climate and its effects." J.B. Robin Matthews, ed., *IPCC, Annex I: Glossary, in* GLOBAL WARMING OF 1.5°C: AN IPCC SPECIAL REPORT ON THE IMPACTS OF GLOBAL WARMING OF 1.5°C ABOVE PRE-INDUSTRIAL LEVELS AND RELATED GLOBAL GREENHOUSE GAS EMISSION PATHWAYS, IN THE CONTEXT OF STRENGTHENING THE GLOBAL RESPONSE TO THE THREAT OF CLIMATE CHANGE, SUSTAINABLE DEVELOPMENT, AND EFFORTS TO ERADICATE POVERTY 539, 542 (Valérie Masson-Delmotte et al. eds., 2018) [hereinafter IPCC ANNEX I]. The Intergovernmental Panel on Climate Change defines "resilience" as "[t]he capacity of social, economic and environmental systems to cope with a hazardous event or trend or disturbance, responding or reorganizing in ways that maintain their essential function, identity and structure while also maintaining the capacity for *adaptation*, learning and *transformation*." *Id.* at 557. *See also* ROB VERCHICK, *THE OCTOPUS IN THE PARKING GARAGE: A CALL FOR CLIMATE RESILIENCE* 37 (2023) (excerpting similar definition).

People living in urban areas are already feeling the effects of global warming, such as torrential rains, heat domes, and smoke from wildfires. HOUSTON HEALTH DEP'T, HURRICANE HARVEY 2017: HOUSTON HEALTH DEPARTMENT RESPONSE REPORT 4 (2017); Elena Shao, *Harvey Hit 5 Years Ago. Its Floodwaters Did Not Strike Equitably*, N.Y. TIMES (Aug. 25, 2022), www.nytimes.com/2022/08/25/climate/hurricane-harvey-climate-change.html; Katie Honan, *Mayor's Map Showed Most of Ida's Victims Lived Where Rainfall Was Riskiest*, THE CITY (Sept. 3, 2021), www.thecity.nyc/environment/2021/9/3/22656482/mayors-map-showed-ida-victims-risk; VERCHICK, *supra*, at 45–48; *Multnomah County Sues Oil Companies Over 2021 Heat Dome Disaster*, MULTNOMAH CNTY. (June 22, 2023), www.multco.us/multnomah-county/news/multnomah-county-sues-oil-companies-over-2021-heat-dome-disaster; J. David Goodman, *In a Texas City, Heat Proved Deadly Even for Those Long Used to It*, N.Y. TIMES (July 13, 2023), www.nytimes.com/2023/07/13/us/texas-heat-deaths-webb-county.html; Marc Lallanilla, *ER Visits Spike Amid Wildfire Smoke: Asthma, Breathing Problems*, N.Y. POST (June 9, 2023), https://nypost.com/2023/06/09/er-visits-spike-amid-wildfire-smoke-asthma-breathing-problems/; Jonathan Mingle, *Even "Safe" Places Are Experiencing Climate Chaos in America*, N.Y. TIMES (July 13, 2023), www.nytimes.com/2023/07/13/opinion/floods-vermont-new-york-heat-climate-change.html; Erin McCormick, *Doctor's Alarmed by Surge in Hospital Visits as Toxic Smoke Engulfs West Coast*, THE GUARDIAN (Sept. 18, 2020), www.theguardian.com/world/2020/sep/18/wildfire-smoke-health-effects-hospitals; Jack Lee, *Are New York City's Orange Skies as Bad as the Bay Area in 2020? Here's How They Compare*, S.F. Chronicle (June 8, 2023), www.sfchronicle.com/weather/article/california-wildfire-smoke-18140289.php.

2. NAT'L ECON. COUNCIL, ECONOMIC REPORT OF THE PRESIDENT 274 (2023) ("Many important areas that are relevant to adaptation, from land use planning and zoning to the regulation of insurance markets, are governed at the State or local level."); VERCHICK, *supra* note 1, at 44, 72 (emphasizing the centrality of local governments in building resilience to climate change); Sheila R. Foster & Chiara Pappalardo, *Local Initiatives, in* GLOBAL CLIMATE CHANGE AND U.S. LAW 361, 378–382 (Michael B. Gerrard, Jody Freeman & Michael Burger eds., 3rd ed. 2022) (identifying land use measures local governments are using to promote adaptation).
3. CITY OF N.Y., COOL NEIGHBORHOODS NYC: A COMPREHENSIVE APPROACH TO KEEP COMMUNITIES SAFE IN EXTREME HEAT 7 (2017); *Interactive Heat Vulnerability Index*, ENV'T & HEALTH DATA PORTAL, https://a816-dohbesp.nyc.gov/IndicatorPublic/key-topics/climatehealth/hvi/ (last visited Apr. 19, 2024); *see also* Foster & Pappalardo, *supra* note 2, at 382–85 (describing local government uses of green infrastructure, including tree planting, to adapt to climate change).

4. On the meaning of vulnerability, *see, e.g.*, Sheila Foster et al., *New York City Panel on Climate Change 2019 Report: Chapter 6: Community Based Assessments of Adaptation and Equity*, 1439 ANN. N.Y. ACAD. SCI. 126, 129 (2019) ("Vulnerability to climate change is defined as the susceptibility of a given population, system, or place to harm from exposure to climate-related shocks and stresses.") (citing INTERGOVERNMENTAL PANEL ON CLIMATE CHANGE, MANAGING THE RISKS OF EXTREME EVENTS AND DISASTERS TO ADVANCE CLIMATE CHANGE ADAPTATION: SPECIAL REPORT OF THE INTERGOVERNMENTAL PANEL ON CLIMATE CHANGE (2012)). For an interesting article scoring neighborhoods in NYC for their vulnerability to various climate risks (such as "coastal and riverine flooding" and heat) and "displacement and social vulnerability," see Marco Tedesco, Sheila Foster, Ana Baptista & Casey Zuzak, A *Multi-Hazard Climate, Displacement and Socio-Vulnerability Score for New York City*, 16 SUSTAINABILITY 1, 1 (2023).

On the greater vulnerability of low-income and Black people to heat, *see, e.g.*, *Interactive Heat Vulnerability Index*, *supra* note 3; Jaime Madrigano, Kazuhiko Ito, Sarah Johnson, Patrick L. Kinney & Thomas Matte, A *Case-Only Study of Vulnerability to Heat Wave-Related Mortality in New York City (2000–2011)*, 123 ENV'T HEALTH PERSPECTIVES (2015); Alana Hansen et al., *Vulnerability to Extreme Heat and Climate Change: Is Ethnicity a Factor?*, 6 GLOB. HEALTH ACTION 21364 1, 1 (2013); Seth B. Shonkoff et al., *The Climate Gap: Environmental Health and Equity Implications of Climate Change and Mitigation Policies in California – A Review of the Literature*, 109 CLIMATIC CHANGE S485, S489 (2011); NAT'L ECON. COUNCIL, *supra* note 2, at 281 (citing Jeremy S. Hoffman, Vivek Shandas & Nicholas Pendleton, *The Effects of Historical Housing Policies on Resident Exposure to Intra-Urban Heat: A Study of 108 US Urban Areas*, 8 CLIMATE 12 (2020) and Susanne Amelie Benz & Jennifer Anne Burney, *Widespread Race and Class Disparities in the Surface Urban Heat Extremes Across the United States*, 9 EARTH'S FUTURE 1 (2021)).

Between 2010 and 2019, ten people died on average each summer "directly from heat" (from heat stress) in New York City; Black people accounted for 43 percent of these deaths, even though only about 23 percent of city residents are Black people. The number of deaths from heat stress has declined recently in New York, but "the racial inequity persists." *2021 NYC Heat-Related Mortality Report*, ENV'T & HEALTH DATA PORTAL, https://a816-dohbesp.nyc.gov/IndicatorPublic/key-topics/climatehealth/2021-heat-report/ [hereinafter N.Y.C. HEALTH] (last visited Mar. 15, 2024); *see also* *QuickFacts: New York City, New York*, U.S. CENSUS, www.census.gov/quickfacts/newyorkcitynewyork (last visited Mar. 14, 2024). Between 2010 and 2018, there were approximately 350 deaths annually "caused indirectly by heat, such as by aggravating an underlying illness." N.Y.C. HEALTH, *supra*. "Heat-exacerbated mortality is higher in neighborhoods that are home to a greater proportion of Black New Yorkers ... [and] people with household incomes below the federal poverty line." *Id.*

Income also is associated with vulnerability to flooding. Eric Tate et al., *Flood Exposure and Social Vulnerability in the United States*, 106 NATURAL HAZARDS 435 (2021). Rebuild by Design reports that "1.3 million New York City residents live within or directly adjacent to the floodplain" and "[m]ore than half of the floodplain residents live in areas with a median income less than $75,120, which is considered low income for New York City for a family of three." *Who Lives in the Floodplain in the Year 2100?*, REBUILD BY DESIGN, https://rebuildbydesign.org/who-lives-in-nycs-floodplain/ (last visited Mar. 15, 2024).

A study by the economist Ana Varela Varela even suggests that coastal flooding can have opposite effects on high-income neighborhoods versus low-income neighborhoods. Varela Varela looked at the change in property values in neighborhoods that were flooded by Superstorm Sandy and found that while, "on average, flooded properties are sold at lower prices" than similar nonflooded properties, in the areas that housed higher income populations prior to Sandy, flooding was associated with a relative price *increase*. *See generally* Ana Varela Varela, Surge of Inequality: How Different Neighborhoods React to Flooding (2023); *see also id.* at 15.

5. Nat'l Econ. Council, *supra* note 2, at 277 ("Mitigation is a classic example of a public good .... In contrast, many adaptation decisions are private goods, in that both the costs and benefits are largely internalized by the decisionmaker."); *see also id.* at 295. On the implications of the cost-benefit structure of adaptation for the allocation of responsibility for it among different levels of government, *see, e.g.*, Matthew Kahn, Adapting to Climate Change: Markets and the Managements of an Uncertain Future 78–79; 87–88 (2021); Daniel A. Farber, *Climate Adaptation and Federalism: Mapping the Issues*, 1 San Diego J. Climate & Energy L. 259 (2009); Robert L. Glicksman, *Climate Change Adaptation: A Collective Action Perspective on Federalism Considerations*, 40 Env't L. 1159 (2010); Alice Kaswan, *Climate Change Adaptation and Land Use: Exploring the Federal Role*, 47 J. Marshall L. Rev. 509 (2013).

6. *Construction Project Areas for East Side Coastal Resiliency*, NYC E. Side Coastal Resiliency Project, www.nyc.gov/site/escr/project-updates/project-updates.page (last visited Mar. 21, 2024); Ian Michaels, *City to Start East Side Coastal Resiliency Construction in East River Park*, NYC Dep't of Design & Constr. (Nov. 1, 2021), www.nyc.gov/site/ddc/about/press-releases/2021/pr-110121-ESCR-construction.page.

   The East Side Coastal Resiliency project, of which the reconstruction of East River Park is a part, involves upgrades to 2.4 miles along Manhattan's East River shore. In addition to rebuilding East River Park, the project includes "improvements" to other parks and playgrounds. Michaels, *supra*; *Construction Project Areas for East Side Coastal Resiliency, supra*. Construction is proceeding in phases; for example, the rebuilt Asser Levy Playground opened in July 2022. Michaels, *supra*; *Mayor Adams Announces First Section of East Side Coastal Resiliency Project Completed as Asser Levy Playground Reopens with New Floodwall and Resilient Play Areas*, NYC Parks (July 18, 2022), www.nycgovparks.org/parks/asser-levy-recreation-center-pool-and-playground/pressrelease/22003.

   On the significance of the East Side Coastal Resiliency project, see, for example, Rob Hotakainen, *In N.Y., Battling Climate Change Means Killing 1,000 Trees*, E&E News (Dec. 22, 2021), www.eenews.net/articles/in-n-y-battling-climate-change-means-killing-1000-trees/; Malcolm Araos, *Democracy Underwater: Public Participation, Technical Expertise, and Climate Infrastructure Planning in New York City*, 52 Theory & Soc'y 1, 2 (2021) (referring to the East Side Coastal Resiliency project as "one of the world's largest and most expensive coastal protection projects").

7. Sara Hughes, *A Meta-Analysis of Urban Climate Change Adaptation Planning in the U.S.*, 14 Urb. Climate 17, 18 (2015).

8. Xinyu Fu, *Measuring Local Sea-Level Rise Adaptation and Adaptive Capacity: A National Survey in the United States*, Cities, July 2020, at 1 ("Unsatisfied with higher-level governmental progress in coping with climate change, local communities in the US are bearing the responsibility for adaptations."); *see also* Kaswan, *supra* note 5, at 523 ("Where systematic adaptation planning has occurred, state and local governments have been the primary drivers."); Tania Lopez-Cantu, Constantine Samaras & Marissa Webber, *Compilation of U.S. City Climate Adaptation Plans*, Carnegie Mellon Univ. (Dec. 4, 2020), https://doi.org/10.1184/R1/13125473.v2. (forty-eight out of eighty-seven cities examined as of 2020 had "a standalone climate adaptation plan (or climate assessment report)"); Foster & Pappalardo, *supra* note 2, at 377 ("In the United States and Canada combined, of the 195

cities surveyed by CDP [Climate Disclosure Project], 180 are taking some form of adaptation action.") (referring to CLIMATE DISCLOSURE PROJECT, CITIES ON ROUTE TO 2030, BUILDING A ZERO EMISSIONS RESILIENT PLANET FOR ALL 33 (May 2021)).

Between 2013 and 2019, the Rockefeller Foundation funded twenty-four U.S. cities as part of its 100 Resilient Cities Program, and this program presumably contributed to local adaptation planning in at least some of these cities. SARA MCTARNAGHAN, JORGE MORALES-BURNETT & REBECCA MARX, *URBAN RESILIENCE: FROM GLOBAL VISION TO LOCAL PRACTICE* 2–3 (2022); Linda Poon, *What Can the World Learn from 100 Resilient Cities?*, BLOOMBERG (Oct. 6, 2022), www.bloomberg.com/news/articles/2022-10-06/what-can-the-world-learn-from-100-resilient-cities.

9. Our list of the twenty most populous cities is based on 2022 population estimates from the U.S. Census Bureau. *See* U.S. CENSUS BUREAU, ANNUAL ESTIMATES OF THE RESIDENT POPULATION FOR INCORPORATED PLACES OF 50,000 OR MORE, RANKED BY JULY 1, 2022 POPULATION: APRIL 1, 2020 TO JULY 1, 2022 *available at* www.census.gov/data/tables/time-series/demo/popest/2020s-total-cities-and-towns.html#tables (last visited June 14, 2024) (listing the top twenty cities by population as of 2022, from highest to lowest as: New York City, Los Angeles, Chicago, Houston, Phoenix, Philadelphia, San Antonio, San Diego, Dallas, Austin, Jacksonville, San Jose, Fort Worth, Columbus, Charlotte, Indianapolis, San Francisco, Seattle, Denver, and Oklahoma City).

For projections developed for ten of the twenty most populous cities, *see, e.g.*, KATHARINE HAYHOE, *ATMOS RSCH. & CONSULTING, CLIMATE CHANGE PROJECTIONS FOR THE CITY OF AUSTIN* 3 (2014) (developed by Atmos Research & Consulting for the City of Austin); CHI. CLIMATE ACTION PLAN, CLIMATE CHANGE AND CHICAGO: PROJECTIONS AND POTENTIAL IMPACTS – EXECUTIVE SUMMARY (2008) (developed by an expert panel for the City of Chicago); GREAT LAKES INTEGRATED SCI. AND ASSESSMENT (GLISA) & UNIV. OF MICH. CLIMATE CTR., CLIMATE CHANGE IN COLUMBUS OHIO (2016) (developed by Great Lakes Integrated Sciences and Assessment (GLISA) and the University of Michigan Climate Center for the City of Columbus); ANNE STONER & KATHARINE HAYHOE, *ATMOS RSCH. & CONSULTING, CLIMATE IMPACT ASSESSMENT FOR THE CITY OF HOUSTON* (2020) (developed by Atmos Research & Consulting for the City of Houston); *Climate Change in the Los Angeles Region*, UCLA IOES (2015), www.ioes.ucla.edu/project/climate-change-in-the-los-angeles-region/ (developed by Center for Climate Science Faculty Director for the City of Los Angeles); NEW YORK CITY PANEL ON CLIMATE CHANGE (NPCC), N.Y.C. PANEL ON CLIMATE CHANGE, CLIMATE RISK INFORMATION 2013: OBSERVATIONS, CLIMATE CHANGE PROJECTIONS AND MAPS 7 (2013) [hereinafter CLIMATE RISK INFORMATION 2013], (developed by an expert panel for the City of New York); *Climate Data & Reports*, CITY OF OKLAHOMA CITY (developed by South Central Climate Adaptation Science Center for the City of Oklahoma City); ICF, USEFUL CLIMATE INFORMATION FOR PHILADELPHIA: PAST AND FUTURE (2014) (developed by ICF for the City of Philadelphia); ICF, THE CITY OF SAN DIEGO: CLIMATE CHANGE VULNERABILITY ASSESSMENT (2020) (developed by ICF for the City of San Diego); S.F. DEP'T OF PUB. HEALTH, SAN FRANCISCO CLIMATE & HEALTH PROFILE 8 (2014) (identifying San Francisco Department of the Environment as one source of climate projections); *see also* CITY AND COUNTY OF SAN FRANCISCO, SAN FRANCISCO SEA LEVEL RISE ACTION PLAN 2–7 (2016) (identifying San Francisco sea level rise vulnerability zone based on sea level rise projections).

In addition to the ten cities listed in the previous paragraph, other cities among the twenty most populous may have published by 2020 projections of local climate impacts;

we did not search every publication released by the other ten cities before 2020 that may include projections of local climate change impacts developed specifically for the local government. Research conducted for this book suggests that, by 2020, some of the remaining most populous cities had published projections of climate impacts relying primarily on assessments of climate impacts at the state or regional levels undertaken by higher levels of government and other sources. Dallas's 2020 environmental and climate plan referred to federal projections of temperature changes. City of Dallas, Dallas Comprehensive Environmental and Climate Action Plan 11 (2020), www.dallasclimateaction.com/_files/ugd/349b65_e4f9a262cebf41258fd4343d9af0504f.pdf. Denver's 2014 adaptation plan referred to projections of climate impacts produced by or for the local water utility, federal and Colorado agencies, and other sources. City & Cnty. of Denver, Climate Adaptation Plan 8–12, 27 (2014), www.denvergov.org/files/assets/public/climate-action/documents/climate_adaptation_final-with-letter.pdf. Seattle's 2013 climate action plan included projections for climate impacts (temperature, precipitation, and sea level changes) but the source of the projections is unclear; as of 2024, the city of Seattle's website includes sea level rise projections based on a study conducted at the University of Washington that was funded by the federal and state governments. Seattle Off. of Sustainability & Env't, Seattle Climate Action Plan 53 (2013), www.seattle.gov/documents/Departments/Environment/ClimateChange/2013_CAP_20130612.pdf; Seattle Pub. Utils., *Projections & Maps* (citing IAN MILLER, Harriet Morgan, Guillaume Mauger, tyler Newton, Ray Weldon, David Schmidt, Mark Welch & Eric Grossman., Projected Sea Level Rise for Washington State (2018), www.wacoastalnetwork.com/wp-content/uploads/2020/02/SLR-Report-Miller-et-al-2018.pdf), www.seattle.gov/utilities/protecting-our-environment/community-programs/climate-change/projections-and-maps (last visited June 4, 2024).

Some cities had published qualitative discussions of potential climate impacts for their locality. *See* Katharine Hayhoe, ATMOS Rsch. & Consulting, Climate Trends in San Antonio and an Overview of Climate Projections for the South Central Region (2015); Adaptation Int'l & Kim Lundgren Assocs., City of San Antonio Sustainability Plan: Climate Vulnerability Assessment 9 (2016).

Some cities among the twenty most populous do not appear to have published projections of local climate change impacts before 2020. *See, e.g.*, *Fort Worth, TX*, ACEEE, https://database.aceee.org/city/fort-worth-tx (Fort Worth); *Jacksonville, FL*, ACEEE, https://database.aceee.org/city/jacksonville-fl (last visited Mar. 15, 2024) (Jacksonville). *But see* Fernleaf & Water Inst., Resilient Jacksonville Vulnerability Assessment 18, 32 (2023) (including localized projections of climate impacts developed by Fernleaf and the Water Institute for the City of Jacksonville in 2023 report).

10. Hughes, *supra* note 7, at 18. *See also* Fu, *supra* note 8, at 1 (finding that, while "local communities in the US are bearing the responsibility for adaptations[,] … coastal localities are more actively investing in adaptation planning than actions.").
11. "A 2016 study of spending in global megacities for resilience and adaptation indicated that New York City ranked first in total spending, ranked second in spending per capita, and tied for third for spending per dollar of GDP for climate change adaptation." Zimmerman et al., *New York City Panel on Climate Change 2019 Report Chapter 7: Resilience Strategies for Critical Infrastructures and Their Interdependencies*, 1439 Annals N.Y. Acad. Scis. 174, 205 (2019) (citing Lucien Georgeson et al., *Adaptation Responses to Climate Change Differ between Global Megacities*, 6 Nat. Clim. Change 584 (2016)).

In 2023, the New York State Comptroller's office issued a report on local government investments in infrastructure related to climate change that underscored that New York City is unique among local governments in the state in the extent to which it is investing in climate adaptation. THOMAS P. DINAPOLI, N.Y. STATE COMPTROLLER, NEW YORK'S LOCAL GOVERNMENTS ADAPTING TO CLIMATE CHANGE: CHALLENGES, SOLUTIONS AND COSTS 2 (2023). The report indicated "that the City's capital commitment plan for FY 2023 alone included $829 million for projects that can be considered full adaptation and resilience and another $1.3 billion that was partially for these purposes. Furthermore, the plan showed commitments for adaptation and resilience (including those that are either fully or partially for this purpose) averaging $1.8 billion or 9.7 percent of average annual commitments for all capital projects for FY 2023 through FY 2026." *Id.* These figures reflect only city capital spending, not spending by the federal or state governments. *Id.*

12. For a general discussion of the politics of adaptation, see Nives Dolšak & Aseem Prakash, *The Politics of Climate Change Adaptation*, 43 ANN. REV. ENV'T & RES. 317 (2018).
13. In the early 2010s, the New York City Department of Health and Mental Hygiene, working with researchers at Columbia University, developed a Heat Vulnerability Index based on analyzing mortality data in the city between 2000 and 2011. The research produced a map showing the vulnerability of neighborhoods in the city to heat. Madrigano et al., *supra* note 4. In 2017, the city released *Cool Neighborhoods NYC: A Comprehensive Approach to Keep Communities Safe in Extreme Heat*, which identified a range of strategies, informed by the Heat Vulnerability Index, to address the risks of heat in the city. CITY OF N.Y., *supra* note 3. The strategies included aiming to plant more trees and install more cool roofs in heat vulnerable neighborhoods identified through the Heat Vulnerability Index and creating a Be a Buddy NYC program to foster community resilience, also especially in heat vulnerable neighborhoods. *Id.* at 11–15, 23–24. In 2020, during the COVID pandemic, the city established a program that distributed over 70,000 air conditioners to older, low-income New Yorkers. Kathryn Lane, Lauren Smalls-Mantey, Diana Hernández, Siobhan Watson, Sonal Jessel, Darby Jack, Leanne Spaulding & Carolyn Olson, *Extreme Heat and COVID-19 in New York City: An Evaluation of a Large Air Conditioner Distribution Program to Address Compounded Public Health Risks in Summer 2020*, 100 J. URBAN HEALTH 290 (2023). At the city's request, New York State regulators additionally provided utility bill assistance to help vulnerable city residents pay to use their air conditioning units on a regular basis. Press Release, City of N.Y., Get Cool NYC: Mayor de Blasio Updates New Yorkers on COVID-19 Summer Heat Plan (June 12, 2020), www.nyc.gov/office-of-the-mayor/news/433-20/get-cool-nyc-mayor-de-blasio-new-yorkers-covid-19-summer-heat-plan; Press Release, City of N.Y., Mayor de Blasio Announces COVID-19 Heat Wave Plan to Protect Vulnerable New Yorkers (May 15, 2020), www.nyc.gov/office-of-the-mayor/news/350-20/mayor-de-blasio-covid-19-heat-wave-plan-protect-vulnerable-new-yorkers. PlaNYC 2023 gave considerable attention to addressing the impacts of warming temperatures, especially for low-income people and people of color. CITY OF N.Y., PLANYC: GETTING SUSTAINABILITY DONE 28–36 (2023) [hereinafter PLANYC 2023]. In the summer of 2024, the city released a new plan to address risks of summer heat, poor air quality, and hurricanes. Press Release, City of N.Y., Mayor Adams, New York City Emergency Management Announce Proactive Safety Plan to Help New Yorkers "Beat the Heat," Resources to Protect against Extreme Summer Weather (May 30, 2024), www.nyc.gov/office-of-the-mayor/news/428-24/mayor-adams-new-york-city-emergency-management-proactive-safety-plan-help-new-yorkers#/0.

As for rainfall flooding, in 2021, New York City released the first map of areas at risk of flooding in rainstorms. In 2022, it updated the stormwater flood maps. N.Y.C. MAYOR'S OFF. OF RESILIENCY, NEW YORK CITY STORMWATER RESILIENCY PLAN 4, 10 (2021); N.Y.C. STORMWATER FLOOD MAPS, https://experience.arcgis.com/experience/6f4cc60710dc433585790cd2b4b5dd0e (last visited Apr. 2, 2024). The 2021 Stormwater Resiliency Plan also addressed strategies to deal with risks of "extreme rainfall." N.Y.C. MAYOR'S OFF. OF RESILIENCY, *supra*, at 12–15. Also in 2021, after Hurricane Ida, the city released NEW YORK CITY, THE NEW NORMAL: COMBATING STORM-RELATED EXTREME WEATHER IN NEW YORK CITY (2021). The 2024 report of the New York City Panel on Climate Change highlighted the multiple flood risks that the city faces – pluvial, fluvial, coastal, groundwater, and compound flooding from the various types of flooding. BERNICE ROSENZWEIG, FRANCO A. MONTALTO, PHILIP ORTON, JOEL KAATZ, NICOLE MAHER, JERRY KLEYMAN, ZIYU CHEN, ERIC SANDERSON, NIRAJAN ADHIKARI, TIMON MCPHEARSON & PABLO HERREROS-CANTIS, NEW YORK CITY PANEL ON CLIMATE CHANGE 4TH ASSESSMENT: CLIMATE CHANGE AND NEW YORK CITY'S FLOOD RISK – INTERIM REPORT (2024), https://climateassessment.nyc/wp-content/uploads/2024/05/NPCC4_FloodingInterimR3.pdf.

For advocacy from environmental justice advocates in New York City to address extreme heat, *see, e.g.*, N.Y.C. ENV'T JUST. ALL., NYC CLIMATE JUSTICE AGENDA: CLIMATE JUSTICE IN A STATE OF EMERGENCY: WHAT NEW YORK CITY CAN DO 4–6 (2017); N.Y.C. ENV'T JUST. ALL., NYC CLIMATE JUSTICE AGENDA: MIDWAY TO 2030: BUILDING RESILIENCY AND EQUITY FOR A JUST TRANSITION 8–15 (2018); WE ACT FOR ENVIRONMENTAL JUSTICE, EXTREME HEAT POLICY AGENDA 2022 (2022). For advocacy to improve stormwater infrastructure to address cloudbursts of rain, *see, e.g.*, N.Y.C. ENV'T JUST. ALL., NYC CLIMATE JUSTICE AGENDA 2020: A CRITICAL DECADE FOR CLIMATE, EQUITY, & HEALTH 54 (2020). *See also* WE ACT FOR ENVIRONMENTAL JUSTICE, 2024 POLICY AGENDA: CAMPAIGNS AND INITIATIVES 21–23 (2023), www.weact.org/wp-content/uploads/2023/11/2024-Policy-Agenda.pdf (describing heat- and flooding-related advocacy priorities).

14. For a recent example of New York City officials framing adaptation as necessary to retain the city's economic base, *see, e.g.*, Press Release, N.Y.C. Office of the Mayor, City Hall in Your Borough: Mayor Announces Capital Project to Protect Seaport from Frequent Flooding (Oct. 26, 2021), www1.nyc.gov/office-of-the-mayor/news/716-21/city-hall-your-borough-mayor-capital-project-protect-seaport-frequent-flooding ("Lower Manhattan is a critical economic hub for New York City, providing 10% of the city's total jobs. Without investments like this, the impacts of climate change in Lower Manhattan will be felt throughout our entire city."). For a critique from the New York City Environmental Justice Alliance of the city's "top-down" approach to resilience and sustainability, see N.Y.C. ENV'T JUST. ALL., NYC CLIMATE JUSTICE AGENDA: CLIMATE JUSTICE IN A STATE OF EMERGENCY: WHAT NEW YORK CITY CAN DO, *supra* note 13, at 17 ("Without an inclusive, long-term decision making process with multiple opportunities for community oversight, the implementation of the City's sustainability and resiliency initiatives remains primarily top-down.... Citywide sustainability and resiliency efforts must be coordinated with grassroots community-based planning to ensure that bottom-up neighborhood priorities are elevated.").
15. In 2017, the New York City Environmental Justice Alliance characterized resiliency initiatives in the city as "top-down." N.Y.C. ENV'T JUST. ALL., NYC CLIMATE JUSTICE AGENDA: CLIMATE JUSTICE IN A STATE OF EMERGENCY: WHAT NEW YORK CITY CAN DO, *supra* note 13, at 17. After describing a number of community-based adaptation

initiatives, the New York City Panel on Climate Change's 2019 Assessment similarly indicated that the community-based organizations surveyed "perceive that they are asked for their input and engagement often after critical decisions have been made, leaving little room for these groups and their communities to meaningfully shape development to meet their needs." Foster et al., *supra* note 4, at 157. Suggestive of a continuing disconnect between community-based resilience initiatives and city government actions, the New York City Panel on Climate Change's 2024 Assessment urges greater "integration and centering of community-based plans in citywide agendas[.]" Deborah Balk, Timon McPhearson, Elizabeth M Cook, Kim Knowlton, Nicole Maher, Peter Marcotullio, Thomas Matte, Richard Moss, Luis Ortiz, Joel Towers, Jennifer Ventrella & Gernot Wagner, *NPCC4: Concepts and Tools for Envisioning New York City's Futures*, 2024 Annals N.Y. Acad. Scis. 16 (2024), https://climateassessment.nyc/assessment/concepts-and-tools-for-envisioning-new-york-citys-futures/. *But see* Sheila R. Foster, Ana Baptista, Khai Hoan Nguyen, Jack Tchen, Marco Tedesco & Robin Leichenko, *Advancing Climate Justice in Climate Adaptation Strategies for New York City: Interim Report*, in *New York City Panel on Climate Change 4th Assessment* 7 (2024), https://climateassessment.nyc/wp-content/uploads/2024/04/NPCC4_EquityInterimR2.pdf ("the City Council and local representatives from EJ organizations have emerged as key players in advancing and institutionalizing environmental justice and equity in the City's long-term climate adaptation planning efforts"). *See also id.* at 15–16, 46–47 (summarizing community-based initiatives since the third assessment in 2019).

There have been community-based efforts to promote resilience at least as far back as 2010. For example, in 2010, the New York City Environmental Justice Alliance established its "Waterfront Justice Project," which the Alliance describes as "New York City's first citywide community-based resiliency campaign." This campaign focused on reducing the risks of industrial pollution during storm surges or other flooding in industrial areas along the city's waterfront. *Waterfront Justice & Coastal Resilience*, N.Y.C. Env't Just. All., https://nyc-eja.org/campaigns/waterfront-justice-and-coastal-resilience/ (last visited May 7, 2024). In 2013, after Hurricane Sandy, "over 40 community, environmental justice, labor and civic groups from New York, New Jersey and Long Island" met in the Sandy Regional Assembly to define a recovery agenda that would address "the needs and priorities of vulnerable groups, particularly in low-income neighborhoods and communities of color[,]" and analyze the city government's Special Initiative for Rebuilding and Resiliency and make recommendations to the federal government on recovering from Sandy. Sandy Regional Assembly: SIRR Analysis: An Assessment of the Mayor's Special Initiative for Rebuilding and Resiliency (SIRR) Plan, and Recommendations for the Federal Hurricane Sandy Rebuilding Task Force 1 (2013). Also after Sandy, "the City's first grassroots community-led resiliency center" was established in Sunset Park, and THE POINT Community Development Corporation launched the "South Bronx Community Resiliency Agenda." N.Y.C. Env't Just. All., NYC Climate Justice Agenda: Strengthening the Mayor's OneNYC Plan 56, 58 (2016), https://nyc-eja.org/wp-content/uploads/2017/10/CJA_041916.pdf. *See also id.* at 53–63 (describing "community-based initiatives" for "climate justice"). In 2015, WE ACT for Environmental Justice led a "community-based planning process" to create the Northern Manhattan Climate Action Plan. *Northern Manhattan Climate Action Plan*, WE ACT for Env't Just., www.weact.org/campaigns/nmca/ (last visited May 7, 2024).

16. Hughes, *supra* note 7, at 22.

The framing of adaptation as a means of protecting the city's assets implicitly aligns adaptation with the traditional local government focus on economic prosperity. Some progressive community-based activists and academics warn that thinking of adaptation in terms of protecting assets and infrastructure risks perpetuating existing inequalities. *Cf.* Linda Shi & Susanne Moser, *Transformative Climate Adaptation in the United States: Trends and Prospects*, 372 SCI. 1, 4–6 (2021). The critics seek a more transformational approach to adaptation that would address "the deep roots and conditions producing vulnerability in the first place." *Id.* at 2.

It is not surprising that advocates have been slower to coalesce around an adaptation agenda, despite the urgency of doing so. In the words of D.J. Rasmussen and his colleagues, "[a]dvocacy coalitions for natural hazard risk management have been slow to emerge in part due to the technical nature of the hazards themselves, which has limited their study largely to scientific communities in government and academia." D.J. Rasmussen, Robert E. Kopp, Rachael Shwom & Michael Oppenheimer, *The Political Complexity of Coastal Flood Risk Reduction: Lessons for Climate Adaptation Public Works in the U.S.*, 9 EARTH'S FUTURE 1, 6 (2021).

17. On the impact of uncertainties about climate risks on policymakers, see, for example, William Solecki & Cynthia Rosenzweig, *New York City Panel on Climate Change 2019 Report Chapter 9: Perspectives on a City in a Changing Climate 2008–2018*, 1439 ANN. N.Y. ACAD. SCI. 280, 301 (2019); HARRIET BULKELEY, CITIES AND CLIMATE CHANGE 142–143 (2013). *See also, e.g.*, *Climate Change*, DENVER WATER, www.denverwater.org/your-water/water-supply-and-planning/climate-change (last visited Apr. 3, 2024) ("[T]here are a wide range of climate-change predictions for Colorado, which makes future water-supply planning difficult. Denver Water is working with climate scientists to best understand how climate conditions may change in our area, as well as to promote the need for better science, modeling and uncertainty planning to meet the needs of water providers.").
18. OFF. OF THE N.Y.C. COMPTROLLER, B. POL'Y & RES., TEN YEARS AFTER SANDY: BARRIERS TO RESILIENCE 30 (2022) [hereinafter TEN YEARS AFTER SANDY], https://comptroller.nyc.gov/wp-content/uploads/documents/Ten-Years-After-Sandy.pdf ("The $15 billion that New York City received as a result of Superstorm Sandy was no doubt instrumental in spurring meaningful resiliency improvements in the last decade.").
19. *Id.* at 12 (After Sandy, New York City "received $4.2 billion of [federal Housing and Urban Development Community Development Block Grant Disaster Recovery] funding" that "came with a use-or-lose timeline that called for recipients to complete spending of federal grant money by 2022. That deadline was recently extended to 2025 as part of the Consolidated Appropriations Act passed by Congress in 2022." (citing Consolidated Appropriations Act of 2022, H.R.2471, 117th Cong. (2022)).
20. Anne Barnard, *Five Ways to Prevent the Next Sandy*, N.Y. TIMES (Oct. 28, 2022), www.nytimes.com/2022/10/28/nyregion/hurricane-sandy-nyc-10-year-anniversary.html.
21. On the effects of the Civil Rights Movement, activism for more public participation, and the environmental protection movement on the construction of urban infrastructure, see ALAN ALTSHULER & DAVID LUBEROFF, MEGA-PROJECTS: THE CHANGING POLITICS OF URBAN PUBLIC INVESTMENT 22–23 (2003). On the development of community participation in land use planning in New York after the Robert Moses era, see SHEILA F. FOSTER & CHRISTIAN IAIONE, CO-CITIES: INNOVATIVE TRANSITIONS TOWARD JUST AND SELF-SUSTAINING COMMUNITIES 165 (2022). On the history of the 1970s era environmental laws and their reliance on public interest litigation, see generally PAUL SABIN, PUBLIC CITIZENS: THE ATTACK ON BIG GOVERNMENT AND THE REMAKING OF AMERICAN LIBERALISM (2021).

22. *See, e.g.*, Geoff Dembicki, *The Progressive Way to Save Cities from Superstorms*, New Republic (Aug. 2, 2023), https://newrepublic.com/article/174664/progressive-way-save-cities-superstorms (critically analyzing Army Corps studies to protect against climate impacts); *Study for City of Boston Coastal Storm Risk Management*, U.S. Army Corps of Eng'r, www.nae.usace.army.mil/Missions/Projects-Topics/City-of-Boston-Coastal-Storm-Risk-Management-Project/ (last visited Apr. 3, 2024); Susan Crawford, Charleston: Race, Water, and the Coming Storm 107–08 (2023); Jenny Staletovich, *Army Corps Agrees to Redo Billion Dollar Plan to Fortify Miami-Dade against Storm Surge*, WUSF (Sept. 8, 2022), www.wusf.org/environment/2022-09-10/army-corps-agrees-to-redo-billion-dollar-plan-to-fortify-miami-dade-against-storm-surge; Katie Watkins, *Army Corps Unveils Updated $26 Billion Project to Protect the Texas Gulf from Storms*, Hous. Pub. Media, (Oct. 30, 2020), www.houstonpublicmedia.org/articles/news/energy-environment/2020/10/30/385009/army-corps-unveils-updated-version-of-its-26-billion-project-to-protect-the-texas-gulf-coast-from-hurricanes-storm-surge/.
23. Press Release, Env't Def. Fund, Advocates Celebrate Breakthrough in Campaign to Overhaul Flawed Army Corps Flooding Plan for NJ-NY Harbor (Nov. 13, 2023), www.edf.org/media/advocates-celebrate-breakthrough-campaign-overhaul-flawed-army-corps-flooding-plan-ny-nj (describing letter from the New York State Department of Environmental Conservation to the Army Corps that will require the Army Corps to "overhaul" its plan so that it addresses multiple types of flood risks in addition to storm surge flooding, and as well as to make other changes to the plan); *New York District, NY & NJ Harbor & Tributaries Focus Area Feasibility Study (HATS), January 2024 Update*, U.S. Army Corps of Eng'rs, www.nan.usace.army.mil/Missions/Civil-Works/Projects-in-New-York/New-York-New-Jersey-Harbor-Tributaries-Focus-Area-Feasibility-Study/ (last visited June 7, 2024) (referring "to a recent request by the States of New York and New Jersey to discuss further flood risk evaluations that may be done as part of the study and as authorized in Section 8106 of the Water Resources Development Act of 2022").
24. *See* Chapters 3 and 4.
25. The assessment was published as "part of a national study commissioned by Congress and carried out by the U.S. Global Change Research Program." Carter B. Horsley & Michele Leight, *Columbia Earth Institute Holds Conference on New Report Outlining Problems for New York Region*, The City Review, www.thecityreview.com/climate.html; *see also* Solecki & Rosenzweig, *supra* note 17, at 280 ("The original work on science-based assessments of climate change impacts in the NYMR [New York Metropolitan Region] began with *Climate Change and A Global City: The Metropolitan East Coast Regional Assessment of Potential Climate Variability and Change* (MEC Report)."); Cynthia Rosenzweig & William D. Solecki, *Columbia Earth Institute, Climate Change and a Global City: The Metropolitan East Coast Regional Assessment* (2001).
26. Solecki & Rosenzweig, *supra* note 17, at 283–84 ("Between the end of the MEC Assessment and the founding of NPCC in 2008, the New York City DEP actively continued to work on climate vulnerability and impacts assessment efforts (NYC DEP, 2008). At the same time, the Mayor's office began efforts to consider climate mitigation for the city as part of PlaNYC.").
27. City of N.Y., N.Y.C. Dept. of Env't Prot. Climate Change Program, Assessment and Action Plan 7 (2008) [hereinafter DEP Assessment and Action Plan]. *See also* Bulkeley, *supra* note 17, at 176–78 (In 2004, the city's Department of Environmental Protection, "established a Climate Change Task Force … as a partnership between scientists and policymakers." Its work "led to a study of the impacts of

sea-level rise on sewer and wastewater treatment, and to new approaches to modelling water availability in the New York catchment area that take account of the effects of climate change.").

In 2003, DEP funded researchers at Columbia University to model local climate change impacts. DEP ASSESSMENT AND ACTION PLAN, *supra*, at 6, 14; *see also id.* at 8 ("DEP has funded the development of a set of regional climate change projections that are based on data from the best available global climate change models. DEP now has the most comprehensive set of climate data that has been produced for New York City and its Watershed Region: Columbia University and NASA have provided annual projections for temperature precipitation and sea level for the 2020s, 2050s, and 2080s."); BULKELEY, *supra* note 17, at 177–78.

DEP "provide[d] funding for Stony Brook University's regional storm surge barrier feasibility study." GARY HEATH, N.Y.C. *BUREAU OF ENV'T PLAN. & ANALYSIS, ASSESSING AND MANAGING CLIMATE CHANGE RISK TO NEW YORK CITY'S WATER SUPPLY AND WASTEWATER TREATMENT SYSTEMS* 5 (2008). *See also* DEP ASSESSMENT AND ACTION PLAN, *supra*, at 56 ("In 2002, the State University of New York at Stony Brook conducted research with sponsorship from New York State Sea Grant and DEP to investigate the feasibility of storm surge barriers to protect most of New York City from the effects of storm surge.").

28. DEP ASSESSMENT AND ACTION PLAN, *supra* note 27, at 4.
29. *Id.* at 10; *see also id.* at 8.
30. CITY OF N.Y., PLANYC: A STRONGER, MORE RESILIENT NEW YORK 23, 32 (2013) [hereinafter SIRR]. In 2007, the Bloomberg administration committed in PlaNYC to working with FEMA to update the floodplain maps. CITY OF N.Y., PLANYC: A GREENER, GREATER NEW YORK 139 (2007) [hereinafter PLANYC 2007].

FEMA did not release the preliminary maps until after Sandy struck in 2012, flooding an area over "one and a half times larger than the 100-year floodplain" in the 1983 maps. SIRR, *supra*, at 23; *see also id.* at 13, 69. A 100-year flood "is the flood that has a 1 percent chance of occurring in any given year." *Id.* at 24.

In January 2013, after Sandy, FEMA issued "interim maps [Advisory Base Flood Elevation Maps, or ABFEs] for New York just as it had done for other communities that did not have up-to-date maps following major storms." *Id.* at 23. In June 2013, FEMA released Preliminary Work Maps (PWMs). *Id.* at 24. These PWMs expanded the 100-year floodplain by "45 percent … over the 1983 FIRMs [Flood Insurance Rate Maps]." *Id.* at 45. FEMA released Preliminary Flood Insurance Rate Maps [PFIRMs] in December 2013, and updated versions of these maps in 2015. CITY OF N.Y., ONE NEW YORK: THE PLAN FOR A STRONG AND JUST CITY 235 (2015) [hereinafter ONE NEW YORK 2015]; *Flood Maps*, N.Y.C. FLOOD MAPS, www.nyc.gov/site/floodmaps/index.page (last visited Apr. 4, 2024); N.Y.C. PLAN., NYC'S FLOODPLAIN BY THE NUMBERS 24 (2020), www.nyc.gov/assets/planning/download/pdf/plans-studies/resilient-neighborhoods/floodplain-by-numbers.pdf. New York City filed an appeal of the 2015 maps based on technical errors, with which FEMA agreed. As of 2023, the city is still waiting for new flood maps from FEMA. Pending the release of these new maps, "flood insurance rates in New York City will continue to be based on the 2007 Effective FIRMs saving coastal households tens of millions of dollars per year; the city's Building Code will continue to reflect the 2015 Preliminary FIRMs." *Appeals*, N.Y.C. FLOOD MAPS, www.nyc.gov/site/floodmaps/appeals/overview.page (last visited Apr. 4, 2024); *see also* N.Y.C. PLAN., *supra*, at 24 ("Building code and zoning will continue to refer to both the 2007 FIRMs and 2015 PFIRMs, whichever is more conservative.").

31. N.Y.C. PANEL ON CLIMATE CHANGE, CLIMATE RISK INFORMATION 4 (Feb. 17, 2009), www.nyc.gov/html/om/pdf/2009/NPCC_CRI.pdf.
32. Michael Bloomberg, *Forewords to Climate Change Adaptation in New York City: Building a Risk Management Response*, 1196 ANN. N.Y. ACAD. SCI. (2010).
33. *New York City Panel on Climate Change 2019 Report: Executive Summary*, 1439 ANN. N.Y. ACAD. SCI. 11, 21 (2019) (citing the 2001 federally funded assessment of climate risks to the Metro East Coast).
34. CITY OF N.Y., PLANYC: A GREENER, GREATER NEW YORK, UPDATE 2011 at 154–55 (2011) [hereinafter PLANYC 2011]. Although the first panel report was published in 2010, in 2009, the NPCC provided climate risk projections for the city. Bloomberg, *supra* note 32; *see also* N.Y.C. PANEL ON CLIMATE CHANGE, *supra* note 31.

    In 2011, the Bloomberg administration committed to "institutionaliz[ing]" the Panel and updating its projections. PLANYC 2011, *supra*, at 155. Under a local law passed by the city council in 2012, the panel is legally required to issue "climate change projections" for New York City after the release of an assessment report of the international intergovernmental panel on climate change, or no less than "once every three years." N.Y.C., N.Y., LOCAL LAW NO. 42 (2012); N.Y.C. ADMIN. CODE § 3-122I(2).
35. RADLEY HORTON ET AL., N.Y.C. PANEL ON CLIMATE CHANGE, APPENDIX A: CLIMATE RISK INFORMATION – CLIMATE CHANGE SCENARIOS & IMPLICATIONS FOR NYC INFRASTRUCTURE 172 (2010). In 2013, the New York City Panel on Climate Change "predict[ed] that, by the 2050s, the city could have as many days at or above 90 degrees annually as Birmingham, Alabama has today – a threefold increase over what New York currently experiences." SIRR, *supra* note 30, at 30.
36. *Executive Summary of Climate Change Adaptation in New York City: Building a Risk Management Response*, 1196 ANN. N.Y. ACAD. SCI. 1, 8 (2010) [hereinafter NPCC 2010 EXECUTIVE SUMMARY]. *See also* Radley Horton et al., *Chapter 3: Climate Observations and Projections*, 1196 ANN. N.Y. ACAD. SCI. 41 (2010).
37. NPCC 2010 EXECUTIVE SUMMARY, *supra* note 36, at 9. *See also* Horton et al., *supra* note 36.
38. Thirteen people died in New York City in 2021 from rain from Hurricane Ida, eleven in flooded basement apartments. Honan, *supra* note 1.
39. HORTON ET AL., *supra* note 35, at 172. *See also id.* at 167 (explaining why the panel offered two projections for sea level rise).
40. Rae Zimmerman & Craig Faris, *Chapter 4: Infrastructure Impacts and Adaptation Challenges*, 1196 ANN. N.Y. ACAD. SCI. 63 (2010).

    The city took steps to acquire more fine-grained information about the risks that the early assessments underscored. In 2010, with funding from the federal Centers for Disease Control and Prevention, the city's Department of Health and Mental Hygiene began studying the human health impacts of higher temperatures. PLANYC 2011, *supra* note 34, at 158, 197; SIRR, *supra* note 30, at 31, 32. DEP committed to modeling the impacts of global warming "on drinking water quality, supply, and demand[,]" and "to quantify[ing] and provid[ing] a more comprehensive understanding of the potential impacts of climate change on drainage, wastewater treatment processes and infrastructure, and harbor water quality." DEP ASSESSMENT AND ACTION PLAN, *supra* note 27, at 44–45. When Sandy struck in 2012 and power outages and storm surge flooding affected ten of the city's "fourteen wastewater treatment plants," DEP was "performing a detailed climate change study for representative wastewater treatment plants, pumping stations, and drainage areas to determine the potential likelihood and severity of various risks, including storm surge." SIRR, *supra* note 30, at 207. *See also id.* at 209, 213–14; N.Y.C. ENV'T PROT., NYC

WASTEWATER RESILIENCY PLAN: CLIMATE RISK ASSESSMENT AND ADAPTATION STUDY 5 (2013) (discussing Hurricane Sandy's impact on New York City's pumping stations and wastewater treatment plants).

41. PLANYC 2011, *supra* note 34, at 158.
42. SIRR, *supra* note 30, at 27, 71–73; N.Y.C. PLAN., *supra* note 30, at 15 ("In 1983, New York City joined the federal National Flood Insurance Program (NFIP), adopting the Flood Insurance Rate Maps (FIRMs) along with federal construction standards for buildings in the floodplain…. These codes are now part of Appendix G of the NYC Building Code. Our analysis shows that buildings that were constructed to these flood-resistant construction standards fared far better during Hurricane Sandy than buildings that were not."); DEP'T OF CITY PLAN., CITY OF N.Y., COASTAL CLIMATE RESILIENCE: URBAN WATERFRONT ADAPTIVE STRATEGIES 3 (2013) [hereinafter URBAN WATERFRONT ADAPTIVE STRATEGIES] ("Since 1983, when FEMA issued the first Flood Insurance Rate Maps for New York City, the city's Building Code has required buildings within the flood zone to incorporate … measures [to avoid 'damage to buildings and their contents']. During Hurricane Sandy, newer buildings built to these standards fared much better than older buildings, demonstrating the effectiveness of such strategies when they are in place. However, 84 percent of the nearly 90,000 buildings in the area inundated by Hurricane Sandy in New York City were built before such standards were required for new construction."). On rezoning of waterfront areas before Sandy to allow more development, see, for example, Samantha Maldonado et al., *Hurricane Sandy Devastated Coney Island 10 Years Ago. So Why Has NYC Added Almost 2,000 Homes to the Area Since?*, THE CITY (Oct. 27, 2022), www.thecity.nyc/2022/10/27/23424718/hurricane-sandy-coney-island-climate-change-development (referring to the rezoning of Coney Island in Brooklyn in 2009); DANIEL L. DOCTOROFF, *GREATER THAN EVER: NEW YORK'S BIG COMEBACK* 278 (2017) (referring to 2009 Coney Island rezoning); DEP'T OF CITY PLAN., CITY OF N.Y., VISION 2020: NEW YORK CITY COMPREHENSIVE WATERFRONT PLAN 36 (2011) [hereinafter VISION 2020] (referring to the 2005 rezoning of Greenpoint-Williamsburg); Tom Angotti, *On the Waterfront*, THE INDYPENDENT (Nov. 19, 2012), https://indypendent.org/2012/11/on-the-waterfront/.

    The 2011 update to PlaNYC indicated that the "current building code requires that new buildings in the FEMA 1-in-100 year flood zone elevate occupied space above the FEMA-designated flood level (the base flood elevation)" and the city currently requires "freeboard" – additional space of "one or two feet" above the base flood elevation – "for critical buildings in flood zones such as hospitals, utility facilities, public safety facilities and schools." PLANYC 2011, *supra* note 34, at 156. The 2011 update also indicated that the city would "pursue amendments to the Building Code to require freeboard for a wider range of buildings to reduce risks associated with sea level rise and more intense coastal storms." *Id.*
43. Retreat, engineering, and nature-based options had already been identified as potential strategies for dealing with coastal flooding risks before Hurricane Sandy. DEP ASSESSMENT AND ACTION PLAN, *supra* note 27, at 56–57; PLANYC 2011, *supra* note 34, at 158.
44. DEP ASSESSMENT AND ACTION PLAN, *supra* note 27, at 12–13; *see also id.* at 48–62 (discussing adaptation strategies but emphasizing the need to better understand the risks that climate change presents and options for addressing these risks before undertaking costly adaptation measures).

    A Stronger, More Resilient New York, the special report that the city released after Hurricane Sandy, implicitly confirms the limited extent of DEP's actions (as opposed to analysis) prior to Sandy, stating that "[t]o prepare for the future, DEP began implementing climate change resiliency measures early, in 2008, when it issued the Climate Change Assessment and Action Plan. Prior to Sandy, DEP was already in the process of performing a detailed climate change study for representative wastewater treatment plants, pumping stations, and drainage areas to determine the potential likelihood and severity of various risks, including storm surge. After Sandy, DEP expanded that study to include all of its wastewater infrastructure across the city to systematically determine risks and resiliency measures to help prevent future disruptions." SIRR, *supra* note 30, at 207.

45. PLANYC 2011, *supra* note 34, at 157.

46. DEP ASSESSMENT AND ACTION PLAN, *supra* note 27, at 60. As of 2011, the Department of City Planning also seemed to think it was too early to invest much in adapting the city to climate change given the uncertainties about its impacts for the city. VISION 2020, *supra* note 42, at 106, 108.

On the obstacles that uncertainty about the future benefits of investing in coastal resilience creates for municipal investments in resilience, see, for example, DAVID L. LEVY ET AL., FINANCING CLIMATE RESILIENCE: MOBILIZING RESOURCES AND INCENTIVES TO PROTECT BOSTON FROM CLIMATE RISKS 3 (2018); KAHN, *supra* note 5, at 79 ("When making an investment decision that features large upfront costs and significant uncertainty about the project's benefits, it can be wise to wait. As time passes, the menu of resilience investment alternatives will change.... The risks of delaying an infrastructure investment is that in the short run it exposes areas to the climate damage posed by the next storm."); Solecki & Rosenzweig, *supra* note 17, at 300–01 ("Policy responses to climate change are also hampered by the generally reactive nature of management organizations. Institutional action is often directed at immediate and obvious problems. Issues that might emerge fully only after several decades are perceived as less pressing."); Rasmussen et al., *supra* note 16, at 6 ("If the primary goal of an elected official is to get re-elected, then it is rational for them to address problems with benefits that are visible to their constituents during their time in office. This includes favoring disaster relief over preparedness.").

47. SIRR, *supra* note 30, at 13 (bar chart illustrating "High-Water Events in Lower Manhattan," showing that the subway system came close to flooding in 1953, 1960 with hurricane Donna, 1992, and 2011 with Hurricane Irene before it flooded in 2012 when Sandy hit New York City); Jose Martinez, *State Comptroller Report Faults MTA for Lack of Climate Change Plans*, THE CITY (Oct. 2, 2023), www.thecity.nyc/2023/10/2/23900353/state-comptroller-faults-mta-climate-change-plans. Notably, in 2011, Dr. Klaus Jacob of Columbia University coauthored a report for New York State that set out detailed projections of how a superstorm would impact the New York City subway system. CYNTHIA ROSENZWEIG ET AL., N.Y. STATE ENERGY RSCH. & DEV. AUTH.,RESPONDING TO CLIMATE CHANGE IN NEW YORK STATE: A SYNTHESIS REPORT 38 (2011); *see also* Klaus Hans Jacob et al., *Transportation, in* RESPONDING TO CLIMATE CHANGE IN NEW YORK STATE 299 (Cynthia Rosenzweig et al. eds., 2011). This chapter referred to some changes that the MTA was making to address flooding in the subway. JACOB ET AL., *supra*, at 333; *see also* Tanya Lewis, *The Scientist Who Helped Save New York's Subway from Sandy*, LIVESCIENCE (July 13, 2022), www.livescience.com/40736-scientist-who-saved-new-york-subway-from-sandy.html. On changes that the MTA made after Sandy, see, for example, *Protecting New York's Transit System from Climate Change*, MTA, https://new.mta.info/climate/completed-resiliency-projects (last visited Apr. 9, 2024); Dan Rivoli, *Seven Years after Hurricane Sandy, the MTA Outlines Prep for Future Storms*, SPECTRUM NEWS N.Y. (Oct. 29, 2019), www.ny1.com/nyc/all-boroughs/

transit/2019/10/30/hurricane-sandy-anniversary-seven-years-later-mta-outlines-prep-for-future-storms; SARAH KAUFMAN ET AL., *RUDIN CENTER FOR TRANSPORTATION, NYU WAGNER GRADUATE SCHOOL OF PUBLIC SERVICE, TRANSPORTATION DURING AND AFTER HURRICANE SANDY* (2012).

48. *See Funding Opportunities*, U.S. CLIMATE RESILIENCE TOOLKIT, https://toolkit.climate.gov/content/funding-opportunities (last visited Apr. 9, 2024); PAUL KIRSHEN ET AL., *SUSTAINABLE SOLUTIONS LAB & UNIVERSITY OF MASSACHUSETTS BOSTON, FEASIBILITY OF HARBOR-WIDE BARRIER SYSTEMS: PRELIMINARY ANALYSIS FOR BOSTON HARBOR* (2018) (describing how coastal barrier alternatives in Boston Harbor range in cost from $6.5 to 11.8 billion dollars, in 2017 dollars).

49. FEMA's Building Resilient Infrastructure and Communities (BRIC) program, which provides funding to localities, states, and others for proactive resilience measures, was launched in 2020. *FEMA Launches Building Resilient Infrastructure and Communities*, FEMA, www.fema.gov/fact-sheet/fema-launches-building-resilient-infrastructure-and-communities (last visited Apr. 9, 2024). BRIC, which replaced the Pre-Disaster Mitigation Program, was established pursuant to 2018 legislation. Stephanie M. Stern, *Climate Transition Relief: Federal Buyouts for Underwater Homes*, 72 DUKE L.J. 161, 175 n.50 & 180 n.75 (2022); *see also* Mark Nevitt, *Destroy, Rebuild, Repeat: How to Break the Climate Disaster Cycle*, 78 VANDERBILT L. REV. (2025) (manuscript at 44, 46).

The Bipartisan Infrastructure Law, passed in 2021, further expanded the funding available for proactive adaptation. Michael Gold et al., *What the Infrastructure Bill Means for the New York Region*, N.Y. TIMES (Nov. 16, 2021), www.nytimes.com/2021/11/15/nyregion/infrastructure-bill-new-york.html. *See also* Sample Letter from EPA Administrator Letter to Governors (Dec. 2, 2021), *available at* www.epa.gov/system/files/documents/2021-12/governors-bil-letter-final-508.pdf (the Bipartisan Infrastructure Law signed by President Biden on November 15, 2021, "includes $50 billion to the EPA to strengthen the nation's drinking water and wastewater systems").

50. Zimmerman et al., *supra* note 11, at 203 ("[W]ith the knowledge that federal funds may be available following a disaster should their facilities incur damage, infrastructure managers may have less of a financial motivation to invest in loss mitigation measures or to purchase insurance to make their systems more resilient in light of potential future disasters."); *id.* at 210 ("Stafford Act funding following a disaster can serve as a disincentive to investment in resilience improvements").

On the benefits of adapting before disaster strikes, see, for example, Hughes, *supra* note 7, at 17 ("Proactive adaptation in cities can be highly cost effective: the National Institute of Building Sciences estimates that every dollar invested in building resilience and reducing exposure to disaster risks (i.e., adaptation) saves $4 in disaster response and recovery."); NAT'L ECON. COUNCIL, *supra* note 2, at 298 (referring to other estimates of the benefits of "proactive adaptation" in reducing harm from climate change).

51. Ning Lin et al., *Physically Based Assessment of Hurricane Surge Threat under Climate Change*, 2 NATURE CLIMATE CHANGE 462 (2012). On Oppenheimer as a member of NPCC2 and 3, see *Building the Knowledge Base for Climate Resiliency: New York City Panel on Climate Change 2015 Report*, 1336 ANN. N.Y. ACAD. SCI. 1, 2 (2015); *Special Issue: Advancing Tools and Methods for Flexible Adaptation Pathways and Science Policy Integration: New York City Panel on Climate Change 2019 Report*, 1439 ANN. N.Y. ACAD. SCI. 1, 6 (2019).

52. Lin et al., *supra* note 51, at 465.

53. The relevant DEP report warned of "the worst-case scenario of a Category 4 hurricane moving north-north westerly and making landfall during high tide near Atlantic City,

New Jersey." DEP ASSESSMENT AND ACTION PLAN, *supra* note 27, at 55. This worst case scenario is mentioned in discussing issues to be addressed in seeking to minimize damages from coastal flooding. The full sentence is: "The larger the magnitude of event (such as the worst-case scenario of a Category 4 hurricane moving north-north westerly and making landfall during high tide near Atlantic City, New Jersey, which would amplify the effect of storm surge through the 'New York Bight'), the more appropriate regional approaches to this problem may be."). *Id.*

54. *Scientist Predicted New York Flooding*, 9 NEWS (Oct. 31, 2012), www.9news.com.au/world/scientist-predicted-new-york-flooding/83fa97d2-2083-49b8-83c1-cbdcbcd10a22.
55. SIRR, *supra* note 30, at 11, 13. For more information about storm surge and Hurricane Sandy, *see generally* ADAM SOBEL, *STORM SURGE: HURRICANE SANDY, OUR CHANGING CLIMATE, AND EXTREME WEATHER OF THE PAST AND FUTURE* (2014).
56. ONE NEW YORK 2015, *supra* note 30, at 216 (44 deaths); SIRR, *supra* note 30, at 11; FURMAN CTR. & MOELIS INST., SANDY'S EFFECTS ON HOUSING IN NEW YORK CITY 3–4 (2013); *see also* SIRR, *supra* note 30, on transportation at 177 and 178 and on wastewater treatment plants at 209.
57. HURRICANE SANDY REBUILDING TASK FORCE, HURRICANE SANDY REBUILDING STRATEGY 21 (2013) ("Hurricane Sandy is the second costliest hurricane in the nation's history."); *Id.* at 21 n.29 ("According to NOAA, the 2013 Consumer Price Index (CPI) cost adjusted value of Hurricane Sandy was $65.7 billion. The costliest storm was Hurricane Katrina, with a 2013 CPI cost adjusted value of $148.8 billion, and the third costliest Hurricane was Hurricane Andrew, with a 2013 CPI cost adjusted value of $44.8 billion."). *Compare* NAT'L OCEANIC & ATMOSPHERIC ADMIN., NAT'L CTRS. FOR ENV'T INFO., COSTLIEST U.S. TROPICAL CYCLONES 1–2 (2024) (identifying Sandy as the fifth costliest U.S. hurricane using "values based on the 2024 Consumer Price Index adjusted cost"), www.ncei.noaa.gov/access/billions/dcmi.pdf (last visited June 7, 2024).
58. SIRR, *supra* note 30, at 69 ("Sandy's impact is illustrative of the city's growing climate risks."); *id.* at 30 (Box "Possible Links Between Sandy and Climate Change," stating that "While it is impossible to attribute any one event such as Sandy entirely to climate change, higher sea levels certainly did increase the extent and magnitude of coastal flooding caused by the storm," that "Sandy is also thought to have gained strength from unusually warm upper ocean temperatures in the North Atlantic" and that "Loss of sea ice as the Arctic warms may possibly have influenced Sandy's path and Intensity"); CLIMATE RISK INFORMATION 2013, *supra* note 9, at 7 ("While it is not possible to attribute any single extreme event such as Hurricane Sandy to climate change, sea level rise already occurring in the New York City area, in part related to climate change, increased the extent, and magnitude of coastal flooding during the storm."). *See also Scientist Predicted New York Flooding, supra* note 54.
59. SIRR, *supra* note 30, at 25 ("The new 100-year floodplain, roughly corresponding to the areas flooded during Sandy, is larger than indicated on the 1983 maps by about 15 square miles, or 45 percent."). Federal agencies also produced other data to help local and state decision-makers in the Sandy region rebuild resiliently, including for determining the 100-year floodplain and "100-year flood elevations." HURRICANE SANDY REBUILDING TASK FORCE, *supra* note 57, at 43. On the Advisory Base Flood Elevation maps, see SIRR, *supra* note 30, at 23.
60. SIRR, *supra* note 30, at 28.
61. *Id.* at 30.
62. *Id.* at 31. *See also* CLIMATE RISK INFORMATION 2013, *supra* note 9, at 5.

The statistics about the current and 2050s floodplain are repeated in successive city government policy documents. *See, e.g.*, N.Y.C. PLAN., NEW YORK CITY COMPREHENSIVE WATERFRONT PLAN 53 (2021) [hereinafter 2021 WATERFRONT PLAN]; ONE NEW YORK 2015, *supra* note 30, at 235.

City policymakers have long recognized the inadequacy of FEMA maps, which are based on historical data, and do not incorporate projections about future climate impacts, such as sea level rise. CLIMATE RISK INFORMATION 2013, *supra* note 9, at 24; PLANYC 2011, *supra* note 34, at 196; 2021 WATERFRONT PLAN, *supra*, at 103. NYC Planning has published flood maps based on NPCC projections for sea level rise. *NYC Flood Hazard Mapper*, N.Y.C. PLAN., https://dcp.maps.arcgis.com/apps/webappviewer/index.html?id=1c37d271fba14163bbb520517153d6d5 (last visited Apr. 17, 2024) (about the map layers).

63. Adalene Minelli, *Adapting New York City: How the Largest US City Is Addressing the Impacts of Climate Change on Its Coastal Communities*, *in* GLOBAL SUSTAINABLE CITIES: CITY GOVERNMENTS AND OUR ENVIRONMENTAL FUTURE 308, 311 (Danielle Spiegel-Feld, Katrina Miriam Wyman & John Coughlin eds., 2023) ("[L]ow-income households and seniors made up a higher-than-average share of the population in the neighborhoods within Hurricane Sandy's surge area, and Black households (and low-income Black households in particular) were more likely to live in these flooded areas." (citing FURMAN CTR., SANDY'S EFFECTS ON HOUSING IN NEW YORK CITY 7–8 (2013) and Jacob W. Faber, *Superstorm Sandy and the Demographics of Flood Risk in New York City*, 43 HUM. ECOLOGY 363 (2015)). *See also* FURMAN CTR., SANDY'S EFFECTS ON HOUSING IN NEW YORK CITY 7–8 (2013) (reporting in March 2013 that "over 150,000 households" in the city had registered with FEMA for assistance after Sandy; 55 percent of the registered households were renters, and roughly "two-thirds of renters … [had] … household incomes of less than $30,000 per year").
64. Faber, *supra* note 63, at 366 ("According to FEMA data, all five boroughs saw flooding, with the worst in Staten Island, southern Brooklyn, and the lower third of Manhattan.").
65. *Id.* at 368–369 ("Analysis of racial and ethnic differences between flooded and dry areas revealed that census tracts with centroids within the storm surge were 43.2% white, while those that did not experience any flooding were just over 30% white … Flooded tracts also had higher black representation (29.2%) than dry tracts (24.8%). Asian and Latino New Yorkers, on the other hand, were more likely to live in dry tracts…. A larger percentage of the population was living below the poverty line in flooded tracts (18.7%) compared to dry tracts (14.7%)…. For white and Asian New Yorkers, there were no statistically significant differences in poverty rates across flood risk. Among blacks and Latinos, however, the poverty rate was slightly, though significantly, higher … among those living in flooded areas, perhaps reflecting the fact that public housing complexes in Red Hook and Coney Island were flooded…. White New Yorkers in flooded census tracts were significantly more likely to be over 65 years old … than those in dry tracts … Additionally, older whites who were directly exposed to the storm surge were almost twice as likely … to be living below the poverty line … than older whites living elsewhere in the city."). NYC Planning released a document in 2020 that provides information about the demographics of the populations living in the city's floodplains; this information is broadly consistent with Faber's complex findings about the demographics of who was more likely to have experienced flooding in Sandy. The NYC Planning document indicates that of the five boroughs, Brooklyn has "the largest population living within both the 1% and 0.2% floodplains"; there is a higher percentage of white people living in the floodplain compared with their share of the city population (45% versus 32%), while there are lower percentages of Black, Hispanic or Latino, and Asian people living in the floodplain than their

shares of the city population (18% [versus 22%], 23% [versus 29%], and 12% [versus 14%], respectively); and a higher share of the population living in the floodplain is over 65 than in the city generally [15% versus 12%]). N.Y.C. PLAN., *supra* note 30, at 2, 13. For a study of the relationship between demographic factors and flood impacts during Sandy based on a "self-administered survey" of 1,231 residents of Long Island, Queens, and Staten Island," see Wil Lieberman-Cribbin et al., *Unequal Social Vulnerability to Hurricane Sandy Flood Exposure*, 31 J. EXPOSURE SCI. & ENV'T EPIDEMIOLOGY 804, 804–05 (2021).

66. N.Y.C. HOUS. AUTH. RECOVERY & RESILIENCE DEP'T., SUPERSTORM SANDY TEN-YEAR ANNIVERSARY 5 (2022), www.nyc.gov/assets/nycha/downloads/pdf/sandy10.pdf. For an effort to quantify the number of affordable housing units at risk from coastal flooding in the US (including in New York City), see Maya K. Buchanan et al., *Sea Level Rise and Coastal Flooding Threaten Affordable Housing*, 15 ENV'T RSCH. LETTERS 124020 (2020).

67. New York City has found that Black New Yorkers are more likely to die directly and indirectly from heat. *See supra* note 4. Also, the city's Heat Vulnerability Index, which maps vulnerability to heat by neighborhood based on the characteristics of residents and neighborhood conditions, underscores that geographically proximate areas of the city differ starkly in their vulnerability to heat. The upscale Upper East Side neighborhood receives a score of 1 out of 5 for heat vulnerability, while East Harlem South – which borders the Upper East Side – receives a score of 4 out of 5. East Harlem North receives a score of 5. *Interactive Heat Vulnerability Index*, *supra* note 3. In the span of less than a mile, the population transitions from the lowest to the highest vulnerability score.

68. SIRR, *supra* note 30 (Mayor's Foreword). In May 2012, months before Hurricane Sandy, the Department of City Planning had started a project on strategies for promoting coastal resilience pursuant to a grant from the federal Department of Housing and Urban Development "to the New York-Connecticut Sustainable Communities Consortium." The study helped to inform the discussion of coastal protection strategies in the report of the SIRR. URBAN WATERFRONT ADAPTIVE STRATEGIES, *supra* note 42, at iii.

69. SIRR, *supra* note 30, at 401 (estimating the plan in the report would cost $19.5 billion; referring to the "10-year horizon" of the plan).

70. SIRR, *supra* note 30, at 401–06.

71. 2021 WATERFRONT PLAN, *supra* note 62, at 89 ("Through PlaNYC: A Stronger, More Resilient New York in 2013, the city identified a series of projects to strengthen areas of the coastline most devastated by Hurricane Sandy and protect against high tide flooding from sea level rise. This plan laid the successful foundation for NYC to pursue federal postdisaster recovery grants totaling approximately $15 billion. Since then, the City has used these funds to plan and design coastal flood protection across the five boroughs. These will comprise an entirely new class of infrastructure that reduces coastal flooding by seamlessly integrating flood barriers into waterfront neighborhoods."); TEN YEARS AFTER SANDY, *supra* note 18, at 4, 12 (After Sandy, the city got $15B in "disaster recovery grants" from the federal government [$10B "in FEMA Sandy grants" and $4.2B in "HUD CDBG-DR grants"]).

72. TEN YEARS AFTER SANDY, *supra* note 18, at 8 (The city has spent $11B of the $15B as of June 2022. In addition, the city has spent its own money on recovery and resilience.).

73. The plan includes a complete chapter setting out what it calls "the City's first comprehensive coastal protection plan." SIRR, *supra* note 30, at 41; *see id.* at 39–65. That plan was strongly focused on protecting against "storm surge," which the report described as the "the greatest risk to coastal areas in New York City." *Id.* at 44. Notably, however, the report referred to the potentially significant impact of sunny day flooding due to sea level rise on the city's coastal areas. It explained that "current projections indicate that, by the

2050s, approximately 43 miles of coastline – 8 percent of the city's total excluding beaches and wetlands – could be at risk of daily or weekly tidal inundation during non-storm conditions." *Id.* at 46. To a lesser extent, the report also addressed other climate risks, such as sudden cloudbursts of rain and rising temperatures. *See, e.g., id.* at 23, 32, 122–29, 183, 218.

The continuity in approach from the late Bloomberg administration through de Blasio administration and to the early Adams administration is suggested by the language in the policy documents produced across the administrations. *See id.* at 50 ("[T]he City believes that the right approach to coastal protection is an integrated system of discrete coastal projects, that together would constitute the elements of a multilayered approach also involving resiliency measures for buildings and protections for critical infrastructure."); ONE NEW YORK 2015, *supra* note 30, at 219 ("A comprehensive climate resiliency plan for New York City was announced in June 2013 and continues to serve as the roadmap for the city's climate adaptation efforts."); N.Y.C. PLAN., ZONING FOR COASTAL FLOOD RESILIENCY: PLANNING FOR RESILIENT NEIGHBORHOODS 8 (2019) [hereinafter ZONING FOR COASTAL RESILIENCY] (referring to the approach of using "multiple lines of defense … [against] coastal flooding" first outlined in One NYC 2015); PLANYC 2023, *supra* note 13, at 39 (referring to "Implement[ing] a multilayered strategy for flood resilience").

74. SIRR, *supra* note 30, at 50, 57–65.
75. *Id.* at 14, 50. PlaNYC 2023 similarly commits the city to "a multilayered strategy for flood resilience." PLANYC 2023, *supra* note 13, at 39.
76. Inside, the report similarly affirmed that "the future of the city lies along its coastline – something that has always been true but is especially true given the nearly 535 million built square feet lying within the city's 100-year floodplain on the PWMs [Preliminary Work Maps] and the million more residents that will move to the already densely settled five boroughs in the coming decades. Given this reality, the city's plan for coastal protection focuses not on retreat – a strategy that may make sense in only very limited circumstances, but is neither possible nor desirable on a larger scale[.]" SIRR, *supra* note 30, at 46; *see also id.* at 79 ("Given the scale of New York's building stock in the coastal area, the fact that buildings can be constructed to address the flood risks faced in the vast majority of coastal neighborhoods, and the limited alternative options for a growing population in New York City and the region, wholesale abandonment or retreat from the city's waterfront is simply not a practical option.").
77. SIRR did mention that the city would "evaluate opportunities for collaboration with the State" in a federally funded buyout program that New York State established in 2013, though the report expected that "a relatively limited number" of properties would be bought out in the city. SIRR, *supra* note 30, at 81. After Sandy, the city "spent about $116 million to buy out 57 properties and acquire 63 … [, and] offered 'resettlement incentives' to tenants and homeowners [to] find other places to live outside the 100-year floodplain." Samantha Maldonado & Christopher Alvarez, *City Eyes New Push to Buy Out Flood-Prone Houses as Climate Change Hits Home*, THE CITY (Oct. 26, 2021), www.thecity.nyc/2021/10/26/22747880/nyc-buy-out-flood-prone-homes-climate-change-sandy-ida.

    New York State had separate buyout and acquisition programs from the city. Under a buyout program, the property could not be rebuilt while it could be if purchased under an acquisition program. *Acquisitions and Buyouts FAQ*, N.Y.C. HOUSING RECOVERY, www.nyc.gov/site/housingrecovery/programs/acquisitions_and_buyouts_faq.page (last visited Apr. 19, 2024).
78. In the 2021 Comprehensive Waterfront Plan, the Department of City Planning bluntly stated that "over time, climate change and sea level rise will make some areas unsuitable

for residential use, and will result in the loss of some existing housing." 2021 WATERFRONT PLAN, *supra* note 62, at 69. The plan indicated that the city would like to develop a standing voluntary buyout program that prioritizes "low-and-moderate income households that are affected by chronic high tide flooding and other compound flooding risks." *Id.* at 81 ("Strategy 3.3: Promote housing stability through flood retrofit and housing mobility services, prioritizing low- and moderate-income households that are affected by chronic high tide flooding and other compound flooding risks.").

In October 2021, "Jainey Bavishi, director of the Mayor's Office of Climate Resilience under Mayor Bill de Blasio, told the City Council" that the city government was seeking Congressional "funding for a possible voluntary buyout program." Maldonado & Alvarez, *supra* note 77. In 2023, the Adams administration committed to developing a "limited voluntary housing mobility and land acquisition program" using federal and state funding for the "limited number of locations where flood resilient infrastructure will not entirely mitigate the risks." PLANYC 2023, *supra* note 13, at 50.

Some cities in the U.S. already have standing buyout programs. *See, e.g.*, CITY OF AUSTIN, OFF. OF THE CITY AUDITOR, AUDIT REPORT: FLOOD BUYOUT PROGRAM (2017) (Austin); *Flood-Prone Property Acquisition*, MET. WATER RECLAMATION DIST. OF GREATER CHI., https://mwrd.org/flood-prone-property-acquisition (last visited Apr. 19, 2024) (Chicago); *Home Buyout Program*, HARRIS CNTY. FLOOD CONTROL DIST., www.hcfcd.org/Activity/Additional-Programs/Home-Buyout-Program (last visited Apr. 19, 2024) (Houston); CITY OF SAN ANTONIO INTERDEPARTMENTAL MEMORANDUM PUB. WORKS DEP'T, ORDINANCE ACQUIRING FEE SIMPLE TITLE AND PAYMENT OF TITLE FEES ASSOCIATED WITH THE PLUMNEAR FLOOD AREA PROJECT (2003) (San Antonio); *Flood Buyout and Elevation Program*, KING CNTY., https://kingcounty.gov/services/environment/water-and-land/flooding/buyout.aspx (last visited Apr. 19, 2024) (Seattle).

79. SIRR, *supra* note 30, at 385; Dana Rubinstein, *Bloomberg Takes His Seaport City Idea a Step Further*, POLITICO (July 31, 2013), www.politico.com/states/new-york/city-hall/story/2013/07/bloomberg-takes-his-seaport-city-idea-a-step-further-008579.
80. The master plan that the de Blasio administration released for flood protections in the South Street Seaport and the Financial District at the end of its time in office, on December 29, 2021, proposed extending the shoreline but creating public spaces in the area. *The Plan*, FIDI AND SEAPORT, https://fidiseaportclimate.nyc/plan (last visited Apr. 19, 2024).
81. *The Geography of New Housing Development*, N.Y.U. FURMAN CTR. (2021), https://furmancenter.org/stateofthecity/view/the-geography-of-new-housing. *See also* Minelli, *supra* note 63, at 315. *See also* N.Y.C. PLAN., *supra* note 30, at 18 (mapping "[r]esidential construction and major alterations in the floodplain, 2013–2018" and indicating that "12% of all citywide units added between 2013–2018 were in the floodplain"); Stefanos Chen, *New Buildings Rise in Flood Zones*, N.Y. TIMES (July 6, 2018), www.nytimes.com/2018/07/06/realestate/luxury/new-buildings-rise-in-flood-zones.html.
82. Nathan Kensinger, *Grading de Blasio: How He Weathered Being the Climate Disaster Mayor*, GOTHAMIST (Dec. 10, 2021), https://gothamist.com/news/grading-de-blasio-how-he-weathered-being-climate-disaster-mayor ("[T]he rezonings of the Harlem River in Inwood, Flushing Creek in Queens and Brooklyn's Gowanus Canal – have been directly at odds with the realities of climate change. These three projects, part of a larger package of rezonings championed by the de Blasio administration, will bring thousands of new residents to flood zones on the city's industrial waterfront and create hundreds of units of affordable housing in places that are expected to repeatedly flood as sea levels rise.").

83. Ryan Chatelain, *City Planners on the Front Lines in Fight against Climate Change*, SPECTRUM NEWS (Dec. 8, 2021), www.ny1.com/nyc/all-boroughs/Climate/2021/12/06/city-planners-play-crucial-role-in-combatting–preparing-for-climate-change (referring to coastal risk districts as "baby step to managed retreat"); *Special Purpose Districts: Citywide*, N.Y.C. PLAN., www1.nyc.gov/site/planning/zoning/districts-tools/special-purpose-districts-citywide.page (last visited Apr. 19, 2024); N.Y.C., N.Y., ZONING RES. § 137–11. *See also* Andrea McArdle, *Managing "Retreat": The Challenges of Adapting Land Use to Climate Change*, 40 *U. ARK. LITTLE ROCK L. REV.* 605 (2018); 2021 WATERFRONT PLAN, *supra* note 62, at 67. In 2022, the administration of Mayor Eric Adams created two more special coastal risk districts in Edgemere; this rezoning grew out of the Resilient Edgemere initiative of the city's Department of Housing Preservation and Development and was initially proposed under the de Blasio administration. Liz Donovan & David Brand, *NYC Council Approves 'Resilient Edgemere' Rezoning Plan*, CITYLIMITS (July 14, 2022), https://citylimits.org/2022/07/14/nyc-council-approves-resilient-edgemere-rezoning-plan-2/.

In 2021, New York City also prohibited the construction of new nursing homes and the expansion of existing nursing homes (by over 15,000 square feet) in a high-risk flood zone. ZONING FOR COASTAL FLOOD RESILIENCY, *supra* note 73, at 27; N.Y.C., N.Y., ZONING RES. § 22–16.

84. 2021 WATERFRONT PLAN, *supra* note 62, at 69.
85. *Id.*
86. TEN YEARS AFTER SANDY, *supra* note 18, at 20. *See* N.Y.C. Building Code 2022, Appendix G: Flood-Resistant Construction, *available at* https://up.codes/viewer/new_york_city/nyc-building-code-2022/chapter/G/flood-resistant-construction#G102 (last visited July 11, 2024) (amended in 2021). On the construction to which Appendix G applies, see *id.* at § G102 (Applicability). On the background to Appendix G, see SIRR, *supra* note 30, at 71–72; Minelli, *supra* note 63, at 314–15.

According to the 2021 Waterfront Plan, "In accordance with NYC Building Code, all new construction situated in the floodplain must be designed to flood resilient standards." 2021 WATERFRONT PLAN, *supra* note 62, at 73; *see also id.* at 102 ("To date, most local regulatory reforms have focused on minimizing exposure to coastal storm surge risk. For example, after Hurricane Sandy – and again in 2021 – the New York City Department of Buildings (DOB) expanded minimum freeboard requirements. These requirements ensure a level of protection for different classes of buildings above the flood elevation. In parallel, the City is exploring how resilient design practices can be applied to other climate risks, including stormwater floods, high tide flooding and extreme heat.").

87. ZONING FOR COASTAL FLOOD RESILIENCY, *supra* note 73, at 3, 6; *Zoning for Coastal Flood Resiliency*, N.Y.C. PLAN., www.nyc.gov/site/planning/plans/flood-resilience-zoning-text-update/flood-resilience-zoning-text-update.page (last visited Apr. 21, 2024). *See also* 2021 WATERFRONT PLAN, *supra* note 62, at 100 (500-year floodplain will "most likely … fall within the 1% annual chance floodplain by the 2050s").
88. TEN YEARS AFTER SANDY, *supra* note 18, at 20 ("Roughly 3.5% of structures in the current 100-year floodplain were built or last altered after the new standards were adopted. The remaining 96.5% of buildings have no obligation to institute resilient measures.").
89. The city developed, and then made mandatory starting in 2026, climate resiliency guidelines for "city capital projects," which include schools. "The Guidelines apply to all City capital projects … except coastal protection projects (e.g., sea walls, bulkheads,

and levees), for which the City is developing separate guidance." N.Y.C. MAYOR'S OFF. OF RESILIENCY, CLIMATE RESILIENCY DESIGN GUIDELINES 5 (2022); *Climate Resiliency Design Guidelines*, N.Y.C. MAYOR'S OFF. OF CLIMATE & ENV'T JUST., https://climate.cityofnewyork.us/initiatives/climate-resiliency-design-guidelines/ (last visited Apr. 21, 2024). In 2021, Local Law 41 codified the Climate Resiliency Design Guidelines into law. They apply to new city facilities, such as schools and affordable housing. 2021 WATERFRONT PLAN, *supra* note 62, at 103.

90. SIRR, *supra* note 30, at 63, 147, 153; Roosevelt Islander, *Roosevelt Island's Coler Hospital Getting $181 Million for Hurricane Sandy Repairs and Future Protection from Storms as Part of $1.6 Billion Commitment from FEMA for NYC Hospitals*, BEN KALLOS (Nov. 5, 2014), https://benkallos.com/press-clip/roosevelt-islander-roosevelt-islands-coler-hospital-getting-181-million-hurricane-sandy; ONE NEW YORK 2015, *supra* note 30, at 242; Sharon Otterman, *Ruth Bader Ginsburg Hospital Comes to Brooklyn. It's Hurricane Resistant*, N.Y. TIMES (May 1, 2023), www.nytimes.com/2023/05/01/nyregion/coney-island-hospital-hurricane.html.

Vast amounts of the city's existing transportation, utility, health care, and other infrastructure are in the 100-year floodplain. TEN YEARS AFTER SANDY, *supra* note 18, at 22 ("79% of citywide land designated for transportation and utility infrastructure sits in the current 100-year floodplain. These areas of the City house our electric and gas utilities, rail yards, airports, docks and piers, bridges, tunnels, and highways.").

Post-Sandy, significant investments were made to improve the resiliency of New York City's transit system using funding from various sources. New York State's Metropolitan Transportation Authority (MTA) allocated "approximately $7.6 billion for projects related to Superstorm Sandy." OFF. OF N.Y. STATE COMPTROLLER, 10 YEARS AFTER SUPERSTORM SANDY: TRACKING MTA CAPITAL SPENDING 1 (2022). Of the MTA's $7.6 billion, $2.9 billion is specifically earmarked for resiliency. *Id.* On the investments that Consolidated Edison made after Sandy to increase the resilience of the electric grid, see VERCHICK, *supra* note 1, at 115–21.

91. SIRR, *supra* note 30, at 50; *see also id.* at 49; ZONING FOR COASTAL RESILIENCY, *supra* note 73, at 8 (referring to the approach of using "multiple lines of defense [against] coastal flooding" first outlined in OneNYC 2015); PLANYC 2023, *supra* note 13, at 39 (referring to "[i]mplement[ing] a multilayered strategy for flood resilience"); *Letter from Rohit Aggarwala to Editor*, N.Y. TIMES (June 21, 2023), www.nytimes.com/2023/06/21/opinion/letters/hunter-biden-donald-trump.html#link-1950d9cf (opposing the idea of building "a barrier at the mouth of New York Harbor" to address coastal flooding risks).

92. SIRR, *supra* note 30, at 49–50.

93. *Id.*

94. *Id.* at 50–51. SIRR described the plan as "the City's first comprehensive coastal protection plan." *Id.* at 41.

95. *Id.* at 50.

96. *Id.* at 40–41. *See also* Seth Barron, *Making More Manhattan*, CITY J. (Spring 2020), www.city-journal.org/de-blasio-plan-to-expand-lower-manhattan ("Legally speaking, the city is free to build out to the pierhead, 500 feet into the river. Beyond that, the Army Corps of Engineers has jurisdiction over all waterways, under the 1899 Rivers and Harbors Act. In practice, 'the city cannot build an inch into the water' without approval from a host of state and federal agencies, according to Roni Deitz, an engineer and resiliency expert for Arcadis, the company heading the inquiry into the feasibility of extending lower Manhattan's shores, on behalf of the NYC Economic Development Corporation (EDC).").

97. N.Y.C. MAYOR'S OFF. OF CLIMATE RESILIENCY, NEIGHBORHOOD COASTAL FLOOD PROTECTION PROJECT PLANNING GUIDANCE app. 1 (Dec. 2021) [hereinafter N.Y.C. FLOOD PROT. GUIDANCE] (listing nine projects and their status). Consistent with this report, the 2022 report from the NYC Comptroller described the pace of implementing recovery and resiliency measures after Sandy as "plodding"; the Comptroller's Office seemed to be referring to measures generally, not solely neighborhood coastal protection projects. TEN YEARS AFTER SANDY, *supra* note 18, at 7, 16.

While none of the projects that the de Blasio administration classified as neighborhood coastal flood protection projects was completed by the end of 2021, many projects were undertaken post-Sandy to rebuild and increase resiliency along the city's shorelines. *See, e.g.*, 2021 WATERFRONT PLAN, *supra* note 62, at 52 (Since Sandy "Hundreds of projects across the city have been completed, including the reconstructed Rockaway Boardwalk and newly restored wetlands in Queens and Staten Island. Others are currently under construction, including the six-mile-long Rockaways-Atlantic Shorefront project in Queens and the East Side Coastal Resiliency project in Manhattan."); *id.* at 91 (referring to coastal protection projects completed since Sandy).

98. N.Y.C. FLOOD PROT. GUIDANCE, *supra* note 97, at app. 1. The appendix lists nine projects; seven were identified as at the design stage and two as under construction. As of 2024, at least three of the projects listed in the appendix as in the design process were under construction (Brooklyn Bridge to Montgomery Coastal Resilience; Battery Coastal Resilience; and the South Battery Park City Resiliency project. (The Appendix refers to the "Battery Park City projects.")). *See* Press Release, City of N.Y., Mayor Adams Breaks Ground on Battery Coastal Resilience to Protect Lower Manhattan from Sea Level Rise and Storm Surge, Calls for Regular Federal Funding for Climate Infrastructure (May 6, 2024), www.nyc.gov/office-of-the-mayor/news/355-24/mayor-adams-breaks-ground-battery-coastal-resilience-protect-lower-manhattan-sea-level (referring to the Battery Coastal Resilience and Brooklyn Bridge-Montgomery Coastal Resilience projects and the South Battery Park City Resiliency project led by the Battery Park City Authority, as under construction).

On the USACE Rockaways Atlantic Shoreline Project, *see, e.g.*, Press Release, N.Y.C. Parks, NYC Parks & United States Army Corps of Engineers Announce 12 Blocks of Rockaway Beach to Reopen Today Ahead of July 4 Weekend (July 1, 2022), www.nycgovparks.org/news/press-releases?id=21990 ($336 million project funded by the U.S. Army Corps of Engineers involving multiple components to address beach erosion between 2020 and 2026).

99. N.Y.C. FLOOD PROT. GUIDANCE, *supra* note 97, at 8.

There is a literature from environmental law professors arguing that the environmental laws legislated in the 1970s, such as the National Environmental Policy Act (NEPA), are an obstacle to decarbonizing electricity. *See, e.g.*, J.B. Ruhl & James Salzman, *The Greens' Dilemma: Building Tomorrow's Climate Infrastructure Today*, 73 EMORY L.J. 1, 10 n.34 (2023); Michael B. Gerrard, *Legal Pathways for a Massive Increase in Utility-Scale Renewable Generation Capacity*, 47 ENV'T L. REP. 10591 (2017); Michael Gerrard, A *Time for Triage*, 39 ENV'T F. 38 (2022). Gerrard suggests in passing that participatory requirements also might need to be relaxed to advance adaptation projects in a timely manner. Gerrard, A *Time for Triage*, *supra*, at 39. Ezra Klein has brought the critique of environmental laws as inhibiting decarbonization to popular attention. Ezra Klein, *What America Needs Is a Liberalism That Builds*, N.Y. TIMES (May 29, 2022), www.nytimes.com/2022/05/29/opinion/biden-liberalism-infrastructure-building.html.

Not all progressives favor relaxing procedural and other laws such as NEPA to deal with climate change. Some, for example in the environmental justice movement, emphasize that they are necessary to prevent disadvantaged communities from disproportionately bearing the burden of decarbonization. *See, e.g.*, Press Release, WE ACT for Env't Just., Environmental Justice Groups and Allied Organizations Urge the White House to Revisit Its Support of Current Permitting Reform Efforts to Ensure Equity (Nov. 14, 2022), www.weact.org/environmental-justice-groups-and-allied-organizations-urge-the-white-house-to-revisit-its-support-of-current-permitting-reform-efforts-to-ensure-equity/; Press Release, Earthjustice, Dirty Permitting Bill Fails Once Again (Dec. 15, 2022), https://earthjustice.org/press/2022/dirty-permitting-reform-fails-once-again; *Principles for Accelerating Clean Energy Deployment Through a Transmission Buildout in an Equitable Clean Energy Future*, EARTHJUSTICE (Dec. 15, 2022), https://earthjustice.org/wp-content/uploads/transmission_principles_12.15.22.pdf; Press Release, Earthjustice, 'Permitting Fix' Is Latest Attack on Environmental Review (Aug. 1, 2022), https://earthjustice.org/press/2022/manchins-permitting-fix-is-latest-attack-on-environmental-review.

100. N.Y.C. FLOOD PROT. GUIDANCE, *supra* note 97, at 24 (referring to the post-Sandy coastal protection projects to protect communities in the city as the "first generation of projects"); *id.* at 29 ("Large-scale neighborhood-wide coastal flood protection projects are a newer form of capital asset in the city and many New Yorkers are unfamiliar with the various physical designs these projects can have and the various levels of protection they can provide").

101. *Id.* at 24, 31, 20, 29; *see also id.* at 18 ("The implementation of neighborhood coastal flood protection projects is inherently complex because they are an entirely new asset class for the City that require holistic, multi-agency engagement and coordination, as well as new approaches to project management. Their physical size and proximity to the coast often means they will overlap with multiple agency assets and jurisdictions. This cross-jurisdictional nature also means that the eventual agency (or collection of agencies) that will permanently operate and maintain the system is not always apparent at the start of the planning and conceptual design process.").

Other factors also likely contributed to the delays in building the neighborhood coastal protection projects, including the COVID-19 pandemic, and community opposition to the projects. *See, e.g.*, Kensinger, *supra* note 82 (referring to COVID and community opposition as contributing to delays in "storm surge and sea level rise infrastructure projects").

102. N.Y.C. FLOOD PROT. GUIDANCE, *supra* note 97, at 24.

103. SIRR, *supra* note 30, at 384 ("Subject to available funding, the City, therefore, will install the first phase of what is intended eventually to be an integrated flood protection system for all of Southern Manhattan, along the coast of the Lower East Side and Chinatown."); E. SIDE COASTAL RESILIENCY PROJECT, FINAL ENVIRONMENTAL IMPACT STATEMENT 2.0-3 (2019).

104. SIRR, *supra* note 30, at 383.

105. East River Park Action v. City of New York, 201 A.D. 3d 73, 76 (N.Y. App. Div. 2021) (noting that the East Side Coastal Resiliency project is "largely located within City parkland"). This case involved an unsuccessful challenge to the ESCR premised in part on the idea that "the project required prior approval from the New York State legislature under the public trust doctrine because its purpose was to prevent coastal flooding in the surrounding community and not just the [p]ark." *Id.* at 78. This public trust challenge underscores that even if building coastal protection infrastructure on publicly owned land is easier for the city, because it avoids the need to assemble the land from private

owners, the city must be careful when using parkland to avoid deploying it for a nonpark purpose, because New York State has a public trust doctrine protecting local parklands.

106. City of N.Y., *Project Background*, N.Y.C. E. SIDE COASTAL RESILIENCY PROJECT, www1.nyc.gov/site/escr/about/project-background.page (last visited Jan. 28, 2024) (the city received a $338 million grant for ESCR). On the goals for the Rebuild by Design competition and the roles of the federal government and the Rockefeller Foundation in supporting it, see HURRICANE SANDY REBUILDING TASK FORCE, *supra* note 57, at 44–47; *see also Rebuild by Design*, U.S. DEPT. OF HOUS. & URB. DEV., www.hud.gov/sandyrebuilding/rebuildbydesign (last visited June 7, 2024).

 The ESCR was one segment of the "Big U," a proposal to protect the 10 mile circumference of Lower Manhattan from storm surge flooding that was developed under the leadership of a Danish architectural firm. U.S. DEP'T OF HOUS. & URB. DEV. ET AL., THE BIG "U" – REBUILD BY DESIGN: PROMOTING RESILIENCE POST-SANDY THROUGH INNOVATIVE PLANNING, DESIGN, & PROGRAMMING 8; ONE NEW YORK 2015, *supra* note 30, at 247.

107. Malcolm Araos, *Democracy Under Water: Public Participation, Technical Expertise and Climate Infrastructure Planning New York City*, 52 THEORY & SOC'Y 1, 12–13 (2023); Michael Kimmelman, *What Does It Mean to Save a Neighborhood?*, N.Y. TIMES (Dec. 2, 2021), www.nytimes.com/2021/12/02/us/hurricane-sandy-lower-manhattan-nyc.html.

 Araos quotes a local activist involved in the East Side Coastal Resiliency project, who describes the planning process in the following terms: "Designers and other folks would come with preliminary designs and ask the community a bunch of questions.... Then they [the designers] would come back again and present how they took that feedback and put it into the plan, then ask even more questions." Araos, *supra*, at 13–14.

108. In November 2017, Anthony Shorris, who had overseen the ESCR as first deputy mayor, announced that he would be leaving the de Blasio administration by the start of the mayor's second term in January 2018. William Neuman, *A Top Deputy Departs the de Blasio Administration*, N.Y. TIMES (Nov. 29, 2017), www.nytimes.com/2017/11/29/nyregion/a-top-deputy-departs-the-de-blasio-administration.html.

109. Araos, *supra* note 107, at 16; Kimmelman, *supra* note 107.

110. Kimmelman, *supra* note 107.

111. Araos, *supra* note 107, at 17–18; Kimmelman, *supra* note 107.

 Perhaps to avoid a recurrence of some of the issues that delayed the ESCR, the 2021 de Blasio planning guidance for neighborhood coastal protection projects urges that "[t]he agencies initially identified to own and operate systems and system components must be fully engaged in the planning and design process from the beginning to ensure that any decisions made are in line with agency standards and resources, and to optimize the effectiveness of the system itself." N.Y.C. FLOOD PROT. GUIDANCE, *supra* note 97, at 21.

112. Araos, *supra* note 107, at 19, 21–27; Kimmelman, *supra* note 107. Opponents of the East Side Coastal Resiliency project and the South Battery Park City Resiliency project unsuccessfully attempted to use litigation to block the projects. *East River Park Action v. City of New York*, 201 A.D. 3d 73 (N.Y. App. Div. 2021); *The Black Inst. v. de Blasio*, No. 160336/2021, 2022 WL 476211 (N.Y. Sup. Ct. Feb. 16, 2022); *Battery Park City Neighborhood Ass'n v. Battery Park City Authority*, No. 160624/2022, 2023 WL 1961153 (N.Y. Sup. Ct. Feb. 08, 2023).

113. New York State Supreme Court Justice Sabrina Kraus similarly recognized the risks of delaying coastal protection projects in ruling against a community group's efforts to

enjoin the Battery Park City Authority's project to increase the resilience of Wagner Park in Lower Manhattan. Justice Kraus noted that:

> The public interest here is incontestable. Residents, employees, and visitors to southern Battery Park City and adjoining areas of Lower Manhattan should not be made to suffer further delay in the accomplishment of this Project .... The Project is in fact a public benefit project meant to protect Lower Manhattan from future storm surge and sea level rise. One of the fundamental purposes of the Project is to ensure that the Park can be enjoyed by generations to come. The parties simply differ on the best way to accomplish this.

Battery Park City Neighborhood Ass'n v. Battery Park City Authority, No. 160624/2022, 2023 WL 1961153, at *4–*5 (N.Y. Sup. Ct. Feb. 08, 2023). *See also* Samantha Maldonado, *Battery Park City Flood Protection Moves Ahead, after Court Denise Request for Pause*, THE CITY (Feb. 10, 2023), www.thecity.nyc/manhattan/2023/2/10/23595002/battery-park-city-wagner-flood-protection-climate-change.

114. Araos, *supra* note 107, at 9.
115. Kellie Zhao, *The East Side Coastal Resiliency Project Breaks Ground, but Opponents Aren't Backing Down*, THE ARCHITECT'S NEWSPAPER (May 28, 2021), www.archpaper.com/2021/05/east-side-coastal-resiliency-project-breaks-ground-opponents-arent-backing-down/.
116. Maldonado, *supra* note 113; Press Release, City of N.Y., *supra* note 98 (referring to Battery Coastal Resilience, South Battery Park City Resiliency, Brooklyn Bridge-Montgomery Coastal Resilience and East Side Coastal Resiliency projects, and "other coastal projects").
117. The city's focus on investing in coastal protection in Lower Manhattan has been criticized as neglecting the risks in other areas, such as Brooklyn, Staten Island, and the Bronx. N.Y.C. ENV'T JUST. ALL., NYC CLIMATE JUSTICE AGENDA: CLIMATE JUSTICE IN A STATE OF EMERGENCY: WHAT NEW YORK CITY CAN DO, *supra* note 13, at 13 ("The City of New York has inequitably allocated funding for coastal protection projects, leaving behind many climate-vulnerable neighborhoods. Nearly five years after Superstorm Sandy, coastal resiliency projects in Lower Manhattan have received over $800 million from the US Department of Housing and Urban Development's (US-HUD) Community Development Block Grant Disaster Recovery Program (CDBG-DR) and City capital-funding streams ..."); N.Y.C. ENV'T JUST. ALL., NYC CLIMATE JUSTICE AGENDA 2020: A CRITICAL DECADE FOR CLIMATE, EQUITY, & HEALTH, *supra* note 13, at 50 ("The City continues to prioritize the financial district in Lower Manhattan for coastal protection investments, while leaving behind other flood-vulnerable communities across the city, including Hunts Point, East Harlem, North Brooklyn, and Sunset Park."). On the economic importance of Manhattan, and in particular Lower Manhattan, *see, e.g.*, NEW NEW YORK, MAKING NEW YORK WORK FOR EVERYONE 10 (2022) (identifying Lower Manhattan as among New York City's "Core Employment Hubs").
118. *See, e.g.*, SIRR, *supra* note 30, at 95–98, 402–04; Steve Overmyer, *City Leaders Break Ground on New Initiative to Better Protect Manhattan against Storm Surges*, CBS NEWS (Oct. 26, 2022), www.cbsnews.com/newyork/news/city-leaders-break-ground-on-new-initiative-designed-to-better-protect-manhattan-from-storm-surges/ (Mayor Eric Adams requests $8.5 billion in federal funding for coastal resilience projects for New York in launching the Brooklyn Bridge-Montgomery Resilience project on the tenth anniversary of Sandy).

119. NAT'L ECON. COUNCIL, *supra* note 2, at 296 ("The costs of major infrastructure projects to manage growing climate risks may be beyond the fiscal reach of many local governments, particularly if climate risks are simultaneously jeopardizing future tax revenue."); DEP ASSESSMENT AND ACTION PLAN, *supra* note 27, at 57 (referring to the potential to build "storm surge barriers in New York Harbor" to protect areas of New York and New Jersey, but warning that "[i]n addition to the large cost and controversial environmental considerations associated with this type of project, it is not clear what agency, other than the U.S. Army Corps of Engineers, or possibly the Port Authority of New York and New Jersey, would have jurisdiction over the construction and operation of such barriers").

The Bloomberg administration's 2013 resiliency report emphasized the need to engage with the USACE's North Atlantic Coast Comprehensive Study (NACCS) to advance the city's many priorities for coastal protection that remained unfunded, notwithstanding the infusion of federal financing after Sandy. SIRR, *supra* note 30, at 41, 50, 57. The 2021 Waterfront Plan, from the de Blasio administration, indicated that the city is working with USACE on the New York and New Jersey Harbor & Tributaries study to "identify a regional coastal flood protection approach and provide a vital blueprint for the region's next generation of coastal resiliency." 2021 WATERFRONT PLAN, *supra* note 62, at 92.

State ownership of navigable and tidal waters, and federal regulation of navigable waters, means that coastal cities cannot simply build coastal protection measures in these waters on their own; they need federal and state approvals at a minimum. JAY AUSTIN & BRUCE MYERS, *ENV'T L. INST.*, *ANCHORING THE CLEAN WATER ACT* (2007); DEP ASSESSMENT AND ACTION PLAN, *supra* note 27, at 67; SIRR, *supra* note 30, at 41; Solecki & Rosenzweig, *supra* note 17, at 300; *see also* BULKELEY, *supra* note 17, at 184 ("Adaptation challenges often cross multiple jurisdictions.").

120. Anne Barnard, *The $119 Billion Sea Wall That Could Defend New York … Or Not*, N.Y. TIMES (Jan. 17, 2020), www.nytimes.com/2020/01/17/nyregion/the-119-billion-sea-wall-that-could-defend-new-york-or-not.html.

121. NAT'L ECON. COUNCIL, *supra* note 2, at 295; Shi & Moser, *supra* note 16, at 6 (warning that constructing a seawall could lead to gentrification in the protected area, and export "vulnerability" to other areas).

Echoing concerns about green gentrification discussed in Chapter 3, progressive critics suggest that by protecting neighborhoods against the effects of climate change – for example, by building new parks to absorb rainfall or barriers to resist storm surge flooding – cities may increase property values and rents in these areas leading to displacement and gentrification as newer whiter, higher-income residents move into the climate-proofed area. Shi & Moser, *supra* note 16, at 6. Higher-income people, the critics suggest, will be able to live in climate-resilient neighborhoods while low-income people are relegated to "climate slums." *Id.* at 4 (using the term "climate slums") (citing Virginia Eubanks, *My Drowning City Is a Harbinger of Climate Slums to Come*, THE NATION (Aug. 29, 2016), www.thenation.com/article/archive/low-water-mark/). For concerns that an Army Corps proposal to protect the New York/New Jersey area from storm surge flooding might lead to climate gentrification, see N.Y.C. ENV'T JUST. ALL. & RESILIENT COASTAL CMTYS. PROJECT, COLUM. CLIMATE SCH. ET AL., PUBLIC COMMENTS ON THE UNITED STATES ARMY CORPS OF ENGINEERS' (USACE) NEW YORK AND NEW JERSEY HARBOR & TRIBUTARIES FOCUS AREA FEASIBILITY STUDY (NYNJHATS) (Mar. 23, 2023) [hereinafter NYNJHATS PUBLIC COMMENTS].

122. The table identifies examples of Army Corps projects to address coastal flooding related to climate change, but does not purport to offer a comprehensive list of such projects.
123. There is a distinction between nonfederal sponsors and nonfederal partners. Whereas nonfederal partners are "States, Tribes, county or local governments, or agencies that … [partner] with USACE to participate in civil works projects," nonfederal sponsors are partners "that are contractual or cost-sharing partners with USACE." U.S. Army Corps of Eng'rs & Inst. For Water Res., Partnering with the U.S. Army Corps of Engineers: A Guide for Communities, Local Governments, States, Tribes, and Non-Governmental Organizations 6 (2019). Sponsors "must have the legal and financial capability to fulfill the requirements of cost sharing and local cooperation" and they must "[p]rovide cash or work-in-kind contributions to meet … cost-share requirements." U.S. Army Corps of Eng'rs, Non-Federal Sponsorship of a U.S. Army Corps of Engineers Project 1 (2014).
124. *Study for City of Boston Coastal Storm Risk Management*, U.S. Army Corps of Eng'rs, www.nae.usace.army.mil/Missions/Projects-Topics/City-of-Boston-Coastal-Storm-Risk-Management-Project/ (last visited Feb. 6, 2025).
125. *Climate Ready Boston and Army Corps Partnership*, City of Boston, www.boston.gov/departments/environment/climate-ready-boston-and-army-corps-partnership (last visited Feb. 6, 2025). (the City is a cost-sharing partner with USACE).
126. U.S. Army Corps of Eng'rs, Charleston Peninsula, South Carolina – Coastal Storm Risk Management Study: Final Feasibility Report/Environmental Impact Statement (2022), www.sac.usace.army.mil/Portals/43/docs/civilworks/peninsulastudy/Final%20FR-EIS/ChsPenStudy%20FR-EIS_April%202022%20-%20Signed.pdf.
127. Pub. L. No. 117-263, Div. H, § 8401(3), 136 Stat. 2395, 3842 (Dec. 23, 2022); *Charleston Peninsula CSRM Study – PED Phase*, U.S. Army Corps of Eng'rs, https://www.sac.usace.army.mil/Missions/Civil-Works/Charleston-Peninsula-CSRM-Project/Preconstruction-Engineering-and-Design-PED-/ (last visited Feb. 7, 2025).
128. U.S. Army Corps of Eng'rs, Chief's Report, Memorandum for the Secretary of the Army,Charleston Peninsula, South Carolina, Coastal Storm Risk Management (June 10, 2022), www.sac.usace.army.mil/Missions/Civil-Works/Charleston-Peninsula-CSRM-Project/Feasibility-Study/.
129. U.S. Army Corps of Eng'rs, Coastal Texas Protection and Restoration Feasibility Study: Final Report (2021), www.swg.usace.army.mil/Portals/26/Coastal%20TX%20Protection%20and%20Restoration%20FINAL%20Feasibility%20Report_20210827.pdf.
130. Pub. L. No. 117-263, Div. H, § 8401(4), 136 Stat. 2395, 3842 (Dec. 23, 2022); *Water Resources Development Act of 2022 Signed into Law*, Coastal Texas Program, https://coastaltexasprogram.com/2022/12/23/water-resources-development-act/ (last visited May 8, 2024). In 2023, the Texas legislature appropriated some funding toward the $34 billion project, which still awaits federal funding. Adam Zuvanich, *Ike Dike Work Closer to Starting After $550 Million Appropriation From Texas Legislature*, Houston Public Media (June 22, 2023).
131. U.S. Army Corps of Eng'rs, Coastal Texas Protection and Restoration Feasibility Study: Final Report, *supra* note 129.
132. *About the Project*, Coastal Tex. Project, https://coastaltexasproject.com/about/ (last visited Feb. 6, 2025).
133. U.S. Army Corps of Eng'rs, Miami-Dade County, Florida, Miami-Dade Back Bay Coastal Storm Risk Management Final Integrated Feasibility

REPORT AND ENVIRONMENTAL ASSESSMENT (2024), https://usace.contentdm.oclc.org/utils/getfile/collection/p16021coll7/id/26750.

134. Pub. L. No. 118-272, Div. A, § 1401, 138 Stat. 2992, 3168 (Jan. 4, 2025).
135. *Miami-Dade County 'Back Bay' Study*, MIAMI-DADE COUNTY, www.miamidade.gov/global/economy/resilience/back-bay.page (last visited May 8, 2024).
136. *NY & NJ Harbor & Tributaries Focus Area Feasibility Study (HATS)*, U.S. ARMY CORPS OF ENG'RS, www.nan.usace.army.mil/Missions/Civil-Works/Projects-in-New-York/New-York-New-Jersey-Harbor-Tributaries-Focus-Area-Feasibility-Study/ (last visited Feb. 6, 2025).
137. *New York District*, *supra* note 23.
138. N.Y. STATE DEP'T OF ENV'T CONSERVATION ET AL., NEW YORK-NEW JERSEY HARBOR & TRIBUTARIES COASTAL STORM RISK MANAGEMENT FEASIBILITY STUDY: DRAFT INTEGRATED FEASIBILITY REPORT AND TIER 1 ENVIRONMENTAL IMPACT STATEMENT i (2022).
139. Pub. L. No. 116-260, Div. AA, § 401(3), 134 Stat. 1182, 2738 (Dec. 27, 2020); *United States Army Corps of Engineers (USACE) Coastal Storm Risk Management (CSRM) Project*, CITY OF NORFOLK, www.norfolk.gov/5282/United-States-Army-Corps-of-Engineers-US (last visited July 11, 2024); Press Release, The White House, FACT SHEET: Biden-Harris Administration Announces Historic Investment to America's Port and Waterway Infrastructure (Jan. 19, 2022), www.whitehouse.gov/briefing-room/statements-releases/2022/01/19/fact-sheet-biden-harris-administration-announces-historic-investment-to-americas-port-and-waterway-infrastructure/; RESILIENT NORFOLK, GHENT TO HARBOR PARK HYBRID FLOOD BARRIER SYSTEM 5 (n.d.), https://usace.contentdm.oclc.org/utils/getfile/collection/p16021coll7/id/23583 (last visited July 11, 2024).
140. *Norfolk Coastal Storm Risk Management Project*, U.S. ARMY CORPS OF ENG'RS, www.nao.usace.army.mil/NCSRM/ (last visited May 8, 2024).
141. *NY & NJ Harbor & Tributaries Focus Area Feasibility Study (HATS)*, *supra* note 136.
142. Robert Yaro & Daniel Gutman, *The Plan to Save New York from the Next Sandy Will Ruin the Waterfront. It Doesn't Have To*, N.Y. TIMES (June 15, 2023), www.nytimes.com/interactive/2023/06/15/opinion/nyc-flood-waterfront-plan.html (identifying the similarity); Anne Barnard, *A $52 Billion Proposal Aims to Protect New York Harbor from Storm Surges*, N.Y. TIMES (Sept. 26, 2022), www.nytimes.com/2022/09/26/nyregion/storm-project-new-york-harbor-flooding.html. *See also* Samantha Maldonado, *Army Corps of Engineers Releases Details of Long-Awaited Coastal Resiliency Plan*, THE CITY (Sept. 26, 2022), www.thecity.nyc/environment/2022/9/26/23373901/army-corps-details-ny-coastal-plan; N.Y. STATE DEP'T OF ENV'T CONSERVATION ET AL., *supra* note 138.
143. Maldonado, *supra* note 142; SIRR, *supra* note 30, at 56; 2021 WATERFRONT PLAN, *supra* note 62, at 92 (USACE has "identified five potential approaches," most of which incorporate "dozens of individual land-based and water-based projects across NYC and the region. These include projects for which the city has long advocated, such as land-based protections for Long Island City, in-water storm surge barriers in Newtown Creek, the Gowanus Canal, Jamaica Bay and a Coney Island tie-off").
144. Tyler Taba, *What Exactly Is the New York-New Jersey Harbor and Tributaries Study (NYNJHATS)?*, WATERWIRE (Jan. 26, 2023), waterfrontalliance.org/2023/01/26/what-exactly-is-the-new-york-new-jersey-harbor-and-tributaries-study-nynjhats/ ("It should also be noted that just because a plan is selected does not mean it has been funded…. The *estimated cost* of the tentatively selected plan (Alternative 3B) is $52.7 billion, but not a dollar of that funding has been authorized by Congress."). The requirement for federal

and nonfederal cost-sharing of projects is in 33 U.S.C. § 2213. For an explanation of the process for selecting Army Corps projects, and the Congressional authorization and appropriation processes for studies and projects, see AM. RIVERS & NAT'L WILDLIFE FED., A CITIZEN'S GUIDE TO THE CORPS OF ENGINEERS 24–47, 101–118 (2009). The States of New Jersey and New York are sharing the estimated $19.4 million cost of the New York/New Jersey Harbor & Tributaries Focus Area Feasibility Study under a 2016 cost-sharing agreement. New York City is a nonfederal partner (as opposed to a nonfederal sponsor) and is not contributing financially to the study. It indicated in commenting on the draft feasibility study that it "will explore ways to become a full nonfederal Partner through the Project Partnership Agreement in order to ensure effective and timely delivery of these projects." *Fact Sheet – New York/New Jersey Harbor & Tributaries Focus Area Feasibility Study*, U.S. ARMY CORPS OF ENG'RS (Feb. 14, 2024), www.nan.usace.army.mil/Media/Fact-Sheets/Fact-Sheet-Article-View/Article/2495552/fact-sheet-new-yorknew-jersey-harbor-tributaries-focus-area-feasibility-study/; NYC MAYOR'S OFF. OF CLIMATE & ENV'T JUST., COMMENTS TO NEW YORK NEW JERSEY HARBOR AND TRIBUTARIES FOCUS AREA FEASIBILITY STUDY, DRAFT INTEGRATED FEASIBILITY REPORT AND TIER 1 ENVIRONMENTAL IMPACT STATEMENT 2 (Mar. 24, 2023).

145. For example, a November 2023 announcement from the Environmental Defense Fund celebrating New York State requesting that the Army Corps revise its approach to the HATS Study mentions that "a broad group of environmental, civic and environmental justice organizations" support the State's letter to the Army Corps. Press Release, Env't Def. Fund, *supra* note 23. The announcement indicates that "[m]ore than 50 organizations in New York and New Jersey have been campaigning for these critical changes." *Id.* By comparison with this list of groups, the advocacy that emerged in response to ESCR seems to have been largely neighborhood based, and not included such a broad coalition of citywide groups. *See supra* notes 103–115 and accompanying text.

The Rise to Resilience Coalition, created in 2019 by the Waterfront Alliance, might be an important precursor to the advocacy to which the Corps' HATS study has given rise. It is a coalition of "more than 100 organizations representing residents, leaders in business, labor community and justice, volunteer organizations, scientists, environmental advocates, and design professionals collectively calling on our federal, state, and local governments to make building climate resilience an urgent priority." *Our Coalition*, RISE TO RESILIENCE, https://rise2resilience.org/our-coalition/ (last visited May 9, 2024). Also of note, in 2021, a group of experts in urban planning, climate change, and other areas launched the first Resilience Political Action Committee (PAC) in the city that seeks to "support candidates who are dedicated to helping New York City's residents, communities and neighborhoods thrive – not just survive – amid the growing challenges of climate change" by endorsing candidates for political offices in the city, including the mayor and city council races. Press Release, Resilience Political Action Committee, Resilience PAC Launch (Mar. 18, 2021), www.resiliencepac.org/press-releases/resilience-pac-launch; Press Release, Resilience Political Action Committee, "Resilience Builders" – Citywide Candidates (Apr. 6, 2021). The creation of the Rise to Resilience coalition and the PAC are relatively recent developments, however, and to our knowledge, there is no multisectoral coalition working to advance an ambitious legislative agenda in the city council comparable to the coalition that proved powerful in getting the City's groundbreaking GHG emissions law, Local Law 97, across the finish line.

146. *See* Kate Boicourt, Env't Def. Fund, Prioritizing Communities and Nature in the Nation's Largest Army Corps Project in New York-New Jersey Harbor (May 8, 2023),

https://blogs.edf.org/growingreturns/2023/05/08/prioritizing-communities-and-nature-in-the-nations-largest-army-corps-project-in-new-york-new-jersey-harbor/ (identifying proposals to improve the Corps' tentatively selected plan as of 2022: prioritizing "front-line communities," including environmental justice communities; focusing on multiple flood risks; advancing "nature-based approaches and … environmental justice"; and using "a phased and adaptive approach and wait[ing] on surge gates" to implement coastal protection); NYNJHATS PUBLIC COMMENTS, *supra* note 121, at 2, 8, 12, 14 (offering four central recommendations: "Advance environmental justice"; "Manage Flood Risk Holistically"; "Deliver Multiple Benefits"; "Consideration for critical EJ communities that are currently excluded").

147. U.S. ARMY CORPS OR ENG'RS, NEW YORK – NEW JERSEY HARBOR AND TRIBUTARIES COASTAL STORM RISK MANAGEMENT FEASIBILITY STUDY DRAFT app.D, 1 (2022) ("The study objective is to evaluate alternative plans that will manage coastal storm risk and reduce coastal storm damages to the existing development on the shorefront and in coastal floodplains and recommend a selected plan."). However, the Water Resources Development Act of 2020, passed as part of the Consolidated Appropriations Act, 2021, states in § 203(a)(4) that "the study for flood and storm damage reduction for the New York and New Jersey Harbor and Tributaries project … is modified to require the Secretary to … evaluate and address the impacts of low-frequency precipitation and sea-level rise on the study area." Also, the Water Resources Development Act of 2022, § 8106 states that if requested by a "nonfederal interest," feasibility studies must "formulate alternatives to maximize the net benefits" from reducing "comprehensive flood risk," including from rainfall and tidal flooding and sea level rise. Referring to these statutes, commenters criticized the Army Corps draft feasibility study for the New York/New York area as having "an overly myopic focus on storm surge." ENV'T DEF. FUND, RE: NY & NJ HARBOR & TRIBUTARIES FOCUS AREA FEASIBILITY STUDY (HATS), TENTATIVELY SELECTED PLAN 3 (Mar. 31, 2023); *see also* N.Y.C. MAYOR'S OFF. OF CLIMATE & ENV'T JUST., *supra* note 144, at 2–3; NYNJHATS PUBLIC COMMENTS, *supra* note 121, at 8; Press Release, Env't Def. Fund, Organizations Voice Concern Over Federal Flooding Plan for NY-NJ Harbor (Aug. 16, 2023) (criticizing the Army Corps' preferred alternative to protect NY-NJ as of September 2022 for focusing myopically on storm surge flooding and not addressing the range of flood risks that the region faces); Letter from John C. Liu, Senator, 16th District, New York State et al. to the Honorable Kathy Hochul, Governor of New York State & Commissioner Basil Seggos, New York DEC Commissioner (Aug. 3, 2023) (urging New York State to request that the Army Corps "develop a more holistic plan that addresses all forms of flood risk"); Letter from Nydia M. Velázquez, Member of Congress et al., to Michael L. Connor, Assistant Secretary of the Army for Civil Works, United States Army Corps of Engineers (Sept. 12, 2023) (urging the Army Corps to address multiple flood hazards and "appropriately center disadvantaged and EJ communities"). After the comment period for the draft feasibility study closed, the states of New Jersey and New York made a request to the Corps "to discuss further flood risk evaluations that may be done as part of the study and as authorized in Section 8106 of the Water Resources Development Act of 2022." *New York District*, *supra* note 23. The Water Resources Development Act of 2024, § 332 created another legal path for nonfederal interests to broaden the scope of the study to address "comprehensive flood risk."

148. Suhail Bhat & Stephon Johnson, *Manhattan Got Less Wealthy while the Bronx Got Less Poor in First Year of Pandemic*, THE CITY (Aug. 2, 2022), www.thecity.nyc/bronx/2022/8/2/23289718/manhattan-got-less-wealthy-and-the-bronx-got-less-poor-in-first-year-of-pandemic-census-data-shows; *see also* NYNJHATS PUBLIC COMMENTS,

supra note 121, at 7, 14–15; Yaro & Gutman, *supra* note 142; N.Y.C. Mayor's Off. of Climate & Env't Just., *supra* note 144, at 3; Shawn M. LaTourette, Commissioner, State of New Jersey, Department of Environmental Protection; Basil Seggos, Commissioner, State of New York, Department of Environmental Conservation; and Rohit Aggarwala, Chief Climate Officer, New York City, Mayor's Office of Climate & Environmental Justice, Non-federal Interest Comments on the New York and New Jersey Harbor and Tributaries Study (HATS) Draft Integrated Feasibility Report and Tier 1 Environmental Impact Statement 3 (Mar. 31, 2023) ("We request that areas with low elevations along the waterfront, especially those with socially vulnerable populations be re-evaluated to identify if flood mitigation features can be included."); Env't Def. Fund, *supra* note 147 at 3 app. A; Press Release, Env't Def. Fund, *supra* note 147.

Commentators attribute the under-protection of environmental justice communities in the Corps' 2022 tentatively selected plan for the New York-New Jersey region (and Corps' coastal protection studies) to the Corps' benefit-cost methodology. NYNJHATS Public Comments, *supra* note 121, at 7. For critiques of the Army Corps's benefit-cost methodology as contributing to inequity more generally, see Columbia University & NAACP, Turning the Tide: Advancing Racial Justice in Federal Flood Infrastructure Projects 42 (2021); Dave McLaughlin, *Five Recommendations for Integrating Equity into Benefit-Cost Analysis for Flood Risk Management*, Env't Def. Fund (Apr. 28, 2023), https://blogs.edf.org/growingreturns/2023/04/28/five-recommendations-for-integrating-equity-into-benefit-cost-analysis-for-flood-risk-management/; David McLaughlin, Eliandro Tavares & Natalie Snider, Env't Def. Fund, Equity and Benefit Cost Analysis: Post-Workshop Summary (2023).

Controversies about the Army Corps' approach to benefit-cost analysis are nothing new. In a book published in 1974, political scientist John Ferejohn identified critiques of the Army Corps's approach to benefit-cost analysis, including an excessively low discount rate and overvaluing project benefits. John A. Ferejohn, *Pork Barrel Politics: Rivers and Harbors Legislation*, 1947–1968, at 44–46 (1974). He also mentioned that there were some "political scientists and economists" who argued that there are "certain projects" that the Army Corps should build "on redistributive grounds" even if they do not pass a benefit-cost test. *Id.* at 44.

149. Press Release, Env't Def. Fund, *supra* note 147 (arguing that the Army Corps' plan for NY-NJ harbor should "maximize[] nature").

150. *See, e.g.*, NYNJHATS Public Comments, *supra* note 121.

Many community-based activists and academics argue for bottom-up, community-based approaches to planning adaptation, instead of a top-down technocratic approach. Amy Chester, *The Right Vision a Decade after Superstorm Sandy*, N.Y. Daily News (Oct. 28, 2022), www.nydailynews.com/opinion/ny-oped-right-vision-decade-after-sandy-20221028-eve466w5ovahbpu2lf63rp4qqu-story.html; Patrick Sisson, *Behind a Billion-Dollar Bid to Save Lower Manhattan*, Bloomberg (July 26, 2022), www.bloomberg.com/news/features/2022-07-26/how-nyc-s-battery-park-city-is-preparing-for-rising-seas; N.Y.C. Env't Just. All., NYC Climate Justice Agenda: Strengthening the Mayor's OneNYC Plan 8 (2016).

151. *See, e.g.*, D.J. Rasmussen, Robert E. Kopp & Michael Oppenheimer, *Coastal Defense Megaprojects in an Era of Sea-Level Rise: Politically Feasible Strategies or Army Corps Fantasies?*, 149 J. Water Res. Plan. Mgmt. 04022077-1 (2023); Greg Allen, *A $4.6 Billion Plan to Storm-Proof Miami*, NPR (June 13, 2020), www.npr.org/2020/06/13/875725714/a-4-6-billion-plan-to-storm-proof-miami (quoting a representative of Miami Waterkeeper as

expressing concern with the proposal for high storm walls and criticizing the Corps for not sufficiently considering nature-based solutions); CRAWFORD, *supra* note 22.

152. Press Release, Env't Def. Fund, *supra* note 23 ("Today, a broad group of environmental, civic, and environmental justice organizations celebrate New York State's action requiring the U.S. Army Corps of Engineers to better protect communities and the region from damaging and frequent flooding harms."); *New York District*, *supra* note 23 (referring "to a recent request by the States of New York and New Jersey to discuss further flood risk evaluations that may be done as part of the study and as authorized in Section 8106 of the Water Resources Development Act of 2022").

153. For discussion of environmentalist opposition to highways, *see, e.g.*, WILLIAM BUZBEE, FIGHTING WESTWAY: ENVIRONMENTAL LAW, CITIZEN ACTIVISM, AND THE REGULATORY WAR THAT TRANSFORMED NEW YORK CITY (2014); ALTSHULER & LUBEROFF, *supra* note 21.

154. NYNJHATS PUBLIC COMMENTS, *supra* note 121, at 16 ("We strongly believe that NYNJHATS must play a key role in bolstering our regional coastal protection. NYNJHATS will only succeed if the project addresses the four concerns we have voiced in these comments and is part of a larger coastal resiliency strategy. Success will also largely be defined by how and if EJ communities are involved and the level of support and coordination the city, state, and federal partners provide.").

155. *See* Noah Berman, *7 Years after Sandy – Part II: The City's Limited Resiliency Efforts Since*, GOTHAM GAZETTE (Sept. 18, 2019); *see also* Minelli, *supra* note 63.

156. On Boston, *see* Linda Shi & Andrew M. Varuzzo, *Surging Seas, Rising Fiscal Stress: Exploring Municipal Fiscal Vulnerability to Climate Change*, 100 CITIES 1, 7–10 (2020). On Charleston, see CRAWFORD, *supra* note 22, at 26, 129–35, 237, 258. On Miami, see Greg Iacurci, *Miami Is "Ground Zero" for Climate Risk. People Are Moving to the Area and Building There Anyway*, CNBC (Apr. 26, 2024), www.cnbc.com/2024/04/26/miami-is-ground-zero-for-climate-risk-people-move-there-build-there-anyway.html. *See also* NAT'L ECON. COUNCIL, *supra* note 2, at 296 ("Several States have seen rapid development in areas exposed to coastal flooding by sea-level rise, with local governments permitting two or three times more construction in these risky areas than in safer regions.") (citation omitted).

157. Crawford discusses the pressure to develop in floodplains in Charleston, 70 percent of which is in a floodplain. CRAWFORD, *supra* note 22, at 38, 258. New York, where 24 percent of the land area could be in the city's 100-year floodplain by the 2050s, still has more land outside of the floodplain than in it. SIRR, *supra* note 30, at 30–31.

158. ENV'T L. INST., The Coastal Property Insurance Crisis: Policy Options in a Time of More Severe Storms and Rising Seas 1, 4–5 (Read Ahead Paper for Mar. 13, 2024 Webinar), www.eli.org/sites/default/files/files-general/2024-03-13%20Coastal%20Property%20Insurance%20Read%20Ahead%20Document.pdf (describing recent increases in federal flood insurance and property insurance rates related to climate change and other factors); FIRST ST. FOUND., THE 9TH NATIONAL RISK ASSESSMENT: THE INSURANCE ISSUE 5 (2023) (describing increases in National Flood Insurance rates and 21 percent drop in the number of policies in force between 2009 and 2021); *Id.* at 28–30 (discussing impact of Risk Rating 2.0, but noting that it "does not yet explicitly include future climate change in its risk assessments"); Debbie Elliott, *10 States and Scores of Local Governments Sue FEMA over Higher Flood Insurance Rates*, NPR (June 1, 2023), www.npr.org/2023/06/01/1179573166/fema-lawsuit-flood-insurance-rate-hikes (describing lawsuit against FEMA for rate hikes from Risk Rating 2.0). There also may be other market failures in addition to the underpricing of insurance contributing to demand

for waterfront properties, such as a lack of awareness of flood risks. *See Reauthorization and Reform of the National Flood Insurance Program: Improving Community Resilience: Hearing before the S. Comm. on Banking, Hous., and Urb. Aff.*, 118th Cong. 12 (2023) (written testimony of Carolyn Kousky, Assoc. Vice President for Econ. and Pol'y, Env't Def. Fund) (noting that a lack of information about flood risks is contributing "to poor decisions and information distortions in housing and mortgage markets").

159. *See, e.g.*, First St. Found., *supra* note 158, at 24 (warning that property values may decline as insurance becomes costlier or unattainable); Christopher Flavelle & Mira Rojanasakul, *As Insurers around the U.S. Bleed Cash from Climate Shocks, Homeowners Lose*, N.Y. Times (May 13, 2024), www.nytimes.com/interactive/2024/05/13/climate/insurance-homes-climate-change-weather.html (describing increases in homeowners insurance rates throughout the U.S. and turn to insurers of last resort); Env't L. Inst., *supra* note 158, at 8 (referring to state-run insurers "in Florida, Louisiana, and California").

160. *See, e.g.*, Dylan E. McNamara et al., *Policy and Market Forces Delay Real Estate Price Declines on the US Coast*, 15 Nature Commc'ns 2209 (2024), www.nature.com/articles/s41467-024-46548-6.

161. Shi and Varuzzo suggest that coastal communities in Massachusetts, including Boston, are continuing to allow new development in waterfront areas because these municipalities depend on property taxes and have limited room to put development elsewhere in their borders. Shi & Varuzzo, *supra* note 156. *See also* Jesse Remedios, *The Seaport Cost Billions to Build. What Will It Take to Save It?*, WBUR (June 16, 2021), www.wbur.org/news/2021/06/16/boston-seaport-fort-point-climate-change-sea-level; Crawford, *supra* note 22, at 129 (Charleston is pursuing the Union Pier Redevelopment because "[t]he city hopes to keep its property tax revenues growing steadily as it plans to somehow build a wall around the lower peninsula that will protect the Union Pier project and the highest-value properties in the tourist area against storm surge, at great public expense"); Kaswan, *supra* note 5, at 524 (referring to the tax revenues that local governments derive from allowing development in floodplains).

162. Shi & Varuzzo, *supra* note 156, at 10 (referring to the "underlying tension between land-based local government finance and climate change adaptation that operate in many contexts"); *see also Racially Just Adaptation + Urban Planning and Climate Inequities + Fate of 100 Resilient Cities and much more with Dr. Linda Shi*, America Adapts: The Climate Change Podcast (Nov. 1, 2022), www.americaadapts.org/episodes/racially-just-adaptation-urban-planning-and-climate-inequities-fate-of-100-resilient-cities-and-much-more-with-dr-linda-shi-re-release. Chapter 3 discusses the focus on redeveloping deindustrialized waterfronts in the late twentieth and early twenty-first centuries.

163. *See* Maldonado et al., *supra* note 42 (describing why New York City is allowing new residential development in waterfront areas such as Coney Island, and mentioning the city's need for affordable housing as a reason for allowing more development in floodplains).

In allowing development to continue, city governments also may be responding to a reluctance on the part of existing waterfront property owners to have new development limited in their areas due to flood risks. Existing property owners may fear that limiting development due to such risks might send a signal that will reduce their property values. Limiting development in certain coastal communities also might be undesirable from an equity perspective. Existing property owners may be from historically disadvantaged communities, raising the specter that property value declines would exacerbate existing inequality. KATHERINE BURGESS ET AL., *LINCOLN INST. OF LAND POL'Y, THE CASE FOR CLIMATE-INFORMED ZONING: A STUDY OF FISCAL IMPACT IN NORFOLK, VA* 1 (2023) ("Governmental recognition of the risk associated with building in particular areas is likely to reduce the value of homes in these locations, further disadvantaging communities already harmed by discriminatory land use policy.").

164. In 2022, ten years after Hurricane Sandy, Seth Pinsky, who headed the Special Initiative for Rebuilding and Resiliency, explained to a reporter the thinking behind the Bloomberg administration's commitment to waterfront development after Sandy. Maldonado et al., *supra* note 42 ("The Bloomberg administration was lauded for climate initiatives like PlaNYC, a strategic blueprint to help the city accommodate roughly one million more residents by 2030 while at the same time combating climate change. But even its climate projections stopped in the middle of this century. Looking further would be too paralyzing, according to Seth Pinsky .... 'The thinking that we had was, if we can protect the city, from 2030 to 2050, then that buys us time to think about the strategy for 2060, 2070, 2080 and 2090,' Pinsky said. 'At some point, technology will change, our focus will change and we'll be able to address the even more dire consequences that are coming behind 2030 and 2050.'").

165. *Cost of Flood Insurance for Single-Family Homes under Risk Rating* 2.0, FEMA, www.fema.gov/flood-insurance/work-with-nfip/risk-rating/single-family-home (last visited May 10, 2024); *see also Reauthorization and Reform of the National Flood Insurance Program: Improving Community Resilience: Hearing before the S. Comm. on Banking, Hous., and Urb. Aff.*, *supra* note 158, at 8–9 (describing impact of Risk Rating 2.0); NAT'L ECON. COUNCIL, *supra* note 2, at 296 (local and state governments "are shielded from the full costs of risky development because of the Federal Government's assumption of disaster risk through the NFIP and disaster relief programs."); Stern, *supra* note 49, at 174 n.47; 189, 202, 204–05, 215–16. New policies are immediately subject to the new risk-rating methodology. *See NFIP's Pricing Approach*, FEMA, www.fema.gov/flood-insurance/risk-rating (last visited May 10, 2024).

166. Benjamin Keys, *Your Homeowners' Insurance Bill Is the Canary in the Climate Coal Mine*, N.Y. TIMES (May 7, 2023), www.nytimes.com/2023/05/07/opinion/climate-change-homeowners-insurance-housing-market.html ("It's estimated that only one-third of households in flood zones have flood insurance"); *see also* SOC'Y OF ACTUARIES, RESIDENTIAL FLOOD RISK IN THE UNITED STATES: QUANTIFYING FLOOD LOSSES, MORTGAGE RISK AND SEA LEVEL RISE (2020); Stern, *supra* note 49, at 215 ("The overall rate of uptake for flood insurance is low, with more than two-thirds of eligible owners lacking insurance.") (citing Carolyn Kousky & Brett Lingle, *The Three Maps that Explain Residential Flood Insurance Purchases*, WHARTON RISK MGMT. & DECISIONS PROCESSES CTR. (Sept. 17, 2018), https://riskcenter.wharton.upenn.edu/lab-notes/the-3-maps-that-explain-residential-flood-insurance-purchases/); *Reauthorization and Reform of the National Flood Insurance Program: Improving Community Resilience: Hearing before the S. Comm. on Banking, Hous., and Urb. Aff.*, *supra* note 158, at 3.

167. *See* NAT'L ECON. COUNCIL, *supra* note 2, at 296–297.

168. *See also* SADIE FRANK ET AL., *BROOKINGS INST., INVITING DANGER: HOW FEDERAL DISASTER, INSURANCE AND INFRASTRUCTURE POLICIES ARE MAGNIFYING THE HARM OF CLIMATE CHANGE* 4 (2021) ("after superstorm Sandy ... special Congressional appropriations allocated between one-third and one half of funding for smart rebuilding – a share much larger than normal disaster recovery programs"); CRAWFORD, *supra* note 22, at 284.

6 AN URBAN CLIMATE CHANGE AGENDA FOR THE EARLY TWENTY-FIRST CENTURY

1. Prominent environmental scholars argue that federal leadership is necessary to reduce GHG emissions but emphasize that climate change law should be an area of concurrent federal and state jurisdiction, not an area of exclusive federal authority. *See, e.g.*, William Buzbee, *Federalism Hedging, Entrenchment, and the Climate Challenge*, 2017 WIS. L. REV. 1037, 1093 (2017). Professor Elinor Ostrom also argued that climate change would require a polycentric approach, with active efforts at multiple levels of governance. Elinor Ostrom, *A Polycentric Approach for Coping with Climate Change* (WORLD BANK POL'Y RES. WORKING PAPER NO. 5095, 2009), www.uncclearn.org/wp-content/uploads/library/wps5095_wdr2010_0021.pdf.

   There is less scholarship from environmental law scholars on allocating responsibility between the federal and subnational governments for adapting to climate change compared to limiting it. Daniel A. Farber, *Climate Adaptation and Federalism: Mapping the Issues*, 1 SAN DIEGO J. CLIMATE & ENERGY L. 259, 259 (2009). For examples of the existing scholarship on the roles that different levels of government should play in adaptation, see *id.*; Robert L. Glicksman, *Climate Change Adaptation: A Collective Action Perspective on Federalism Considerations*, 40 ENV'T L. 1159 (2010); Alice Kaswan, *Climate Change Adaptation and Land Use: Exploring the Federal Role*, 47 J. MARSHALL L. REV. 509, 528–31 (2013); Janet E. Milne, *Storms Ahead: Climate Change Adaptation Calls for Resilient Funding*, 39 VERMONT L. REV. 819 (2015).
2. On the role of state governments as conduits for federal funding, and the importance of intermediaries in helping smaller cities access funding from the federal and state governments, see JOSEPH SCHILLING, CATHERINE TUMBER & GABI VELASCO, *LINCOLN INST. OF LAND POL'Y, GREENING AMERICA'S SMALLER LEGACY CITIES* 56, 67 (2023); N.Y. STATE CLIMATE ACTION COUNCIL, NEW YORK STATE CLIMATE ACTION COUNCIL SCOPING PLAN 406–407 (2022), https://climate.ny.gov/resources/scoping-plan/.
3. The Biden administration called for a "whole-of-government effort" to tackle climate resilience. DAVID J. HAYES, *STAN. WOODS INST. FOR THE ENV'T, FORGING NEW GROUND: IMPLEMENTING A CLIMATE RESILIENCE AGENDA ACROSS THE U.S. FEDERAL GOVERNMENT* 3 (2022). However, the administration appears to have put less emphasis on developing the institutional framework needed for ongoing coordination with state and local governments.
4. Alan Rappeport, *Cities Face Cutbacks as Commercial Real Estate Prices Tumble*, N.Y. TIMES (Mar. 15, 2024), www.nytimes.com/2024/03/14/business/commercial-real-estate-tax-revenue.html.
5. Arpit Gupta, Vrinda Mittal & Stijn Van Nieuwerburgh, *Work from Home and the Office Real Estate Apocalypse* 1 (2023), https://ssrn.com/abstract=4124698 ("A decline in office and adjacent retail real estate valuations may activate a fiscal 'urban doom loop' that lowers the quality of life for urban residents, worsens the business climate, and leads to population loss."); Thomas Edsall, *How a "Golden Era For Large Cities' Might Be Turning into an 'Urban Doom Loop,"* N.Y. TIMES (Nov. 30, 2022), www.nytimes.com/2022/11/30/opinion/covid-pandemic-cities-future.html. For a post-COVID pandemic plan to revitalize New York City, *see, e.g.*, "NEW" NEW YORK PANEL, NEW YORK: MAKING NEW YORK WORK FOR EVERYONE (2022), https://edc.nyc/sites/default/files/2023-02/New-NY-Action-Plan_Making_New_York_Work_for_Everyone.pdf.
6. There also are environmental problems that addressing will yield benefits at intermediate scales, such as at the regional or national level.

7. *See, e.g.*, Mark Nevitt, *Destroy, Rebuild, Repeat: How to Break the Climate Disaster Cycle*, 78 VANDERBILT L. REV. (2025) (manuscript at 52 n.226).
8. *See generally, e.g.*, ERIC KLINENBERG, HEAT WAVE: A SOCIAL AUTOPSY OF DISASTER IN CHICAGO (2nd ed. 2015) (chronicling the devastating 1995 heat wave in Chicago, which killed over 700 people); Eric Klinenberg, *Denaturalizing Disaster: A Social Autopsy of the 1995 Chicago Heat Wave*, 28 THEORY & SOC'Y 239, 256, 272–76 (1999). *See also* Ted Nordhaus, *Did Exxon Make It Rain Today?*, THE NEW ATLANTIS (Winter 2024), www.thenewatlantis.com/publications/did-exxon-make-it-rain-today (referring to Galveston's efforts to address the risks of storm surge flooding in the twentieth century after a hurricane in 1900). Nordhaus does not mention the current proposal for the "Ike Dike," the region's latest proposal to address storm surge impacts. *See* Jake Bittle, *The "Ike Dike" Is the Army Corps of Engineers' Largest Project Ever. It May Not Be Big Enough*, GRIST (Apr. 24, 2023), https://grist.org/extreme-weather/houston-ike-dike-army-corps-flooding/.
9. Nevitt, *supra* note 7, at 75 ("climate change is challenging environmental models traditional conception of stationarity").
10. Kate Marvel et al., *Chapter 2: Climate Trends* 2-16–2-21, *in* Allison R. Crimmins et al., eds., FIFTH NATIONAL CLIMATE ASSESSMENT (Allison R. Crimmins et al., eds., U.S. Glob. Climate Change Rsch. Program, 2023).
11. On the economic costs of extreme heat, *see, e.g.*, ATLANTIC COUNCIL, ADRIENNE ARSHT-ROCKEFELLER FOUNDATION RESILIENCE CTR. & VIVIDECONOMICS, EXTREME HEAT: THE ECONOMIC AND SOCIAL CONSEQUENCES FOR THE UNITED STATES (2021), www.atlanticcouncil.org/wp-content/uploads/2021/08/Extreme-Heat-Report-2021.pdf; JOINT ECONOMIC COMM. DEMOCRATS, 118TH CONG., THE MOUNTING COSTS OF EXTREME HEAT (Comm. Rep. 2023), www.jec.senate.gov/public/index.cfm/democrats/2023/8/the-mounting-costs-of-extreme-heat.
12. Glicksman, *supra* note 1, at 1173; Sheila R. Foster & Chiara Pappalardo, *Chapter 12: Local Initiatives, in* GLOBAL CLIMATE CHANGE AND U.S. LAW 361, 372, 382 (Michael B. Gerrard, Jody Freeman & Michael Burger eds., 3d ed. 2023); *see also* THOMAS DINAPOLI, N.Y. STATE COMPTROLLER, NEW YORK'S LOCAL GOVERNMENTS ADAPTING TO CLIMATE CHANGE: CHALLENGES, SOLUTIONS AND COSTS 4 (2023), www.osc.ny.gov/files/local-government/publications/pdf/climate-change-2023.pdf (local governments in New York State maintain "85 percent of the State's road network and the vast majority of its utilities, including drinking water systems, wastewater treatment plants, sewers and stormwater sewers"); Rob Walker, *City Tech: Getting Smart about Surfaces*, LAND LINES (Feb. 27, 2024) www.lincolninst.edu/publications/articles/2024-02-city-tech-smart-surfaces?utm_source=pardot&utm_medium=email&utm_term=publication_climate&utm_content=lle2403_la&utm_campaign=land_lines (describing local initiatives in various cities to adjust surfaces to reduce temperatures).
13. *See* N.Y.C. MAYOR'S OFF. OF CLIMATE RESILIENCY, NEIGHBORHOOD COASTAL FLOOD PROTECTION PROJECT PLANNING GUIDANCE 12 (2021) ("New York City has 520 miles of coastline.... The strategies to protect New York City's waterfront neighborhoods are as diverse as the neighborhoods themselves.... There is no archetypal project that should be applied across neighborhoods."); Glicksman, *supra* note 1, at 1164, 1172 (decentralizing control over adaptation is justified by differences in the climate risks that jurisdictions face, and the potential that different communities will require different strategies even if they face identical climate risks).
14. Glicksman, *supra* note 1, at 1172; Yi Yin, Liyin He, Paul O. Wennberg & Christian Frankenberg, *Unequal Exposure to Heatwaves in Los Angeles: Impact of Uneven Green Spaces*, 9 SCI. ADV. (2023) (finding "persistent negative correlations between daytime

land surface temperature (LST) and median household income across the Los Angeles metropolitan area" and referring to other scholarship finding disparities in heat exposure based on race and income); Marco Tedesco, Sheila Foster, Ana Baptista & Casey Zuzak, *A Multi-Hazard Climate, Displacement, and Socio-Vulnerability Score for New York City*, 16 *Sustainability* 1, 1 (2023) (finding significant differences among New York City neighborhoods in terms of risks for "climate hazards ...displacement and social vulnerability").

15. *See, e.g.*, Tedesco et al., *supra* note 14, at 15 (discussing differences in vulnerability to flooding and heat in New York City neighborhoods based on race and health conditions [asthma and diabetes]); Alique G. Berberian, David J.X. Gonzalez & Lara J. Cushing, *Racial Disparities in Climate Change-Related Health Effects in the United States*, 9 Current Env't Health Rep. 451 (2022) (discussing differences in health impacts of climate change based on race); Rachel Morello-Frosch & Osagie K. Obasogie, *The Climate Gap and the Color Line – Racial Health Inequities and Climate Change*, 388 N. Eng. J. Med. 943 (2023) (discussing differences in vulnerability to climate impacts such as heat, flooding, and wildfires based on race and income); Janet L. Gamble & John Balbus, *Chapter 9: Populations of Concern, in* U.S. Glob. Change Rsch. Program, The Impacts of Climate Change on Human Health in the United States: A Scientific Assessment 247 (2016) (discussing, for example, the differences in health impacts of climate change for low-income people, children, pregnant women, older people, outdoor workers, and people with disabilities). With respect to wildfires, Morello-Frosch and Obasogie note that people of color and low-income people may not only be more vulnerable but also more exposed due to a greater likelihood of working outdoors and living in poor housing conditions. Morello-Frosch & Obasogie, *supra*, at 946.
16. *See, e.g.*, David L. Levy, *Sustainable Solutions Lab, Univ. of Mass. Boston, Financing Climate Resilience: Mobilizing Resources and Incentives to Protect Boston from Climate Risks* 40 (2018) ("Total Needs in Boston until 2030, exclusive of a harbor barrier, are estimated at $1–$2.4 billion. It is not realistic for the City of Boston to finance 100% of its resilience needs from existing general tax revenues and capital budgets.").
17. Farber, *supra* note 1, at 267 ("[S]pillover effects are relevant to adaptation issues. When watersheds cross state lines, flood control efforts in one area may affect another. In arid areas, failure by water users in one state to conserve may mean that less water is available for downstream users."); Glicksman, *supra* note 1, at 1165, 1184–85 (discussing reasons why federal leadership on adaptation may be necessary, including spillover effects, and providing hypothetical examples of spillover effects from state action or inaction in response to climate change); Kaswan, *supra* note 1, at 528–31 (arguing for mandatory federal adaptation risk assessment and planning requirements for subnational governments partly based on the "extra-jurisdictional" impacts of subnational actions or inaction).
18. N.Y.C. Admin Code § 3–122 (New York City Panel on Climate Change). *See also* William Solecki & Cynthia Rosenzweig, Chapter 9: Perspectives on a City in a Changing Climate 2008–2018 297, *in* New York City Panel on Climate Change 2019 Report (2019) (explaining how the first three reports of the panel were funded, and emphasizing the need to identify secure sources of funding for the panel's work); Deborah Balk, Christian Braneon, Robin Leichenko, Richard Moss & Joel Towers, *Climate Risk and Equity: Advancing Knowledge toward a Sustainable Future – Introduction*, in *New York City Panel on Climate Change 4th Assessment* 9 (2024), https://climateassessment.nyc/assessment/sample-assessment-mollis-amet-cras-ullamcorper-sem-nibh-sollicitudin-amet-etiam/ (panel members are volunteers, similar to the Intergovernmental Panel on Climate Change; New York City

paid for "report administration, support, and production" for the fourth assessment, but the city did not allocate funds until "almost three years after the panel was seated").

19. The provision of technical information is a classic role for the federal government in environmental policy that can be rationalized on the basis that the federal government enjoys economies of scale in generating information. *See, e.g.*, Buzbee, *supra* note 1, at 1048; Glicksman, *supra* note 1, at 1177–78, 1181–82. Information about climate risks also might be regarded as a public good. Madison Condon, *Climate Services: The Business of Physical Risk*, 55 ARIZ. ST. L.J. 147, 155 (2023) (public good); *id.* at 179–80 (emphasizing the greater needs that small localities have for climate risk information compared with large cities).
20. NAT'L OCEANIC & ATMOSPHERIC ADMIN., *Climate Mapping for Resilience and Adaptation*, https://resilience.climate.gov (last visited May 10, 2024); Press Release, Nat'l Oceanic & Atmospheric Admin., Biden Administration Launches Portal to Help Communities Assess Exposure to Climate Hazards (Sept. 8, 2022), www.noaa.gov/news-release/biden-administration-launches-portal-to-help-communities-assess-exposure-to-climate-hazards. In a 2014 article, Professor Alice Kaswan identified earlier federal sources of information available to subnational governments about climate risks and options for addressing them. Kaswan, *supra* note 1, at 536–37.
21. NAT'L ECON. COUNCIL, ECONOMIC REPORT OF THE PRESIDENT TRANSMITTED TO CONGRESS TOGETHER WITH THE ANNUAL REPORT OF THE COUNCIL OF ECONOMIC ADVISERS 293 (2023), www.whitehouse.gov/wp-content/uploads/2023/03/ERP-2023.pdf.
22. Condon, *supra* note 19, at 155, 193–95 (arguing for a National Climate Service, and describing history of proposals for National Climate Service).

    States also can increase the capacity of local governments to assess their local exposure and vulnerability to climate risks. California has an online tool, Cal-Adapt, and produces regional climate change risk assessments, to help local jurisdictions understand their climate risks. *See Explore Tools, Data, & Scientific Studies*, STATE OF CAL., GOVERNOR'S OFF. PLANNING & RSCH., https://resilientca.org/tools// (last visited May 10, 2024). CAL FIRE maps fire hazard severity in the state. *Fire Hazard Severity Zones*, CAL. OFF. OF THE STATE FIRE MARSHAL, https://osfm.fire.ca.gov/what-we-do/community-wildfire-preparedness-and-mitigation/fire-hazard-severity-zones (last visited May 10, 2024). New York State has a climate impacts assessment that includes reports with the risks facing different regions of the state. New York State Climate Impacts Assessment: Understanding and Preparing for Our Changing Climate, N.Y. STATE ENERGY RSCH. & DEV. AUTH., https://nysclimateimpacts.org/ (last visited May 10, 2024).
23. KLINENBERG, HEAT WAVE, *supra* note 8, at 91; *id.* at xxiii-xxiv (referring to his comparison of North Lawndale and South Lawndale and different death rates in two other neighborhoods); Klinenberg, *Denaturalizing Disaster*, *supra* note 8, at 265.
24. Cities, such as Denver, New York, and San Francisco, and states, such as Michigan, Minnesota, New York, Vermont, and Wisconsin, have developed indices to rank the vulnerability of communities within their borders to heat, based on social and environmental factors, to enable adaptive resources (such as tree planting and green infrastructure) to be targeted to vulnerable areas. Kathryn C. Conlon et al., *Mapping Human Vulnerability to Extreme Heat: A Critical Assessment of Heat Vulnerability Indices Created Using Principal Components Analysis*, 128 ENV'T HEALTH PERSP. 097001 (2020); *Health Equity*, CITY OF DENVER, www.denvergov.org/Government/Agencies-Departments-Offices/Agencies-Departments-Offices-Directory/Public-Health-Environment/Health-Equity#section-4 (select health equity data to reach heat vulnerability index) (last visited May 10, 2024); *Heat Vulnerability Index*, N.Y. STATE

Dep't of Health, www.health.ny.gov/environmental/weather/vulnerability_index/ (last visited May 10, 2024); Vt. Dep't of Health, Heat Vulnerability in Vermont 14 (2016), www.healthvermont.gov/sites/default/files/documents/2016/12/ENV_EPHT_heat_vulnerability_in_VT_0.pdf; *Climate and Health: Vulnerability Indices*, Wis. Dep't of Health Serv., https://www.dhs.wisconsin.gov/climate/wihvi.htm (last visited July 11, 2024); *Interactive Heat Vulnerability Index*, City of N.Y., https://a816-dohbesp.nyc.gov/IndicatorPublic/data-features/hvi/ (last visited May 10, 2024). In 2024, the federal Department of Health and Human Services launched the online Heat and Health Index, which local governments and others can use to identify communities at risk from extreme heat at the ZIP code level, based on "historical temperature, heat illness and community characteristics data." U.S. Ctrs. for Disease Control & Prevention, *Heat & Health Tracker, Heat and Health Index*, https://ephtracking.cdc.gov/Applications/heatTracker/ (last visited June 8, 2024); U.S. Dep't of Health & Hum. Servs., *Biden-Harris Administration Launches Nationwide Heat and Health Tool to Protect Communities Most Impacted by Extreme Heat* (May 31, 2024), www.hhs.gov/about/news/2024/05/31/biden-harris-administration-launches-nationwide-heat-health-tool-protect-communities-most-impacted-extreme-heat.html.

For a reference to an "analysis of social vulnerability to flooding and sea level rise in New York City," which emphasizes disparate vulnerability within the city, see Sheila Foster et al., *New York City Panel on Climate Change 2019 Report: Chapter 6: Community Based Assessments of Adaptation and Equity*, 1439 Ann. N.Y. Acad. Sci. 126, 132–33 (2019) (referring to Nature Conservancy, Coastal Resilience New York Mapping Portal (2013)). *See also* NYC Mayor's Office of Climate & Environmental Justice, EJNYC: A Study of Environmental Justice Issues in New York City 153 (2024), https://climate.cityofnewyork.us/wp-content/uploads/2024/04/EJNYC_Report_FIN_20240424.pdf (the city is developing a "Flood Vulnerability Index …, which maps differential vulnerability to coastal flooding in the New York City context").

Other cities have sought to map social vulnerability to climate change. *See* Foster et al., *supra*, at 138, tbl. 6.5; 161, tbl. 6.15; 163, tbl. 6.16 (describing efforts to map climate social vulnerability in Boston, Philadelphia, and Baltimore) (citing S. Atyia Martin, *A Framework to Understand the Relationship between Social Factors that Reduce Resilience in Cities: Application to the City of Boston*, 12 Int. J. Disaster Risk Reduct. 53 (2015) and Philadelphia Mayor's Off. of Sustainability & ICF Int'l, Growing Stronger: Toward a Climate-Ready Philadelphia (2015), www.phila.gov/media/20160504162056/Growing-Stronger-Toward-a-Climate-Ready-Philadelphia.pdf).

On the theory underlying vulnerability analyses, *see, e.g.*, Sheila R. Foster, *Vulnerability, Equality and Environmental Justice: The Potential and Limits of Law*, *in* The Routledge Handbook of Environmental Justice 136, 137, 142–46 (Ryan Holifield, Jayajit Chakraborty, & Gordon Walker, eds., 2017).

25. Tedesco et al., *supra* note 14.
26. *Heat Island Cooling Strategies*, Env't Prot. Agency, www.epa.gov/heatislands/heat-island-cooling-strategies (last visited May 10, 2024). Some cities are already attempting to plant more trees, install permeable pavement, and introduce other forms of green infrastructure in low-income neighborhoods, communities of color, and other climate vulnerable areas to reduce outdoor temperatures and help absorb stormwaters from sudden cloudbursts in these areas. *See, e.g.*, Nathaniel R. Mattison & Kyle McKenney, *Equity in Green Infrastructure* 18–30 (Lincoln Institute of Land Policy, Working Paper WP24NM1, 2024), www.lincolninst.edu/publications/working-papers/equity-in-green-infrastructure (discussing the increasing attention to distributive justice in siting

green infrastructure in Chicago, Denver, Los Angeles, and New York City). Advancing equity in the siting of green infrastructure is a priority for environmental justice and other community-based advocates in large cities. *See, e.g.*, *Heat, Health, & Equity*, WE ACT FOR ENV'T JUST., www.weact.org/campaigns/heat-health-equity/ (last visited May 10, 2024); *New York State Extreme Heat Coalition*, WE ACT FOR ENV'T JUST. www.weact.org/campaigns/extreme-heat-coalition/ (last visited May 10, 2024); WE ACT FOR ENV'T JUST., 2024 POLICY AGENDA: CAMPAIGNS AND INITIATIVES 23 (2023), www.weact.org/wp-content/uploads/2023/11/2024-Policy-Agenda.pdf; *Grassroots Action for Green Infrastructure Equity (GAGE)*, N.Y.C. ENV'T JUST. ALL., https://nyc-eja.org/campaigns/climate-justice-community-resiliency/ (last visited May 10, 2024); *Infrastructure Justice*, INFRASTRUCTURE JUST. FOR LA COAL., www.infrastructurejusticela.org/infrastructure-justice (last visited May 10, 2024); GROUNDWORK USA, https://groundworkusa.org/ (last visited May 10, 2024).

27. *See, e.g.*, Foster & Pappalardo, *supra* note 12, at 380 (warning that using zoning and "development strategies" to shift development to climate-safer areas might lead to "displacement and gentrification in core urban areas to which development is being directed") (citing Jesse M. Keenan et al., *Climate Gentrification: From Theory to Empiricism in Miami-Dade County, Florida*, 13 ENV'T RSCH. LETTERS 054001 (2018)); Sheila R. Foster et al., *Advancing Climate Justice in Climate Adaptation Strategies for New York City*, in *New York City Panel on Climate Change 4th Assessment* 4, 31–33 (2024), https://climateassessment.nyc/assessment/advancing-climate-justice-in-climate-adaptation-strategies-for-new-york-city/ (recommending that New York City measure climate change displacement and adopt policies to prevent it, and summarizing literature on climate change displacement).

28. *See, e.g.*, REBUILD BY DESIGN, ATLAS OF DISASTER 668 (2022) ("At the federal level, BCAs [benefit-cost analyses] are mandated by the Office of Management and Budget, although many agencies have their own specific stipulations for BCAs. Use of BCAs as a decision making or funding tool at the state and local levels is inconsistent."); George C. Homsy & Ki Eun Kang, *Zoning Incentives: Exploring a Market-Based Land Use Planning Tool*, 89 *J.* AM. *PLANNING* ASSOC. 61, 63 (2023) (noting that many communities do not use cost-benefit analyses, but that anecdotal evidence indicates their use is rising).

Notably, however, the Bloomberg administration used cost-benefit analysis in preparing its post-Sandy report for increasing New York City's resilience to climate change. CITY OF NEW YORK, MAYOR MICHAEL R. BLOOMBERG, A STRONGER, MORE RESILIENT NEW YORK 33–36, 50, 57 (2013), https://s-media.nyc.gov/agencies/sirr/SIRR_spreads_Hi_Res.pdf.

29. Emily Pape, *Improving Benefit-Cost Analyses for Rural Areas*, HEADWATERS ECON. (Nov. 15, 2021) https://headwaterseconomics.org/equity/improving-benefit-cost-analyses/; N.Y.C. MAYOR'S OFF. OF CLIMATE RESILIENCY, *supra* note 13, at 29, 44. On the Army Corps' use of benefit-cost analysis, *see, e.g.*, Department of Defense, Department of the Army, Corps of Engineers, Corps of Engineers Agency Specific Procedures To Implement the Principles, Requirements, and Guidelines for Federal Investments in Water Resources, 89 Fed. Reg. 103992 (Dec. 19, 2024); Dave McLaughlin, *Five Recommendations for Integrating Equity into Benefit-Cost Analysis for Flood Risk Management*, ENV'T DEF. FUND (Apr. 28, 2023), https://blogs.edf.org/growingreturns/2023/04/28/five-recommendations-for-integrating-equity-into-benefit-cost-analysis-for-flood-risk-management/; DAVID MCLAUGHLIN, ELIANDRO TAVARES & NATALIE SNIDER, EQUITY AND BENEFIT COST ANALYSIS: POST-WORKSHOP SUMMARY (2023), https://blogs.edf.org/growingreturns/wp-content/blogs

.dir/52/files/2023/04/EDF-Equity-and-Benefit-Cost-Analysis-Post-Workshop-Summary-FINAL-04-30-23-002.pdf.

30. Rebuild by Design, *supra* note 28, at 668 (advocating for changes to the BCA framework so that it prioritizes "justice-centered resilient infrastructure projects with multiple benefits and uses").

31. *Id.* at 669–71 (recommending that agencies consider using "equity weights" in benefit-cost analyses and recognizing that FEMA made changes to the use of benefit-cost ratios for the BRIC and Flood Mitigation Assistance programs to reduce the ratios that proposals must satisfy under certain conditions); *see also* NYC Mayor's Office of Climate & Environmental Justice, *supra* note 24, at 157 ("there are limitations with the Benefit-Cost Analysis (BCA) formulas used to allocate FEMA funds, including a failure to explicitly consider 'distributional factors' such as income, race, or geographic location"); Pape, *supra* note 29.

32. Rebuild by Design, *supra* note 28, at 668–69.

33. For express governmental statements of the importance of public consultations in developing climate infrastructure, see, for example, N.Y.C. Mayor's Off. of Climate Resiliency, *supra* note 13, at 12, 24; N.Y. State Climate Action Council, *supra* note 2, at 410.

34. Klinenberg distinguishes governmental efforts to increase resilience to climate change through "social infrastructure," which he defines as "the people, places, and institutions that foster cohesion and support," and physical infrastructure. Eric Klinenberg, *Adaptation*, New Yorker (Dec. 30, 2012); *see also* Eric Klinenberg, Palaces for the People: How Social Infrastructure Can Help Fight Inequality, Polarization, and the Decline of Civic Life (2018).

35. *See, e.g.*, Linda Shi & Susanne Moser, *Transformative Climate Adaptation in the United States: Trends and Prospects*, 372 Science eabc8054, at 1–2 (2021), www.science.org/doi/10.1126/science.abc8054 ("Growing civic discourse and bodies of research advocate for transformative adaptation that redresses the underlying drivers of societal vulnerability to climate change. The complexity and magnitude of the current multistressor crisis (health, economic, climate, and racism) illustrate that incremental efforts 'aimed at accommodating change, rather than contesting it' no longer suffice. Whereas dominant approaches to adaptation address 'end-point vulnerability' (the most visible symptoms of past development patterns, societal relations, and human-environment interactions), transformative adaptation responds to 'starting-point vulnerability' (the deep roots and conditions producing vulnerability in the first place).") (citations omitted). *See also* Tedesco et al., *supra* note 14, at 18.

36. Klinenberg, Heat Wave, *supra* note 8, at xxiii, 32; Klinenberg, *Denaturalizing Disaster*, *supra* note 8, at 260.

37. In 2020, during the COVID pandemic, New York City established a program that distributed over 70,000 air conditioners to older, low-income New Yorkers. Kathryn Lane, Lauren Smalls-Mantey, Diana Hernández, Siobhan Watson, Sonal Jessel, Darby Jack, Leanne Spaulding & Carolyn Olson, *Extreme Heat and COVID-19 in New York City: An Evaluation of a Large Air Conditioner Distribution Program to Address Compounded Public Health Risks in Summer 2020*, 100 *J. Urban Health* 290 (2023). At the city's request, New York State regulators additionally provided utility bill assistance to help vulnerable city residents pay to use their air conditioning units on a regular basis. Press Release, City of N.Y., Get Cool NYC: Mayor de Blasio Updates New Yorkers on COVID-19 Summer Heat Plan (June 12, 2020), www.nyc.gov/office-of-the-mayor/news/433-20/get-cool-nyc-mayor-de-blasio-new-yorkers-covid-19-summer-heat-plan. The New York City

Environmental Justice Alliance and WE ACT for Environmental Justice advocate for funding for cooling technologies. *See, e.g.*, N.Y.C. Env't Just. All., Climate Justice & Community Resiliency, https://nyc-eja.org/campaigns/climate-justice-community-resiliency/ (last visited July 11, 2024); WE ACT for Env't Just., 2023 Extreme Heat Policy Agenda 4 (2023), www.weact.org/wp-content/uploads/2023/07/2023-Extreme-Heat-Policy-Agenda-FINAL.pdf.

38. City of N.Y., Cool Neighborhoods NYC: A Comprehensive Approach to Keep Communities Safe in Extreme Heat 23–24 (2017); Mayor's Office of Climate and Environmental Justice, Be a Buddy, https://climate.cityofnewyork.us/initiatives/be-a-buddy/ (last visited May 15, 2024); WE ACT for Env't Just., *supra* note 37, at 17; N.Y.C. Env't Just. All., NYC Climate Justice Agenda 2020: A Critical Decade for Climate, Equity, & Health 57 (2020) (urging "dedicated funding" for the Be a Buddy program); NYC Mayor's Office of Climate & Environmental Justice, *supra* note 24, at 148 (describing Be a Buddy program).

39. City of N.Y., PlaNYC: Getting Sustainability Done 35, 43, 54 (2023) [hereinafter PlaNYC 2023].

40. Kristin Baja, *Urb. Sustainability Dir. Network, Resilience Hubs: Shifting Power to Communities and Increasing Community Capacity* 7 (2019). For a map of the cities with resilience hubs and developing them, see Bryn Grunwald, Mia Reback & Ryan Warsing, *Weathering Climate Disasters with Resilience Hubs*, RMI (Oct. 26, 2022), https://rmi.org/weathering-climate-disasters-with-resilience-hubs/. *See also* Klinenberg, *supra* note 34.

41. On the broad aspirations of transformative climate adaptation, *see, e.g.*, Shi & Moser, *supra* note 35, who describe it as potentially encompassing "changing economic paradigms." On differential vulnerability to flooding and heat, *see, e.g.*, Eric Tate et al., *Flood Exposure and Social Vulnerability in the United States*, 106 Natural Hazards 435 (2021); Nat'l Econ. Council, *supra* note 21, at 281 (2023) ("Minority and low-income areas within cities, including formerly redlined neighborhoods, are substantially hotter than wealthier, whiter, and nonredlined areas.") (citing Jeremy S. Hoffman, Vivek Shandas & Nicholas Pendleton, *The Effects of Historical Housing Policies on Resident Exposure to Intra-Urban Heat: A Study of 108 US Urban Areas*, 8 Climate 12 (2020); Susanne Amelie Benz & Jennifer Anne Burney, *Widespread Race and Class Disparities in the Surface Urban Heat Extremes across the United States*, 9 Earth's Future 1 (2021)).

42. *See, e.g.*, Clayton P. Gillette, *Local Redistribution and Local Democracy* 1–5 (2011) (describing Chicago's 2006 law increasing the local minimum wage).

43. *See* Paul Peterson, City Limits 217–219 (1981).

44. *See id.* at 32–38, 43, 50 (citing Charles M. Tiebout, A *Pure Theory of Local Expenditures*, 64 *J. Pol. Econ.* 416 (1956)).

45. Shi and Moser seem to address their arguments for transformative adaptation to the federal government. Shi & Moser, *supra* note 35.

46. Christopher Flavelle et al., *Mississippi Crisis Highlights Climate Threat to Drinking Water Nationwide*, N.Y. Times (Sept. 1, 2022), www.nytimes.com/2022/09/01/us/mississippi-water-climate-change.html.

47. In 2022, the New York State Comptroller surveyed a subset of local governments in the state about their spending to adapt infrastructure to address climate risks. The study found that New York City's capital commitment for projects fully or partially related to climate adaptation for FY 2023 was $859 million, and an average of $1.8 billion a year between FY 2023 and FY 2026. DiNapoli, *supra* note 12, at 1–2. "Among the projects considered

either full or partial adaptation and resilience, the biggest cost drivers were sewer projects ($2.3 billion over the four years), water pollution control ($1.8 billion) and the broad category of resiliency, technology and equipment ($1.6 billion). Planned commitments for sewer to include storm and combined sewer projects as well as work on green infrastructure and bluebelts." *Id.* at 2. The other ninety-five local governments that responded to the survey "reported a total of $1.34 billion in actual and anticipated expenditures between 2017 and 2026 on projects. They estimated that about 55 percent ($737 million) of this total was in response to climate change-related hazards, with flooding and increased storm activity far outweighing other hazards.... The most expensive category was rebuilding or retrofitting critical infrastructure other than buildings. This category included major changes to wastewater treatment facilities, which were especially expensive to address. This action category cost $632 million in total, $401 million (64 percent) of which was attributed to climate change adaptation." *Id.* at 1–2.

48. *See* Letter from Env't Def. Fund et al. to Michael Connor, Assistant Sec'y of the Army, Civil Works, U.S. Army Corps of Eng'r 2 (Nov. 10, 2021), *available at* www.edf.org/sites/default/files/documents/National%20USACE%20Sign-On%20Letter%2011-10-21.pdf (identifying examples of nature-based approaches).
49. David Schleicher, *In a Bad State: Responding to State and Local Budget Crises* 9, 160 (2023).
50. DiNapoli, *supra* note 12, at 1. The data referenced in the text do not include findings from discussions with New York City.

The local focus on upgrading water infrastructure reflects the significance of flooding as a climate risk in New York State. N.Y. State Climate Action Council, *supra* note 2, at 414.

51. "The 1988 Stafford Act commits the federal government to provide 75% of the cost of rebuilding damaged roads, bridges and other infrastructure once the President declares a federal disaster area." Levy, *supra* note 16, at 12. Robert T. Stafford Disaster Relief and Emergency Assistance Act, Pub. L. No. 93–288, §§ 403(b), 406(b)(1), 503(a) (1974). *See also* Levy, *supra* note 16, at 3 ("In general, large-scale federal funding in the United States is mostly available post-disaster."); *id.* at 34 (identifying "[p]rograms for post-disaster recovery" as a category of funding for resilience); Milne, *supra* note 1, at 830–31 (describing federal assistance available after a federal disaster declaration, and the process by which a disaster is declared).
52. *See, e.g.*, U.S. Dep't of Homeland Sec., Hazard Mitigation Assistance Program and Policy Guide 28–30 (2023) (discussing FEMA's Hazard Mitigation Grant Program).
53. *Id.* at 35; *see also id.* at 31–33 (describing BRIC). In practice, the requirement for a disaster declaration is unlikely to be a major obstacle to applying for BRIC funding. "Ninety percent of U.S. counties ... experienced a federal climate disaster between 2011–2021[.]" Rebuild by Design, *supra* note 28, at 10. Every state was "eligible to apply in fiscal year 2023" for BRIC funding. U.S. Dep't of Homeland Sec., FEMA, Before You Apply for Building Resilient Infrastructure and Communities (BRIC) Funds, www.fema.gov/grants/mitigation/building-resilient-infrastructure-communities/before-apply (last visited June 13, 2024).

BRIC funding comes with many restrictions, including a cap of $50 million per project. *Id.*; *Reauthorization and Reform of the National Flood Insurance Program: Improving Community Resilience: Hearing before the S. Comm. on Banking, Hous., and Urb. Aff.*, 118th Cong. 4 (2023) (written testimony of Carolyn Kousky, Assoc. Vice President for Econ. and Pol'y, Env't Def. Fund). For eligibility for BRIC funding, see *Before You*

Apply for Building Resilient Infrastructure and Communities (BRIC) Funds, FEMA, www.fema.gov/grants/mitigation/building-resilient-infrastructure-communities/before-apply#eligibility (last updated Oct. 20, 2023); WHITE HOUSE, BUILDING A BETTER AMERICA: A GUIDEBOOK TO THE BIPARTISAN INFRASTRUCTURE LAW FOR STATE, LOCAL, TRIBAL, AND TERRITORIAL GOVERNMENTS, AND OTHER PARTNERS 277 (2022) [hereinafter BUILDING A BETTER AMERICA] (describing local governments as recipients of BRIC funding). On the BIL's increase in funding for BRIC, see *Bipartisan Infrastructure Law Provides Historic Levels of Funding for Resilience Projects Nationwide*, FEMA, www.fema.gov/fact-sheet/bipartisan-infrastructure-law-provides-historic-levels-funding-resilience-projects (last updated May 19, 2023).

54. There are other issues with disaster assistance as well. *See, e.g.*, NYC MAYOR'S OFFICE OF CLIMATE & ENVIRONMENTAL JUSTICE, *supra* note 24, at 157 (referring to "research" indicating that "FEMA disaster response … perpetuates existing inequities by funding more efforts in wealthier, whiter communities").
55. On the benefits of adapting before disaster strikes, see, for example, Sara Hughes, *A Meta-Analysis of Urban Climate Change Adaptation Planning in the U.S.*, 14 URB. CLIMATE 17 (2015) ("Proactive adaptation in cities can be highly cost effective… [T]he National Institute of Building Sciences estimates that every dollar invested in building resilience and reducing exposure to disaster risks (i.e., adaptation) saves $4 in disaster response and recovery."); NAT'L ECON. COUNCIL, *supra* note 21, at 298 (referring to other estimates of the benefits of "proactive adaptation" in reducing harm from climate change); Nevitt, *supra* note 7, at 17 ("By one measure, for every dollar spent on pre-disaster hazard mitigation, six dollars are saved in disaster response – an extraordinary return on investment.") (citing Sierra Killian & Rebecca Kihslinger, *Before Disaster Strikes: Pre-disaster Mitigation Funding*, Environmental Law Institute: National Institute of Building Standards Multihazard Mitigation Council (Nov. 28, 2018)).
56. *See also* Stephanie M. Stern, *Climate Transition Relief: Federal Buyouts for Underwater Homes*, 72 DUKE L.J. 161, 174 (2022) (noting that the Flood Mitigation Assistance program is the only FEMA program funding buyouts that does not "arise from provisions of the Stafford Act, a disaster relief statute enacted decades prior to national awareness of climate change"); U.S. DEP'T OF HOMELAND SEC., *supra* note 52, at 33–34; LEVY, *supra* note 16, at 36, tbl. 5 (Federal Grant and Other Funding Programs) (listing federal sources of funding for resilience).
57. BUILDING A BETTER AMERICA, *supra* note 53, at 271; *Flood Mitigation Assistance Grant Program FY 2022 Subapplication and Selection Status*, FEMA, www.fema.gov/grants/mitigation/flood-mitigation-assistance/after-you-apply/fy22-status (last visited May 30, 2024); U.S. DEP'T OF HOMELAND SEC., *supra* note 52, at 35. NYC has received funding from the FMA to study the potential to use backwater valves to reduce flooding from sewer backups. PLANYC 2023, *supra* note 39, at 45.
58. *Reauthorization and Reform of the National Flood Insurance Program: Improving Community Resilience: Hearing before the S. Comm. on Banking, Hous., and Urb. Aff.*, *supra* note 53; Press Release, FEMA, Biden-Harris Administration Announces an Additional $160 Million to Build Climate and Disaster Resilience Nationwide, Including Over $50 Million for Tribal Nations (May 19, 2023), *available at* www.fema.gov/press-release/20230519/biden-harris-administration-announces-additional-160-million-build-climate.
59. Ysabelle Kempe, *Communities Hoping to Build Disaster Resilience Request Record $8 Billion in FEMA Grants*, SMART CITIES DIVE (Mar. 21, 2024), www.smartcitiesdive.com/news/disaster-resilience-fema-grants-record-request-flood-fires-heat/710963/. Kousky mentioned in testimony to a Senate Committee that in 2022, the demand for funding

also outstripped the availability of funding for BRIC. *Reauthorization and Reform of the National Flood Insurance Program: Improving Community Resilience: Hearing before the S. Comm. on Banking, Hous., and Urb. Aff.*, *supra* note 53.

See also ROB VERCHICK, THE OCTOPUS IN THE PARKING GARAGE: A CALL FOR CLIMATE RESILIENCE 215 (2023) ("Federal programs fall dramatically short in supporting climate adaptation efforts generally and migration efforts in particular. Most adaptation resources come through ad hoc agency projects that are driven by primary missions (i.e., secure housing, sound transportation) that, while relevant to climate impacts, exist independent of them.").

60. Press Release, City of N.Y., Transcript: Mayor Eric Adams Breaks Ground on Major Coastal Resilience Project (Oct. 26, 2022), www.nyc.gov/office-of-the-mayor/news/782-22/transcript-mayor-eric-adams-breaks-ground-major-coastal-resilience-project [hereinafter Press Release]; *see also* VERCHICK, *supra* note 59, at 216.

61. Press Release, *supra* note 60; *see also* Press Release, City of N.Y., Mayor Adams Breaks Ground on Battery Coastal Resilience to Protect Lower Manhattan from Sea Level Rise and Storm Surge, Calls for Regular Federal Funding for Climate Infrastructure (May 6, 2024), www.nyc.gov/office-of-the-mayor/news/355-24/mayor-adams-breaks-ground-battery-coastal-resilience-protect-lower-manhattan-sea-level ("Mayor Adams today also called on the federal government to create a regular, recurring source of federal funding for coastal infrastructure that would enable New York City to complete critical resiliency projects."); VERCHICK, *supra* note 59, at 216–17 (advocating "perpetual and reliable revenue streams").

On federal formula funding for highways and transit, see BRAD LANDER, N.Y.C. COMPTROLLER, SHIFTING GEARS: STEERING FEDERAL INFRASTRUCTURE FUNDS TO SUPPORT NYC'S TRANSPORTATION FUTURE 14–17 (2023). On examples of the federal government providing funding to states and cities during the COVID pandemic using various formulas, see SCHLEICHER, *supra* note 49, at 133.

62. Press Release, *supra* note 60.

63. Ysabelle Kempe, *FEMA Climate Resilience Grants Unevenly Distributed Among Communities*, SMART CITIES DIVE (Sept. 27, 2023), www.smartcitiesdive.com/news/fema-climate-disaster-resilience-grants-bric-funding/694911/; *see also* Ysabelle Kempe, *What Mayors Really Think about the Inflation Reduction Act*, SMART CITIES DIVE (Mar. 20, 2024) [hereinafter Kempe, *What Mayors Really Think*] (citing KATHERINE LEVINE EINSTEIN, DAVID M. GLICK, MAXWELL PALMER, STACY FOX & ERIN LEBLANC, 2023 *Menino Survey of Mayors: Building for a Green Future: Cities and the IRA* (B.U. Initiative on Cities, 2023) (referring to concerns voiced in a survey of mayors that large cities have an edge in competing for federal grants under the Inflation Reduction Act and other programs); Kris Smith, *FEMA's BRIC Program Continues to Fund Innovative Risk Reduction – But Community Capacity Limits Access*, HEADWATERS ECONOMICS (Sept. 5, 2023), https://headwaterseconomics.org/headwaters/femas-bric-program-continues-to-fund-innovative-risk-reduction-but-community-capacity-limits-access/ ("In this year's national competition, 3% of funding ($50 million) went to projects in low-capacity counties, and 83% ($1.5 billion) went to projects in high-capacity counties.").

64. *See also* Farber, *supra* note 1, at 269–72 (outlining the "'beneficiary pays' principle" for adaptation); N.Y.C. ENV'T JUST. ALL., NYC CLIMATE JUSTICE AGENDA: CLIMATE JUSTICE IN A STATE OF EMERGENCY: WHAT NEW YORK CITY CAN DO 16 (2017) ("The City must commit to creating a continuous funding stream for phased construction of coastal infrastructure that does not rely on federal funding.").

65. LEVY, *supra* note 16, at 6, 19, 23. *See also* N.Y. STATE CLIMATE ACTION COUNCIL, *supra* note 2, at 411 (recommending that New York State authorize "all municipalities to establish community preservation funds"); Farber, *supra* note 1, at 270 (recommending the use of "climate change adaptation districts" and "special tax assessments" on the beneficiaries of adaptation projects to fund adaptation); Press Release, Bill Dodd, Cal. State Sen., Senate Dist. 3, Governor Signs Sen. Dodd's Climate Resilience Bill (Sept. 9, 2022) (Senate Bill 852 authorizes "cities, counties or special districts ... [to] establish climate resilience financing districts" and "raise revenue through tax increment funding, voter-approved supplemental property taxes, property benefit assessments or fees."); Milne, *supra* note 1, at 840, 848–66 (identifying new sources of revenue to fund); MATTHEW E. KAHN, *ADAPTING TO CLIMATE CHANGE: MARKETS AND THE MANAGEMENT OF AN UNCERTAIN FUTURE* 81–82 (2021) (recommending that landowners pay taxes "earmarked for significant upgrades in local infrastructure" or, alternatively, municipalities "issue bonds to finance infrastructure upgrades"). Bonds are a major source of financing for infrastructure. ELLA MURE ET AL., *RMI*, *SUPPORTING LOCAL GOVERNMENTS AS CLIMATE CHANGE THREATENS THEIR COMMUNITIES* (2023) ("Municipal bonds fund about two-thirds of all infrastructure projects, making them the most prominent funding mechanism for rebuilding climate-resilient infrastructure.").

    Cities have sued fossil fuel companies for damages to offset the costs of adapting to climate change. These suits are winding their way through the courts, and it is unclear whether they will ultimately generate funds for governments. On local governments as plaintiffs in litigation involving climate change and other pressing policy issues, see, for example, Zachary D. Clopton & Nadav Shoked, *The City Suit*, 72 EMORY *L.J.* 1351 (2023). Another option might be for legislatures – at the federal or state levels – to require fossil fuel companies to contribute to a fund that would fund adaptation efforts. *See, e.g.*, Alisa White, *Rising Tides – Toward a Federal Climate Resilience Fund*, 52 ENV'T *L. REP.* 10703 (2022). Legislators in California, Maryland, and Massachusetts have considered or are considering bills that would require oil and gas producers to pay into a state fund to finance climate adaptation. Adam Aton & Lesley Clark, *A Superfund for Climate? These States Are Pushing for It*, CLIMATEWIRE (Mar. 6, 2024), www.eenews.net/articles/a-superfund-for-climate-these-states-are-pushing-for-it/. In 2024, Vermont became the first state to pass law that will charge fossil fuel companies based on their historical emissions and use the proceeds to help fund climate adaptation, and New York State also passed a "climate superfund" law to charge oil companies to pay for adaptation. Manuela Andreoni, *Vermont to Require Fossil-Fuel Companies to Pay for Climate Change*, N.Y. TIMES (May 31, 2024), www.nytimes.com/2024/05/31/climate/vermont-law-fossil-fuel-climate-damage.html; Food & Water Watch, NY Assembly Passes Climate Change Superfund Act (June 8, 2024), www.foodandwaterwatch.org/2024/06/08/ny-assembly-passes-climate-change-superfund-act/.

66. LEVY, *supra* note 16, at 19 ("A state mandated surcharge on all property and casualty insurance policies has been proposed to generate funding for an Adaptation Trust Fund for the New York metropolitan region."); Milne, *supra* note 1, at 858–62 (discussing the potential to help fund adaptation with "adaptation fees or taxes on impervious surfaces" that contribute to stormwater runoff).

67. *But see* SCHLEICHER, *supra* note 49, at 9 (2023) ("The United States has always relied on state and local governments to build and maintain most of our civic infrastructure.... Only rarely, like during the height of the interstate highway system, has the federal government even provided a majority of the capital funding for even particular types of infrastructure like roads."); *see also id.* at 25–26 (same).

68. *Flood Risk Management,* U.S. Army Corps of Eng'rs, www.usace.army.mil/Missions/Civil-Works/Flood-Risk-Management/ (last visited May 20, 2024); *Brief History: Bureau of Reclamation,* U.S. Bureau of Reclamation, www.usbr.gov/history/2011NEWBRIEFHISTORY.pdf (last visited May 20, 2024); Daniel Rothberg, *The Coming Crisis along the Colorado River,* N.Y. Times (Aug. 4, 2022), www.nytimes.com/2022/08/04/opinion/drought-climate-colorado-river.html. The Army Corps' long-term efforts to protect New Orleans from flooding may be the closest (if not particularly encouraging) precedent for the novel coastal protection infrastructure under consideration in large cities along the eastern seaboard. D.J. Rasmussen, Robert E. Kopp & Michael Oppenheimer, *Coastal Defense Megaprojects in an Era of Sea-Level Rise: Politically Feasible Strategies or Army Corps Fantasies?,* 149 *J. Water Res. Plan. & Mgmt.* 04022077-1 (2023) (Table 2: An incomplete list of erected USACE coastal flood protection projects, which includes unadjusted cost figures for Corps coastal protection projects, including in New Orleans, underscoring the scale of the New Orleans efforts); Nat'l Acad. of Eng'g & Nat'l Rsch. Council of the Nat'l Acads., The New Orleans Hurricane Protection System: Assessing Pre-katrina Vulnerability and Improving Mitigation and Preparedness 15 (2009), https://nap.nationalacademies.org/read/12647/chapter/1.
69. Department of Defense, Department of the Army, Corps of Engineers, Corps of Engineers Agency Specific Procedures To Implement the Principles, Requirements, and Guidelines for Federal Investments in Water Resources, 89 Fed. Reg. 103992 (Dec. 19, 2024). *See also* Jim Morrison, *A Proposed Army Corps Change Could Affect Hundreds of Billions in Federal Funding,* Virginia Mercury (Feb. 29, 2024), https://virginiamercury.com/2024/02/29/a-proposed-army-corps-change-could-affect-hundreds-of-billions-in-federal-funding/.
70. Commenting on the proposed rule changes, experts on the Army Corps' project planning process emphasized that the effects would depend on implementation. *See* Morrison, *supra* note 69.
71. *See, e.g.,* McLaughlin *supra* note 29; McLaughlin, Tavares & Snider, *supra* note 29, at 6–8; Letter from Env't Def. Fund et al., *supra* note 48. For research suggesting that the Army Corps' historical approach to benefit-cost analysis might lead to less protection of socially disadvantaged coastal areas and populations, see Jeremy Martinich et al., *Risks of Sea Level Rise to Disadvantaged Communities in the United States,* 18 *Mitigation and Adaptation Strategies for Global Climate Change* 169, 175–182 (2013); Columbia University & NAACP, Turning the Tide: Advancing Racial Justice in Federal Flood Infrastructure Projects 42 (2021).
72. Letter from Env't Def. Fund et al., *supra* note 48.
73. N.Y.C. Env't Just. All. & Resilient Coastal Cmtys. Project, Colum. Climate Sch. et al., Public Comments on the United States Army Corps of Engineers' (USACE) New York and New Jersey Harbor & Tributaries Focus Area Feasibility Study (NYNJHATS) (Mar. 23, 2023); *see also* Geoff Dembicki, *The Progressive Way to Save Cities from Superstorms,* The New Republic (Aug. 2, 2023), https://newrepublic.com/article/174664/progressive-way-save-cities-superstorms (describing problems with the Army Corps' approach to designing large coastal protection infrastructure to address climate risks).
74. Relatedly, the U.S. has a federal flood insurance program, but no federal fire insurance or heat insurance programs. Should there be federal insurers of last resort against these hazards as well, as some have proposed? *Reauthorization and Reform of the National Flood Insurance Program: Improving Community Resilience: Hearing before the S. Comm. on*

Banking, Hous., and Urb. Aff., *supra* note 53, at 3. ("The need for more inclusive insurance is an important policy topic for other disaster and property insurance beyond flooding, as well.") (citing CAROLYN KOUSKY & KARINA FRENCH, INCLUSIVE INSURANCE FOR CLIMATE-RELATED DISASTERS: A ROADMAP FOR THE UNITED STATES (2023)).

75. The National Climate Adaptation and Resilience Strategy Act, introduced in the Senate in 2022, would require the appointment of a Chief Resilience Officer who would be charged with developing a "whole-of-government effort to build resilience," meaning a whole-of-federal government approach. S. 3531, 117th Cong. § 3(a) (2022). The bill does recognize the importance of "non-Federal partners" (including local governments) in adapting to climate change; for example, the bill required that the proposed National Climate Adaptation and Resilience Strategy include "strategies for the Federal Government, in partnership with non-Federal partners," to address climate vulnerabilities. S. 3531 § 2(15) (defining non-Federal partner), § 6(a)(3).
76. CITY OF NEW YORK, A STRONGER, MORE RESILIENT NEW YORK 49–50 (2013); LEVY, *supra* note 16, at 9; NAT'L ECON. COUNCIL, *supra* note 21, at 290; Sarah Pruitt, *How Levee Failures Made Hurricane Katrina a Bigger Disaster*, HISTORY (Aug. 25, 2023), www.history.com/news/hurricane-katrina-levee-failures; *Infrastructure Failure – Levee Failure*, NOLA READY, https://ready.nola.gov/hazard-mitigation/hazards/infrastructure-failure-levee-failure/ (last visited May 20, 2024).
77. NAT'L ECON. COUNCIL, *supra* note 21, at 277–79 (describing the private incentives that individuals have to adapt, and the limitations of these incentives); KAHN, *supra* note 65, at 14, 16–17, 71–73 (emphasizing the private incentives to adapt, but noting that lack of access to wealth and capital may impede adaptation for lower income people); Nevitt, *supra* note 7, at 25–35 (describing lack of access to climate information and urging more transparency about risks from climate change).
78. Laurie Mazur, *How Climate Resilience Can Curb a Crisis in Homeowners' Insurance*, U.S. NEWS (Mar. 9, 2024), www.usnews.com/news/health-news/articles/2024-03-09/climate-resilience-can-curb-a-crisis-in-homeowners-insurance; Christopher Flavelle & Mira Rojanasakul, *As Insurers Around the U.S. Bleed Cash from Climate Shocks, Homeowners Lose*, N.Y. TIMES (May 13, 2024), www.nytimes.com/interactive/2024/05/13/climate/insurance-homes-climate-change-weather.html; FIRST STREET FOUNDATION, THE 9TH NATIONAL RISK ASSESSMENT: THE INSURANCE ISSUE 5 (2023) (describing increases in National Flood Insurance Program rates and a 21 percent drop in the number of policies in force between 2009 and 2021); *Id.* at 28–30 (discussing impact of Risk Rating 2.0, but noting that it "does not yet explicitly include future climate change in its risk assessments"); Nevitt, *supra* note 7, at 50–51 ("Private insurance companies are fleeing climate-exposed states, while NFIP [the National Flood Insurance Program] continues to issue new policies. Meanwhile, insurance rates are increasing….").
79. On the importance of land use for adaptation, see, for example, Kaswan, *supra* note 1, at 513–17.
80. *See, e.g.*, KATHERINE BURGESS ET AL., *LINCOLN INST. OF LAND POL'Y, THE CASE FOR CLIMATE-INFORMED ZONING: A STUDY OF FISCAL IMPACT IN NORFOLK, VA* 20 (2023).
81. SUSAN CRAWFORD, CHARLESTON: RACE, WATER, AND THE COMING STORM 38–39 (2023) (citing LAND ELEVATION & FLOOD RISK (WITHIN UGB), shown during City of Charleston City Plan Water Lab Meeting (Sept. 23, 2020)).
82. *But see* BURGESS ET AL., *supra* note 80, at 21–23 (studying the impact of Norfolk's "climate-informed" reforms to land use policy and concluding that the policy

changes did not impact sales prices in areas where development was limited between 2018 and 2021).

83. Burgess et al., *supra* note 80, at 1 ("Governmental recognition of the risk associated with building in particular areas is likely to reduce the value of homes in these locations, further disadvantaging communities already harmed by discriminatory land use policy."). On the history of redlining, see Richard Rothstein, The Color of Law (2017).
84. Burgess et al., *supra* note 80, at 20–21. *See also generally* Nicholas R. Williams, *Coastal TDRs and Takings in a Changing Climate*, 46 The Urban Lawyer 139 (2014).
85. Burgess et al., *supra* note 80, at 20–21.
86. *See* Stern, *supra* note 56, for an excellent discussion of the literature on buyouts. Stern argues that buyouts should be targeted to economically vulnerable households rather than be universally available, as universal buyouts might induce more (and inefficient) investment in vulnerable areas since the availability of buyouts would act as a form of insurance against downside risk. *Id.*
87. *Id.* 164 (noting 48,000 buyouts); *see also* Michael Pappas & Victor B. Flatt, *Climate Changes Property: Disasters, Decommodification, and Retreat*, 82 Ohio St. L.J. 331, 342–43 (2021) (referring to federal funding for local buyouts).
88. Stern discusses existing federal programs for funding buyouts. Stern, *supra* note 56, at 173–78. On inequities in FEMA buyout programs, see Linda Shi et al., *Equitable Buyouts? Learning from State, County, and Local Floodplain Management Programs*, 174 (3–4) Clim. Change 29 (2022).
89. N.Y. State Climate Action Council, *supra* note 2, at 414–15 (recommending changes to state building codes as part of state's response to increasing extreme heat risk).
90. Press Release, Rob Bonta, Cal. Att'y Gen., Attorney General Bonta Issues Guidance to Local Governments to Mitigate Wildfire Risk from Proposed Developments in Fire-Prone Areas (Oct. 10, 2022), https://oag.ca.gov/news/press-releases/attorney-general-bonta-issues-guidance-local-governments-mitigate-wildfire-risk; *see also* Levy, *supra* note 16, at 52–53, app. B (evaluating resilience investments: return on investment and cost-benefit analysis) (referring to changes that existing buildings might make to increase their resilience to flooding).
91. Levy, *supra* note 16, at 13; Farber, *supra* note 1, at 268; Verchick, *supra* note 59, at 40, 209–10.
92. Nat'l Econ. Council, *supra* note 21, at 296–97 (referring to the "moral hazard" that federal disaster assistance and subsidized flood insurance create for local and state governments in establishing "zoning, building codes, and land-use management").
93. U.S. Dep't of Homeland Sec., Partial Implementation of the Federal Flood Risk Management Standard for Hazard Mitigation Assistance Programs (2022); Christopher Flavelle, *As Climate Toll Grows, FEMA Imposes Limits on Building in Flood Plains*, N.Y. Times (July 10, 2024), www.nytimes.com/2024/07/10/climate/fema-flooding-construction-rules.html; *but see* Christopher Flavelle, *FEMA Quietly Eases Rules Meant to Protect Buildings in Flood Zones*, N.Y. Times (Feb. 14, 2025), https://www.nytimes.com/2025/02/14/climate/fema-quietly-eases-rules-meant-to-protect-buildings-in-flood-zones.html (describing FEMA's decision to "pause" the enforcement of the Federal Flood Risk Management Standard). On the history of the rule, see, e.g., Verchick, *supra* note 59, at 113–14; Rebecca Bratspies, *Protecting the Environment in an Era of Federal Retreat: The View from New York City*, 13 *FIU L. Rev.* 5, 7 (2018).
94. Stern, *supra* note 56, at 191–92 ("[T]he NFIP requires communities to adopt floodplain management plans for residents to qualify for flood insurance. However federal

regulations for these plans primarily require elevating and floodproofing new construction, except in more strictly regulated floodways (i.e., the channel of the watercourse and its immediate banks). There are also significant enforcement issues, with research reporting local noncompliance with the NFIP building and other regulations ranging from 15 percent to 42 percent." (citing 42 U.S.C. 4022(a)(2)(A) and 42 U.S.C. 4102)); *Reauthorization and Reform of the National Flood Insurance Program: Improving Community Resilience: Hearing before the S. Comm. on Banking, Hous., and Urb. Aff.*, *supra* note 53, at 3. (referring to need for updates to FEMA requirements); NAT'L ECON. COUNCIL, *supra* note 21, at 299 (referring to FEMA proposal for flood disclosure requirements); Kaswan, *supra* note 1, at 520 (referring to weaknesses of NFIP requirements).

95. NAT'L ECON. COUNCIL, *supra* note 21, at 300 ("provisions of the Bipartisan Infrastructure Law lower the non-Federal share of certain grants for transportation projects prioritized in a State's Resilience Improvement Plan").
96. Glicksman, *supra* note 1, at 1176; *see also id.* at 1184; Farber, *supra* note 1, at 265. Farber provides the example of a potential requirement that "all levees be adequate even if climate change increases future flooding." *Id.* Kaswan argues that "the federal government should … require land use related climate impact assessments and adaptation planning and, to a limited extent, … define certain minimum parameters to guide state and local adaptation planning and programs." Kaswan, *supra* note 1, at 510; *see also id.* at 535 ("[F]ederal rules could establish clear adaptation-related goals that state and local plans must achieve, like limiting development in areas that currently, or will in the future, face high risks of property and environmental loss").
97. *See also* Glicksman, *supra* note 1, at 1167.
98. Jonathan B. Wiener, *Think Globally, Act Globally: The Limits of Local Climate Policies*, 155 *U. PA. L. REV.* 1961, 1967 (2007).
99. States can take various attitudes to local climate action. Some, like New York State, may permit it, others may incentivize it, and still others may limit it through preemption. *See, e.g.*, SCHILLING, TUMBER & VELASCO, *supra* note 2, at 22; *id.* at 58 (Box: Intergovernmental Dynamics: Federal Regulation and State Preemption vs. Local Government Independence).
100. *See also* Richard B. Stewart, *States and Cities as Actors in Global Climate Regulation: Unitary vs. Plural Architectures*, 50 *ARIZ. L. REV.* 681, 705–06 (2008) (arguing that "[u]nder optimal conditions," a "unitary" approach to climate regulation, led by the U.S. with a federal cap-and-trade program, would be preferable but that under real-world conditions a plural model that includes a role for states and local governments is preferable); Jonathan H. Adler, *Jurisdictional Mismatch in Environmental Federalism*, 14 *N.Y.U. ENV'T L.J.* 130, 175–76 (2005) (climate change should be regulated at the federal level); Wiener, *supra* note 98, at 1965 (noting that, "because GHGs mix globally and have global impacts, local abatement actions pose local costs, yet deliver essentially no local climate benefits"); JOSEPH STIGLITZ, SCOTT BARRETT & NOAH KAUFMAN, *HOW ECONOMICS CAN TACKLE THE "WICKED PROBLEM" OF CLIMATE CHANGE* 15 (2024), https://igp.sipa.columbia.edu/sites/igp/files/2023-12/How-Economics-Can-Tackle-the-Wicked-problem-of-Climate-Change.pdf ("Carbon prices work best when combined with other policies"). *But see* Ostrom, *supra* note 1, at 22–27, 35 (questioning the conventional wisdom that large geographic units are likely to be more successful in addressing climate change and arguing for policies at multiple scales).
101. As mentioned earlier, the smaller the regulating entity, the less likely it will be willing to impose the stringent regulations that are necessary to rapidly decarbonize, because

these regulations will be costly for local actors and the benefits of GHG reductions are distributed around the whole world.

102. In the debate about establishing a New York State-level cap and invest program to reduce GHG emissions, representatives of business interests are warning that the program "could drive more businesses and people to leave the state or companies to raise prices." Marie J. French, *New York's Cap-and-trade Proposal Threatens State's Climate Goals*, POLITICO (Mar. 8, 2024) (referring to the state Business Council).

103. 16 U.S.C. § 824(b)(1). *See also* Alexandra B. Klass & Elizabeth J. Wilson, *Interstate Transmission Challenges for Renewable Energy: A Federalism Mismatch*, 65 VAND. L. REV. 1801, 1829–1830 (2012) (emphasizing "[t]he need for greater federal involvement (or at least regional siting authorities) … in the area of transmission line siting, which, unlike energy facility siting, is inherently interstate … because, for the most part, states consider only in-state benefits in their siting determinations even though the benefits of the projects are primarily regional."). On efforts by the Federal Energy Regulatory Commission to promote the construction of new long-distance electricity transmission, see, e.g., Ethan Howland, *FERC Issues Landmark Transmission Planning, Cost Allocation Rule, with Dissent over State Roles*, UTILITY DIVE (May 14, 2024), www.utilitydive.com/news/ferc-transmission-planning-cost-allocation-rule/716018/.

104. JOHN LARSEN ET AL., RHODIUM GROUP, A TURNING POINT FOR US CLIMATE PROGRESS: ASSESSING THE CLIMATE AND CLEAN ENERGY PROVISIONS IN THE INFLATION REDUCTION ACT (2022), *available at* https://rhg.com/research/climate-clean-energy-inflation-reduction-act/; INTERSOLAR NORTH AMERICA, ONE YEAR IN: THE INFLATION REDUCTION ACT IN REVIEW (2024), https://discover.divcom.com/rs/756-FWJ-061/images/ISNA-2024-eBook%20The%20Inflation%20Reduction%20Act.pdf.

105. *See* Ostrom, *supra* note 1, at 32–36 (arguing that climate change requires a polycentric approach, involving actions by governments at different levels, as well as private entities).

106. New York State's Climate Scoping Plan for decarbonizing the state draws attention to the GHG emissions from solid waste management facilities (landfills) and wastewater treatment plants, and recommends state regulation to reduce these emissions. N.Y. STATE CLIMATE ACTION COUNCIL, *supra* note 2, at 333–34. In New York City, Local Law 97's GHG reduction targets for New York City are a reason for the city to focus on reducing methane emissions from wastewater treatment plants. N.Y.C. Council Comm. on Env't Prot., Resiliency & Waterfronts, Preliminary Budget Hearing – Environmental Protection, March 7, 2023 (testimony of Rohit Aggarwala, Chief Climate Officers & Commissioner, NYC Department of Environmental Protection, Tr. at 73–74) [hereinafter Aggarwala Testimony].

107. *See, e.g.*, David Propper, *City Island Residents Clamor for Ferry Stop in Bronx Enclave as $15 Congestion Pricing Looms: "A Very Attractive Option,"* N.Y. POST (Apr. 3, 2024), https://nypost.com/2024/04/03/us-news/city-island-locals-clamor-for-ferry-as-congestion-pricing-nears/.

108. In 2023, New York City approved a series of zoning changes to facilitate decarbonization. *See* N.Y.C. Dep't of City Plan., *City Planning Commission Review Session + Special Public Meeting*, YOUTUBE (Apr. 24, 2023), www.youtube.com/watch?v=10-8NynzlRY (City of Yes for Carbon Neutrality presentation); Press Release, Mayor Adams, Speaker Adams Celebrate Passage of Zoning Changes that Fights Climate Change by Opening Doors to Cleaner Air, Lower Energy Costs (Dec. 6, 2023), www.nyc.gov/office-of-the-mayor/news/935-23/

mayor-adams-speaker-adams-celebrate-passage-zoning-changes-fights-climate-change-by.

109. *See, e.g.*, *What Is a Transit Overlay District? How TOD Zoning Supports Bus Rapid Transit*, RALEIGH (Jan. 4, 2024), https://raleighnc.gov/planning/what-transit-overlay-district. *See also* Sam Mellins, *How Hochul Plans to Build Hundreds of Thousands of Homes New Train Stations*, N.Y. FOCUS (Feb. 2, 2023), www.nysfocus.com/2023/02/02/hochul-housing-transit-oriented-development-zoning/.

See also, e.g., Marcia D. Lowe, *Alternatives to the Automobile*, 57 EKISTICS 269, 278 (1990) ("A reasonably high gasoline tax, such as the $1 to $2 per gallon taxes now common in Europe, would discourage driving, encourage people to use public transport where it is available, and raise revenues to expand transit service where needed."). The economists Edward Glaeser and Matthew Kahn have found evidence that higher gas taxes are associated with greater density in practice; in a study of seventy cities around the world, they found that "when countries move from having low gas taxes to high gas taxes, the density of development increases by more than 40 percent." EDWARD GLAESER, *TRIUMPH OF THE CITY: HOW OUR GREATEST INVENTION MAKES US RICHER, SMARTER, GREENER, HEALTHIER, AND HAPPIER* 172 (2011) (citing Edward L. Glaeser & Matthew E. Kahn, *Sprawl and Urban Growth*, *in* HANDBOOK OF REGIONAL AND URBAN ECONOMICS 2481, 2499–2500 (J. Vernon Henderson & Jacques-François Thisse, eds., 2004)).

Similarly, a national price on carbon that increased the cost of heating residences using oil and natural gas might incentivize building owners to conserve heat and hot water and/or electrify these systems so they could be powered by renewable energy sources. If the federal government does not establish energy efficiency regulations to reduce excessive use of renewable electricity to limit its nonclimate environmental and social harms, such as the impacts of large scale solar and wind farms on landscapes and wildlife, then states and local governments might establish such regulations. On the environmental and social harms that utility-scale solar installations can cause, see, for example, Hillary Angelo, *Boomtown*, HARPER'S MAG. (Jan. 2023), https://harpers.org/archive/2023/01/boomtown-beatty-nevada-solar-farms-death-valley/. For a discussion of some of the environmental impacts of wind energy production, see Daniel Y. Choi, Thomas W. Wittig & Bryan M. Kluever, *An Evaluation of Bird and Bat Mortality at Wind Turbines in the Northeastern United States*, 15 PLOS ONE (2020).

110. For example, the longstanding Production Tax Credit and Investment Tax Credit for wind and solar. *See* 26 U.S.C. §§ 45, 48.

111. *See, e.g.*, I.R.A., Pub. L. No. 117–169 §§ 22003, 23002–03, 30002, 40004, 40007, 60105, 60110, 60114, 60201, 60506. For an argument that the IRA's preference for tax incentives over grants reflects the political difficulties of getting Congress to approve direct funding for climate investment, *see* Sadek Wahba, *The Inflation Reduction Act Shows the Way Forward on Climate*, FORBES (Feb. 2, 2023), www.forbes.com/sites/forbesfinancecouncil/2023/02/02/the-inflation-reduction-act-shows-the-way-forward-on-climate/?sh=309af90e76de ("In its reliance on incentives, the IRA is responsive to political realities. In our polarized political environment, a direct funding program on the scale of the IIJA is unlikely to be repeated anytime soon. With its focus on the private sector, I believe the IRA provides a go-forward model.").

112. Historically, subsidies have been criticized as inefficient compared with taxing pollution or regulating it through cap and trade programs. *See, e.g.*, Richard B. Stewart, *A New Generation of Environmental Regulation?*, 29 CAP. U. L. REV. 21, 98 (2001). Yet, some economists have recently suggested that subsidies are an efficient tool for decarbonizing

electricity while simultaneously trying to grow renewable energy generation to supply electrified transportation and home heating. They emphasize that increasing the price of electricity through taxes or cap and trade would reduce the incentives for consumers to shift from fossil fuels to electricity for transportation and heating. Severin Borenstein & Ryan Kellogg, *Carbon Pricing, Clean Electricity Standards, and Clean Electricity Subsidies on the Path to Net Zero Emissions* 15–19 (Nat'l Bureau of Econ. Rsch., Working Paper No. 30263, 2022), www.nber.org/papers/w30263; Lydia DePillis, *Pace of Climate Change Sends Economists Back to Drawing Board: They Underestimated the Impact of Global Warming, and Their Preferred Policy Solution Floundered in the United States*, N.Y. TIMES (Aug. 25, 2022), www.nytimes.com/2022/08/25/business/economy/economy-climate-change.html (referring to new openness among some economists to subsidies and other approaches in light of the need to rapidly reduce GHG emissions) (citing Borenstein & Kellogg, *supra*).

There also are historical precedents for the federal government subsidizing local governments to make environmental improvements, sometimes even without complementary federal regulations. *See, e.g.*, MARTIN V. MELOSI, *THE SANITARY CITY: ENVIRONMENTAL SERVICES IN URBAN AMERICA FROM COLONIAL TIMES TO THE PRESENT* 137–138 (2008) (describing federal funding in the 1930s for water supply and sewage system); ROBERT V. PERCIVAL ET AL., *ENVIRONMENTAL REGULATION: LAW, SCIENCE AND POLICY* 94 (9th ed. 2022) (referring to post-World War II funding to spur municipal construction of sewage treatment plants and to "encourag[e] the states to adopt pollution control measures of their own"); Glicksman, *supra* note 1, at 1167; Robin Kundis Craig, *There Is More to the Clean Water Act than Waters of the United States: A Holistic Jurisdictional Approach to the Section 402 and Section 404 Permit Programs*, 73 CASE WESTERN RESERVE L. REV. 349, 357 (2022) (referring to grant program in 1972 Clean Water Act for sewage treatment plants); William L. Andreen, *Of Fables and Federalism: A Re-examination of the Historical Rationale for Federal Environmental Regulation*, 42 ENV'T L. 627, 653–55 (2012) (federal funding for local and state air pollution control offices in 1960s).

113. For a pre-IRA history of failed Congressional legislative efforts to mandate reductions in GHG emissions, see MATTO MILDENBERGER, CARBON CAPTURED: HOW BUSINESS AND LABOR CONTROL CLIMATE POLITICS (2020).

114. Since the Obama era, the federal government has been regulating GHG emissions from new motor vehicles. Jody Freeman, *The Obama Administration's National Auto Policy: Lessons From the "Car Deal,"* 35 HARV. ENV'T L. REV. 343 (2011). The Obama administration's Clean Power Plan to regulate GHG emissions from existing power plants never took effect. West Virginia v. E.P.A., 597 U.S. 697, 699–700 (2022). GHG emissions from new, modified, and reconstructed power plants have been regulated under the Clean Air Act since 2015. *NSPS* for *GHG Emissions from New, Modified, and Reconstructed Electric Utility Generating Units*, ENV'T. PROT. AGENCY, www.epa.gov/stationary-sources-air-pollution/nsps-ghg-emissions-new-modified-and-reconstructed-electric-utility (last updated Apr. 25, 2024). *See also* Util. Air Regul. Grp. v. Env't Prot. Agency, 573 U.S. 302 (2014); LINDA TSANG & ALEXANDRA M. WYATT, CONG. RSCH. SERV., R44480, CLEAN POWER PLAN: LEGAL BACKGROUND AND PENDING LITIGATION IN WEST VIRGINIA V. EPA 3–4 (2017) ("As a practical matter, *UARG* affirmed EPA's ability to regulate roughly 83% of U.S. stationary-source GHG emissions under PSD and Title V permitting programs[.]").

115. Coral Davenport, *Biden Administration Announces Rule Aimed at Expanding Electric Vehicles*, N.Y. TIMES (Mar. 20, 2024), www.nytimes.com/2024/03/20/climate/biden-phase-out-gas-cars.html (the rule is intended "to ensure that the majority of new passenger cars and light trucks sold in the United States are all-electric or hybrids by 2032"); Env't Prot. Agency, Final Rule, Multi-pollutant Emissions Standards for Model Years 2027 and Later Light-Duty and Medium-Duty Vehicles, 89 Fed. Reg. 27842 (Apr. 18, 2024) [hereinafter Multi-pollutant Emissions Standards for Vehicles]; Lisa Friedman, *E.P.A. to Exempt Existing Gas Plants from Tough New Rules, for Now.*, N.Y. TIMES (Feb. 29, 2024), www.nytimes.com/2024/02/29/climate/epa-climate-power-plant-emissions.html; *Biden-Harris Administration Finalizes Suite of Standards to Reduce Pollution from Fossil Fuel-Fired Power Plants*, U.S. ENV'T PROT. AGENCY (Apr. 25, 2024), www.epa.gov/newsreleases/biden-harris-administration-finalizes-suite-standards-reduce-pollution-fossil-fuel; New Source Performance Standards for Greenhouse Gas Emissions from New, Modified, and Reconstructed Fossil Fuel-Fired Electric Generating Units; Emission Guidelines for Greenhouse Gas Emissions from Existing Fossil Fuel-Fired Electric Generating Units; and Repeal of the Affordable Clean Energy Rule, 89 Fed. Reg. 39798 (May 9, 2024) [hereinafter New Source Performance Standards]. *See also USDOT Finalizes New Fuel Economy Standards for Model Years 2027–2031*, U.S. DEP'T OF TRANSP., NAT'L HIGHWAY TRAFFIC SAFETY ADMIN. (June 7, 2024), www.nhtsa.gov/press-releases/new-fuel-economy-standards-model-years-2027-2031.
116. Brad Plumer, David Gelles & Karen Zraick, *Tracking Trump's Biggest Climate Moves*, N.Y. TIMES (Feb. 13, 2025), https://www.nytimes.com/2025/02/13/climate/tracking-trumps-biggest-climate-moves.html. Even if the Democrats had held onto the presidency, the Biden administration's climate regulations would have faced legal risks due in part to recent Supreme Court decisions inhospitable to environmental regulations. *See* West Virginia v. E.P.A., 597 U.S. 697 (2022); Loper Bright Enters. v. Raimondo, 603 U.S. 369 (2024); *see also* Sackett v. E.P.A., 598 U.S. 651 (2023).
117. Lisa Friedman, Brad Plumer & Harry Stevens, *Trump Is Freezing Money for Clean Energy. Red States Have the Most to Lose*, N.Y. TIMES (Feb. 11, 2025), https://www.nytimes.com/2025/02/10/climate/trump-clean-energy-republican-states.html.
118. *See* Buzbee, *supra* note 1, at 1066 (emphasizing the "protective benefits" of concurrent federal and state authority over climate change). According to the Center for Climate and Energy Solutions, "[t]wenty-four states plus the District of Columbia have adopted specific greenhouse gas reduction targets to reduce climate change." Center for Climate and Energy Solutions, State Climate Policy Maps, www.c2es.org/content/state-climate-policy/ (last visited May 27, 2024).
119. N.Y. STATE CLIMATE ACTION COUNCIL, *supra* note 2, at 183, 188–91 (noting how compliance standards should "align with New York City's Local Law 97").
120. In December of 2022, the Biden administration announced a building performance standard (BPS) for federal buildings that commits to "zero scope 1 emissions in 30 percent of the building space owned by the Federal government by square footage by 2030." *Federal Building Performance Standard*, OFF. OF THE FED. CHIEF SUSTAINABILITY OFFICER, www.sustainability.gov/federalbuildingstandard.html (last visited May 27, 2024). With 300,000 existing federal buildings, such a BPS could make a real difference, not only in lowering the emissions profile of the government's own buildings, but also in helping to scale emergent markets for low-carbon building goods and services. Press Release, White House, Fact Sheet: Biden-Harris Administration Proposes Plan to Protect Federal Supply Chain from Climate-Related Risks (Nov. 10, 2022), www.whitehouse

.gov/briefing-room/statements-releases/2022/11/10/fact-sheet-biden-harris-administration-proposes-plan-to-protect-federal-supply-chain-from-climate-related-risks/.

121. Additional federal – and state – subsidies likely will be necessary to decarbonize and electrify existing multifamily buildings, especially privately owned affordable housing, and public housing. New York State's Public Service Commission recognizes that governmental assistance is necessary to decarbonize "affordable multifamily buildings." Marie J. French, *N.Y. Utility Regulator Reshapes Energy Efficiency Programs to Support Climate Law*, E&E NEWS (July 21, 2023). For examples of existing federal subsidies for retrofitting affordable housing, see, e.g., Press Release, U.S. Dep't of Housing & Urb. Dev., HUD Announces More than $837 Million from President Biden's Investing in America Agenda to Improve Housing Quality and Reduce Energy Costs for Undeserved Communities (May 11, 2023), www.hud.gov/press/press_releases_media_advisories/HUD_No_23_093 (announcing funding to retrofit HUD-subsidized multifamily housing).

122. However, in 2012 New York City adopted a series of zoning changes (Zone Green) to encourage green buildings, and in December 2023 the City Council passed another series of zoning changes to facilitate the city's transition to carbon neutrality. *Zone Green: Text Amendment – Approved!*, N.Y.C. PLAN., www.nyc.gov/assets/planning/download/pdf/plans/zone-green/zone_green.pdf (last updated Apr. 30, 2012); *City of Yes: Carbon Neutrality*, N.Y.C. PLAN., www.nyc.gov/site/planning/plans/city-of-yes/city-of-yes-carbon-neutrality.page (last visited May 27, 2024).

123. *See* Jonathan Rosenbloom, *Outsourced Emissions: Why Local Governments Should Track and Measure Consumption-Based Greenhouse Gases*, 92 U. COLO. L. REV. 451, 465 (2021) ("A typical Sector-based Inventory lists 'stationary energy' as the large majority of GHGs, with 'residential buildings' and 'commercial and institutional buildings and facilities' being the largest sector-based emissions. In Sector-based Inventories, transportation typically amounts to the second-highest amount of GHG emissions, with waste ranked third, accounting for only a small percentage of sector-based GHG emissions."); *id.* at 463–64 (comparing sectors and subsectors recommended by the Global Protocol for Community-Scale Greenhouse Gas Emissions Inventories, which include land use, to the inventory used by Chicago, which does not include land use and is "surprisingly similar" to other local governments' inventories); *see also* N.Y.C. MAYOR'S OFF. OF CLIMATE & ENV'T JUST., *NYC Greenhouse Gas Inventories*, https://climate.cityofnewyork.us/initiatives/nyc-greenhouse-gas-inventories/ (last visited May 27, 2024).

124. Katrina Wyman, Danielle Spiegel-Feld, Adalene Minelli & Sara Savarani, *Valuing Density: An Evaluation of the Extent to Which American, Australian and Canadian Cities Account for the Climate Benefits of Density through Environmental Review* 3–6 (Lincoln Institute of Land Policy, Working Paper WP22KW1, 2022).

125. Jane Margolies, *Awash in Asphalt, Cities Rethink Their Parking Needs*, N.Y. TIMES (Mar. 7, 2023), www.nytimes.com/2023/03/07/business/fewer-parking-spots.html.

126. N.Y.C. Dep't of City Plan., *City Planning Commission Review Session + Special Public Meeting*, YOUTUBE (Apr. 26, 2023), www.youtube.com/watch?v=10-8NynzlRY (City of Yes for Carbon Neutrality presentation) (referring to existing zoning that limits the ability to install rooftop solar, solar panels in residential areas).

127. *See, e.g.*, Mark Chediak, *California NIMBYs Threaten Biden's Clean Energy Goals*, BNN BLOOMBERG (July 29, 2021), www.bnnbloomberg.ca/california-nimbys-threaten-biden-s-clean-energy-goals-1.1634351 (describing cases where resident complaints blocked renewable energy installations); Erin Conlon, *Battery*

Storage at 315 Berry Street Could Help Us Meet Climate Goals. Tenants Have Concerns, GREENPOINTERS (July 28, 2023), https://greenpointers.com/2023/07/28/battery-storage-at-315-berry-street-could-help-us-meet-climate-goals-tenants-have-concerns/ (describing opposition by building tenants in Brooklyn to a battery storage project); Jerusalem Demsas, *Not Everyone Should Have a Say*, THE ATLANTIC (Oct. 19, 2022), www.theatlantic.com/ideas/archive/2022/10/environmentalists-nimby-permitting-reform-nepa/671775/.

128. MATTHEW EISENSON, *SABIN CTR. FOR CLIMATE CHANGE LAW*, *OPPOSITION TO RENEWABLE ENERGY FACILITIES IN THE UNITED STATES: MAY 2023 EDITION* 1–2, 3 (2023); *see also* Kempe, *What Mayors Really Think*, *supra* note 63 (reporting on a study that highlights the desire of mayors for local control of permitting for constructing renewable energy).
129. On the environmental and social harms that utility-scale solar installations can cause, *see supra* note 109.
130. ANUSHREE CHAUDHURI & LAWRENCE SUSSKIND, MIT RENEWABLE ENERGY CLINIC, SHIFTING TO STATE PREEMPTION: THE IMPLICATIONS OF NEW RENEWABLE ENERGY SITING FRAMEWORKS IN THE U.S. (2024), https://drive.google.com/file/d/1928U15GIQnCpRsbxffO6FdDPyeeg2UG_/view (referring to California, Michigan, and New York). In 2024, New York State passed reforms to facilitate transmission siting in the state. Marie J. French, *Transmission Permitting Changes in New York Get Support. But Challenges Remain.*, E&E NEWS (Mar. 8, 2024); Renewable Action through Project Interconnection and Deployment (RAPID) Act, 2024 N.Y. Sess. Laws ch. 58, pt. O, § 11 (McKinney) (to be codified at N.Y. PUB. SERV. Law §§ 136–148).
131. We are certainly not the first scholars to call for this sort of reform. *See, e.g.*, Michael B. Gerrard, *Legal Pathways for a Massive Increase in Utility-Scale Renewable Generation Capacity*, 47 ENV'T L. REP. 10591 (2017). *See also* Tracy Hester, *Legal Pathways to Negative Emissions Technologies and Direct Air Capture of Greenhouse Gases*, 48 ENV'T L. REP. 10413 (2018); Rayan Sud, Sanjay Patnaik & Robert L. Glicksman, *How to Reform Federal Permitting to Accelerate Clean Energy Infrastructure: A Nonpartisan Way Forward*, BROOKINGS 2 (Feb. 14, 2023), www.brookings.edu/wp-content/uploads/2023/02/20230213_CRM_Patnaik_Permitting_FINAL.pdf.
132. In 2023, the New York City Department of City Planning initiated the City of Yes for Carbon Neutrality zoning text amendment to facilitate the siting of renewable energy facilities in New York City and achieve other climate goals. On opposition among environmentalists to specific renewable energy proposals, see Jim Tankersley et al., *The Clean Energy Future Is Roiling Both Friends and Foes*, N.Y. TIMES (Aug. 18, 2023), www.nytimes.com/interactive/2023/08/12/climate/wind-solar-clean-energy.html.
133. *State Preemption of Local Zoning Laws as Intersectional Climate Policy*, 135 HARV. L. REV. 1592 (2022); Amy E. Turner, *Legal Tools for Achieving Low Traffic Zones (LTZs): LEZ, ULEZ & Congestion Pricing in U.S. Law Context*, 50 ENV'T L. REP. 10329 (2020). Pricing car travel on city streets by imposing congestion or vehicles per mile charges might also reduce car travel and its associated GHG emissions. REG'L PLAN ASS'N, *The Fourth Regional Plan*, http://fourthplan.org/action/tolling (last visited May 28, 2024) ("Charge drivers to enter Manhattan, price highways, and transition to vehicle-miles tolling.").
134. *See, e.g.*, *State Preemption of Local Zoning Laws*, *supra* note 133 (arguing that encouraging density will limit climate change and promote housing affordability

and reduce racial segregation, and state preemption of local zoning is justified to increase density); Liam Dillon & Taryn Luna, *California Bill to Dramatically Increase Home Building Fails for the Third Year in a Row*, L.A. TIMES (Jan. 30, 2020), www.latimes.com/california/story/2020-01-29/high-profile-california-housing-bill-to-allow-mid-rise-apartments-near-transit-falls-short (noting that SB 50, an iteration of Scott Wiener's proposal, was again rejected); Cara Eckholm, *Will Ambitious Plans for a 'New' New York Get Crushed in Albany?*, N.Y. TIMES (Mar. 29, 2023), www.nytimes.com/2023/03/29/opinion/housing-future-new-york-city.html (describing political opposition to proposal to require zoning "for an average of 50 units per acre in areas within a half a mile of Metropolitan Transportation Authority stations to create more sustainable communities"); Ross Barkan, *The Many Enemies of Affordable Housing*, N.Y. MAG. (Apr. 24, 2023), https://nymag.com/intelligencer/2023/04/kathy-hochuls-plan-for-affordable-housing-was-doomed.html (referring to opposition from suburban mayors and legislators and their constituents to Governor Hochul's Housing Compact). *But see* Press Release, Scott Wiener, Governor Newsom Signs Senator Wiener's Housing Density Legislation (Sept. 16, 2021) (noting that SB 10 was signed into law).

135. On opposition to transportation-related changes, see, for example, Noah M. Kazis, *Transportation, Land Use, and the Sources of Hyper-Localism*, 106 IOWA L. REV. 2339 (2021).
136. On the YIMBY movement, see, e.g., Conor Dougherty, *The Surprising Left-Right Alliance That Wants More Apartments in Suburbs*, N.Y. TIMES (Mar. 9, 2024), www.nytimes.com/2024/03/09/business/economy/yimby-housing-conference.html.
137. PLANYC 2023, *supra* note 39, at 63, 107–08. Some local (and state and federal) climate policies already recognize the impact of their jurisdictions on GHG emissions through consumption. For example, policies to transition government-owned vehicles to electric vehicles seek to reduce GHG emissions through government purchasing.
138. In the Biden administration, the federal government developed pilot low-carbon standards for construction materials for projects funded by the Inflation Reduction Act. Press Release, U.S. Gen. Serv. Admin., GSA pilots Buy Clean Inflation Reduction Requirements for low embodied carbon construction materials (May 16, 2023), www.gsa.gov/about-us/newsroom/news-releases/gsa-pilots-buy-clean-inflation-reduction-act-requirements-for-low-embodied-carbon-construction-materials-05162023. *See also* Sebastian Obando, *NY Announces First-in-the-Nation State Concrete Mandate*, DIVE BRIEF (Sept. 25. 2023), www.constructiondive.com/news/new-york-buy-clean-concrete/694551/.
139. Press Release, City of N.Y., Mayor Adams Commits to Reducing City's Food-Based Emissions by 33 Percent by 2030 after Releasing New Greenhouse Gas Emissions Inventory Incorporating Emissions from Food (Apr. 17, 2023), www.nyc.gov/office-of-the-mayor/news/263-23/mayor-adams-commits-reducing-city-s-food-based-emissions-33-percent-2030-after-releasing#/0; *see also* PLANYC 2023, *supra* note 39, at 52.
140. Press Release, *supra* note 139.
141. *See generally* Xiaoming Xu et al., *Global Greenhouse Gas Emissions from Animal-Based Foods Are Twice Those of Plant-Based Foods*, 2 NATURE FOOD 724 (2021).
142. PLANYC 2023, *supra* note 39, at 20–21.
143. Katrina Wyman & Emma Dietz, *Integrating Food into Local Climate Policy*, 24 N.Y.U. J. OF LEGIS. & PUB. POL'Y 725, 728 (2022).

144. Emma G. Fitzsimmons, *Did Eric Adams, an Avowed Vegan, Eat Fish? (Yes, and It Was No Fluke)*, N.Y. Times (Feb. 7, 2022), www.nytimes.com/2022/02/07/nyregion/eric-adams-fish-vegan.html.

145. *See, e.g.*, *The NYC Climate Justice Agenda*, N.Y.C. Env't Just. All., https://nyc-eja.org/campaigns/climate-justice-community-resiliency/ (last visited May 28, 2024) (referring to reports extending back to 2016); WE ACT for Env't Just., Emergency Preparedness: Climate Ready Uptown Plan, www.weact.org/campaigns/crup/ (last visited July 11, 2024); WE ACT for Env't Just., 2024 Policy Agenda: Campaigns and Initiatives, *supra* note 26.

In 2010, the New York City Environmental Justice Alliance established its "Waterfront Justice Project," which the Alliance described as "New York City's first citywide community-based resiliency campaign." This campaign focuses on reducing the risks of industrial pollution during storm surges or other flooding in industrial areas along the city's waterfront. *Waterfront Justice & Coastal Resilience*, N.Y.C. Env't Just. All., https://nyc-eja.org/campaigns/waterfront-justice-and-coastal-resilience/ (last visited May 28, 2024). In 2013, after Hurricane Sandy, "over 40 community, environmental justice, labor and civic groups from New York, New Jersey and Long Island" met in the Sandy Regional Assembly to define a recovery agenda that would address "the needs and priorities of vulnerable groups, particularly in low-income neighborhoods and communities of color," and analyze the city government's Special Initiative for Rebuilding and Resiliency and make recommendations to the federal government on recovering from Sandy. Sandy Regional Assembly, SIRR Analysis: An Assessment of the Mayor's Special Initiative for Rebuilding and Resiliency (SIRR) Plan, and Recommendations for the Federal Hurricane Sandy Rebuilding Task Force 1 (2013).

146. In 2017, the New York City Environmental Justice Alliance characterized resiliency initiatives in the city as "top-down." N.Y.C. Env't Just. All., *supra* note 64, at 17. For other less explicit references to adaptation as top-down, see, e.g., Foster et al., *supra* note 24, at 157; Deborah Balk, Timon McPhearson, Elizabeth M. Cook, Kim Knowlton, Nicole Maher, Peter Marcotullio, Thomas Matte, Richard Moss, Luis Ortiz, Joel Towers, Jennifer Ventrella & Gernot Wagner, *Concepts and Tools for Envisioning New York City's Futures*, in *New York City Panel on Climate Change 4th Assessment* 16 (2024), https://climateassessment.nyc/assessment/concepts-and-tools-for-envisioning-new-york-citys-futures/. *But see* Sheila R. Foster, Ana Baptista, Khai Hoan Nguyen, Jack Tchen, Marco Tedesco & Robin Leichenko, *Advancing Climate Justice in Climate Adaptation Strategies for New York City*, in *New York City Panel on Climate Change 4th Assessment* 7 (2024), https://climateassessment.nyc/assessment/advancing-climate-justice-in-climate-adaptation-strategies-for-new-york-city/ ("the City Council and local representatives from EJ organizations have emerged as key players in advancing and institutionalizing environmental justice and equity in the City's long-term climate adaptation planning efforts"); *id.* at 15–16, 46–47 (summarizing community-based initiatives since the third assessment in 2019).

Notably, in 2023, over twenty-five environmental, social, and other organizations formed a coalition to urge the Army Corps of Engineers to make major changes to its proposed approach to protecting the New York/New Jersey Harbor from coastal flooding. This is an example of community-based pressure for adaptation. Press Release, Env't Def. Fund, Organizations Voice Concern Over Federal Flooding Plan for NY-NJ Harbor (Aug. 16, 2023), www.edf.org/media/

organizations-voice-concern-over-federal-flooding-plan-ny-nj-harbor. *See also* Press Release, Env't Def. Fund, Advocates Celebrate Breakthrough in Campaign To Overhaul Flawed Army Corps Flooding Plan for NY-NJ Harbor (Nov. 13, 2023), www.edf.org/media/advocates-celebrate-breakthrough-campaign-overhaul-flawed-army-corps-flooding-plan-ny-nj (over "50 organizations in New York and New Jersey have been campaigning for" changes to the Army Corps' study of coastal protection measures in the two states).

CODA

1. Lyndon B. Johnson, *Special Message to the Congress on Conservation and Restoration of Natural Beauty – February* 8, 1965, 1965 PUB. PAPERS 155 (1965). The Congressional Record for February 8, 1965 states: "The SPEAKER laid before the House the following message from the President of the United States; which was read and referred to the Committee of the Whole House on the State of the Union and ordered to be printed." 111 Cong. Rec. 2085 (1965). *See also id.* at 2245 ("The PRESIDING OFFICER (Mr. HARRIS in the chair). The Chair lays before the Senate a message from the President of the United States on natural beauty. This message has been read in the House of Representatives; and, without objection, the message will be printed in the RECORD without reading, and appropriately referred.").
2. Johnson, *supra* note 1, at 155.
3. *Id.* at 156.
4. *Id.* at 157 ("The primary purpose of the Open Space Program has been to help acquire and assure open spaces in urban areas. I propose a series of new matching grants for improving the natural beauty of urban open space.... Our city parks have not, in many cases, realized their full potential as sources of pleasure and play. I recommend on a matching basis a series of federal demonstration projects in city parks to use the best thought and action to show how the appearance of these parks can better serve the people of our towns and metropolitan areas.").
5. *Id.* at 161.
6. Dana Nuccitelli, *Scientists Warned the US President about Global Warming 50 Years Ago Today*, THE GUARDIAN (Nov. 5, 2015), www.theguardian.com/environment/climate-consensus-97-per-cent/2015/nov/05/scientists-warned-the-president-about-global-warming-50-years-ago-today.
7. *See generally* Chapter 3. *See also* TRUST FOR PUBLIC LAND, 2024 CITY PARK FACTS (last visited June 16, 2024) ("In the most recent 2023 fiscal year, $11.2B was invested in city parks across the 100 most populous U.S. cities, up from $9.7B in 2022 and the most since pre-2007 Great Recession even after adjusting for inflation.").
8. Johnson, *supra* note 1, at 161. However, the impacts of climate change, such as increasingly prevalent and severe wildfires, heat and droughts, are contributing to air pollution in urban areas such as Los Angeles. *See, e.g.*, *State of the Air 2024: Key Findings*, AM. LUNG ASS'N www.lung.org/research/sota/key-findings (last visited June 16, 2024); *Wildfire Smoke in Los Angeles County*, CNTY. OF L.A. PUB. HEALTH, www.publichealth.lacounty.gov/eh/safety/wildfire-smoke.htm (last visited June 16, 2024); Tony Briscoe, *Pollution from California's 2020 Wildfires Likely Offset Decades of Air Quality Gains*, L.A. TIMES (June 17, 2022), www.latimes.com/environment/story/2022-06-17/2020-california-wildfires-offset-decades-of-air-quality-gains; Ezra Romero, *A New Study Explores the Role of Climate Change in Worsening Fires*, NPR (Jan. 10, 2025), https://www.npr.org/2025/01/10/nx-s1-5253063/a-new-study-explores-the-role-of-climate-change-in-worsening-fires.

9. Johnson, *supra* note 1, at 156 ("This means that beauty must not be just a holiday treat, but a part of our daily life. It means not just easy physical access, but equal social access for rich and poor, Negro and white, city dweller and farmer.").
10. Simon Evans & Verner Viisainen, *Analysis: Trump Election Win Could Add 4bn Tonnes to US Emissions by 2030*, Carbon Brief (Mar. 6, 2024), www.carbonbrief.org/analysis-trump-election-win-could-add-4bn-tonnes-to-us-emissions-by-2030/.
11. Matt McGrath, *Trump Vows to Leave Paris Climate Agreement and "Drill, Baby, Drill,"* BBC (Jan. 20, 2025), https://www.bbc.com/news/articles/c20px1e05w0o (last visited Feb. 1, 2025).
12. *See U.S. State Greenhouse Gas Emissions Targets*, Ctr. for Climate & Energy Sols., www.c2es.org/document/greenhouse-gas-emissions-targets/ (last visited May 7, 2024).

Index

Adams, Eric, 95, 104
  administration, 71
adaptation to climate change, 72
  cities and, 88–89, 90–91, 104, 106
  constraints, 81
  fiscal limitations, 74, 76–77
  incentives, 72, 88
  plans, 72–73, 75–76, 89–90
Aggarwala, Rohit, 58, 60
air pollution, 17, 20–21
  anti-smoke ordinances, 18
  heating, 44–45
  interstate pollution, 20–21
  New York City, 44–45
Araos, Malcolm, 82
Army Corps of Engineers, 74, 75, 80, 82, 84, 91, 95, 96

Barber, Benjamin, 7
Battery Park City Authority, 6
Bautista, Eddie, 37, 50, 53
benchmarking, 60–62
bicycle paths, 29
Biden, Joseph, 52, 69, 71, 100, 106
Bipartisan Infrastructure Law, 34, 35, 94, 100, 101
Bloomberg Philanthropies, 7, 61
Bloomberg, Michael, 27, 36, 38, 53, 79
  administration, 28, 30, 36–37, 38–45, 58–59, 75, 78
borough equity, 50
Boston, 45, 69, 74, 82, 85, 95
Brooklyn Bridge Park, 42, 54
brownfields, 43–44
buildings
  decarbonization, 101
  emissions, 23, 44–45, 57, 60
  energy consumption, 61
  federal standards, 23, 69, 101
  mandates, 64, 68–69
  regulation, 60, 68–70, 79, 80, 98, 101
Bush, George W., 63
Buzbee, William, 148, 229, 232

C40 Cities Climate Leadership Group, 7
California, 6, 7
carbon dioxide emissions. *See* greenhouse gas emissions
Central Park, 18, 20, 29, 40
Chambers, Mark, 69
Charleston, 74, 82, 85, 95, 97
Chicago, 18, 19, 63, 90, 92, 105
China, 11
cities
  as defined, 15–16
  fiscal limitations, 26, 74, 76–77
  global networks, 7
  grassroots advocacy in, 9, 10, 11, 26, 29–31, 32, 33
  land use regulation, 12, 19, 23, 72, 89, 96–98, 100, 101–3
Civil Rights Movement, 20
Clean Air Act, 7, 21, 44, 100
Clean Water Act, 7, 23, 33, 40, 100
climate change
  adaptation. *See* adaptation to climate change
  cities and, 6, 8, 11–12, 17, 33–35, 55–56, 63, 72, 87, 88, 101, 106
  decarbonization. *See* decarbonization
  grassroots advocacy and, 34, 104
  inequitable distribution of vulnerability, 78, 89, 90, 92
  political parties, 31
Climate Works for All, 65, 66–67
Clinton, Bill, 37
Columbia University's Earth Institute, 75
Community Parks Initiative, 47

community-based advocacy. *See* grassroots advocacy
congestion pricing, 39, 44, 53, 60
Constantinides, Costa, 65
COVID-19 pandemic, 31, 46, 70, 92
Creative Class theory, 28–29, 36

Dallas, Texas, 63
de Blasio, Bill, 37, 45, 63
  administration, 30, 37–38, 45–48, 64, 80
decarbonization
  cities and, 12, 14, 33–35, 55–56, 63, 99
  consumption patterns, 103–4
  electric/zero-emission vehicles, 100
  federal policy, 99–101
  grassroots advocacy, 30, 34, 65–68
  natural gas bans, 69–70
  in New York City, 58–63, 70–71
development
  brownfield remediation program and, 43–44
  climate-safer neighborhoods, 97
  waterfront, 78, 79, 85–86, 98
Dinkins, David, 50
Doctoroff, Daniel, 27, 28, 36, 38–39, 53
drinking water, 12, 17–18, 88, 89
drought, 10, 72, 88, 89

Earth Day, 20
East River Park, 6, 10, 81, 82
East Side Coastal Resiliency project, 6, 10, 72, 81–82
economics
  decarbonization, 57, 59
  deindustrialization, 29
  environmental protection and, 29, 73
  equity, 46
  inequality, 92–93
  office-based economy, 87
  population growth, 27–28
  property taxes, 39
Energy Policy and Conservation Act, 70
environmental, as defined, 15
environmental justice, 20, 30, 33, 48–52, 68, 84, 89, 106
environmental justice communities, 53, 69, 84
environmental policy
  benefit-cost analysis, 91
  economic growth, 36–37, 46
  environmental justice and, 48–52
  federalization of, 7, 20–21, 22–23, 35
  New York City, 11, 14–15, 38–45, 46–52
  public health and, 18, 19, 20
Environmental Protection Agency (federal), 44, 100
environmental protection measures
  benchmarking, 60–62
  cities and, 6, 8–10, 25–26, 32, 101, 106
  coastal protection infrastructure, 79, 80–81
  economic growth and, 29, 53–54, 59, 70
  federal government assistance, 20–21, 84

Federal Emergency Management Agency, 75, 78, 91, 94
federal government
  air pollution and, 20–21, 44
  assistance, 12, 14, 20–21, 74, 84, 87, 93–95, 98, 104
  automobile emission standards, 21, 23
  Building Resilient Infrastructure and Communities program, 92, 94
  climate adaptation, 86, 95–96
  competitive grant programs, 95
  Council on Environmental Quality, 69
  decarbonization and, 99–101
  disaster relief, 77, 78, 86
  environmental law and, 6, 7, 20–21, 22–23, 35
  Environmental Protection Agency, 44, 100
  Federal Emergency Management Agency, 75, 78, 91, 94
  Flood Mitigation Assistance, 94
  funding, 12, 74, 76–77, 78, 80, 84, 85, 93–95
  National Building Performance Standards Coalition, 69
  National Flood Insurance Program, 86, 94, 98
  National Oceanic and Atmospheric Administration, 90
  National Weather Service, 90
  whole-of-government approach, 13, 104
flooding, 10, 72, 88
  Federal Emergency Management Agency, 75, 78
  Federal Emergency Management Agency flood maps, 78
  National Flood Insurance Program, 86, 94, 98
  New York City, 1–6, 76–78
Frug, Gerald, 22

gentrification, 20, 29, 37, 43, 46, 47–48, 90, 97
Gerrard, Michael, 197, 219, 233, 253
Gillette, Clay, 30
Giuliani, Rudolph, 50
Global Parliament of Mayors, 7
global public goods, 33–35, 88
Goldstein, Eric, 161, 167
grassroots advocacy, 26, 29–31, 33
  climate adaptation and, 84–85, 104
  decarbonization, 30, 34, 65–68
  environmental justice, 9, 30, 33
  in New York City, 37–38, 48–52, 53, 65–68

green roofs, 23
Greener, Greater Buildings Plan, 60–61
greenhouse gas emissions, 10–11
  benchmarking, 60–62
  in China, 11
  in cities, 7, 9, 10, 23, 25, 33–35, 55–56, 63, 71, 99
  electric/zero-emission vehicles, 100
  electricity, 55
  federal decarbonization policy, 99–101
  food emissions, 103–4
  grassroots advocacy, 30, 65–68
  natural gas bans, 69–70
  in New York City, 11, 25, 38, 58–63, 71
  in the United States, 11
greenhouse gas inventories, 59
greenspaces, 9, 10, 17, 18, 32, 39–42, 72. *See also* parks

heat waves, 72, 76, 88, 89, 90, 92
Holloway, Cas, 71
Hudson River Park, 1, 41, 54
Hughes, Sara, 72
Hurricane Ida, 76
Hurricane Katrina, 77, 80, 96
Hurricane Sandy, 2, 14, 62, 64, 77, 95

incentives
  for adaptation, 72
  bottom-up approach, 9, 26, 29–31, 34
  for local environment, 9, 32, 36–37, 38–39, 53
  top-down approach, 9, 25–26, 28–29, 33–34
Inflation Reduction Act, 12, 34, 99, 100, 101, 106
infrastructure
  climate-risk resistant, 93
  coastal protection, 1–6, 79, 89, 93, 95–96
  gentrification and, 47–48
  green, 23, 47–48, 90, 93
  grey, 23, 93
  nature-based solutions, 80, 84, 93
  social, 92
International Council for Local Environmental Initiatives, 63
Izeman, Mark, 161

Jackson, Mississippi, 93
Johnson, Lyndon B., 105–6
Joshi, Meera, 95

Kennedy, Robert F., 22
Kerr, Laurie, 39
Kimmelman, Michael, 81
Klinenberg, Eric, 90, 92
Kresge Foundation, 7
Kyoto Protocol, 63

Lake Michigan, 19
League of Conservation Voters, 67
Lee, John, 65
levees, 80, 96
local governments
  federal government and, 26–27
  fiscal limitations, 92–93, 95–96
  limitations on, 26–27, 54, 55, 88
  local economic growth, 25, 27, 29
  local elites and, 9, 25–26, 28–29, 32
  protest politics, 57, 63, 66–68 71
  state governments and, 26–27
Local Law 97 (New York City), 9, 30, 57, 64–69, 70
local public goods, 10, 17, 32–33, 72, 88
London, 39
Los Angeles, 7, 105
Loughran, Kevin, 47

Mayors Climate Protection Agreement, 63
Miami, 74, 82, 85, 95
migration to the suburbs, 22
Moses, Robert, 28

National Building Performance Standards Coalition, 69
National Flood Insurance Program, 86, 94, 98
National Oceanic and Atmospheric Administration, 90
natural gas bans, 69–70
Natural Resources Defense Council, 67
nature-based barriers, 80, 84, 93
New Jersey, 21–22
New Orleans, 33, 80, 96
New York & New Jersey Harbor & Tributaries Focus Area Feasibility Study, 84
New York City
  adaptation to climate change, 73–75, 85
  affordable housing crisis, 43, 45, 70
  air quality, 21–22, 44–45
  Bronx, 84
  Brooklyn, 42, 79, 84
  Brooklyn Bridge Park, 42, 54
  brownfield remediation program, 43–44, 46
  building regulations, 80
  Central Park, 18, 20, 29, 40
  Clean Heat Program, 45
  coastal flooding protection, 1–6, 73, 79, 80–81, 85, 95
  Commercial Waste Zones Law, 51
  Community Air Survey, 44
  Community Parks Initiative, 53
  community-based parks, 37, 47–48
  congestion pricing, 44, 60
  decarbonization, 58–63, 70–71

New York City (cont.)
Department of Environmental Protection, 1, 71, 75
Department of Sanitation, 51
East River Park, 6, 10, 81, 82
East Side Coastal Resiliency project, 6, 10, 72, 81–82
economic growth, 36–37, 46
environmental justice, 33, 37–38, 48–52, 84
Environmental Justice Advisory Board, 52
environmental policy, 14–15, 38–45, 46–52, 58–63
Financial District, 6, 79
flooding, 1–6, 76, 77
food emissions, 103
Fresh Kills landfill, 42, 49–50
garbage disposal. *See* New York City, waste management
gentrification, 20, 29, 37, 43, 46, 47–48
Gowanus Canal, 84
grassroots advocacy in, 37–38, 48–52, 53, 65–67, 84–85
Greener, Greater Buildings Plan, 60–61
greenhouse gas emissions, 11, 25, 38, 58–63, 71
greenhouse gas inventories, 59
greenspaces, 39–42
High Line, 41–42
Hudson River Park, 1, 41, 54
Hurricane Sandy, 2, 14, 62, 64, 77, 95
improvement of physical environment, 36–37, 38–39, 46
integrated inventory, 103
Little Island, 1
Local Law 97, 9, 30, 57, 64–69, 70
Lower East Side, 81
Mayor's Office of Climate Resiliency, 81
Mayor's Office of Long-Term Planning and Sustainability, 38, 39, 58, 62
Newtown Creek, 84
North Brooklyn, 53
One City: Built to Last, 65
OneNYC, 47, 54
Panel on Climate Change, 75, 78
parks, 39–42, 106
Parks Department, 82
PlaNYC, 38–45, 53, 58, 70
population growth, 27–28, 39, 45
public housing, 81
Queens, 79
Red Hook, 50
Seaport City, 79
September 11th attacks, 36
sewage, 23, 33
South Bronx, 47, 53
South Street Seaport, 79
Southeast Queens, 53
Special Initiative for Rebuilding and Resiliency, 78, 80
Staten Island, 21, 42, 49, 79
stop-and-frisk, 37
subway, 76
Sunset Park, 47, 50, 53
tourism, 39–40
tree planting, 43, 76
waste collection franchising system, 51–52
waste equity, 38, 48–52
waste management, 19, 37–38, 48–52, 106
water supply system, 18, 23, 29
waterfront, 1, 40, 78, 79, 80–85, 85–86
Williamsburg-Greenpoint, 43, 47, 50
zoning, 19, 43, 46, 76
New York City Economic Development Corporation, 39
New York City Environmental Justice Alliance, 50, 67
New York City Panel on Climate Change, 75, 78
New York Communities for Change, 66, 70
New York Lawyers for the Public Interest, 50
New York Public Interest Research Group, 70
New York State, 18, 70
Nixon, Richard, 20
Norfolk, Virginia, 76, 95
NYU Furman Center, 79

Ocasio-Cortez, Alexandria, 66
Olympic Games, 2012, 38–39
OneNYC, 47, 54
Oppenheimer, Michael, 77
Organization of Waterfront Neighborhoods, 50

Paris Agreement, 63, 65
parks, 18, 29, 39–42, 105
Brooklyn Bridge Park, 42, 54
Central Park, 18, 20, 29, 40
community-based parks, 37, 47–48
East River Park, 6, 10, 81, 82
Hudson River Park, 1, 41, 54
Pataki, George, 50
People's Climate March, 65
Peterson, Paul, 26, 29, 46
Philadelphia, 18, 29, 45
Pittsburgh, 18
PlaNYC, 38–45, 53, 58, 70
policymakers
in cities, 8–10, 25
local economic growth, 25, 27
local elites and, 9, 25–26, 28, 32
pollution
air pollution, 17, 18, 21–22, 44–45
brownfields, 43–44

environmental justice, 30
garbage, 19, 48–52
heating, 44–45
interstate pollution, 17, 21–22
water, 17
public goods
global, 33–35, 88
local, 10, 17, 32–33, 72, 88
public health, 18, 19

Raleigh, North Carolina, 76
Real Estate Board of New York, 67
Rebuild by Design competition, 81
renewable energy credits, 68
renewable energy facilities, 102
retreat, 97–98
Revesz, Richard, 110, 137
Reynoso, Antonio, 51
Rockefeller Foundation, 75
Rosenzweig, Cynthia, 75

Sabin Center for Climate Change Law, 102
Schragger, Richard, 30
sea level rise, 2, 76, 89
sewage treatment, 10, 18, 20, 23, 29, 32
Shepard, Peggy, 52
Sikora, Pete, 66, 67
social resilience, 92
Solecki, William, 75
Special Initiative for Rebuilding and Resiliency, 78, 80
St. Louis, Missouri, 20
state governments
interstate pollution, 21–22
local governments and, 26–27
Stewart, Richard, 7
storm surge, 2, 88, 89
storm surge barriers, 80, 82, 84, 93
Sze, Julie, 50

Taylor, Dorceta, 33
Tiebout, Charles, 124, 128, 129, 239
Transform Don't Trash NYC coalition, 51
transportation
automobile emission standards, 21
congestion pricing, 39, 44, 53, 60
federal automobile emission standards, 23
tree planting, 43, 72, 76, 90
Trump, Donald, 9, 62–63, 65–66, 71, 106
administration, 34, 35, 57, 100, 101
Trust for Public Land, 42

Urban Green Council, 66

Wagner, Robert F., Jr., 21
Waring, George, 19
Washington, D.C., 25, 69
waste management, 19, 29, 32, 37–38, 48–52
water quality, 1
water supply systems, 17, 18, 23, 29
waterfront areas, 1, 40
WE ACT for Environmental Justice, 52, 67, 70
whole-of-government approach, 13, 87, 104
wildfires, 10, 72, 88, 89
Williams, Jumaane, 65

Yes in my backyard movement, 103

Zarrilli, Dan, 65
zoning, 19, 23, 43, 46, 97, 100, 102

Printed by Integrated Books International,
United States of America